Ability, Merit and Measurement

ABILITY, MERIT AND MEASUREMENT

Mental Testing and English Education
1880–1940

by
GILLIAN SUTHERLAND

in collaboration with Stephen Sharp

CLARENDON PRESS · OXFORD
1984

Oxford University Press, Walton Street, Oxford OX2 6DP

London Glasgow New York Toronto
Delhi Bombay Calcutta Madras Karachi
Kuala Lumpur Singapore Hong Kong Tokyo
Nairobi Dar es Salaam Cape Town
Melbourne Auckland

and associated companies in
Beirut Berlin Ibadan Mexico City Nicosia

Oxford is a trade mark of Oxford University Press

Published in the United States
by Oxford University Press, New York

British Library Cataloguing in Publication Data
Sutherland, Gillian
Ability, merit and measurement: mental testing
and English education, 1880–1940.
1. Students, Rating of 2. Mental tests —
Great Britain — History
I. Title II. Sharp, Stephen
371.2'6 LB1117
ISBN 0-19-822632-2

Library of Congress Cataloging in Publication Data
Sutherland, Gillian.
Ability, merit, and measurement.
Bibliography: p.
Includes index.
1. Educational tests and measurements — Great
Britain — History. 2. Mentally handicapped children —
Education — Great Britain — Ability testing — History.
3. Intelligence tests — Great Britain — History.
4. High schools — Great Britain — Entrance examinations —
History. I. Sharp, Stephen. II. Title.
LB3056.G7S9 1984 371.2'6'0942 83-19478
ISBN 0-19-822632-2 (Oxford University Press)

Typeset by Hope Services, Abingdon
Printed in Great Britain
at the University Press, Oxford

For Alister

Acknowledgements

Many debts have been incurred in the making of this book. The bulk of the work upon which it is based was funded by the Social Science Research Council; and the book constitutes the final report on project HR 4204/2, completing and to some degree superseding the interim reports on the work represented by the progress reports to the SSRC and the articles 'The magic of measurement' (*TRHS* 1977) and 'Measuring intelligence' (published in both *The Meritocratic Intellect*, ed. Smith and Hamilton and *Biology, Medicine and Society*, ed. Webster). I am grateful to the editors and copyright holders concerned for allowing me to repeat some points made in these.

The generous support of the SSRC enabled me to seek guidance on issues in statistics and the psychology of individual differences from Professor V.R. Cane and Dr A.W. Heim. It also enabled Dr Stephen Sharp to work with me for two years, providing essential statistical and psychological expertise and doing much of the 'leg work' upon which chapters seven and eight, in particular, are based. We must be uniquely placed to provide a version of the Historical Manuscripts Commission *Guide to Record Repositories in Great Britain* annotated to take account of local government reorganization and cross-referenced to the CAMRA *Good Beer Guide*. Dr Sharp has read, criticized and helped to rewrite successive drafts; but the responsibility for the final version, warts and all, is mine alone.

The SSRC is currently funding a further, complementary study of mental testing and English education 1940–70 (C/00/23/0025/1). The principal research worker on this is Dr Deborah Thom. I have profited greatly from regular discussions with her over the past year; and we have both learnt from our contacts with the team at the Institute of Education in London, led by Professor Harvey Goldstein, whose work on assessment in the 1970s and 1980s is also being supported by the SSRC.

Joan Austoker, Keith Hope, Joanna Innes, Patricia Potts, Peter Searby, Alister Sutherland, Rick Trainor and Charles Webster read all or parts of the draft and I have benefited greatly from their advice, even when — as they will see — I have chosen not to act upon it. The support of the Principal and Fellows of Newnham College has been more than formal. They established an important precedent within Cambridge by agreeing to administer the SSRC grant and provide office space for Dr Sharp. The comments of the then Principal, Mrs Jean Floud, whose own work has done so much to illuminate our understanding of the class-stratified nature of English education, were invaluable in the early planning of the work. My fellow historians, Rosamond McKitterick and Margaret Spufford, shouldered administrative burdens while I was on sabbatical leave; and when the leave was ended and there were still many things left to do, provided a support and an understanding which have roots in their own high standards of scholarship.

I am obliged to the Comptroller of Her Majesty's Stationery for permission to quote in full Form 306M and at length from *The Health of the School Child, 1935*; and for permission to cite Crown Copyright material in the Public Record Office. I am obliged to the Marquess of Salisbury and Lord Medway, to all those local authorities responsible for the archives listed in the first section of the Bibliography below, to the National Union of Teachers, to the Principal and Governors of the College of Ripon and York, St. John, and to the Trustees of the Godfrey Thomson Unit for Educational Research, University of Edinburgh, for permission to cite copyright material. I am also indebted to the British Psychological Society for permission to quote in full the six 'A' series tests from Godfrey Thomson's 1921 article, 'The Northumberland Mental Tests'; to the Greater London Council for permission to quote in full Test 25 from Cyril Burt's *Mental and Scholastic Tests* (1921); and to the Trustees of the Godfrey Thomson Unit for permission to quote the 1934 Moray House Report for the Education Committee of Lancashire County Council in full, as an appendix to chapter 7.

Dr Sharp and I received much help from many local education authority officers and from the staffs of the various archives listed below, in the Bibliography. But we should like in particular to thank Mr A.R. Neate, the Record-Keeper to the Greater London Council, for his help not only with material relating to Sir Cyril Burt but also in checking items when the records were being moved from County Hall to Clerkenwell; those members of the Public Record Office staff who enabled us to work on Ed 77/- and Ed 110/- while the move from Ashridge to Kew was taking place; and those present and former members of the Godfrey Thomson Unit, who not only allowed the records of Moray House up to 1940 to travel to Cambridge on loan for a period, but also hunted out additional material, answered questions and read and commented on chapter 7 in draft.

Finally, I am extremely grateful for the expert help of Miss Christine Northeast, who typed the final version of the text, and Mrs Margaret Anderson, who made the Index.

Gillian Sutherland

Contents

Figures

Abbreviations frequently used

AEC	Association of Education Committees
AR	Annual Report
BJEP	*British Journal of Educational Psychology*
BJP	*British Journal of Psychology*
BPS	British Psychological Society
CBC	County Borough Council
CC	County Council
GSQ 1975	Questionnaire circulated by the author in 1975 (see Appendix II below)
GSQ 1976	Questionnaire circulated by the author in 1976 (see Appendix II below)
HESC	Higher Education Sub-Committee
HMI	Her/His Majesty's Inspector of Schools
LCC	London County Council
LEA	Local Education Authority
MHA	Moray House Arithmetic test
MHE	Moray House English test
MHT	Moray House Intelligence test
MOH	Medical Officer of Health
NIIP	National Institute of Industrial Psychology
NUT	National Union of Teachers
P.P.	Parliamentary Papers
SMO	School Medical Officer
SSRC	Social Science Research Council
TRHS	*Transactions of the Royal Historical Society*

Exact locations and details of all manuscript collections cited are given below in the Bibliography.

Introduction

My objective in embarking on the work presented in this book was to investigate the roles played by the idea and techniques of measurement in the English public education system in the late nineteenth and early twentieth century. Studies of social policy-making in England have characteristically laid considerable stress on the importance of quantification, of precise measurement, in any given policy. It has been suggested that the power of the evidence, once properly assembled and measured, could on occasion be sufficient to dissolve previous certainties and act as a catalyst of new thought.[1] There are surely links between this aspect of the historiography of social policy and the preoccupation of English social thought with empiricism, a preoccupation which led sometimes to the presentation of empiricism as an alternative to social theory.[2] Both these characteristics enhance the importance of attempts to assess the role of measurement in any given field of policy and to confront directly the questions of its autonomy and the power of its advocates.

Education is a key field in which to test hypotheses about social policy-making. It is by definition a social activity; and it can generate elaborate and expensive attempts at social engineering. An investigation of the initial impact on English education of mental testing, that is, the techniques associated with the psychology of individual differences for measuring the capacities and aptitudes of individuals, thus had obvious

---

[1] e.g. O.R. McGregor, 'Social Research and Social Policy in the Nineteenth Century', *British Journal of Sociology* viii (1957), pp. 146–57; O.O.G.M. MacDonagh, 'The Nineteenth Century Revolution in Government: A Reappraisal', *Historical Journal* i (1958), pp. 52–67.

[2] Philip Abrams, *The Origins of British Sociology: 1834–1914* (Chicago, 1968); Eileen Yeo, 'Social Science and Social Change: A Social History of Some Aspects of Social Science and Social Investigation in Britain 1830–1890' (unpublished Sussex D.Phil. thesis, 1973); M.J. Cullen, *The Statistical Movement in Early Victorian Britain: The Foundations of Empirical Social Research* (Hassocks, Sussex, 1975).

attractions. The interest and importance of the study were enhanced, moreover, by the close connections between mental testing and some of the major innovations in statistical method of the early twentieth century, with the application of the normal curve of distribution to social phenomena, the development of correlation and of factor analysis.

The pursuit of this objective led me first to look at notions of classification in general in English state schools in the second half of the nineteenth century and then to follow through the developing concern for the identification and proper care of mentally handicapped children. It was in this context that the techniques of mental measurement were first used in the public education system. The first three chapters therefore deal with these themes.

The remaining seven chapters deal with the emergence of the form of mental measurement much more familiar to most readers (especially if they are old enough once upon a time to have taken the 'eleven-plus' examination), namely, the group intelligence test and its early uses. There are of course important links between the measurement of mental handicap and efforts to discriminate between the abilities of 'normal' children. But they nevertheless remain two distinct case-studies with different dynamics and crucially different rhythms of activity. And consideration of efforts to measure the abilities of normal children leads us into a consideration of the development of selective examinations in the English public education system and ultimately to a consideration of English versions of meritocracy.

While the work for this book was under way, the row about Sir Cyril Burt and the provenance of his data broke into print. There is no need to rehearse the details of the arguments here; and Dr Sharp and I have commented on some aspects elsewhere.[3] But this row has formed part of the

---

[3] Gillian Sutherland and Stephen Sharp, ' "The fust official psychologist in the wurrld": aspects of the professionalization of psychology in early twentieth century Britain', *History of Science* xviii (1980), pp. 181–208. For the main lines of the row, see Oliver Gillie, 'Sir Cyril Burt and the great IQ fraud', *New Statesman* 24 Nov. 1978, pp. 688–94; L.S. Hearnshaw, *Cyril Burt, psychologist* (London, 1979) and 'A balance sheet on Burt', Supplement to the *Bulletin of the British Psychological Society* xxxiii (1980).

larger argument about the proper uses of mental testing which has been going on since at least the early 1950s in both Britain and the USA. The debate has been a less dramatic one in Britain than in the USA because class is a less explosive issue than race;[4] but the issues are none the less real. I am well aware that some of the readers of this book will want to treat it as a contribution to this debate; and one, at least, of my psychologist friends who has been kind enough to read drafts, has already challenged my 'spurious neutralism'. But the attempt at neutralism has been real enough. I set out to see why educationists took to measurement, what they did with it, and what they thought it did for them. I have tried to write about it in terms which are not only intelligible to my contemporary audience, but which might also make some sense to the actors themselves.

To say this is not to disclaim all views on the uses of testing. And perhaps it will deflect some readers from forcing debates of 1880-1940 into frames of reference derived from the debates of the 1970s and 1980s, or from hunting through the book for concealed value-judgements, if I offer some clear targets and blatant value-judgements now. In certain rather carefully defined situations, mental measurement does seem to me to have uses. The development of individual mental tests greatly refined the diagnosis and assessment of mental handicap. It seems impossible to dispute that Binet and Simon's tests were a great improvement on the methods of diagnosis and assessment that had gone before; and while supplemented, they have not yet been declared redundant.[5] Stephen Jay Gould has described Binet as testing 'in order to identify and help';[6] and, like Gould, I approve of this.

---

[4] On the context of the American debate, see the illuminating work of Jonathan Harwood, including most recently 'Nature, Nurture and Politics: A Critique of the Conventional Wisdom' in *The Meritocratic Intellect. Studies in the History of Educational Research*, ed. James V. Smith and David Hamilton (Aberdeen, 1980), pp. 115-29 and 'American Academic Opinion and Social Change: recent developments in the nature–nurture controversy', *Oxford Review of Education* viii (1982), pp. 41-67.

[5] A.D.B. and A.M. Clarke, eds., *Readings from Mental Deficiency: The Changing Outlook* (London, 1978) (a selection, with an additional chapter, from the 3rd edition of their *Mental Deficiency* (London, 1974), p. 2.

[6] Stephen Jay Gould, *The Mismeasure of Man* (New York and London, 1981), p. 153.

Group tests are very much more of a blunt instrument than an individual test, sympathetically administered by a skilled investigator. But there is a distinction to be drawn between the decision to select, a decision taken on social, political and economic grounds, and the choice of techniques, when once the decision to select has been taken. Selection was the order of the day in England in the inter-War years. I therefore find myself in sympathy with the position taken by Godfrey Thomson: if it is to be done, let it be done as fairly as we know how; a sympathy reinforced by what I have learnt about local authorities' examining procedures in general in the period.

To express such sympathy does not entail committing one-self to the view that intelligence tests were entirely objective and free of class and cultural bias. It is simply to suggest that they were less blatantly subjective and biased than many of the other selection methods being used at the time. If, however, the issue of selection as such is part of the agenda, as it begins to be in the 1950s, then the terms of the debate change and the limitations of *all* methods of selection are a part, although not the whole, of the case for its dismantling. To approve of Godfrey Thomson's position in the 1930s — and Binet's position in the 1910s — is to make relative judgements, not absolute ones.

Sympathy for and knowledge of positions taken in earlier phases of debate about a great issue ought to inform but not to dictate positions adopted in the contemporary phase of that debate. Conversely, a position adopted in a contemporary debate ought to inform but not to strait-jacket efforts to understand earlier phases of that debate. Writing and reading history ought to extend one's experience, albeit vicariously, rather than simply provide reinforcement and endless re-duplication of entrenched positions and prejudices. Trying to reconstruct and describe past arguments, the contexts of past decisions, one develops strong likes and strong dislikes — the writing would be desperately wooden without them. But the strength of these feelings underlines the historian's responsibility to deal as even-handedly as she can with the issues and the personalities involved, to try, as the German historian, Thomas Nipperdey, once remarked, 'to restore to the past the freedom of choice it once had'.

Chapter 1
The Beginnings of Classification

According to the authors of the standard contemporary work on mental deficiency, 'the need to classify is deeply embedded in human beings, indeed it appears to be a fundamental basis of cognitive activities'.[1] Historians find themselves uncomfortable with this kind of biological determinism. Categories of classification which are socially and/or politically effective tend to involve institutional provision; and much of this, whether for the sick, the poor, the young, or the aged, is a product of the recent past. It does seem, however, that once the commitment to institutional forms of treatment has been made, pressure to refine and sophisticate the categories of classification, forming subgroups within the institution or spilling over into new institutions, is likely to build up. Classification of children, whether in terms of ability or achievement, or both, thus seems to follow on from the development of mass formal schooling.

The English came relatively late to mass formal education by comparison with Scotland and much of Western Europe. From 1833 government grants were available for promoters of schools meeting certain conditions. Legislation for a national network of elementary schools was carried only in 1870. The new local education authorities, school boards, were allowed to adopt powers to compel attendance if they wished; and in 1876 it became possible to create school attendance committees with similar powers in non-school-board areas. Legislation requiring compulsory attendance nationally was at last carried in 1880. Thus only in the last two decades of the nineteenth century did teachers and school managers begin really to face the full variety of children's needs and conditions.

In such circumstances the grosser abnormalities were likely to attract attention first, and a study of notions and modes of mental measurement must begin with the efforts of

[1] Clarke and Clarke, *Mental Deficiency*, p. 19.

teachers and school administrators to cope with mentally handicapped children. The 1880s saw the first stage in this, a sustained public discussion of the health and capacities of school children of quite a new kind. By the end of the decade mentally handicapped or defective children had been isolated as one of several groups of children with special needs. In the 1890s the focus upon them sharpened; and although they proved difficult both to identify and to classify with precision, various local authorities experimented with special schools for their care, finally precipitating the government into permissive legislation in 1899.

I The condition of England's children

It was thus only after 1880 that teachers and school managers began to face the full variety of children's needs and conditions. But this variety was dramatized for them by the system of government grant then prevailing, the system known as 'payment by results'. Under this system, the bulk of the government grant, which provided at least half a school's annual income, depended upon the performance of each child each year in examinations in the three Rs conducted by HM Inspector. Children who attended regularly but failed any or all of the examinations for their 'Standard' earned their school only a much reduced grant. This Procrustean system had been introduced in the 1860s, ostensibly to prevent teachers focusing their attention on the handful of bright children in the class and neglecting the others, but actually to save money. In the short run it certainly did the latter; and whether or not it distributed teachers' attention more evenly between pupils, it forced them, faced with fluctuating and often very large classes, increasingly to resort to mechanistic teaching and drill-like methods.[2]

In essence this system assumed that the vast majority of children, if not all, were 'normal', the norms being very precisely delimited by a sequence of arbitrarily imposed tests of numeracy and literacy. The crudity of this had been attacked from the beginning, not least by the teachers and

---

[2] For more detail see Gillian Sutherland, *Policy-Making in Elementary Education 1870–1895* (London, 1973), pp. 6–9, chs. 7, 8, and 9.

their unions; but compulsory attendance gave the attack a new dimension. The 1880 Education Act was at the time of its passage seen by many as simply a kind of tidying-up, ensuring that children would actually go to these expensive new schools. But compelling all children to go to school was in the long run seen to entail also the provision of appropriate schooling for all children and not simply for those who were 'normal'. The 1880s saw the beginning of the shift from the former to the latter; and what came to be known as the great 'over-pressure' row inaugurated a prolonged and unprecedented public discussion of the condition, physical and mental, of school children.

Problems of diagnosing and treating mental strain among schoolchildren had been debated by medical men — and Dr Elizabeth Garret Anderson — in the correspondence columns of *The Times* in the spring of 1880.[3] But the question only really hit the headlines in the summer of 1883, when from various quarters attack was being mounted on the new 'Code', the detailed regulations for the payment of grant under the system of payment by results, issued by the Education Department. Some of the government's critics, the campaigners against 'over-education' from the Anglican voluntaryist right wing of the Tory party, thought the expectations represented by the new Code excessive. The National Union of Elementary School Teachers (NUET) by contrast distinguished sharply between 'over-education' and 'over-pressure' and attacked the system of grant as such, their Secretary, T.E. Heller, making the most of an invitation to address the combined Health and Education Sections of that year's Social Science Congress, on the question 'Is the modern system of education any deleterious influence upon the health of the country?'[4]

The Education Department declared its belief that 'the course of instruction under the Code, so far as it is obligatory, can be easily mastered by a child of ordinary health and intelligence, who attends school with fair regularity'. The NUET retorted that 'it is because the Code proceeds upon the general assumption that all scholars can progress at

---

[3] See ibid. pp. 245–57 for a full and fully documented account, on which the following paragraphs are largely based.
[4] *The Times* 5 Oct. 1883, p. 8 and 9 Oct. 1883, p. 4.

the same rate, irrespective of capacity or attendance, that over-pressure exists'.[5]

Fuel was added to the flames in 1884 by the intervention of Dr James Crichton-Browne, formerly Director of the West Riding Lunatic Asylum, founder-editor of *Brain* and now one of the Lord Chancellor's Visitors in Lunacy. Mundella, the Vice-President of the Committee of Council on Education, made one major gesture to what had now become a very noisy coalition of right-wing Tories, concerned school managers, militant teachers and a sprinkling of doctors, by inviting Crichton-Browne to look into conditions in London schools. The two of them disagreed afterwards as to whether Crichton-Browne had been formally invited to report to the Department or informally invited 'to look into the question' and the Opposition had to intervene to secure the publication of his report. But when it came, it was somewhat less imposing scientifically than his credentials. After making visits of observation to fourteen schools in the worst areas of London, he classified 20 per cent of the children as bright, 60 per cent as of moderate intelligence and 20 per cent as backward. He acknowledged the importance of malnutrition in rendering children vulnerable to strain — 'to educate a half-starved child at all is to over-press it'. He then jumped straight to a consideration of national health statistics and, deriving from them an increase in lunacy, in the suicide rates, and in hydrocephalus in the age group 5-20, he ended up with a declaration that the present system of elementary education was the major cause of these disturbing figures.[6]

The Education Department was well able to defend itself against the loose modes of argument used by Crichton-Browne; and detailed investigation of each of the twenty-two individual cases in which it had been alleged that over-pressure had caused a child's illness or death, failed to substantiate any of the claims.

By the early months of 1885 the agitation was gradually subsiding. No direct hits had been scored; but neither was it completely without effect. The advent of a Conservative administration that summer brought a Royal Commission on

    [5] Ibid., 17 Nov. 1883, p. 6 and 30 Nov. 1883, p. 6.
    [6] P.P. 1884 ff. 259-311, *Report of Dr Crichton-Browne upon the alleged Over-pressure*: the quotation comes from f. 268.

elementary education, under the chairmanship of Viscount Cross, and the Lord President and the Vice-President of the Committee of Council on Education were under pressure to make Crichton-Browne a Commissioner. But as the Vice-President, Sir Henry Holland, put it, 'he has taken so prominent – and disputed – a part that he should not be a commissioner but should be a witness'.[7] This same government had already, as a response to quite separate pressures, appointed a Royal Commission on the education of the blind; and at the beginning of 1886 it changed and extended its composition and terms of reference to include not only the deaf and dumb but also 'such other cases as from special circumstances would seem to require exceptional methods of education', thereby enabling the members of the Cross Commission to leave consideration of what they called 'feeble-minded' children entirely to this second Commission, chaired by Lord Egerton of Tatton.[8]

Royal Commissions usually bring a lull in public controversy and politicians are not and were not averse to using them in this way. But while specific allegations of over-pressure died away, the health and capacities of elementary schoolchildren seemed now established as a continuing topic for investigation and concern. A whole section of the first series of Charles Booth's inquiries into *London Life and Labour* was devoted to 'School Life'. First published in 1891, this was forthright in its denunciation of the rigidities of payment by results. As Mary Tabor, Booth's research worker, put it, 'The buildings, the staff, the educational appliances,

[7] Cranbrook Papers, HA 43/L: T501/259 Holland to Cranbrook, 23 Dec. 1885. See also ibid., same to same 27 Dec. 1885, and Salisbury Papers, Salisbury to Cranbrook 29 Dec. 1885.

[8] D.G. Pritchard, *Education and the Handicapped 1760–1960* (London, 1963), pp. 93–7. Pritchard makes a rare error in saying that the Cross Commission was appointed after the reconstruction of the Commission on the education of the blind. The membership of the Cross Commission was announced on 15 Jan. 1886 (P.P. 1886 xxv ff. 3–4) and the reconstruction of the Commission on the blind was announced on 20 Jan. 1886 (P.P. 1889 xix f. 13). Lord Egerton of Tatton, who became the new chairman of the blind, deaf, dumb, and handicapped enquiry, was at one stage considered as a possible chairman for the elementary education enquiry (Cranbrook Papers, HA 43/L: T501/259 Holland to Cranbrook 23 Dec. 1885), strengthening the probability that the reconstruction of the blind enquiry was seen as complementing the establishment of the elementary education enquiry, as well as responding to the lobby on behalf of the deaf.

the requirements of the Code, are the same for every class. It is the children alone who vary.'[9]

Nor were Booth and his assistants the only investigators to be found in the London schools at the end of the 1880s. In August 1888 Dr Francis Warner, Physician to the London Hospital, addressed the Psychology Section at the annual meeting of the British Medical Association in Glasgow on 'A Method of Examining Children in Schools as to their Development and Brain Condition.'[10] Roughly speaking, it involved surveying a class-room of children, then making them file slowly past, and noting on a prepared schedule those children displaying one or more physical abnormality. His colleagues responded with a committee, whose members employed Warner's methods to look at 100,000 school-children between 1888 and 1894.[11]

Booth's attention had first been drawn to schools and to the way in which the implementation of compulsory attendance had brought under scrutiny many aspects of working-class life, by a remark of Joseph Chamberlain's to the Royal Commission on Housing. In his evidence, Chamberlain had mentioned that the Birmingham Council had found the extensive knowledge of each family possessed by school attendance officers very helpful in preparing slum-clearance schemes. Following this up, Booth secured the permission of the London School Board to interview attendance officers and use their information to check and amplify the evidence of census schedules and his sample of households, when he embarked on his survey in 1886.[12]

Booth's survey is the paradigmatic social survey of modern Britain; and the key part played in it by the information of the attendance officers[13] serves to establish concern with the

[9] Charles Booth, *Life and Labour of the People in London* (London, 1902, consolidated edition) vol.3, p. 206.

[10] *British Medical Journal* 22 Sept. 1888, pp. 659–60.

[11] *Journal of the Royal Statistical Society* lix (1896), pp. 125–68, 'Mental and physical conditions among 50,000 children. . . .'. See also 'Preface' and ch.3 of *The Feeble-Minded Child and Adult* (London, 1893) pub. by the Charity Organization Society in their *Charity Organization series.*

[12] Beatrice Webb, *My Apprenticeship* (London, 1936), pp. 225–9.

[13] See Booth, *London Life and Labour*, 3, p. 195: 'In describing the streets and various portions of London we have drawn upon many sources of information, but it must be borne in mind that the classification of the people rests in effect upon what the School Board attendance officers have told us of the homes and parents of the children in elementary schools.'

state of schoolchildren as a distinct and important strand in what might be called 'the rediscovery of the Condition-of-England Question'. It has become almost a commonplace of recent historical writing that the 1880s saw an upsurge of interest in and concern for social and economic conditions and problems, comparable in intensity and extent with that of the 1830s and 1840s, so memorably characterized by Carlyle in his essay on 'Chartism' as 'The Condition-of-England Question'.[14] Much of what was said was hardly new;[15] but somehow it caught attention, occupied the public prints and the speeches of politicians as social comment and criticism had not done since the 1830s and 1840s. The publication of Andrew Mearns's pamphlet, *The Bitter Cry of Outcast London*, in 1883 is usually taken to signal the beginning of the public discussion, and it was soon continued in other pamphlets and before governmental inquiries such as the Royal Commission on Housing 1884-5, the House of Lords' Select Committee on 'Sweating' 1888-90 and the series of inquiries into 'Dangerous Trades' launched by the Board of Trade in the early 1890s.

The debate of the 1830s and 1840s had evoked a response ultimately even among the writers of fiction; and Disraeli's *Sybil*, Dickens's *Hard Times*, Mrs Gaskell's *Mary Barton*, and Charles Kingsley's *Alton Locke* are the classical 'social novels'.[16] The debate beginning in the 1880s did not evoke a comparable response among the novelists of the day. The most resonant texts in the literature of social comment in the period from the 1880s to the turn of the century have seemed to be neither social novels nor passionate, almost

[14] Thomas Carlyle, *Chartism*, 1839, reprinted in vol.6 of *Critical and Miscellaneous Essays* in the shilling edition of 1888. Helen M. Lynd, *England in the Eighteen-Eighties* (New York, 1945); Herman Ausubel, *In Hard Times. Reformers Among the Late Victorians* (London, 1960); Andrew Mearns, *The Bitter Cry of Outcast London*, edited with an Introduction by Anthony S. Wohl (Leicester, 1970); Gareth Stedman Jones, *Outcast London. A Study in the Relationship between Classes in Victorian Society* (Oxford, 1971), ch.16; José Harris, *Unemployment and Politics. A Study in English Social Policy 1886-1914* (Oxford, 1972).

[15] Stedman Jones, *Outcast London*, ch. 13 and E.P. Hennock, 'Poverty and social theory in England: the experience of the eighteen-eighties', *Social History* i (1976), pp. 67-91.

[16] Kathleen Tillotson's discussion in *Novels of the Eighteen-Forties*, first published in Oxford in 1954, still seems the most helpful.

apocalyptic polemics, like Carlyle's 'Chartism' or Engels's *Condition of the Working Class in England in 1844* but rather the social surveys, above all Booth and B. Seebohm Rowntree's house-to-house study of York, published in 1901 as *Poverty; A Study of Town Life* — and the account of the beginning of a life committed to social enquiry in Beatrice Webb's *My Apprenticeship*. To assert this is not to imply that either Booth or Rowntree — or Beatrice Webb — was passionless or to deny that all three had strong views on what needed to be done, which they proceeded to act out politically.[17] Nor is it intended to belittle the importance of the surveys carried out in the 1830s and 1840s, best symbolized by Edwin Chadwick's *The Sanitary Condition of the Labouring Population of Great Britain* (1842). It is simply an attempt to convey something of the tone of discussion at the end of the century and dramatize the dominance achieved by then of the empiricist mode in English social thought and criticism.[18]

The causes of this upsurge of concern, investigation and comment among the political nation in general and the intelligentsia in particular, have been much discussed. Was it fear of the developing urban ghettoes, sharpened by slowing economic growth? Was there a sense of the limitations of orthodox political economy after several decades of sustained trial? Whatever the roots of this 'class-consciousness of sin' as Beatrice Webb was to call it,[19] compulsory schooling ensured that the condition of the nation's children became an object for study and concern in a way that it had not been before. Children in mines and factories, in agricultural gangs, cleaning chimneys, had indeed attracted attention earlier; but as

[17] See F.R. Leavis's comments on the status of *My Apprenticeship* in his 'Introduction' to *Mill on Bentham and Coleridge* (London, 1950), pp. 18-29. For Booth see T.S. and M.B. Simey, *Charles Booth Social Scientist* (London, 1960) and for Rowntree, see Asa Briggs, *Social Thought and Social Action. A Study of the Work of Seebohm Rowntree 1871-1954* (London, 1961).

[18] See Abrams, *The Origins of British Sociology*; Yeo, 'Social Science and Social Change'; Cullen, *The Statistical Movement*; Reber N. Soffer, *Ethics and Society in England. The Revolution in the Social Sciences 1870-1914* (California and London, 1978); and Stefan Collini, *Liberalism and Sociology. L.T. Hobhouse and Political Argument in England 1880-1914* (Cambridge, 1979) and 'Political Theory and the Science of Society in Victorian Britain', *Historical Journal* xxiii (1980), pp. 203-32.

[19] Webb, *My Apprenticeship*, p. 182.

particular and distinct groups of victims. In the 1880s social commentators began to take an interest in the state of the child population *as a whole*. The invitation to the Secretary of the NUET to address the Social Science Congress in 1883 on the question 'is the modern system of education exerting any deleterious influence upon the health of the country?' was thus not simply a propaganda bonus for him in the fight against payment by results. It was also more generally symptomatic. And Dr James Crichton-Browne proved to be but the first of a procession of investigators and commentators to tramp through schools.

II The sharpening focus on mental defect

The Cross Commission had placed the question of mentally handicapped children firmly before the Egerton Commission and, interestingly, managed to inquire into over-pressure without calling Crichton-Browne as a witness. The Egerton Commission dodged him too. As we have seen, consideration of education for defective children other than the blind, had been tacked on to their terms of reference at a late stage. The timing and the looseness of phrasing concerning handicaps other than blindness and deafness[20] combined to make it look as though they were being sent on a general fishing expedition, during which the public controversy would have time to die down. And although the Commissioners did make a serious gesture towards children with other handicaps, not unnaturally, the bulk of their time and energy was devoted to blind and deaf children.

Given the public controversy, it was not surprising either to find the Commissioners, in making their gesture, interpreting 'other cases requiring exceptional methods of education' as meaning primarily children with mental defect. Their two medical witnesses on this subject were Dr Francis Warner and Dr G.E. Shuttleworth, Superintendent of the Royal Albert Asylum. Shuttleworth was perhaps a less celebrated but also a less controversial medical psychologist than Crichton-Browne; and his involvement correspondingly enables us to disentangle more clearly the part played by

[20] See above, p. 9.

doctors in general and medical psychologists in particular, in pressing for the identification and separate treatment of the mentally handicapped. Again, the establishment of an institutional framework of care seems to be the essential pre-condition for this differentiation.

By the late eighteenth century private madhouses were a well-established phenomenon. The state began to concern itself with patterns and standards of care for those with obvious mental malfunction in the early nineteenth century and a permanent supervisory body, the Lord Chancellor's Commissioners in Lunacy, with power to inspect, report on and license madhouses, was established in 1845.[21] Already by then it was becoming clear that a proportion of those consigned to madhouses were not mentally ill, but mentally deficient, and commentators, both medical and lay, began regularly to draw a distinction between dementia, the disturbance of mental function, and amentia, the absence of mental function.[22] The refinement of classification within the second of these broad groupings, and its relation to public policy is, of course, one of the major themes of this study. Classification proceeded — and proceeds — along two parallel, occasionally intersecting, paths: the aetiology of mental defect and the measurement of its severity. Both have implications for care and treatment, but given that a high proportion of mental defects are congenital and not (so far) susceptible of cure as such, the latter is of independent and enduring importance.

At first, however, precision appeared more easily attainable on the aetiological front. At the beginning of the nineteenth century the words 'cretin', 'idiot' and 'imbecile' had been used more or less interchangeably. But the accumulation of evidence about the association of cretinism with thyroid deficiency and the efficacy of treatments involving iodine, first isolated and then greatly reduced its incidence. In 1866

[21] See William Ll. Parry-Jones, *The Trade in Lunacy. A Study of Private Madhouses in England in the Eighteenth and Nineteenth Centuries* (London, 1972); Kathleen Jones, *A History of the Mental Health Services* (London, 1972), Part I; and Andrew Scull, *Museums of Madness. The Social Organization of Insanity in Nineteenth-Century England* (London, 1979), chs. 1–3.

[22] Jones, *Mental Health Services,* Part II, s.8, L. Kanner, *A History of the Care and Study of the Mentally Retarded* (Springfield, Illinois, 1964), p. 102.

Dr John Langdon Haydon Down set out the classical description of what, using racial stereotypes, he called Mongolism, and we now know as Down's Syndrome.[23] When, in 1877, W.W. Ireland published his *On Idiocy and Imbecility*, which one leading twentieth-century American authority has called 'the first well-organized and medically oriented textbook of mental deficiency', he set out no less than twelve subdivisions of idiocy: '1) Genetous [*sic*], 2) microcephalic, 3) eclampsic, 4) epileptic, 5) hydrocephalic, 6) paralytic, 7) traumatic, 8) inflammatory, 9) sclerotic, 10) syphilitic, 11) cretinism, 12) idiocy by deprivation'.[24]

The expansion of work in medical psychology and the emergence of neurophysiology as a medical specialism had much to do with David Ferrier's successful demonstration of cerebral localization of function;[25] and it is perhaps not entirely fanciful to see reverberations of this in the positive obsession of most late nineteenth-century medical writers on mental defect with physical and often cranial abnormalities — what they came to call the *stigmata* of mental defect. Warner, it should be said, came to concern himself with defective children through earlier work on their motor development rather than on mental illness or the brain. But this again led him to focus intensively upon the child's physical appearance and co-ordination.[26] This approach had its limitations, as some doctors were very willing to acknowledge. In the second edition of what proved a very successful textbook, *Mentally Deficient Children*, in 1900 Dr Shuttleworth commented that of the 100,000 children supposedly covered by the Warner inquiries between 1888 and 1894, only 18,127 were actually individually examined, 'no note being taken of

[23] John Langdon Haydon Down, 'Observations on an Ethnic Classification of Idiots', *London Hospital Reports* 3 (1866), pp. 259-62, reprinted in Down, *Mental Affections of Childhood and Youth* (London, 1887), pp. 210-13. For a brief account of Down, see Lord Brain, 'Chairman's Opening Remarks: Historical Introduction', in CIBA Foundation Study Group No.25, *Mongolism, in commemoration of Dr John Langdon Haydon Down*, ed. G.E.W. Wolstenholme and Ruth Porter (London, 1967), pp. 1-5. The *cause* of Down's syndrome — the presence of an extra chromosome — was of course a twentieth century discovery.

[24] Kanner, *Care and Study of the Mentally Retarded*, p. 106.

[25] See Robert M. Young, *Mind, Brain and Adaptation in the Nineteenth Century* (Oxford, 1970).

[26] See e.g. chapters 1-3 of Francis Warner, *Lectures on the Growth and Means of Training the Mental Faculty* (Cambridge, 1890).

the 81,900 children not presenting obvious physical defect, or not reported by teachers as mentally dull'.[27]

The range of Shuttleworth's experience had shown him that neither 'stigmata' nor teacher's assessments were completely comprehensive or infallible. Besides his work at the Royal Albert Asylum he had also, in the early 1880s, begun to consider what might be done for children whose defect was not so severe as to require residential care.[28] At the same time the effect of the 1886 Idiots Act had been to enlarge the group of children coming into residential care. Hitherto it had been possible for an asylum to accept a child only if the parents and two doctors were prepared to certify him or her under the Lunacy Acts, with all the enduring legal disabilities which that brought. Now a parent could apply for the admission of a child simply on the basis of one medical statement that the child was an imbecile.[29] Shuttleworth was beginning to grapple with questions of treatment and care and thus with measuring the severity of mental defect on a larger scale than ever before. And he was to dedicate his textbook to Edouard Séguin who, as Superintendent of the School for Idiots at the Bicêtre in Paris 1842-8 and then as Superintendent of the Massachusetts School for Idiots and Feeble-Minded Youths 1848-80, had first shown both Western Europe and the USA how systematic training could help even severely defective children to cope better with the management of their daily lives.

All of this made Shuttleworth a witness of far greater value than Warner to the Egerton Commission. Warner's grand scheme of surveys carried with it no prescription for action once the defective children had been identified; and, as the Commissioners rather dismissively remarked, 'Dr Warner's views are not at present generally accepted, but they are under examination.'[30] Shuttleworth, on the other hand,

[27] G.E. Shuttleworth, *Mentally Deficient Children* (2nd edition, London, 1900), pp. 13-14. The first edition had been published in 1895; this, considerably expanded, second edition followed in 1900 and further editions followed in 1910, 1915, and 1922: from 1910 Shuttleworth was assisted by Dr W.A. Potts. For Warner's enquiries, see above, p. 000.

[28] Pritchard, *Education and the Handicapped*, p. 106, n. 1.

[29] P.P. 1889 xix *Report and Minutes of Evidence of the Royal Commission on the Blind, Deaf and Dumb, etc., of the United Kingdom* (Egerton), *Report*, paras. 628-30.   [30] Ibid., para. 723.

they embraced whole-heartedly and their report and recommendations concerning children with mental defect are
largely a summary of his evidence.

The Commission's recommendations make it plain that the
elaboration of categories in the aetiological description of
defect achieved by the end of the 1880s, whether as exemplified by Warner, or Ireland, or indeed by Shuttleworth
himself, in the relevant chapters of *Mentally Deficient
Children*, could not be matched with a comparable elaboration in the classification of defect by degree of severity.
Although acknowledging what had become a conventional
distinction between idiocy (sometimes 'idiotcy') and imbecility, namely that the former was a more severe condition
of the latter, the Commissioners saw this only as a difference
of degree and went on to use the terms interchangeably.
They accepted Shuttleworth's grouping of 'the idiot class'
into three: 'those capable of learning to read and write;
secondly, those capable of benefiting in a minor degree by
school instruction and discipline; and thirdly; the ineducable
class'. They talked also of children who were 'weak-minded'
or 'backward', a category of defect they considered less
severe than idiocy.[31] But the effective distinction between
these children and Shuttleworth's first class of idiots seems
to have been that their parents chose to send them to elementary schools rather than to asylums. The Commissioners
and Shuttleworth might propose four groups but in effect
they were describing a continuum of defect, shading from
the very severe through to the nearly normal, and suggesting
that children could be placed with assurance somewhere in
that continuum only through the trial and error of attempting to teach them.

The fishing expedition had served to reveal an issue of
great complexity, about which expertise and experience were
only just beginning to accumulate. The tentative tone of the
Commissioners' recommendations about mentally defective
children contrasted sharply with the assurance and detail of
their proposals for the blind, deaf and dumb children, as did
the pattern of public response.

For blind and deaf and dumb children, the Egerton

---

[31] Ibid., paras. 651, 660, 661 and subhead, and 709-24.

Commissioners recommended the provision of special schools, the bulk of the cost to be borne by the state, and compulsory attendance, for blind children between the ages of five and sixteen, for the deaf and dumb between the ages of seven and sixteen. Efforts to turn these recommendations into legislation began at once, both inside and outside government, and by 1893 achieved success.[32]

In the case of feeble-minded children, the Commissioners had suggested that the school attendance officer be required to notify these and to obtain a medical report on their educability. On receipt of this and on application from the parent, 'The school authority should have the power and be required to send the child to an institution and contribute to its maintenance.'[33] To this there was no response within the central government and no pressure group hastened to sponsor a bill.

But the Report did not disappear into a void. No education authority had made much effort to compel the attendance of children with severe mental defects, those likely to need residential care, and they did not begin to do so now. However, many children with less severe defects had — as the Commission had recognized — found their way into the elementary-school system, where they constituted a considerable teaching problem. For these children — and indeed for some physically handicapped and delicate children — the annual graded examinations of the Elementary Education Code were an almost insuperable barrier: they were, in fact, the most likely victims of over-pressure, if it existed. They were usually to be found clustered together with the seven-year-olds in Standard I, or occasionally, in large schools, in a separate Standard 'O'.[34] Since 1890 Major-General F.J. Moberley, chairman of the London School Board's sub-committee on the blind and deaf, had been campaigning for the Board to act on the Egerton Commission's recommendations and establish special schools for the feeble-minded;

[32] Education Department and Board of Education Papers, Ed 31/8 and Pritchard, *Education and the Handicapped*, pp. 102–11. The different ages for compulsion were based on the misconception that systematic language training for the deaf and dumb children could not be started before they had reached the age of seven.

[33] P.P. 1889 xix *Egerton Report*, p. cvi, recommendation 1.

[34] Pritchard, *Education and the Handicapped*, pp. 116–17.

and the first of these was at last opened in the autumn of 1892. That same summer, the inspector employed by the Leicester School Board had taken it upon himself, apparently quite independently, to establish a special class for feeble-minded children at Milton Street School. By 1897 there were twenty-seven special schools in London alone and six other school boards besides Leicester, Nottingham, Birmingham, Bradford, Brighton, Bristol and Plymouth, had begun to make separate provision for the feeble-minded. Altogether, 1,300 children were attending special schools and classes.[35]

Unlike the Leicester Board, the London Board had consulted the Education Department before acting and persuaded it to treat children in special schools as infants, i.e. under seven, for the purposes of grant under the Code. But defective children cost more than normal infants and in 1894 the Board began to lobby both for increased grant and the extension of the system of special schools as established by the 1893 Blind and Deaf Act, to cover mentally defective children. Now the pressure groups began to form; and London and the other Boards were reinforced by a special committee under no less a person than Lord Egerton of Tatton, and by the Charity Organization Society and its newest offspring, the National Association for Promoting the Welfare of the Feeble-Minded. At the end of 1896 the government took refuge in another inquiry, this time a departmental one.[36]

One of its functions was undoubtedly to buy time — it did not report until 1898 — but it was very much more than a fishing expedition. Its terms of reference were tightly and precisely drawn:

To inquire into the existing systems for the education of feeble-minded and defective children not under the charge of Guardians [i.e. the Poor Law authorities] and not idiots or imbeciles and to advise as to any changes, either with or without legislation, that may be desirable.

To report particularly upon the best means for discriminating on the one hand between the educable and non-educable classes of feeble-minded and defective children, and on the other hand between

[35] P.P. 1898 xxvi, *Report and Minutes of Evidence of the Departmental Committee on Defective and Epileptic Children,* f. 7; qq. 3569–72.

[36] Ed 14/43 and Ed 50/29. For the Charity Organization Society and the National Association for Promoting the Welfare of the Feeble-Minded, see below, pp. 27–34.

those children who may properly be taught in ordinary elementary schools by ordinary methods and those who should be taught in special schools.

To inquire and report as to the provision of suitable elementary education for epileptic children and as to any changes that may be desirable.[37]

The sharp focus of this brief enabled the official hard core of the committee, two HMIs and two Examiners, to explore systematically what the medical psychologists had to say and to see what the two newly emerging groups of experts, Medical Officers of Health, and teachers and managers of special schools, along with the more miscellaneous persons now appearing to take an interest, could contribute. Dr Shuttleworth was a member of the committee; Dr Warner appeared once more as a witness, along with Dr F.H. Walmsley from the Darenth Asylum, Dr Fletcher Beach from the Epileptic Colony at Chalfont and the most distinguished neurophysiologist of them all, Dr David Ferrier, now Professor of Neuropathology at King's College, London. Dr W.R. Smith, MOH to the London School Board, was another member of the committee and the witnesses included his assistant Dr F.D. Harris, and Dr James Kerr, MOH to the Bradford School Board, the only other Board in the country to employ a MOH full time. Mrs E.M. Burgwin, the Superintendent of the London special schools, was yet another committee member and the witnesses also included General Moberley, Miss Annette Verrall, the head of the Brighton special school, Henry Major, the Leicester School Board's inspector, and the Revd. J.J. Martin of the Bristol School Board. Other interested parties included, on the committee itself, Miss Pauline Townsend, member of the council of the Association for Promoting the welfare of the Feeble-Minded, and among the witnesses, Miss F.A. Cooper, its Secretary, C.S. Loch, Secretary to the Charity Organization Society, and Sir Douglas Galton, geographer, hospital planner, cousin of Francis Galton and representing the British Association for the Advancement of Science, who had supported some of Warner's work. Everybody who could conceivably have a view — except the parents and the children — appeared to be in the act.

<hr>

[37] P.P. 1898, xxvi, *Defective and Epileptic Children,* f. 5.

The real challenge to all this experience and expertise lay in the second paragraph of their terms of reference: to report upon 'the best means of discriminating' first between educable and non-educable children and then between children who could attend an ordinary elementary school and those who should be in a special school. On this the committee and its witnesses had nothing of substance to add to the Egerton Report. As the Committee's Secretary, Hugh Orange of the Education Department, acknowledged frankly to the Treasury in January 1899: 'None of the witnesses were [*sic*] able to offer any verbal definition of the degree of want of intelligence which constitutes a defective child.'[38]

They had discussed it exhaustively of course; and again, much was made of 'stigmata', Dr James Kerr of Bradford being much preoccupied with 'curved fingers' as well as 'arched palates' and 'lobeless ears'. But when pressed really hard, he admitted that it was extremely difficult to be rigorous in the description of physical signs of defect. 'There is something that eludes description in diagnosis — you must take the whole case.' Likewise, Dr Francis Warner admitted at one point, 'it is difficult to define what physical conditions seen, as apart from mental tests, indicate the child as unfitted for the usual methods of education'.[39]

Professor David Ferrier was quite frank in admitting the great difficulty of attempting to distinguish between idiocy and feeble-mindedness. He commended the London School Board's practice of involving the district HMI and the Superintendent of special schools, as well as the MOH, in the examination of children selected by the class teachers in the elementary schools for consideration for admission to special schools. He agreed with the committee that the MOH should be involved in the process, but, alone of the medical witnesses, argued that his should not be the decisive voice until he

[38] Ed 31/16 Memorandum on the Definition of Defective, headed with a pencilled note showing it was prepared for transmission informally to Spring-Rice at the Treasury by Orange, at the same time as the official letter and Memorandum from the Permanent Secretary of the Education Department, 25 Jan. 1899 (see below, p. 23). Henceforward cited as 'Orange's Unofficial Memo. January 1899'.

[39] P.P. 1898 xxvi, *Defective and Epileptic Children*, qq. 566-9 (Kerr), 752 (Warner). See also Shuttleworth's Appendix I and the evidence of Drs Fletcher Beach and Harris, esp. qq. 1067-8 and 1071.

had had at least eighteen months' experience of the work.[40]

Paragraph fourteen of the committee's eventual report, dealing with the description of feeble-minded children, was a positive masterpiece of evasion.

Feeble-minded children are, in the great majority of cases, marked by some physical defect or defects discernible by the trained observer, and to some extent also by the untrained. The most conspicuous of such defects are irregularity in general bodily conformation, malformation of the head, the palate, tongue, lips, teeth, and ears, defective power either of motion or control in almost any of the different forms of muscular action, as shown in balance, attitude, and movement, and defects in some one or more of the sensory functions, besides the ordinary varieties of deformity and ill-health. A child may be abnormal in one or more of these respects without necessarily being feeble-minded; and there is no formula which will enable an untrained observer to pick out the precise point at which a combination of abnormalities constitutes a strong presumption of mental deficiency, and to identify the combination as that of a feeble-minded child. This is a matter which requires not only medical knowledge, but some special medical study; but we need not discuss whether a combination of physical signs is by itself, to a trained mind, a sufficient ground, without other proofs, for an opinion as to the mental powers of the child. Information can always be obtained as to the child's habits, conduct, and power of learning, and generally also as to its history, and there is no reason why these most important factors should ever be neglected.[41]

But whatever the continuing uncertainties of classification, it was hardly possible to dispute that the special schools and classes were having a beneficial effect on the children who found their way into them and neither the Committee nor its witnesses seriously attempted to do so.[42] Those authorities who had experimented had come to constitute a not inconsiderable vested interest. The Report therefore came firmly down in favour of requiring all local education authorities to provide special schools or classes for mentally defective children aged seven and upwards, deemed to be educable. On the thorny question of selection, they endorsed the London practice of involving class and special school

[40] Ibid., qq. 5215-36.
[41] Ibid., f. 10; see also f. 15, para. 22 on distinguishing educable from non-educable children.
[42] Ibid., f. 34, paras. 73-5; also qq. 456-68 and 495-501 (Kerr); qq. 1007-115, 1220-1 (Harris); qq. 1406-10, 1419-24 (Chard) and qq. 1582-1695 (Blackmore).

teachers, the HMI and the MOH, and recommended that the parent should always be invited to attend the examination.[43] The Education Department thus had a firm brief, from a committee which had included four of its own senior men; although the first draft of a bill produced within the Department by the committee's secretary, Hugh Orange, differed crucially from the Report in being permissive, not compulsory.[44] The first draft of the Blind and Deaf Bill in 1890 had likewise been permissive and on that occasion Kekewich, the Permanent Secretary, himself had strengthened it.[45] But he took no such action on this occasion, in part, at least, because of the continuing problem of defining mental defect.

The Lord President, the eighth Duke of Devonshire, might have been indolent and often somnolent, but he had an unerring eye for the central issue. He responded to Orange's draft with the comment that special schools were likely to cost money and the Treasury had better be squared first. And when the Chancellor of the Exchequer, Hicks Beach, noted that unless the definition of mental defect was tightly and precisely drawn, a large number of children might find their way into special schools, he took the point immediately.[46] Orange therefore prepared for Kekewich a letter and a memorandum for the Treasury on the likely cost of the proposals. The burden of these was that the bill would make very little difference. Much play was made with its permissive nature: Orange and Kekewich forecast that a good number of local education authorities would not bother to respond.[47]

Orange, as befits a Civil Service 'flyer', also had his own informal channels of communication with the Treasury; and he reinforced the official letter and memorandum with an additional memorandum of his own. In this, as has been

[43] Ibid., ff. 17-18, paras. 28 and 29.
[44] Ed 31/16 printed heads of bill, Minute H.W. Orange to Sir George Kekewich 18 Nov. 1898 and Kekewich's Minute to Vice-President 21 Nov. 1898.
[45] Ed 31/8 Kekewich's amendments to the draft bill of March 1890.
[46] Ed 31/16 Devonshire's Minute 27 Nov. 1898, Hicks Beach to Devonshire 13 Jan. 1899 and Devonshire's Minute 17 Jan. 1899. On Devonshire as Lord President, see A.I. Taylor, 'The Church Party and Popular Education 1893-1902' (unpublished Cambridge Ph.D. thesis, 1981), pp. 102-6.
[47] Ed 31/16 Memorandum 5 Jan. 1899 with annotation 'as sent to Treasury enclosed in letter 25 January 1899', Orange's draft of a letter to the Treasury 23 Jan. 1899 and Kekewich's Minute 24 Jan. 1899.

noted, he freely admitted that the Departmental Committee had failed to come up with a watertight definition of 'the degree of want of intelligence that constitutes a defective child'. But he offered an expansion of the words in his original draft, replacing 'children, who not being imbecile, are incapable of receiving proper benefit from the instruction in ordinary schools' with 'children, who not being imbecile, and not being merely backward or dull children are, by reason of mental defect incapable of receiving proper benefit from the instruction in ordinary schools'. And he went on to argue that the draft bill's requirement of reports from both teacher and MOH in standard form, the retention of the ultimate power of decision in the hands of the Education Department, and the fact that, in spite of extra grant, some of the extra cost of special schools would fall on the local authority, would all combine to discourage them from 'acting frivolously'.[48]

The Treasury allowed itself to be persuaded and the bill proceeded on its way in essentially this form through the Cabinet and to Parliament. The only amendments of substance accepted in the Commons brought the parents of a child thought to be defective more explicitly into the process of examination, although thereby also enhancing the importance of the doctor. They turned the medical report into a medical certificate, gave the parent the right to insist on this before his child was admitted to a special school, and gave him the right and the local authority the discretion to require re-examination of the child at periodic intervals.[49]

The bill received the Royal Assent on 9 August 1899. The 1890s had seen no significant advances in either the aetiology or the treatment of mental defect. But the local initiatives and the accumulation of experience in the care of mentally defective children had proved enough to get permissive legislation on to the statute-book.

---

[48] Ibid. Orange's Unofficial Memo., January 1899. From 1902 to 1910 Orange was Director-General of Indian Education; from 1910 to 1912 he was Chief HMI for Elementary Schools and from 1912 to 1928 Accountant-General of the Board of Education, retiring with a KBE.

[49] Ibid. Mowatt to Kekewich 8 Feb. 1899, annotated order paper 27 July 1899. 62 & 63 Vict. c. 32.

Chapter 2

Towards a National Policy for the Subnormal Child

The decade and a half up to the outbreak of the First World War saw a further intensification of interest in and activity on behalf of mentally defective children. In 1914 legislation *requiring all* local education authorities to provide special schools, reached the statute-book. By that time also a sophisticated system of classifying mental defect by degree of severity had been developed.

It is tempting to postulate some causal connections between these developments; and it would be satisfyingly tidy to be able to argue that sophisticated classification made a national system possible. But contentious social legislation seldom has tidy origins. It is in fact possible to explore the pressures which build up to produce the Act of 1914 with virtually no reference to the parallel technical developments; and before examining these technical developments it is necessary to look at the pressures for action. This entails in turn discussion of the extent to which the campaign to provide for defective children was caught up with and related to the campaign primarily concerned with adult defectives, which resulted in the Mental Deficiency Act of 1913. The earliest manifestation of this campaign, spearheaded by the Charity Organization Society, concerned itself with what one protagonist called 'social waste'. Later campaigners came increasingly to use the language of Social Darwinism and, in some cases, of eugenics.

The relationship between these movements and attempts to provide for children are obviously of great intrinsic interest and importance. The interest and importance are enhanced because it has been argued that such ideas provided the primary impulse for the legislative provision of 1913 and 1914 together.[1] This seems to me both to overstate and to

---

[1] Jones, *Mental Health Services,* pp. 185-210, R.A. Lowe, 'Eugenicists, Doctors and the Quest for National Efficiency: An Educational Crusade 1900–1939', *History of Education* viii (1979), pp. 293-306, acknowledges the distinctive position of the Board of Education in general and Dr George Newman in particular, but inclines to present them as responding essentially defensively to

over-simplify the relationship. As the previous chapter attempted to show, a campaign to make special provision for mentally defective children had got under way by the end of the 1880s. Certainly the concern of those preoccupied with the 'social waste' represented by defective adults, and then the articulation of Social Darwinist notions about the threat to the race provided powerful reinforcements for this. And in so far as the debate about 'national efficiency' which developed following the Boer war focused particularly on the children of the nation, more intensively even than the discussion of the 1880s, the campaign for special schools gained significantly in momentum. Nevertheless, the provision for mentally defective children decided upon in 1913-14 remained distinct from that for mentally defective adults. Its primary object was education rather than custody. The commitment to a national system of special schools cannot be seen as a straightforward triumph for the eugenists.

I From 'social waste' to 'national efficiency'

Mention has already been made of the involvement of the Charity Organization Society in the campaign for special schools in the 1890s and the formation of the National Association for Promoting the Welfare of the Feeble-Minded in 1896.[2] These mark the increasing interaction between the campaigns for the care of adult defectives and the campaign on behalf of children. The treatment of adults first becomes a topic of public debate in the early 1870s in the context of concern about the mismanagement and waste of human resources in the society. The roots of this concern, however, lie even further back, in the moralization of political economy in the first half of the nineteenth century and the successful marriage between the Evangelical commitment to personal service and the methods of investigation and models

the great monolith of the eugenics movement. This view of both the Board and of eugenics seems to me an extravagant and also a somewhat simplistic one; and as will be clear from this chapter and chapters 1 and 3, I differ from Mr Lowe on the interpretation of the sources at a number of points.

[2] Above, pp. 19-20.

of economic and political organization developed by the
political economists.[3]

Classical political economy taught that indiscriminate
alms-giving undermined the economic system of the country
by eroding and ultimately destroying the labouring man's
incentive to work. The logical consequence was the abolition
of all poor relief — never a politically viable course. And it
was Edwin Chadwick's triumph in the Poor Law Amendment
Act of 1834 to devise a scheme both politically and intellectually acceptable. Poor relief was to continue, but only within
the workhouse and at subsistence level, consequently presenting itself as less attractive or 'eligible' than the freedom
and modest standard of living to be achieved by honest toil.
This doctrine of 'less eligibility' rested, of course, on two
assumptions: first, that full employment was the norm and
second, that wages provided more than subsistence. Considerations of the theoretical and practical adequacy of
political economy apart, there were of course times and
places in nineteenth-century England when neither of these
held. Poor relief, as it actually operated after 1834, left
ample scope for the earnest Evangelical to act out his commitment. He — or equally often, she — might concern himself
with the proper organization of his local workhouse; he
might concentrate his attention on the care of those un-
fortunates who were clearly not able-bodied adult economic
man — the sick, the aged and small children — and thus
respectable exceptions to the general rule of less eligibility.[4]

The Charity Organization Society, founded in 1869,
exemplified the extent to which Evangelicals and political
economists found it possible to combine. The immediate
object of the founders, Octavia Hill, Canon Samuel Barnett,
the Revd W.H. Fremantle and C.S. Loch, was 'to organize
charitable assistance so as to prevent over-lapping and competition between the innumerable and heterogeneous

---

[3] A key figure in this process was the Revd Thomas Chalmers — see the extended discussion in Boyd Hilton, *The Age of Atonement* (forthcoming).

[4] Mark Blaug, 'The Myth of the Old Poor Law and the Making of the New',
Journal of Economic History xxiii (1963), pp. 151–84 and 'The Poor Law Report
Re-examined', ibid. xxiv (1964), pp. 229–45; Geoffrey Best, *Mid-Victorian
Britain 1851–75* (London, 1971), pp. 133–48; F.K. Prochaska, *Women and
Philanthropy in Nineteenth-Century England* (Oxford, 1980).

agencies'. From this they wanted to move to refine and ultimately to reduce charitable assistance by the practice of systematic social case-work. Beatrice Webb characterized their basic principles thus:

> patient and persistent personal service on the part of the well-to-do; an acceptance of personal responsibility for the ulterior consequences, alike to the individual recipient and to others who might be indirectly affected, of charitable assistance; and finally, as the only way of carrying out this service and fulfilling this responsibility, the application of the scientific method to each separate case of a damaged body or a lost soul; so that the assistance given should be based on a correct forecast of what would actually happen, as a result of the gift, to the character and circumstances of the individual recipient and the destitute class to which he belonged.[5]

One of the problems with which the Charity Organization Society early concerned itself was the herding together in many workhouses of various categories of pauper who, in its view, would benefit from separate treatment. Edwin Chadwick had originally envisaged specialization within the workhouse and distinct and separate regimes for the adult able-bodied, the sick, the aged and the children. For reasons of cost, if nothing else, many Boards of Guardians disregarded such refinements and built or adapted general workhouses.[6] But in the larger institutions in particular, the efficient management of paupers who were never likely to work again, such as the disabled and the aged, could be clearly distinguished from that of the able-bodied adults who were to be given every incentive to quit the workhouse as soon as possible. And this was one of the considerations in the prolonged and complex public debate which led eventually to the Metropolitan Poor Act of 1867. This compelled the combination of the individual Poor Law authorities in the metropolitan area, to form the Metropolitan Asylums

---

[5] Webb, *My Apprenticeship*, pp. 196–7. See also e.g. Charity Organisation Series (*sic*), *The Feeble-Minded Child and Adult*, London, 1893, p. xv. Beatrice Webb's discussion of the Charity Organization Society — 'my friend, my enemy' — pp. 193–215, remains a far more vivid and telling one than the pieties of Charles Loch Mowat, *The Charity Organization Society 1896–1913. Its Ideas and Work* (London, 1961).

[6] S.E. Finer, *The Life and Times of Sir Edwin Chadwick* (London, 1952), pp. 85–6; Michael E. Rose, *The Relief of Poverty 1834–1914* (London, 1972), pp. 35–9.

Board, charged to provide specialized institutions for the care of the sick, infirm and insane poor of London.[7] In the nineteenth-century workhouse, as in the nineteenth-century madhouse, pressure developed thus for the categorization and specialist treatment of the assorted inmates. Distinct provision for the insane poor of the metropolis under the 1867 Act was a logical extension of the principle of specialization of care – and one which had already been urged by the Lord Chancellor's Commissioners in Lunacy.[8] The Metropolitan Poor Act enabled the transfer of imbeciles and the chronic insane from London workhouses to the new asylums, and by the early 1870s there were in existence two new institutions for adults, at Leavesden and Caterham, and a training school for imbecile children at Darenth. The creation of this last institution was an important stage in the differentiation of the mentally defective from the mentally ill, to which reference has already been made;[9] and it was at this point that the Charity Organization Society entered the fray. In 1875 it set up a 'Committee for Considering the Best Means of making a Satisfactory Provision for Idiots, Imbeciles and Harmless Lunatics'. The committee contained an impressive array of the great and the good – peers such as the Earls of Devon and Lichfield, distinguished public servants such as Sir Charles Trevelyan and Sir James Kay-Shuttleworth (initially trained as a doctor), and a battery of medical specialists including Drs Langdon Down, Fletcher Beach, W.W. Ireland and Daniel Hack Tuke; and when they reported in 1877 they recommended, in effect, that the principle of the Metropolitan Poor Act should be extended to cover the whole country.

When in May 1877 they waited in a great deputation upon the President of the Local Government Board to present their report, they were accompanied by none other than the seventh Earl of Shaftesbury, not actually a member of the Charity Organization Society but on this matter entirely in agreement with them. He recalled that he had been a

---

[7] Ruth G. Hodgkinson, *The Origins of the National Health Service. The Medical Services of the New Poor Law, 1834–1871* (London, 1967), pp. 500–1. For the debate, see the preceding sections of ch.14.

[8] Ibid. Ch. 15.

[9] Above, p. 14.

Commissioner in Lunacy for fifty years, and he spoke in support particularly of schemes for training schools for mentally defective children:

this class can be vastly benefited by being brought under proper treatment and are capable of receiving such comfort in the perfection of the training that they may discharge their duty as members of society.

He argued also that the attempt to care for one mentally defective member often pulled down whole families into pauperism; and wound up:

I know that all classes of our people have the strongest possible objections against what is called 'paternal government', but 'paternal government' is of two kinds, that which is over children and that which is over adults. It is, I think, the duty of the State to come in when they see children altogether without care. The State does so where the children have no parents; and so, where the parents are unable to do justice to imbecile children, I think it is the duty of the State to come forward and, *in loco parentis*, give all the aid which humanity and Christianity dictates as necessary to be given. We have in this matter not only the principles of political economy in the utilisation of now wasted labour: but we have, beyond all, the great lesson taught in Scripture, that in all our work there should be no 'waste'; for the Saviour of Mankind, after feeding the multitude, commanded to 'gather up the fragments that remain, so that nothing be lost'. I urge upon Her Majesty's Government that these poor creatures of whom we speak are the fragments of humanity whom it is our duty, as civilised beings and as Christians, to 'gather up' and store in the public garner.[10]

For all their courteous reception at the Local Government Board, nothing happened; although it has been suggested that Charity Organization Society pressure contributed to the passage of the Idiots' Act of 1886, which, as we have seen, made it possible for mentally defective persons to be admitted to asylums without the full panoply of certification as lunatics.[11]

The rediscovery of the Condition-of-England Question in

[10] Charity Organization Society, *Report of the Committee for Considering the Best Means of Making a Satisfactory Provision for Idiots, Imbeciles and Harmless Lunatics* and *Idiots, Imbeciles and Harmless Lunatics, their Education and Care. Report of a Deputation to the Local Government Board.* ... (London, 1877), direct quotation from pp. 54–5.

[11] Above, p. 16 and Jones, *Mental Health Services*, p. 185. She states that Shaftesbury 'headed' the deputation. He did not and his speech makes his special supporting role quite plain.

the 1880s, as one might expect, profoundly altered the context in which the Charity Organization Society worked. In some senses the Charity Organization Society constituted the advance guard of rediscovery, particularly through its insistence upon systematic social case-work and the 'scientific method'. But the upsurge of concern and comment spread far beyond the Charity Organization Society and its hard core of support in the professional middle class; and it gradually found itself but one of a number of groups competing to offer social diagnosis and prescription — a situation dramatized as some of its members, most notably two of the founders, Canon Barnett and his wife Henrietta, moved beyond their co-founders towards an explicit Socialist commitment.[12]

But the changed climate was also one in which a number of campaigns initiated or supported by the Charity Organization Society were able to flourish. Having focused initially on provision for those with severe mental defect, it turned its attention in the later 1880s to the so-called feeble-minded, both child and adult. In concert with the National Vigilance Association and the Metropolitan Association for Befriending Young Servants, it helped bring about the creation, between 1887 and 1896, of eleven homes for feeble-minded girls over school age.[13] It strongly supported Dr Francis Warner's surveys of schoolchildren and in 1893 published a summary of these along with a report from its own committee on *The Feeble-Minded Child and Adult*. This added its voice to the swelling chorus in support of special schools.

All this activity, as might have been expected, eventually in 1896 brought forth a specialist pressure group, the National Association for Promoting the Welfare of the Feeble-Minded, providing a national framework and forum for two redoubtable campaigners, Miss Mary Dendy and Mrs Ellen Pinsent. Both had come to the work initially through school board membership, Miss Dendy in Manchester and Mrs Pinsent in Birmingham. Miss Dendy was the archetypal committed case-worker — not unlike Octavia Hill in the field of housing — and was the prime mover in the foundation and running of a

[12] Webb, *My Apprenticeship*, p. 215. See also Stedman Jones, *Outcast London*, pp. 296–314.
[13] Pritchard, *Education and the Handicapped*, p. 180.

colony for mentally handicapped adults and children at Sandlebridge in Cheshire, which opened its doors in 1902. Mrs Pinsent exhibits more dramatically the transformation well under way, of the nineteenth-century lady who engaged in good works, into the middle-class woman of the early twentieth century, whose formal position might remain that of a voluntary worker, but whose engagement in pressure-group tactics, organization and administration was wholly professional in its quality and extent.[14]

Miss Dendy and Mrs Pinsent concerned themselves not simply with social waste but with what they saw as social danger. The arrangements at Sandlebridge laid as much emphasis upon custodial care as upon training. The children were expected in due course to move from the residential school to a permanent home in the adult colony. Writing was discouraged in the school, for fear it might lead to undesirable communication between the sexes in adulthood; and the adult quarters were strictly segregated by sex. A paper delivered by Mrs Pinsent to a conference on 'Treatment of the Mentally Defective' in Leicester in 1902, was a rousing call for a national and complete system of such schools and colonies. In this way, she declared,

children who were unfit to face life on their own responsibility. . . . would never be allowed the liberty which they can only misuse to their own degradation and to the degradation of the society in which they live. Theoretically it may be hard to decide what degree of mental deficiency renders people morally irresponsible for their actions, but when it comes to the practical side, the question as to which cases will ever become independent of help and self-supporting, it is not nearly so hard a matter. Let us face the worst that might happen. Let us grant that a very small percentage of the feeble-minded would be kept in a colony who might have gone through life without serious harm to themselves or to others and then let us weigh this evil — for I grant it would be an evil — against the infinite amount of suffering and moral degradation caused by the fact that people of defective intellect are allowed the full liberty of responsible citizens, that they are allowed to make the lives of their own families miserable and to leave behind them

[14] M. Cruikshank, 'Mary Dendy 1855–1923' *Journal of Educational Administration and History* viii (1976), pp. 26–9; Mary Dendy, *Appendix* to C. Paget Lapage, *Feeble-Mindedness in Children* (London, 1911); Jones, *Mental Health Services.* Mrs Pinsent, or Dame Ellen Pinsent, as she later became, would be well worth a biography.

others as defective as themselves. Ultimately such people do have some restriction or other put upon their personal liberty; too often in gaol, too often in penitentiaries, and most often, perhaps, in the workhouse. We are only asking for restriction a few years sooner and we offer, instead of the usual story of crime, shame and pauperism, that these years should be spent happily and safely and filled with pleasant and honest labour.

Central to such proposals was the belief that mental defect was predominantly an inherited condition and could be reduced, if not stamped out, by discouraging or preventing the mentally defective from marrying and breeding. Mrs Pinsent concluded her paper, 'a thorough and complete system of state intervention would lead to a steady decrease in the numbers of the mentally deficient'.[15] It was a view which gained ground rapidly in the 1890s. Some measure of the extent and speed of the shift is given by a comparison of Mrs Pinsent's remarks with the Report of the Charity Organization Society Committee ten years earlier. Its members, too, considered heredity to play a major part in mental defect, but they were rather less convinced that custodial detention and segregation would provide the solution:

And though feeble-mindedness is largely due to heredity, in a great number of cases it makes its appearance independently of known hereditary taint. Also in the course of hereditary transmission degenerate conditions are transmitted so that the imbecile or feeble-minded child is more frequently the offspring of a consumptive or a scrofulous than of a mentally deficient person. . . . We may conclude then that the extent of the mischief due to this cause [i.e. absence of custodial detention] has been somewhat exaggerated.

And they left custodial detention firmly 'an open question'.[16]

Dr Shuttleworth had, inevitably, been a member of this Charity Organization Society Committee and, yet again, he constitutes an admirable barometer. In his evidence to the Egerton Commission, he had described the origins of mental defect as very varied, and concentrated on training schemes. The training schemes recommended by the Charity Organization Society in 1893 were substantially his. These themes remained prominent in the first edition of *Mentally Deficient*

[15] Ellen F. Pinsent, 'On the Permanent Care of the Feeble-Minded', *The Lancet*, 21 Feb. 1903, pp. 513-15.
[16] *The Feeble-Minded Child and Adult*, p. 136 (see also p. 13).

Children, published in 1895. But in his second edition in 1900 there was a new emphasis upon the inheritance of defect in his discussion of its causes. In his final chapter, he rebutted charges that the training of mentally defective children would increase their chances of eventual marriage and thus child-bearing. He admitted, however, that he was in favour of the legal detention of mentally defective adults, although thinking this likely to be politically unacceptable. 'There is no doubt', he went on, 'that in the interests of society a permanent Home, apart from the ordinary population, is, in the majority of feeble-minded cases, a desideratum. It must never be forgotten that mental feebleness is as a rule hereditary, and consequently transmissable to another generation.' In this edition, too, he was but the first of many to commend especially Mary Dendy's plans for Sandlebridge, now about to open its doors.[17]

Therefore, before we can turn at last to a consideration of the campaigning in the years after 1900, we must attempt some unravelling of one further major strand in the swelling debate about the care of the mentally defective; that represented by Social Darwinism and eugenics.

Darwin's cousin, Francis Galton, wrote that,

The publication in 1859 of the *Origin of Species* by Charles Darwin made a marked epoch in my own mental development, as it did in that of human thought generally. Its effect was to demolish a multitude of dogmatic barriers by a single stroke, and to arouse a spirit of rebellion against all ancient authorities whose positive and unauthenticated statements were contradicted by modern science.[18]

Galton found in Darwin encouragement to react against the strains of associationist psychology and environmentalism so powerful in English social thought at that period, and to focus instead on heredity. In 1869 he published *Hereditary Genius*. He explained in the preface:

The idea of investigating the subject of hereditary genius occurred to me during the course of a purely chronological inquiry into the mental

[17] G.E. Shuttleworth, *Mentally Deficient Children* (2nd edition, London, 1900), direct quotations from pp. 138-9, 149. Compare ch.XI, 'Results and Conclusions' with ch.IX, 'Results and Conclusions' of the first edition, 1895.

[18] Francis Galton, *Memories of My Life* (London, 1908), p. 287. This still conveys the man more vividly than the recent thorough and informative study by D.W. Forrest, *Francis Galton: The Life and Work of a Victorian Genius* (London, 1974).

peculiarities of different races; when the fact, that characteristics cling to families, was so frequently forced on my notice as to induce me to pay special attention to that branch of the subject. I began by thinking over the dispositions and achievements of my contemporaries at school, at college and in after life, and was surprised to find how frequently ability seemed to go by descent. Then I made a cursory examination into the kindred of about four hundred illustrious men of all periods of history, and the results were such, in my own opinion, as completely to establish the theory that genius was hereditary, under limitations that required to be investigated.

Galton used genius as a synonym for natural ability and later regretted that he had not used the latter term.[19] The bulk of the book is really an elaborate series of family trees of groups of men who had made their mark in various ways, ranging through judges, scientists, divines and Senior Classics, to oarsmen and North Country wrestlers — 'I propose to supplement what I have written about brain by two short chapters on muscle'[20] — with a discussion of the role played by heredity in the distinction of each group.

In conclusion he turned from patterns of inheritance among individuals to those among races: 'Every long-established race has necessarily its peculiar fitness for the conditions under which it has lived, owing to the sure operation of Darwin's law of natural selection.' After arranging the major races of the world in an hierarchy of ability, he sounded a warning note.

The needs of centralization, communication, and culture, call for more brains and mental stamina than the average of our race possess. We are in crying want for a greater fund of ability in all stations of life; for neither the classes of statesmen, philosophers, artisans nor labourers are up to the modern complexity of their several professions. . . . When the severity of the struggle for existence is not too great for the powers of the race, its action is healthy and conservative, otherwise it is deadly, just as we may see exemplified in the scanty wretched vegetation that leads a precarious existence near the summer snow-line of the Alps — and disappears altogether a little higher up. We want as much backbone as we can get, to bear the racket to which we are henceforth to be exposed, and as good brains as possible to contrive machinery, for modern life to work more smoothly than at present. We can, in some degree, modify the conditions to suit his nature. It is clearly right that both these powers should be exerted, with the view of bringing his

[19] *Hereditary Genius* (2nd edition, London, 1892), pp. viii–ix.
[20] *Hereditary Genius* (1st edition, London, 1869), p. 305.

nature and the conditions of his existence into as close harmony as possible.[21]

In these last two sentences he appeared even-handed, considering the possibility of changes in nurture as well as in nature. But it was the latter that fascinated him and it became the central preoccupation of the remainder of his long life. Once again, his own account of his intellectual trajectory cannot be bettered. In his *Memories* in 1908 he wrote:

After I had become satisfied of the inheritance of all the mental qualities into which I had inquired, and that heredity was a far more powerful agent in human development that nurture, I wished to explore the range of human faculty in various directions in order to ascertain the degree to which breeding might, at least theoretically, modify the human race. I took the moderate and reasonable standpoint that whatever quality had appeared in man and in whatever intensity, it admitted of being bred for and reproduced on a large scale.[22]

'To explore the range of human faculty', he began to experiment with various tests, both anthropometric and of sensory perception; and we shall return to these and some of their implications later on.[23] For the purposes of the present discussion, it is the linked propositions first, that a struggle for survival takes place in human society as well as in the plant and animal kingdoms; and second, that patterns of human reproduction can and ought to be managed, christened by him in 1883 'eugenics',[24] that are of importance.

Galton had begun the drafting of what was to become *Hereditary Genius* in the early 1860s, prefiguring its main argument in a paper published in 1864. In his monumental *Life* of Galton, Karl Pearson wrote, 'and then — in 1864 — we suddenly find the whole doctrine of eugenics as the salvation of mankind, developed half-a-century too early'.[25] 'Half a century' is an exaggeration; but Pearson is right to draw attention to the interesting time-lag between the initial enunciation of Galton's ideas and widespread public discussion

---

[21] Ibid., pp. 336, 345-6.

[22] Galton, *Memories*, p. 266. He died in 1911.

[23] Below, pp. 114-18.

[24] Francis Galton, *Inquiries into Human Faculty and its Development* (London, 1883), p. 24, n.1.

[25] Karl Pearson, *The Life, Letters and Labours of Francis Galton* (3 vols., Cambridge 1914-1930), ii (1924), p. 77.

and popularization of social Darwinist and eugenic propositions. Dr Langdon Down's choice of the label 'mongolism'
in 1866 is an exception,[26] and, in the context of our present
discussion, an important one. But in general, this widespread
public discussion was a feature more of the years after 1885
than before it.

In the preface to the second edition of *Hereditary Genius*
in 1892, Galton himself remarked that, 'At the time when
the book was written the human mind was popularly thought
to act independently of natural laws and to be capable of
almost any achievement, if compelled to exert itself by a will
that had a power of initiation'[27] and a view of social and
economic life as a battlefield, on which the weak are ultimately destroyed, was not easily assimilable to mid-Victorian
optimism, what Michael Sadleir once called 'a consciousness
of national well-being which bordered on the sanctimonious'.[28]
But the rediscovery of the Condition-of-England Question in
the 1880s and beyond reflected in part, at least, the dis-
solution of old certainties; and images of conflict and struggle
acquired increasing resonance as inquiries into the conditions
of life in the urban slums multiplied. In her contribution on
'London Children' to Booth's *Life and Labour of the People
of London* Mary Tabor wrote,

Puny, pale-faced, scantily-clad and badly shod, those small and feeble
folk may be found sitting limp and chill on the school benches in all the
poorer parts of London. They swell the bills of mortality as want and
sickness thin them off, or survive to be the needy and enfeebled adults
whose burden of helplessness the next generation will have to bear.[29]

For some, the images of Social Darwinism functioned
primarily as dramatic metaphor; for others they became the
organizing principles of their view of the world; and there
were many intermediate stages between these two positions.
It is not difficult to see how the language of Social Darwinism
might mesh most effectively with a concern about 'social
waste' like that expressed by the Charity Organization
Society. But it could issue then in either a plea to reduce

[26] Above, p. 15.
[27] Galton, *Hereditary Genius,* 2nd edition, 1892, p. vii.
[28] Michael Sadleir, *Trollope: A Commentary* (London, 1927), p. 9.
[29] Booth, *London Life and Labour* 1902 coll. edn., iii, p. 207.

state or charitable intervention and allow nature to take its course and eliminate the unfit, or a plea for greatly enhanced intervention, to manage and accelerate the process of survival of the fittest. It is possible to find both socialists and un-reconstructed political economists deploying very similar images in their initial diagnoses, before going on to offer diametrically opposed prescriptions. Likewise, not all who used the language of Social Darwinism were prepared to go as far as Galton in contemplating and exploring the possibility of selective human breeding.

The language, moreover, acquired additional resonance as international rivalries intensified in the later 1890s. Then between October 1899 and 1900 the early disasters of the Boer War disposed of the last vestiges of high Victorian complacency. Drama – or perhaps melodrama – and dark images of national decay increasingly pervaded social com-ment – as in the essays edited by C.F.G. Masterman in 1901, subtitled soberly, 'Discussions of Problems of Modern City Life in England, with an Essay on Imperialism', but entitled *The Heart of the Empire* and with an epigraph from a lecture by J.W. Mackail on William Morris, beginning, 'The times are strange and evil'. The need for 'national efficiency' became part of every politician's rhetorical stock-in-trade; and the language of Social Darwinism achieved even wider currency, at times approaching the status of cant.

The impact and diffusion of Social Darwinist ideas and the use and abuse of the label 'eugenist' is in fact a massive topic which has already generated a large and distinguished secondary literature.[30] The preceding crude sketch can add little to this. But an attempt to explore the extent to which, and ways in which Social Darwinist and eugenic ideas pro-vided momentum and context for the campaign to provide

---

[30] e.g. Bernard Semmel, *Imperialism and Social Reform* (London, 1960); H.C.G. Matthew, *The Liberal Imperialists. The Ideas and Politics of a post-Gladstonian Elite* (London, 1973), esp. chs. v and vii; Michael Freeden, *The New Liberalism. An Ideology of Social Reform* (Oxford, 1978), esp. chs. iii and v; Collini, *Liberalism and Sociology*, esp. ch.6; Greta Jones, *Social Darwinism and English Thought. The Interaction between Biological and Social Theory* (Hassocks, Brighton, 1980); and especially G.R. Searle, *The Quest for National Efficiency* (Oxford, 1971), *Eugenics and Politics in Britain, 1900–1914* (Leyden, 1976) and 'Eugenics and Class' in *Biology, Medicine and Society 1840–1940*, ed. Charles Webster (Cambridge, 1981), pp. 217–42.

for mentally defective children, does encourage the view that the labels 'Social Darwinist' and 'eugenist' are not in themselves very informative about either configurations of attitudes or policy commitments; and they need to be both elaborated and qualified before they can be used to 'place' people or campaigns with any precision.

II The making of mental deficiency legislation

The end of the fighting in South Africa brought revelations about the poor physical condition of many of the troops and in turn precipitated the most serious concern yet about social and economic conditions.[31] The National Association for Promoting the Welfare of the Feeble-Minded was quick to take advantage of this ferment and a heavyweight petition calling for a Royal Commission on the treatment of the feeble-minded duly reached the Home Secretary in April 1903.[32] The Home Secretary, Akers Douglas, was, interestingly, not initially convinced that a Royal Commission was necessary and appointed a departmental committee to advise him. This, reporting early in 1904, advised that children could be dealt with quite simply by rendering the 1899 Act compulsory; but the problems of adults were too intractable and complex to be dealt with without the thorough investigation which a Royal Commission would bring.[33] In the autumn of 1904, therefore, Mrs Pinsent found herself a member of a Royal Commission charged to inquire into the care and control of the feeble-minded, both child and adult, in company with, amongst others, W.H. Dickinson MP, the chairman of the National Association, Dr A.F. Tredgold, its consulting physician and C.S. Loch, the Secretary of the Charity Organization Society.

This Royal Commission reported in 1908, arguing that

---

[31] The best account of this still seems to me to be Bentley B. Gilbert, *The Evolution of National Insurance in Great Britain. The Origins of the Welfare State* (London, 1966), pp. 81–101.

[32] Pritchard, *Education and the Handicapped*, p. 183, n. 2.

[33] Ed 50/24, Report of the Committee 7 Mar. 1904, with covering note from H. Cunynghame to Secretary, Board of Education, 15 June 1904. (Legislation in 1899 had brought the Education Department at the Privy Council Office and the Science and Art Department at South Kensington together as the Board of Education.)

mental defect was predominantly an inherited condition, proposing certification and custodial care, to be managed by new central and local authorities, but stopping short of sterilization, a policy now beginning to be actively canvassed in both England and the United States.[34]

Legislation did not, however, reach the statute-book until 1913 and 1914. The Mental Deficiency Act of 1913 provided for the ascertainment and where necessary, the custodial care of adult idiots, imbeciles, feeble-minded persons and 'moral defectives', under a new central authority, the Board of Control, working with special committees of county and county borough councils as local authorities. The ascertainment of child defectives was the responsibility of the local education authority; and only those assessed as ineducable came under the jurisdiction of the local control authority. The Elementary Education (Defective and Epileptic Children) Act of 1914 compelled all local education authorities to exercise the powers already available under the 1899 Act for the creation of special schools.[35]

The length of the interval and the emergence of two statutes rather than one are worth examination. A number of factors were, of course, involved. But in exploring the arguments between the Home Office and the Board of Education it is possible to gauge the extent to which the concern for mentally defective children had autonomy, and to see why and how the provision remained, as it had begun, within an educational rather than a custodial framework, one which therefore, in theory at least, was dynamic, stressing the possibilities of development, rather than static, entailing possibly permanent segregation from society at large.

The members of the National Association had displayed no lack of initiative or sophistication in following up the Royal Commission's Report. The year 1908 saw also the publication of A. F. Tredgold's *Mental Deficiency*. This, which was to become one of the standard English medical

[34] P.P. 1908 xxix Cd 4202, *Report of the Royal Commission on the Care and Control of the Feeble-Minded*. On sterilization laws in the US, see Leon J. Kamin, *The Science and Politics of I.Q.* (Potomac, Maryland, 1974), pp. 10–12; and Kanner, *Care and Study of the Mentally Retarded*, pp. 136–7.

[35] 3 & 4 Geo, V, c. 28, esp. ss. 1, 2, 30 and 31, and 4 & 5 Geo. V, c. 45.

textbooks on the subject,[36] made more widely available the substance of the Report in a language free from some of the circumlocutions beloved of Royal Commission draftsmen. A joint committee, headed by the Archbishops of Canterbury and York, was formed to lobby for legislation, and circulars and pamphlets poured forth. In 1910 the Eugenics Education Society, founded at the end of 1907 to publicize Galton's work, formally joined the campaign. By 1912 the campaigners were driven to use the goad of private members' bills.[37]

They were, however, but one of a number of groups clamouring for the government's attention — and this, after all, was the Liberal administration currently engaged in taking on the House of Lords, building Dreadnoughts, reorganizing the Army, fending off suffragettes and just about to take on the doctors and the approved societies in the preparation of health and unemployment insurance.[38] The Home Office had begun the process of consultation in December 1908;[39] and in his spell at the Home Office, February 1910 to October 1911, Churchill took an interest in the subject of mental defect, circulating to the Cabinet copies of Tredgold's address to the AGM of the National Association in 1909, and announcing that a bill was being drafted.[40] But he moved to the Admiralty before any of this came to fruition; and the troubles experienced by his successor, McKenna, when he finally did introduce a bill, underline the fact that, despite the unanimity of the Royal Commission and the sophistication of the National Association's

[36] It went into five editions between 1908 and 1929. The eighth edition in 1952 acknowledged the assistance of R.F. Tredgold; and *Tredgold's Mental Retardation*, technically the eleventh edition, edited by K. Soddy and R.F. Tredgold in 1970, still contains some portions of the original.

[37] Jones, *Mental Health Services*, pp. 196-7, 200; Searle, *Eugenics and Politics*, ch. 9; Jayne Woodhouse, 'Eugenics and the feeble-minded: the Parliamentary debates of 1912-14', *History of Education* xi (1982), pp. 130-1.

[38] Gilbert, *The Evolution of National Insurance*, chs. 6 and 7; Neal Blewett, *The Peers, The Parties and the People. The General Elections of 1910* (London, 1972), esp. Part II; Bruce K. Murray, *The People's Budget 1909-10* (Oxford, 1980).

[39] Ed 24/284 Newman's Memorandum for Permanent Secretary on Home Office conference 17 Dec. 1908.

[40] Ed 24/167, dated from the Board of Education covering notes 4 and 5 Mar. 1911; but see also ibid., Runciman to Churchill 8 July 1910.

operation, this was a highly sensitive and complex subject on which to attempt to legislate at all. The government bill of 1912, which was lost, and that of 1913, which eventually scraped through, were both subjected to one of the most sustained and dramatic parliamentary filibusters of the twentieth century, led by Colonel Josiah Wedgwood, in the name of the liberty of the subject.[41]

In addition, before ever a bill could be introduced at all, the Home Office had had to come to terms with the absolute determination of the Board of Education to retain control of the care of feeble-minded children and not cede it to any new mental deficiency authority. This determination was rooted in a complex set of considerations, among which deeply felt positions of principle shaded into and were inextricably blended with vested interests.

At one level, the Board of Education was simply defending a very straightforward and recognizable vested interest. With the 1899 Act it had been in the field first; and the Home Office committee of 1904 in fact acknowledged this by suggesting the Board promote a bill to make that Act compulsory, leaving a Royal Commission to consider only the case of adult defectives.[42] The logic of this split was administrative, however, rather than political; and with the opposition to the 1902 Education Act still reverberating, it is not surprising that the Board of Education did not choose to expose itself to attack again so soon. But by the time it became a question of responding to the Royal Commission's Report, the Board was entirely ready to go on to the offensive to retain and strengthen its control of special schools. As soon as rumours began to spread about Churchill's intentions in the summer of 1910, Walter Runciman, the President of the Board of Education, and the Parliamentary Secretary, Charles Trevelyan, were briefed to challenge him directly.[43]

---

[41] Jones, *Mental Health Services*, pp. 200–4. Searle, *Eugenics and Politics*, pp. 109–11; Woodhouse, 'Eugenics and the feeble-minded', pp. 131–6. See also the problems encountered in drafting regulations under the mental deficiency legislation – Ed 50/115, and Ed 50/116.

[42] Above, p. 39 n. 3.

[43] Ed 24/167 typewritten, undated and unsigned 'Memorandum on the Problem of the Feeble-Minded', addressed 'Mr Trevelyan [the Parl. Sec. to the Board] and President'. It can in fact be dated because scribbled on the top is the first draft of a letter from Walter Runciman (the President) to Churchill of 8 July

Pressure was maintained at this, the highest, level. Runciman countered Churchill's circulation of Tredgold's pamphlet to the Cabinet in February 1911 with a lengthy paper.[44] And when the Under-Secretary at the Home Office principally involved, W.P. Byrne, wrote in some haste to the Permanent Secretary of the Board of Education, Robert Morant, asking for the Education 'line' on policy towards the feeble-minded, to include in a brief for Churchill, who was about to meet a London County Council deputation on the subject, he was put down in magisterial fashion: 'The questions at issue', wrote Morant,

go to the roots of local government and to the roots of the Feeble-Minded Problem. Their solution as between this Department and the Home Office clearly cannot be arrived at without earnest discussion between the Ministers; they are not points of technical detail as between officials, simply.[45]

Such loftiness had not, however, prevented Morant from harassing Byrne throughout 1911, once Churchill had identified him as the relevant official.[46]

The Board of Education 'line', moreover, had been clear from the beginning of serious discussions in mid-1910 and was to remain so until the bitter end. 'Educable children must remain under our jurisdiction', telegraphed the President to the Permanent Secretary in June 1913, as the Home Office ministers fought the Mental Deficiency Bill through the Commons and the Board of Education worried about the

1910, a later draft of which is also in the file. From the content, in particular, the confidence and the detail of the medical discussion, the author is almost certainly Dr George Newman, the Chief Medical Officer of the Board. Normal procedure, powerfully reinforced by factors set out below, pp. 48-52, would, however, have required endorsement of the Memo by the Permanent Secretary, Sir Robert Morant, before it went to the Ministers. Henceforward it is referred to as 'Newman's Memorandum of July 1910'.

[44] Ibid. Cabinet Paper 14 Mar. 1911. See also ibid., Runciman to Churchill 14 Mar. 1911, Minute from Morant to H.G. Maurice (Runciman's private secretary) 15 May 1911, Maurice to Eddie Marsh (Churchill's private secretary) 15 May 1911, and Marsh to Maurice 18 May 1911.

[45] Ibid. Morant to Byrne 14 Nov. 1911.

[46] Ibid. Minute Morant to Newman 14 Jan. 1911, Morant to Byrne 7 Mar. 1911, Byrne to Morant 8 Mar. 1911, Morant to Byrne 5 May 1911, Byrne to Morant 9 May 1911 with 'Mr Byrne's Notes of 9 May 1911'; also the exchanges between Morant, Maurice, and Marsh noted above, n. 44. Edward Troup to Morant 10 July 1911 and Morant's Minute 8 Nov. 1911.

amendments they might be driven to accept.[47] It was just that it took the Home Office a long time to accept this. Its vested interest, if it can be so called, was different. Its central preoccupation was with arrangements for the care and control of mentally defective adults, in which a custodial element bulked large. It was easy, therefore, to put the children, the next generation of mentally defective adults, within the same frame. This view had begun to emerge even before the Royal Commission was established. The section of the departmental committee's report in 1904 dealing with children, while recommending the extension of the 1899 Act, contained an ominous coda:

We are fully aware that the making of further public provision for the care and maintenance of feeble-minded children, while it would seem consonant with humanity, might have disadvantages. For although the chief object of such provision is and should be to improve the physical and mental condition of the children and make them better fitted to contribute to their own support, we think that it may involve the nursing and preservation of large numbers of helpless defectives, and that if these numbers are returned into the world, and left to propagate their species, the gain to society on the whole result of the experiment might be questionable.[48]

The Home Office officials, therefore, saw no problems in accepting the recommendations of the Royal Commission that the new central and local authorities for mental defect should be responsible for the children as well as for the adults, and that central and local education authorities should cease to have any responsibility for mentally defective children, except where the local mental deficiency authority might call on the LEA to continue or to start special schools or classes, as its agent.

As a coherent administrative system, there was much to be said for this; and in May 1911 Byrne, for the Home Office, elaborated its case by pointing out, first that, according to the Royal Commission, three out of four of the LEAs in England and Wales had never adopted the 1899 Act; second, that those local education authorities operating the Act had no jurisdiction over 'children who are "imbecile" or worse,

---

[47] Ed 24/620 Pease to Selby-Bigge 13 June 1913; see also the remainder of this file.
[48] Ed 50/24 Report, 7 Mar. 1904.

these latter being perhaps the largest section of the Feeble-minded'; and third, the Royal Commission had been sceptical about the effectiveness of existing special schools.

the restricted class with which the Board [of Education] is now concerned is not in the Acts limited by any scientific definition; it purports to include children who cannot be benefited by the training of the ordinary elementary school but who can be benefited by the training of special schools and classes established under the Defective Children Acts. That is to say, the Acts attempt not a scientific but a practical definition: and in practice the definition has been found to be an imperfect guide. Largely because of the limitations which must attach to the efforts of a merely educational authority attempting to deal with the wider problem of the Feeble-minded the system of the Defective Acts is, in the opinion of the Royal Commission, a practical failure. It amounted in their opinion to beginning to try to do in England what had been abandoned as hopeless in America, the pioneer country in this matter. The problem of the Feeble-minded is not largely an educational problem: and Education Acts, however enlightened, touch only a fringe of it.[49]

In line with this, the 'Heads of a Bill' produced by the Home Office in July referred simply to power for the new mental deficiency local authority 'to make arrangements with any local education authority for the education of children'.[50]

The initial Board of Education tactic was to refuse to take anything of this level of generality seriously.[51] But when in November 1911 the Home Office began to propose a time-table for the introduction of such a bill,[52] more became necessary. From the Board of Education's point of view, the timing was diabolical. Since March that year the President, Runciman, and the Permanent Secretary, Morant, who were not, anyway, on the closest of terms, had been under sustained public attack over the affair of the Homes Circular, a memorandum for circulation within the department only, highly critical of some of the ex-teachers employed in LEA inspectorates, which had been leaked to the NUT. Finally, in November Runciman was moved to the Board of Agriculture and Morant resigned; although Lloyd George fetched him

[49] Ed 24/167 Mr Byrne's Notes of 9 May 1911, quotation from para. 9.
[50] Ibid. 'Mental Infirmity Bill', para. 12; see also accompanying letter, Edward Troup to Morant 10 July 1911.
[51] Ibid. Morant to Maurice 15 May 1914, Minute Morant to Newman 17 July 1911 and Minute Newman to Morant 7 Nov. 1911.
[52] Ibid. Morant's Minute of discussion with Byrne 8 Nov. 1911.

back prematurely from the first holiday he had had for years to head the new National Insurance Commission.[53]

The responsibility for a considered response to the Home Office and the briefing of a new President, J.A. Pease, and a new Permanent Secretary, L.A. Selby-Bigge, fell therefore upon the Chief Medical Officer, Dr George Newman, who proved fully equal to the task. He pointed out first that LEAs were continuing to adopt the 1899 Act in increasing numbers; twice as many were now operating under its provisions as had been when the Royal Commission was taking evidence. (The numbers continued to increase throughout 1912; while fifty Poor Law Unions organized a petition to make the 1899 Act compulsory.[54] There are all the signs of a carefully orchestrated campaign, although it is not clear where the initiative was coming from.) Second, Newman argued that the Royal Commission had underestimated the extent to which the mentally defective were educable and the importance of the accumulation of experience in special schools and classes. Finally, he pointed out that the identification and care of defective children was now, since 1908, properly located within a comprehensive system of school medical inspection.

Medical Inspection has been established in every Public Elementary School in England and Wales. There are 995 School Doctors now at work and every child is examined for mental defect. The machinery for enquiry, sifting and classification of all feeble-minded children is therefore now in existence under statute.

He concluded:

The Local Education Authorities acting under the Board of Education must continue to be held responsible for providing (a) clearing houses for catching and sifting all feeble-minded children; and (b) education

[53] Bernard M. Allen, *Sir Robert Morant. A Great Public Servant* (London, 1934), pp. 254–69; Violet Markham, *Friendship's Harvest* (London, 1956), pp. 188–9; and Gillian Sutherland, 'Administrators in education after 1870: patronage, professionalism and expertise' in *Studies in the Growth of nineteenth century Government*, ed. Gillian Sutherland (London, 1972), pp. 282–5. Allen, as at so many other points, is vague about precise dates and sequences. Violet Markham has Morant resigning in August 1911. In fact, both new appointments were announced in the Commons on 28 Nov. 1911, but Runciman's move had been arranged earlier — see Ed 24/167 Morant to Byrne 14 Nov. 1911. My source for the details in Morant's case is personal information from his daughter.
[54] Ed 50/148.

for all of the 48,000 who are educable. The Royal Commission found that two-thirds of the 48,000 (that is 32,000) were educable, but by the newer methods of education it is probable that many of the 16,000 for whom it was proposed to provide custody only are also capable of some training. Using the term 'education', therefore, as something which is going to produce ultimately a person capable of earning his own living, partly or wholly, whether under supervision or otherwise, it may be said that not less than 32,000 of these feeble-minded children are educable, and all 48,000 of them would be the better for some training which at least would enable them to assist in raising some revenue for the custodial institutions in which they are placed. . . . It may be convenient to make it clear here that 'custody' does not mean a more or less prolonged sojourn in a custodial institution, but it means, in the view of the Royal Commission, permanent detention (for life). Whatever may be said in favour of such treatment of adults, it seems to me a monstrous proposition to apply such treatment to young children whose powers are growing and concerning whose future we know little or nothing.

Pease, like Newman a Quaker by birth and schooling, found this wholly convincing and in fact sent on the minute from which the preceding quotations are taken, to McKenna, now Home Secretary, as setting out the Board's considered position.[55] The reshuffle at Education, therefore, brought no relief to the Home Office.

The Board of Education's most powerful weapon in its battle with the Home Office, fully revealed at last, was school medical inspection. More important than its vested interest in the form of existing special schools and classes here and there, was the Board's firm control of already existing machinery for assessing the incidence of defect in the population as a whole. In his Notes of May 1911 W.P. Byrne had been forced to acknowledge that,

the Educational System is at present, in many places an effective agency in ascertaining the number and requirements of the Feeble-minded young: in the future it will be the universal and almost the only indispensable [sic] agency for ascertaining their numbers in the new generations. It is clear that local Education Authorities must have duties in regard to hunting up the Feeble-minded as well as others of school age and that these duties must be carried out under the Regulations of the Central Education Authority.[56]

[55] Ed 24/167 'The Education of Feeble-Minded Children', Minute for the President 24 Nov. 1911; Pease's annotation 11 Dec. 1911.
[56] Ibid. Mr Byrne's Notes of 9 May 1911, para. 10.

Had it not been for this, the Home Office might have tried to legislate without reference to education authorities. But it had to concede — indeed it needed — this diagnostic function and machinery. McKenna, perhaps softened up by the experience of his own spell at the Board of Education, January 1907-April 1908, and exposure to Morant's powerful personality and plans,[57] seems to have accepted the substance of Pease's case without too much argument;[58] and from this point on, separate legislation became increasingly likely, though finally decided upon only in the autumn of 1912.[59]

The Board of Education remained nervous throughout, both of the Home Office's good faith and of the reverberations of the parliamentary row over the bills providing for mentally defective adults. This row indeed brought about the loss of its first bill in 1913, which ran out of time, and prolonged the discussion on the second bill in 1914.[60] But the 1913 Mental Deficiency Act confirmed the role of the local education authorities in assessing the ability of all children at the age of seven. It required them to hand over to the care of the local mental deficiency authorities only those deemed ineducable. The 1914 Education Act complemented this by requiring all LEAs to provide special schools.[61]

The replacement of Morant by Newman as the Board of Education's key spokesman on provision for mental defect from the end of 1911[62] and the central role of the school medical service in the argument were neither of them fortuitous. Newman and Morant had been hand in glove all along. The Memorandum prepared — probably by Newman, but if

[57] Gilbert, *The Evolution of National Insurance*, p. 128.
[58] Ed 24/167 Pease's note of 11 Dec. 1911 on Newman's Minute of 24 Nov. 1911.
[59] Ed 24/620, Ed 24/622, and Ed 31/190.
[60] Ed 31/194, Ed 31/196, Ed 24/620 (1912–13), and Ed 24/640 (1914).
[61] 3 & 4 Geo. V, c. 28 ss. 2, 31; 4 & 5 Geo. V, c. 45.
[62] Besides Ed 24/167 Newman's Minute for the President 24 Nov. 1911, see also ibid., Newman's Minute for the President 17 Nov. 1911, Ed 24/620 Summary of exchanges with the Home Office to date drawn up for the Permanent Secretary (now Selby-Bigge) by Warburton on Newman's instruction 23 Jan. 1912 (in effect a summary of the contents of Ed 24/167, as it existed in 1976, although a check in 1981 revealed the disappearance of a number of items), Ed 24/620 Minute Newman to Selby-Bigge 19 Mar. 1912, Minute Newman to Selby-Bigge 3 May 1912, Ed 31/190 Minute Newman to Selby-Bigge 18 Oct. 1912, Ed 31/196 Minute Newman to President (Pease) 23 May 1913 (second copy in Ed 50/150A).

so, undoubtedly approved by Morant — to equip Runciman to tackle Churchill in July 1910 had pointed out that

since the Royal Commission was appointed, great advance has been made in the machinery of the State for dealing with this question. There has been medical inspection and treatment has been introduced with a complete network of school doctors for detecting and following up these cases.

And it concluded that retention of the care of feeble-minded children by the Board of Education was 'both practicable and compatible with the evolution of the state medical service at the centre of government and at the periphery in the local areas'.[63] Then early in 1911 the two of them combined to persuade Runciman and Trevelyan to sanction an expansion of the activities of the Board's medical inspectorate *vis-à-vis* special schools — a kind of pre-emptive strike, or, as Newman put it, 'fixing and strengthening the present policy with regard to the education of the feeble-minded rather than letting the present position get weaker and weaker in order that the Royal Commission and Home Office may step in to end it'.[64]

Their partnership was one of the most influential in twentieth-century welfare provision. It dated formally from August 1907, when Morant had engineered the passage of the Education (Administrative Provisions) Bill, which required LEAs to 'provide for the medical inspection of children' and also 'to make such arrangements as may be sanctioned by the Board of Education for attending to the health and physical condition of children educated in public elementary schools'. From the deliberate vagueness of 'such arrangements' developed the school medical service. Those LEAs who did not already have medical officers had to begin to find them; while in September 1907 the appointment of Dr George Newman as Chief Medical Officer to the Board of Education

[63] Ed 24/167 Newman's Memorandum 7 July 1910; see above, p. 000. This line of argument was prefigured in Newman's contribution to the Home Office Conference of December 1908, when he suggested that before they rushed to create a new central authority, they should look at the 'periphery' and see what services already existed and could be utilized — Ed 24/284, Newman's Memorandum for Permanent Secretary on Home Office Conference 17 Dec. 1908.

[64] Ed 50/22 Minute Newman to Morant 27 Feb. 1911, Minute Morant to Trevelyan and President 28 Feb. 1911, and their annotations of 1 Mar. and 9 Mar. 1911 respectively. Also above, note 51.

was announced, and he and Morant set about creating a small medical department within the Board — 'of good men and no juniors'.[65]

It might be argued that in the defence of this newly burgeoning empire against the encroachments of the Home Office, we are again seeing the defence of a vested interest. This element was undoubtedly present: Morant, in particular, was a man of powerful ambition.[66] But for both much more was at stake. Both Morant and Newman saw in the school medical service the embryo of national health care and both were prepared to go to considerable lengths to accelerate its growth. Sir Lawrence Brock, who worked under Morant from 1912 to 1920, reflected long after on the implications and effect of that vague little Act of 1907:

> Morant knew . . . but did not tell his Minister, that medical inspection would reveal such a mass of disease and defect that no Government subsequently would be able to resist the demands of the Local Education Authorities to provide treatment. Morant told me himself that he foresaw what would happen and *meant it to happen* . . .[67]

Morant seldom 'went public', as it were. He operated best behind the scenes and had perhaps too well-developed a talent for presenting arguments in the terms and language his hearers found most acceptable. But in so far as it is possible to reconstruct his motives, he appears as a passionate and committed advocate of national efficiency, both responding and contributing to the debates that followed the Boer War. He told the annual dinner of the Society of Medical Officers of Health in 1909 'we have now to think of the English people in competition with other races, and if we neglected the health of the race . . . we should lose in the racial competition

[65] Gilbert, *The Evolution of National Insurance*, pp. 127-32. The chapter, 'The children of the nation', of which these pages form a part, is an excellent discussion of the whole complex subject and forms the basis for what follows, except where otherwise indicated.

[66] The case for a modern biography of Morant is overwhelming. Allen, *Sir Robert Morant*, is coy on this subject as on so many others and his account of a man who evoked the strongest feelings, both for and against him, among his contemporaries, is staggeringly bland. A much more vivid if partisan picture is conveyed by Violet Markham, *Friendship's Harvest*, pp. 167-207. She stoutly denies that Morant was personally ambitious, but on that see Taylor, 'The Church Party and Popular Education', pp. 249-57 and chapters 11, 12, and 13, esp. pp. 315-63, 383-90 and 412-15.

[67] Quoted in Markham, *Friendship's Harvest*, pp. 200-1, his emphasis.

of this world'.[68] The Social Darwinist overtones of this are particularly well developed; yet at no stage can Morant be found promoting policies with a distinctively hereditarian cast.

Newman, too, was prepared to use the language of national efficiency.[69] But again his policy preoccupations can more easily be characterized as environmentalist than hereditarian. The Memorandum prepared to equip — perhaps to incite — Runciman to tackle Churchill about Home Office intentions in June/July 1910, comments as follows on the work of the Royal Commission on the Care and Control of the Feeble-Minded:

I must remind you that though there is no absolutely conclusive evidence one way or the other, the Royal Commission took up the position that the disease known as 'feeble-mindedness' was mainly a disease transmitted by heredity and that therefore a great need of the future was to prevent these feeble-minded children growing up and marrying and so propagating their kind. This question is one of considerable intricacy, partly because of the difficulty of exactly defining the disease from a medical point of view (in point of fact the Royal Commission defined the disease in social terms only, a definition which is open to very considerable criticism, especially in view of the proposition that the disease is hereditary), and partly because of the extreme difficulty of furnishing reliable evidence that heredity rather than environment has been the main cause.[70]

Newman had of course begun his career as a doctor as Medical Officer first in Bedfordshire and then in Finsbury; and it might be suggested that Medical Officers as a group were likely to be preoccupied with environmental factors in the broadest sense, since this was their bread and butter. But this argument equally can be turned on its head, to suggest that doctors with these interests might well choose public health as a specialist field. Newman belongs at least as much to the sequence of distinguished doctors stretching back to Sir

---

[68] Gilbert, *The Evolution of National Insurance*, p. 148, n. 106.

[69] Ibid., p. 125; Jane Lewis, *The Politics of Motherhood* (London, 1980), pp. 29–30.

[70] Ed 24/167 Newman's Memorandum of July 1910. Newman's approach to the problem of high child mortality is also of interest here. As both Jane Lewis op. cit. and Carol Dyhouse ('Working Class Mothers and Infant Mortality in England 1895–1914', in *Biology, Medicine and Society*, ed. Webster, p. 74) point out, he had a positive obsession with maternal ignorance as a key causal factor. But this again is an environmentalist rather than an hereditarian preoccupation.

John Simon, if not to Thomas Southwood Smith, who exploited their expertise and medical standing to urge the state towards positive action on health,[71] as he does to the advocates of national efficiency. And while Newman and Morant, like the National Association for Promoting the Welfare of the Feeble-Minded, were concerned to secure a more efficient nation, they chose to go about it in a different way.

III Technical breakthrough

One of the Home Office's lines of challenge to the Board of Education had been the lack of precision involved in the definition of mental defect — 'the Acts attempt not a scientific but a practical definition: and, in practice, the definition has been found to be an imperfect guide'.[72] As we have seen, the definition had given a lot of trouble in 1898 and 1899;[73] and all the evidence collected by the Royal Commission on the subject between 1904 and 1907 indicated that the methods of identification and classification were not significantly different from those described by witnesses to the Departmental Committee 1897-8, or indeed by Dr Shuttleworth to the Egerton Commission in 1889. That is to say, teachers and medical officers were putting together what they saw of a child's physical peculiarities and competence, and intellectual and scholastic performance in trying to decide whether the child was 'merely dull and backward', 'feeble-minded' or 'imbecile'.[74]

Newman, as we have also seen, argued stoutly that 'since the Royal Commission was appointed we have had 6 years'

[71] See e.g. Cullen, *The Statistical Movement*; Hodgkinson, *Origins of the National Health Service*; Royston Lambert, *Sir John Simon and English Social Administration 1816-1904* (London, 1963); Gillian Sutherland, 'Introduction' to *Studies in the growth of nineteenth century government*, ed. Sutherland, pp. 2-3 and 8; and Gilbert, *The Evolution of National Insurance*, p. 93.

[72] Above, p. 45.

[73] Above, pp. 21-4.

[74] e.g. *Royal Commission on the Care and Control of the Feeble-Minded: Minutes of Evidence etc.* P.P. 1908 xxxv Cd 4215 ff. 583-5 and p. 690 (London and Kilburn), P.P. 1908 xxxvi Cd 4216 q. 12984 (Bolton), P.P. 1908 xxxviii Cd 4219 ff. 225-6 (Sheffield) and Appendix: Halifax forms. See also Newman's attempt to systematize these kinds of procedures in Circular 582 of 1908, P.P. 1910 xxiii Cd 5426, Appendix to Chief Medical Officer's Report.

further experience of this question' and what had been learnt would make it possible to help far more of these children manage without custodial care.[75] It remains finally to consider whether Newman was simply putting a brave face on things. Whether, to put the same question another way, provision for a national framework of special schools had been achieved while the methods of identifying and classifying mentally defective children remained as imprecise, as much dependent on experience and trial and error, as they had been in the 1890s. The answer to this is 'no', although for all most of the protagonists knew, it might well have been 'yes'.

To resolve this paradox, we need to go back for a moment to Galton. As has been mentioned, he began to experiment with tests of mental ability, focusing in the main on tests of sensory perception. He was followed by others, in England, the USA and Germany; but such tests had been found to be of limited value in assessing the mentally defective since, in the main, they tested individual simple skills and reactions. In France at the same time, however, Alfred Binet and Victor Simon were pursuing an opposite hypothesis, namely, that the higher and more complex mental processes could only be measured by tests which engaged them directly. Heavily involved in the work of *La Société libre pour l'étude psychologique de l'enfant* and then of the Commission for the Abnormal, set up by the Ministry of Public Instruction, they attempted to devise tests of vocabulary, spatial perception, memory, inductive and deductive reasoning, and even 'judgement' and 'moral sense'. They tried their tests out on hundreds of Paris schoolchildren, relating the results to what the teachers told them about normal and abnormal performances, revising, redesigning and adjusting. In 1905 they published a first series of tests. A revised version followed in 1908, with an age-related scale for scoring the results; and a second revision in 1911 — the year in which Binet died.[76]

Here at last was an instrument of classification both subtle and precise. It explicitly set out to assess the widest possible

---

[75] Ed 24/167 Newman's Memorandum July 1910, see also ibid. Minute Newman to President 24 Nov. 1911.

[76] Theta H. Wolf, *Alfred Binet* (Chicago, 1973), esp. chs. 4 and 5; also below, pp. 123-7.

range of mental abilities and provided a means of combining them into an overall figure referred to as the child's mental age. Thus a child was said to have a mental age of six years if his performance matched that of the average six-year-old. This index provided a measure which was intuitively interpretable and which allowed children to be compared in a more precise manner than was possible previously. In particular, the gap between mental age and chronological age was an easily intelligible gauge of the severity of defect, while at the same time allowing for fine grading in difference of degree between children. Finally, the existence of a *sequence* of age-related tests made it possible to measure development and growth.

Ironically, the French themselves took little interest in the tests, but the response from other countries was rapid and dramatic. The German psychologist William Stern made it even easier for the lay mind to grasp the key relationship between mental and chronological age through the device of the intelligence quotient or IQ. He divided mental age by chronological age, multiplied by 100 and rounded off to eliminate the fractions, and came up with a single number, which could be used to describe the abilities of one child and contrast that one with any other. In California Lewis Terman and in Liverpool Cyril Burt began work on the standardization of Binet and Simon's tests on American and English schoolchildren respectively. They began also to experiment with the possibility of a group test, that is, one that could be administered in written form, not orally, to a number of people simultaneously and the results scored by an unskilled individual or even by a machine.

The practical use and economy of a group test are obvious; and a dramatic demonstration of its possibilities was given in 1917 and 1918, when the Alpha and Beta Tests devised by the consultant psychologists to the American Army enabled the overwhelmed authorities to begin to distinguish between eager volunteers who ought not to be trusted with a rifle and those who were potential officer material.[77]

[77] Wolf, *Binet; A History of Psychology in Autobiography* (Worcester, Mass., 1930-36), 4 vols., vols. 1-3 ed. C.A. Murchison, vol. 4 ed. E.G. Boring, H.S. Langfeld, H. Werner, and R.M. Yerkes; P.H. Dubois, *A History of Psychological Testing* (Boston, Mass., 1970); Daniel J. Kevles, 'Testing the Army's Intelligence: Psychologists and the Military in World War I', *Journal of American History* IV

But well before this, the practical possibilities of the individual test had been appreciated in England. Dr James Kerr, by now translated from Bradford to the employment of the LCC Education Committee, first drew attention to Binet and Simon's tests in his report for 1909; and the prolonged and complex negotiations between 1911 and 1913, which led in the end to the appointment of Cyril Burt as part-time psychologist to the LCC, to assist in the 'examination of children nominated for admission to schools for the mentally defective', both showed the LCC inspectorate to be well-informed and served to inform the LCC Special Schools Sub-Committee about the tests.[78]

There was no love lost between Kerr and Newman, Kerr having himself aspired to the post of Chief Medical Officer of the Board of Education.[79] In spite — or perhaps because — of this, Newman was quick to follow in drawing attention to Binet and Simon's work. In his Report for 1910 he mentioned the 1908 revision in general terms.[80] In his Report for 1911 he presented his usual summary of the items to be included in the properly conducted physical examination of a child thought to be mentally defective; then continued, 'in assessing the intelligence, however, which is, broadly speaking, the chief criterion for differentiation of the normal child from the feeble-minded, the mental tests designed by Binet and Simon are recommended'. He went on to set out the scheme of tests as presented in the 1911 revision, to give a lucid and succinct account of the method of calculating the mental age of the child from the results and concluded by stressing that the tests should supplement the teacher's report and the physical examination.[81]

(1968), pp. 565–81.

[78] Sutherland and Sharp ' "The fust official psychologist" ', pp. 183–6. The direct quotation is taken from LCC committee minutes. Burt later claimed that his responsibilities were much wider than this and his biographer is inclined to follow him — Hearnshaw, *Cyril Burt* pp. 33–6, 82–3. Certainly he came to interpret them more widely. But for an extended consideration of the relation between Burt's later recollections and the surviving contemporary sources, see Sutherland and Sharp, ' "The fust official psychologist" '.

[79] Gilbert, *The Evolution of National Insurance*, pp. 133–7.

[80] P.P. 1911 xvii Cd 5925 Report of the Chief Medical Officer, ch. x.

[81] P.P. 1912–13 xxi Cd 6530 Report of the Chief Medical Officer, Appendix E.

The drafting of this must have overlapped with the arguments with the Home Office. With the benefit of hindsight, one might wonder why he did not make more of Binet and Simon and the burgeoning new specialism of 'mental measurement'. But this is to expect too much. The tests were too new for anyone to be certain quite how important they would become; and the wonder is, rather, that Newman and Kerr picked them up as quickly and as positively as they did. Neither was a specialist on mental defect in particular. But both, whatever their personal jealousies, were deeply committed to improving the health of the schoolchild and thus, presumably, on the alert for new developments, in whatever direction.[82]

In so far as there was a causal relationship between sophisticated techniques for measuring defect and the campaign to make special provision for mentally defective children, it seems that the pre-existence of the latter ensured a rapid response to the former. The strongest version of this relationship came, of course, in France, where the preoccupation of *La Société libre* with provision for mentally defective children acted as a kind of forcing-house for the ideas and experiments of Binet and Simon. In England the mental deficiency legislation of 1913 and 1914 would have reached the statute-book even if Kerr, the LCC and Newman had never heard of the tests of Binet and Simon.[83] Those tests, however, represented considerable reinforcement for the contention that the care of children with mental defect should properly be located within the educational system.

[82] Dr George Auden, School Medical Officer for Birmingham (and father of the poet) was also well-informed on the subject at a very early stage — Lowe, 'Eugenists, Doctors and the Quest for National Efficiency', pp. 295-6 and 'Eugenics and Education: a note on the origins of the intelligence testing movement in England' *Educational Studies* vi (1980), pp. 2-3. On the other hand, there is no mention of Binet in the third edition of Shuttleworth's *Mentally Deficient Children* in 1910.

[83] The evidence presented by Lowe in 'Eugenics and Education', pp. 1–3 does not seem adequate to warrant his conclusion that 'the concentration of Burt and Auden on the problem [of psychometrics] was a necessary part of the debate leading up to the more extensive enactments of 1913 and 1914. In this way the pioneer psychometricians initiated policy....'

Chapter 3

'Impossible statutory obligations'

The 1914 Elementary Education (Defective & Epileptic Children) Act received the royal assent six days after the outbreak of war; and the imperialism which had characterized activity in this as in so many other fields of social policy since 1906, came to an abrupt halt. There was no significant increase in the provision of special-school places in England and Wales during the wartime period.[1]

In 1917 the Ministry of Reconstruction invited the Board of Education to comment on a Memorandum from the National Association for Promoting the Welfare of the Feeble-Minded, now transmogrified into the Central Association for the Care of the Mentally Defective, complaining of the non-implementation of the 1913 and 1914 Acts. Newman reported bitterly that it was entirely the central government's fault — 'the abeyance is due *directly* to the stripping of the medical staffs'.[2] He did his best, however, to remind local education authorities of their responsibilities.[3]

The ending of hostilities was to bring very little relief. In the bleak economic climate prevailing after 1918 the plans of 1913 and 1914 for the training and care of the mentally defective came to look more and more like extravagant fantasies. Experience in the management and treatment of mental defect continued to accumulate and feed knowledge about its nature and causes; and the new technology of mental measurement in particular developed apace. But the patterns of interaction between these developments and national policy were very different from those prevailing before the War. Lack of money drove the Board of Education first to reappraise the role of special schools and then to cease positively to campaign for them. The reappraisal drew

---

[1] See below, Appendix I, Table 3.

[2] Ed 50/151 CACMD Memorandum 24 Oct. 1917, Minute E.H. Pelham to G. Newman 21 Nov. 1917, Minute Newman to Pelham 1 Dec. 1917.

[3] ARMOH for 1917, P.P. 1918 ix Cd 9206, ch. vii, 'The Mentally Subnormal Child'.

quite heavily upon the new techniques of mental measurement; and it has been suggested that the Board of Education's
increasing commitment to these was a symptom of an increasing commitment to an hereditarian, 'eugenist' approach.
The further implication of this is that there was a retreat not
simply from the special school as a practical device for
helping mentally defective children, but more generally
from the whole position articulated by Newman between
1910 and 1914, that the bulk of mentally defective children
were educable and it was the Board's duty to educate them
to the limits of their abilities, whatever those might prove to
be. This line of argument is open to serious challenge. Mental
measurement did indeed come to play an important part in
the Board of Education's approach to mental defect. But
acceptance of it was not seen by them as entailing abandon-
ment of a developmental approach. The real constraints on
such an approach were financial and it is to these we must
turn first.

I The strait-jacket of finance

The first year of peace brought more characteristic exhort-
ations from Newman to the local education authorities to
tackle at last the problem of the mentally defective child;
although from now on, Newman's energies, as Medical
Officer not only to the Board of Education but also to the
newly created Ministry of Health, would be engaged on a
much wider front.[4] The next year HMI Dr Alfred Eichholz,
the Inspector principally responsible for special schools, was
sent on a special mission to ginger up the particularly backward Welsh authorities.[5] The Birmingham authority commissioned a special report on the city's needs from Cyril Burt.[6]

[4] ARMOH for 1919, P.P. 1920 xv Cmd 995, ch. vi. See also ARMOH for
1919-20, P.P. 1921 xi Cmd 1522, s. viii. On the creation of the Ministry of
Health, see B.B. Gilbert, *British Social Policy, 1914–39* (New York, 1970) Part 3,
and Kenneth and Jane Morgan, *Portrait of a Progressive. The Political Career of
Christopher, Viscount Addison* (Oxford, 1980), pp. 94, 133–4.

[5] Ed 50/153 Eichholz's Report 14 May 1920. Like Newman, Eichholz had
started his career as a Medical Officer of Health and had been heavily involved in
the pre-War discussions and campaigns — see Gilbert, *Evolution of National
Insurance*, pp. 89, 133.

[6] Cyril Burt, *Report of an investigation upon backward children in Birmingham* (Birmingham, 1921).

Nationally the figures suggest some initial effort to respond;[7] and Part V of the consolidatory Education Act of 1921 reiterated the provisions of 1913 and 1914. But even as this reached the statute-book and the LEA response got under way, the brakes were being slammed on. The Geddes Committee, set up in August 1921 to review the estimates and make economies, was severely critical of the cost of special schools — as A.H. Wood later acknowledged in an internal Board of Education Minute:

You could, for instance, send a young man to Oxford or Cambridge for an Honours course for the same amount that you spend on sending to a residential special school a mentally defective child from 7 to 16, who at the end of it may be locked up permanently in a colony of lunatics.[8]

And well before the Geddes Committee actually reported in February 1922, the Board, urged on by the President, H.A.L. Fisher, was seeking ways and means of economizing. A much more critical scrutiny of proposals from LEAs for new special schools was begun in 1921 and LEAs were told that their expenditure on special schools in 1922-3 must not exceed that of 1921-2. Circular 1297 of January 1923 revised downwards the staffing and accommodation requirements for special schools.[9]

The effects of this Circular were minimal: in the first eight months of its operation, nineteen special-school staff were shed and a further 887 places were 'found'.[10] Small savings like these made it possible to rebut charges of

[7] See below, Appendix I, Table 3.

[8] Ed 50/146 Minute A.H. Wood to Newman Apr. 1924. On the full range of Geddes proposals, see Geoffrey Sherington, *English Education, Social Change and War, 1911-20* (Manchester, 1981), pp. 163-7; on the political context and the general retreat from innovation in social policy see Kenneth O. Morgan, *Consensus and Disunity: The Lloyd George Coalition Government 1918-22* (Oxford, 1979), pp. 280-95.

[9] Ed 50/150B Minute on President's behalf to A.H. Wood 9 Nov. 1921; Minute H.A.L. Fisher to Wood 4 Dec. 1921; Minute Wood to Newman and Eichholz 10 Jan. 1922; Circular 1297 Jan. 1923. See also the recurrent criticisms made at the conference on mental defect organized by the CACMD, now the Central Association for Mental Welfare, in the summer of 1922, reported in *The Times Educational Supplement* 5 Aug. 1922, p. 366 and Ed 50/146 Minute A.H. Wood to Newman April 1924. Fisher was particularly concerned to protect his restructuring of teachers' salary scales — on this see Sherington, op. cit. and H.A.L. Fisher, *An Unfinished Autobiography* (London, 1940), p. 104.

[10] Ed 50/146 Minute A.H. Wood to Newman April 1924.

extravagance but could make little impact on the larger problem, the massive cost, both capital and running, entailed in providing the complete national network of special schools envisaged in the legislation. Estimated total expenditure on special schools of *all* types, that is for physically as well as mentally handicapped children, for 1923-4 was £1,260,383. To provide adequate additional places for mentally defective children alone would, Eichholz estimated, involve capital expenditure of the order of £3m. and additional annual expenditure of around £1.25m.[11]

Clearly this kind of extra money would not be forthcoming in the foreseeable future. But without it the law could not be uniformly and effectively enforced. Neither the civil servants nor the doctors at the Board of Education found this situation professionally tolerable — and the position was not made any easier by constant harassment from the Board of Control, Mrs Pinsent, now one of its Commissioners, to the fore.[12]

Officials of the Board of Education began to consider, therefore, whether the position could be rationalized by, in effect, changing the rules. The prime mover was A.H. Wood, who launched a long Memorandum in July 1923, 'Mentally Defective Children . . . on the future policy of the Board'. His initial point was a very familiar one:

the definition of a mentally defective child for the purposes of the Education Act 1921 is quite a vague one. The child for whom the local education authority has to remain responsible is one who is capable of profiting by instruction in a Special School; but the nature of a Special School is nowhere defined in the Act. It is simply a school to which suitable children can be sent.

It would be profitable, he thought, to consider the consequences if different standards of referral were applied:

it is obvious that the correct standard is open to considerable doubt, and in an endeavour to fix it, it does not seem unreasonable to consider *inter alia* what its effect would be. If the effect should prove to be entirely impracticable, it would be necessary for the Board to consider

[11] Ed 50/150B Memorandum Eichholz 1 June 1923, Memorandum A.H. Wood, dated from covering note 8 June 1923.
[12] e.g. Ed 50/119 Note of interview 3 Nov. 1922 and interview Memorandum 19 Apr. 1923; items in Ed 50/121 listed below in note 14; Ed 50/112.

whether some more practicable standard complied fairly with a reasonable interpretation of the Acts, and if not, whether some modification of the present law was required.[13]

The problem was not simply a medico-psychological one; it was also a legal one, in senses other than that already described. Not only did the legislation not define a special school, it offered definitions of degrees of mental defect which at points overlapped. Specifically, s. 1 (b) of the 1913 Act defined an imbecile child as one suffering from mental deficiency so pronounced that he was incapable of managing his own affairs or being taught to do so. Such a child was the responsibility of the Board of Control and the local control authority. Sections 2 and 21 of that Act and Part V of the 1921 Education Act, however, asserted the responsibility of the Board of Education and the LEA for all mentally defective children capable of benefiting from instruction in special schools. The two definitions were not mutually exclusive; it was perfectly possible for a child to benefit from instruction in a special school and yet not be capable of managing his affairs on his own.

Wood had hoped that the problem facing the Board of Education might be somewhat reduced by transferring part of it elsewhere: specifically, by transferring some of the children with severe mental defect from special schools to the custodial care of the local control authorities — although these were no less starved of resources. But the ruling from the Board's legal adviser, W.R. Barker, was emphatic — and showed, interestingly, that for once the grey area in law was a faithful reflection of real problems and uncertainties in diagnosis and classification. Wood summarized Barker's opinion to the Board of Control:

he advises that we are acting in harmony with the intention of the relevant Acts in refusing to treat as imbeciles children who are incapable of managing themselves or their affairs, but with regard to whom it is doubtful whether they can be taught to do so. He thinks that it is clear that the point at which the child would be treated as an imbecile does not arise until it is established that he cannot be so taught. The only place in which as a rule this criterion can be applied is the Special School. Every mentally defective child therefore who is capable of receiving benefit from instruction in a Special School

[13] Ed 50/155.

should be given a trial in such a school and should not be notified until it is established that the influence of the school is powerless to teach him to manage his own affairs. While, therefore, all children in special schools should be reviewed at regular intervals to see whether they fall below this standard, it must be regarded as possible for the decision to be delayed till quite late in school life and even in many cases till they are nearly about to leave school at sixteen years of age.[14]

On the face of it, new legislation might tidy things up. But none of Wood's colleagues thought this worth the effort: it was a controversial field and new definitions might confound confusion. The only immediate fruit of his initiative was another gloomy circular, 1341 of September 1924, urging economy and making the best of what was acknowledged to be a bad job.[15]

Simultaneously, the Board had been grappling with the problems presented by the very different practices of LEAs in the ascertainment of mentally defective children. Some authorities, amongst which Birmingham was notorious, would not admit to the existence of a mentally defective child unless they had a special-school place for him. Others identified the children but then ran into difficulties as to whether, in the absence of enough special-school places, they could or should compel the children's attendance at an ordinary public elementary school and claim grant for them. In addition, the variety of practice made the aggregate national statistics and any projections of need derived from them, highly unreliable. Wood and Newman argued for pressure on LEAs to secure uniformity of ascertainment. The Permanent Secretary, Selby-Bigge, and the Parliamentary Secretary, Lord Onslow, disagreed — 'we should place ourselves in a false position and give the idea that we are going to take steps which we know we are not able to at the present moment'. But the President, Edward Wood (later Lord Halifax), apparently felt quite able to cope with any demands

[14] Ed 50/121 letter A.H. Wood to Sir F. Willis '5/2' date-stamped 24 Sept. 1924. See also Minute Wood to W.R. Barker 25 Jan. 1924, Minute Barker to Wood 28 Jan. 1924, Note of interview with officers of the Board of Control date-stamped 24 Sept. 1924.
[15] Ed 50/121, Ed 50/155, see especially Minute A.H. Wood to Newman 23 Apr. 1924. Circular 1341 September 1924.

for increased expenditure which might result and authorized Wood and Newman to go ahead.[16]

These variations and problems of ascertainment reinforced A.H. Wood's determination to try to secure greater rationality and even-handedness in procedures and their enforcement: a full-scale inquiry might bring these, if only by exposing the full illogicality and embarrassment of the present position. Moreover while the inquiry deliberated, the Board would have a respectable defence for not enforcing the existing law more aggressively. In the course of 1924, therefore, Newman was persuaded to set up a committee to inquire into the national incidence of mental deficiency. Initially the committee was concerned only with children. But in 1925 the brief was extended to cover adults as well. All the interested parties were there: Wood, Dr Crowley, Cecil Eaton and N.D. Bosworth-Smith from 'M' Branch; Miss Hilda Redfern, HMI for schools for mentally defective children until 1927 and thereafter an inspector for the Board of Control; Mrs Pinsent from the Board of Control and her successor as major-general of the voluntary organizations, Miss Evelyn Fox, Honorary Secretary of what had now become the Central Association for Mental Welfare; Dr A.F. Tredgold, 'Lecturer in Mental Deficiency, London University' and still one of the Association's leading lights; Dr F.C. Shrubsall, senior MOH, and Dr Cyril Burt, psychologist, from the LCC; and Dr F. Douglas Turner, the medical Superintendent of the Royal Eastern Counties Institution.[17]

The Committee deliberated for nearly five years, reporting in 1929. As the members themselves acknowledged, they were covering much of the ground covered by the Royal Commission on the Care and Control of the Feeble-Minded, twenty years before;[18] and their Report provides an admirable

[16] Ed 50/119, direct quotation from Lord Onslow's Minute 6 Oct. 1923. For examples of variation see ARMOH for 1913, P.P. 1914–16 xviii Cd 7730, para. 242; *The Health of the School Child, 1923* (London, 1924), s. vi; *Report of the Mental Deficiency Committee* (London, 1929), 3 vols. (henceforward Wood Report), i, ch. 1, para. 2.

[17] Ed 50/150B 'Memorandum on the Board's policy towards special schools', A.H. Wood, dated from covering note 8 June 1923; Ed 24/1199 Note by Wood for the new Permanent Secretary, Sir Aubrey Symonds, on the origins of the Committee, 23 Oct. 1925; Wood Report, i, preface and list of members.

[18] Wood Report, iii, ch. 1, p. 1.

measure of continuities and changes in attitudes to mental
defect in those twenty years. One of the leading American
authorities on mental defect has described the years 1910-35
as representing a 'great lull' in the study and treatment of
mental defect, brought to an end only by the Norwegian,
Fölling's isolation and identification of phenylketonuria, an
enzyme deficiency condition which, if not corrected by
rigorous diet, could lead to mental handicap.[19] This indeed
was a dramatic advance in the aetiology of defect, comparable with the linkage established between thyroid deficiency
and cretinism in the nineteenth century, and with work after
the Second World War on chromosomal abnormalities. But
there were other, less spectacular changes in attitudes towards
the causes of mental defect which are none the less important because they combined to erode and to undermine
the centrality of heredity in such explanations.

Like the Royal Commission, the Wood Committee formu-
lated a definition of mental defect which was essentially
social, and acknowledged it as such. But unlike the Royal
Commission, it distinguished between three groups of causal
factors, congenital defects, brain damage brought about by
illness or accident, and the possible temporary effects of
mental illness. The Royal Commission, it noted, had considered only the first.[20]

The whole range of problems associated with brain damage
after birth had been forcibly brought home to the Board of
Control, and to a lesser extent, to the Board of Education, by
a serious outbreak of encephalitis lethargica in 1925-6.
Children and adolescents who suffered brain damage from
this, as, indeed, from meningitis and other infections which
attacked the central nervous system, could not be brought
within the framework of the existing mental deficiency
legislation and care, since that specified that the defect must
have existed 'from birth or a very early age'. Eventually in
1927 the Board of Control had secured amending legislation,
redefining mental defect as 'a condition of arrested or incomplete development of mind existing before the age of
eighteen years, whether arising from inherent causes or

[19] Kanner, *Care and Study of the Mentally Retarded*, p. 141.
[20] Wood Report, i, ch. 2.

induced by disease or injury' — but not without another
passage of arms with Colonel Wedgwood.[21]

The Wood Committee's approach to classification of
defect by degree of severity also bore the impress of developments since 1908. Given the wild variations not only in
LEAs' assessments of the incidence of defect but also in the
assessments made by local control authorities, its members
had to embark on their own sample survey;[22] and the procedures used to classify children in this show just how great
the impact of Binet and Simon's mental tests had been. The
Committee's special investigator, Dr E. O. Lewis, was a Board
of Control inspector, but had an impressively wide range of
qualifications and experience. He had taught in both elementary and secondary schools; after reading Natural Sciences
at Aberystwyth he had taken Part II of the Moral Sciences
Tripos at Cambridge. Subsequently he had taken a doctorate
in psychology at London, had lectured in educational
method at a training college and in educational psychology
at the University of St. Andrews. To all this he had then
added medical qualifications and work as an assistant MOH
for the LCC.[23] In consultation with the Committee he chose
and investigated in depth six areas, each with a population of
approximately 100,000. In investigating the incidence of
defect among children he first surveyed the populations of
the special schools and classes in the area. In addition, the
class teachers in the elementary schools in each area were
asked to select the 15 per cent of their classes who were the
most backward. These children were then given a group
mental test and those with the lowest scores were given
further individual mental tests and, in some cases, a physical
examination also.[24]

On the basis of this survey, the Wood Committee concluded
that in the country as a whole, beside the 33,000 defective
children already identified by MOHs and teachers, only half
of whom were actually in special classes or schools, there

[21] Ed 31/252; 17 & 18 Geo. V, c. 33, s. 1 (2); Jones, *Mental Health Services*,
pp. 215–16.
[22] Wood Report, i, ch. I, paras. 2, 5 and 6.
[23] Ibid., i, ch. I, para. 8.
[24] Ibid., iii, ch. I esp. pp. 21–8.

were another 72,000 unascertained.[25] The Committee also pronounced on the standards for ascertainment being used by LEAs. It was apparently becoming conventional to regard children with IQs of below 70 as mentally defective. But while some authorities might treat these children as suitable candidates for a special school or class, others would refer them to the local control authority as ineducable. The Committee recommended that only children with an IQ of below 50 should be so referred. Children with IQs between 50 and 70 should be grouped together with those with IQs between 70 and 80, coming conventionally to be identified as the 'dull and backward'; and this new category, to be labelled 'retarded', should be given special care within the framework of the ordinary elementary school, not segregated in a special school.[26] The technology of mental measurement was thus employed by the Wood Committee both to calculate the extent of mental defect among the child population nationally and to provide local education and control authorities with clear-cut criteria for the ascertainment and referral of children.

But full implementation of these proposals required legislation. The Committee's Secretary, Bosworth-Smith, summed up the position crudely, but not unfairly, in a Minute to his fellow committee member, Dr Ralph Crowley, in November 1929:

under the present law any appreciable extension of the special school system is impossible. . . .the only way of getting anything done for the large numbers of M.D. children now attending Public Elementary Schools is to amend the law so that M.D. and dull and backward children can be dealt with in a single system.[27]

And as the Committee had also thrown in the proposal that 'retarded' children should be kept at school till the age of sixteen, any attempt to legislate was bound to bring in its train the vexed question of the repeated deferment of the raising of the school-leaving age for all children.[28]

[25] Ibid., i, ch. IV paras. 55-6, ch. V paras. 83 and 93. Even so, this did not take account of the children notified to and in the custodial care of the local control authority — see ch. IX p. 154 ss. 3(b) and (c).

[26] Ibid., i, ch. VIII esp. paras. 151, 156, 163-5 and ch. IX p. 157.

[27] Ed 50/124 Minute N.D. Bosworth-Smith to Dr Ralph Crowley 12 Nov. 1929.

[28] On the problems associated with this, see e.g. Rodney Barker, *Education and Politics 1900–1951, A Study of the Labour Party* (Oxford, 1972), pp. 60-4.

When the Report was published, all the usual lobbies swung into action, mostly in support of the recommendations concerning children; and the Board of Education went through the motions of preparing various schemes, according to various assumptions. But the Board was distinctly half-hearted about it, and with reason. While the Committee sat, there had been a struggle every single year with the Treasury over its expenses — which never, in any year, exceeded £1,000; and the economic blizzard of 1931 finally put paid to any hope of action — even to the gesture of another gloomy circular.[29]

Even without legislation, the Report brought the Board one gain which it is difficult to imagine was not foreseen, at least by A.H. Wood. It had challenged the orthodoxy, prevailing since the early 1890s, that special schools made the best provision for mentally defective children. Thereby, the Report gave the Board of Education a most respectable alibi, intellectual as well as financial, for taking no further steps to expand special-school provision — which it was not above invoking. Memorandum 344, advising HM Inspectors in 1934 on the right approach to the education of mentally defective children in their area, urged them to seek the referral of all children with IQs of under 50 to the local control authority and to encourage provision for other children of low IQ within the existing public elementary schools, both on grounds of cost and on the basis of the Wood recommendations.[30]

Failure to act on the Wood Report was of course only a tiny part of the cuts inflicted by the crisis of 1931. For education potentially the most serious cut, with ramifications throughout the service, was the ending of the percentage grant system, initiated by s. 44 of Fisher's 1918 Education Act. Under this the central government was required to meet half the total expenditure by an LEA on elementary or higher education, provided the Board's regulations had been complied with. The Treasury had always regarded this as subversive of Treasury control and an incentive

[29] For the dealings with the Treasury, see Ed 23/319; for lobbying, draft schemes and attempts at a circular, see Ed 50/124.
[30] Ed 22/109.

to extravagance by local authorities; and Lord Eustace Percy, President of the Board from 1924 to 1929, was inclined to agree, although he and the Treasury differed over the appropriate form of block grant.[31] Selby-Bigge, the Permanent Secretary from 1911 to 1925, vehemently disagreed, however, pointing out first that in 1922–3 and 1923–4 the Board had been able to impose a 'rationing' of expenditure, while in 1926 its hand had been strengthened further by s. 12(1) of the Economy (Miscellaneous Provisions) Act, which read

For the purpose of removing doubts it is hereby declared that the Board of Education shall not ... be bound to recognize as expenditure in aid of which parliamentary grants should be made to a local education authority and expenditure which in the opinion of the Board is excessive, having regard to the circumstances of the area of the authority and the general standard of expenditure on corresponding services in other areas, or which in the opinion of the Board unreasonably exceeds any estimates of expenditure made by the authority.[32]

Despite this, the May Committee — the 'Geddes Committee' of 1931 — successfully argued for the complete abolition of the percentage grant system in education and its replacement by block grants.[33]

---

[31] Lord Percy of Newcastle, *Some Memories* (London, 1958), p. 98 and Ed 24/1198. I owe the last reference to Kevin Jefferys who is completing a Ph.D. thesis for the University of London on 'The Educational Policies of the Conservative Party 1918–44' and from whose comments this chapter and chapter 6 have benefited particularly.

[32] D.N. Chester, *Central and Local Government. Financial and Administrative Relations* (London, 1951), pp. 6–7 and Sir Lewis Amherst Selby-Bigge, *The Board of Education* (London, 1927), pp. 98–114. See also the comment of C.D. Foster, R. Jackman and M. Perlman, *Local Government Finance in a Unitary State* (London, 1980), p. 183, that 'There was no evidence to suggest that percentage grants encouraged extravagance by local authorities.' Selby-Bigge's discussion of the grant structure is far and away the most lucid and detailed available. It is a pity that nothing comparable exists for the period after 1927.

[33] On the May proposals for education as a whole, see Brian Simon, *The Politics of Educational Reform 1920–1940* (London, 1974), pp. 171–8. See also U.K. Hicks, *The Finance of British Government 1920–1936* (Oxford, 1938, reprinted 1970), p. 153. The proportion of costs met by grant duly fell, from 56.8 per cent in 1929–30 to 48 per cent in 1932–3 (ibid.). On the other hand, spending per head in elementary education went up from £12.4s. in 1922, to almost £15 in 1936, despite the fall in prices and the components of this increase, the fall in the child population (see my Appendix I, Fig. 1), reorganization etc. have never been satisfactorily analysed — Hicks, p. 54, also diagram facing p. 39 and Appendix 6. I suspect that Selby-Bigge drew a distinction between 'extravagance' and 'maintenance of standards/acceptable improvement' which the Treasury was never prepared to recognize. If so, the issue then becomes one of the rate of deceleration — how near zero growth could the Board of Education and the local authorities be brought — rather than one of absolute cut-backs.

These changes underpinned a complete embargo on new special-school provision (and also new nursery-school provision) between 1931 and 1934,[34] and an unprecedented review of expenditure on school medical services 1932–3. As A.W. Maudslay put it to Newman:

In normal times . . . it is not part of the Board's work to exercise a very meticulous control over expenditure so long as there is no gross extravagance. The present times, however, are very far from normal. . . .

Unless they themselves investigated the variation in unit cost of school medical services, they were likely to have some independent investigative body thrust upon them. Newman took the point; and the effect of the Board's own inquiry was to pin-point nine apparently extravagant authorities, Beckenham, Manchester, Reigate, Bath, Leicester, Todmorden, Halifax, West Sussex and Staffordshire, all of which were warned. Sadly, the five really *low*-spending authorities also identified, Hyde, Shrewsbury, Birmingham, Somerset and Darlington, were not correspondingly instructed to raise their standards;[35] although by 1936 the officials of the Board were becoming increasingly worried about chronic underspending on special schools and school medical services in the depressed (confusingly 'special') areas, where the evidence of malnutrition among the child population was building up.[36] Against this background, it is hardly surprising that special-school provision remained static during the 1930s; although the continuing fall in the child population made this less of a problem for LEAs than it might have been.[37]

II Mental measurement and its context

Eustace Percy recalled his Shadow, Sir Charles Trevelyan, quoting Browning at him from the Opposition Front Bench in the mid-1920s to warn him 'that it could never be "glad confident morning again"' in educational policy-making.[38] The treatment of special schools in particular and the

[34] Ed 50/48.
[35] Ed 50/105, direct quotation from Maudslay's Minute to Newman 26 Aug. 1932. [36] Ed 50/181.
[37] See below, Appendix I, Table 3 and Fig. 1; also the comments of Dr Henry Herd, SMO Manchester, 'The Education and Notification of Mentally Defective Children', *Education* 23 Dec. 1938, p. 678.
[38] Percy, *Some Memories*, p. 98.

provision in general for mentally defective children in the inter-War years were as powerful illustrations as any of what he meant. Between 1910 and 1914 Newman and Morant argued a case on principle. Costings were made, but they did not determine choices. By 1925 their plans had come to be seen as grandiose fantasies. A.H. Wood, briefing the new Permanent Secretary about the doings of the Committee of which he, Wood, was Chairman, wrote plaintively,

you will see we are not wild men about finances. In fact we have shown over and over again that we are trying to reduce impossible statutory obligations within the bounds of possibility.[39]

In due course his Committee reported, in effect, that there was no real need for these expensive special schools: educable children with mental defect ought to be coped with within the existing elementary schools. The administrative and financial attractions of such a solution are obvious; but of course the principal argument used to defend the proposal was educational. Since mentally defective children in practice constituted a continuum of ability, shading all the way through from the severe to the normal, rather than a clear-cut category like blind children, it was inappropriate to segregate them. And the new technology of mental measurement, in particular the device of the IQ, made the idea of a continuum or spectrum of ability far more easily assimilable than ever before.

The Wood Report and its reception bring sharply into focus the fundamental question about the nature and springs of policy towards mentally defective children in the inter-War years. Were financial constraints as overwhelming as to shape, subordinate, deform even, all else? There is an air of unreality certainly about some of the Wood recommendations concerning children. They rejected a clear line of demarcation between the elementary and the special school, while accepting a much more important one, that between the educable and the ineducable child. They hardly engaged at all with the argument from experience deployed by the special-school teachers: these children flourish and develop with our favourable staffing ratios and specially adapted curriculum. What

---

[39] Ed 24/1199 handwritten note to accompany the typewritten note from A.H. Wood to the Permanent Secretary 23 Oct. 1925.

hope is there for them in the already grossly overcrowded classes of unreorganized elementary schools? To make the new proposals work would need an injection of resources into the elementary school system comparable to that needed for extra special schools. As the editor of the Association of Education Committees' journal, *Education*, remarked, with exceptional politeness — or perhaps elaborate irony —

It is almost a paradox that while 300,000 children are to receive a form of education which is provided at present for only 15,000, the report is quite definite in noting that little, if any, expansion of the special school system is possible.[40]

It is as if the members of the Wood Committee — the official ones anyway — knew that nothing would actually *happen* as a result of their Report. It becomes tempting to see the invocation of mental measurement, the careful parade of psychological and medical expertise, as partially or even primarily devices to reduce or evade these 'impossible statutory obligations'. As both mental measurement and financial constraints appear to pull in the same direction, it becomes very difficult to establish their respective weights. We shall never know what the impact of mental measurement would have been on policy towards mentally defective children, had the Board of Education's room for financial manœuvre remained as extensive as it had seemed from 1910 to 1914. On the other hand, there is ample evidence that the Board of Education's commitment to the principles of mental measurement and the developing field of the psychology of individual difference antedated and extended well beyond any possible financial pay-off. More money would have affected the extent and the name of the provision for mentally defective children — either more special schools or accelerated and more lavish reorganization of elementary schools — but it is unlikely significantly to have altered the conceptual framework of discussion.

Special schools were principally the responsibility of 'M'

---

[40] *Education* 17 May 1929, p. 552. See also the exchange between Maudslay and Leah Manning of the NUT on the need for certification of mentally defective children, or some equivalent in Ed 50/266, Interview Memorandum 24 Sept. 1936; and the comments on the uses of segregation by Dr Henry Herd in the article cited above, note 37.

branch at the Board of Education;[41] and both its civil servants
and its doctors seem gradually to have built up a respectable
body of expertise on mental measurement. It was Newman,
of course, who had given Binet and Simon's tests their first
large-scale English publicity in his pre-War reports;[42] and as
has been mentioned, he returned to the fray even before the
end of the War. In his report for 1917 he not only repeated
the substance of his 1912 report, commending the tests of
Binet and Simon, but also drew the attention of School
Medical Officers to the discussion in Cyril Burt's special
report to the LCC, published in 1917 as *The Distribution
and Relations of Educational Ability*.

In 1921 the Chief Medical Officer's report was separated
from the Board's Annual Report and published separately as
an annual semi-official paper, *The Health of the School
Child*. This, if anything, increased the opportunities for
Newman and his colleagues to spread themselves; and the
pattern set in that 1917 report, a clear exposition and usually
some critical discussion of the latest work in the field, was
maintained, lasting also through Newman's retirement in
1935 and replacement by Dr Arthur McNulty. Chapter VIII,
'The Diagnosis of Mental Deficiency' in *The Health of the
School Child, 1935* (published in 1936) is fuller than in some
years, but overall may be taken as a characteristic example.
The sections 'Preliminaries to Examination' and 'Cooperation
with Teachers' discussed the initial screening of children in
infants and lower junior schools, suggesting that a group test,
as used by some LEAs, might be helpful, and drawing attention to some recently-developed non-verbal tests, but
stressing that

The teachers from their close contact with the children have that knowledge of their temperaments, their special abilities, and their home and
school circumstances which cannot be revealed by tests and which must
be available to the school medical officer if he is to draw proper conclusions from his examination.

The section on the conduct of the examination dealt first
with the proper treatment of family history,[43] then with the

---

[41] Created in 1911 — Ed 50/27 Procedure Minute E 15/11, M. 1 signed R.L.M.
30 June 1911.
[42] See above, p. 55.   [43] See also below, pp. 88-9.

importance of testing hearing and sight before all else:

it is difficult — it might almost be said to be impossible to distinguish between mental deficiency and the retardation, physical and mental, which may be caused by blindness in a child who has never been to a blind school.

Only if a child with a sight defect failed to make any headway at a school for the blind (or a child with a hearing defect at a school for the deaf) should he be suspected of mental defect. Finally there was guidance on the importance of securing the child's relaxed participation — 'if he is frightened, or even if he feels in strange surroundings or with a strange person, or is nervous, or at all upset, a true picture of his mind cannot be seen' — and an extended discussion of types of mental tests worth quoting in full.

The Test of Intelligence

After the child has been set at his ease and the school medical officer has obtained the other particulars he requires, he usually gives an intelligence test to determine the general mental level. The test which is generally used for this purpose is the Binet test either in the Stanford Revision of Terman* or the London Revision of Burt+. Outside London the Stanford Revision is more generally used, although it was standardised on American children, possibly because the test booklets and material are of a very handy form and the book of directions is very explicit as well as full. The version used should be specified on Form 306 M in the space provided. Although school medical officers have been using this test for many years, it is not superfluous to remind them that the assessment of mental age derived from their testing is valueless, unless they have adhered word for word to the directions for administration. The change of an expression to another which seems to mean the same may alter the difficulty of a test item by a year or more. It is not permissible to vary the wording to make things clear to a child who does not understand: the test is one of understanding.

The Binet Test.

In a recent book on mental tests† the writer claims that there is less scientific evidence for the validity of the Binet test as a measure of the central intellective factor in ability which Spearman calls 'g' than there is for many of the more recent tests, and he therefore does not include a detailed description of it in his manual. He enumerates some of its

---

* L.M. Terman: The Measurement of Intelligence, London, Harrap.
+ C. Burt: Mental and Scholastic Tests, London, P.S. King.
† R.B. Cattell. A Guide to Mental Testing. 1936, London University Press.

other defects, the small number of items, its inadequacy at the higher
mental ages, its dependence on experience and schooling, and the large
influence of the personal contact of tester and child. Lest school
medical officers should feel that they are out of date in using this test,
perhaps something should be said here about its use for purposes of
diagnosis of mental deficiency.

It may be admitted that the Binet test was compiled and revised in
its present form before the scientific techniques of analysis were
developed to their present state. Originally it was a more or less empirical scale, and though its revisers improved and standardised it
against various criteria, yet as an instrument of scientific precision for
measuring the general ability which may be taken to underlie all cognitive acts, it cannot rank as high as some other tests. The small number
of items compared with the large number in more recent tests does give
more scope to chance, and the scale is admittedly unsuitable for bright
children at the higher age levels. Years ago Burt showed that the score
on it was influenced by the amount of schooling a child had had. On
the other hand, very few alternatives have had anything like so much
attention bestowed on them by psychologists, and few are nearly so
well or so widely standardised. Only one or two tests besides Binet can
be used on the lower levels of intelligence, particularly below a mental
age of 8, which are just those most used for diagnosis of mental deficiency. Those which can be used are either of a performance or a
'non-language' type, demanding either manipulation and constructive
ability or the interpretation of printed signs or pictures, but neither
spoken nor written language. They are most useful for assessing an
abstract intelligence level, for scientific and clinical purposes, and for
children with a special linguistic defect, but in examining the ordinary
child for mental deficiency it is as well to have a measure which includes as one factor verbal ability, as this figures so prominently in
school work and has such a bearing on the child's ability to profit by it.

The criticism that the Binet test is dependent to some extent on
schooling is a serious one, and cannot be ignored; but if it is recognised
by users of the test that it is only if the child has had a reasonably
normal environment and reasonably adequate schooling for his age
that the Binet test gives a valid result little harm can be done. Where it
is used on children who have had an abnormal upbringing, such as gipsy
children, canal boat children, children in institutions, children who have
been ill for long periods and lost many attendances at school, children
from homes which have afforded them an abnormally narrow existence
without the usual privileges of childhood, the mental age ascertained
will be too low and allowance must be made for these depriving circumstances. This of course may vitiate the obtained intelligence quotient as
a scientific result, but it makes no difference to the usefulness of the
Binet test as an instrument of diagnosis. There is no other single test in
general use by which the examiner can learn so much about the child,
his social type, his disposition, his method of tackling problems and his
language ability, although the test is not designed to give separate
measures of these. The very fact that that this is a series of conversational

situations and not a pencil and paper examination is all to the good for these purposes, if the examiner is trained and takes every precaution to avoid personal bias in his administration. If there are no untoward circumstances the intelligence quotient obtained will be a good index of the child's probable scholastic future even though there may be better indices of his 'g'. Even if the child's past history makes one hesitate to take the numerical intelligence quotient as a valid measure, one has still amassed a great quantity of information valid for diagnostic purposes.

In drawing conclusions from the results of the Binet test the mental age or intelligence quotient is not the only thing to be considered. It should always be kept in mind that the numerical result is valid only if there have not been irrelevant factors which might prevent the child showing his ability at the time of the test. One method of scrutinising the results to see if there is any evidence that this has not been so, is to note whether there is an abnormally large amount of 'scatter' in the responses to the test items. A small 'scatter' is to be expected: few children progress with success up to a given point and fail consistently thereafter, but 'scatter' over several years calls for comment by the tester.

An example will make this plain. One recent case of a child aged 10 years 8 months showed that he passed on the Stanford Revision all the VI year tests, 4 of the VII year tests, 1 of the VIII year tests, 4 of the IX year tests and none further. His mental age therefore was 7 years 6 months and intelligence quotient 70. It was a doubtful case on other counts than intelligence quotient, which was probably to be the deciding factor. Examination of tests passed and failed showed that he failed early on tests of a similar type to others he later passed, making it fairly likely that he possessed abilities which had not shown themselves. The fact that he did 4 out of 6 tests for year IX (one of the failures being in the date, which was excusable as he was not at school) made it seem probable that his actual mental level was nearer 8 1/2 than 7 1/2 and his intelligence quotient over 75, and suggested that a retest might show surprisingly different results. As the failures were mainly in tests requiring an oral response, it was possible that the child was temporarily out of sympathy with the examiner. In such a case a note should be made that in the examiner's opinion the ascertained intelligence quotient may not be really representative of the child's potential ability, and a retest should be made (preferably by another examiner) after a short interval and before any action is taken concerning the child. The examiner in this instance was a comparatively inexperienced assistant school medical officer who had probably carried out the test in a mechanically accurate manner, without making sure that he had the child's interest. Fortunately, he had obeyed the instruction to go on till the child failed to do a complete year of the tests. If he had stopped at the end of the VIII year series (as many people might with some justification have done) the intelligence quotient would have turned out to be 64 and the child would have been certified without doubt. The same 'scatter' is often found in the test results from children of the unstable type.

Corroboration by a second test.

Even with the best and most reliable tests the variability from day to day of the performance of the child, especially the unstable child, may be so great that it is never advisable to make a diagnosis upon one test, on one occasion. It would be a good rule if the results of not less than two applications of a test were available to a school medical officer before he made his final decision. Where there is any reason to believe that variability of response is due to undeveloped linguistic ability a performance test should be used either as a supplement to or in substitution for the Binet test, and in all cases the greatest possible caution should be used before arriving at a diagnosis of mental deficiency.

Performance Tests.

The fullest scale of performance tests readily available in this country is that of Drever and Collins*. It is composed of a number of well-known tests, together with some new ones, and is standardised as a whole, not part by part. It requires a good deal of time for its administration and the scores have a fairly wide range. It is not therefore so open as some performance tests are to the charge that it samples only a small part of the mind. The main objection to its use as a routine is the amount of time involved, and it may be found possible to use it only on doubtful cases where a full report has to be made. The Merrill-Palmer tests are widely used by psychologists, and school medical officers who are interested in testing might well follow their example. Separate tests like the Porteous Mazes, Kohs Blocks or the Seguin or Healy Boards take little time to give, but have a small range of scores. Certifying officers should use one or more of them, in addition to the Binet test. If the performance mental age is lower than the Binet mental age the indication of mental deficiency is strengthened: where it is higher there is the likelihood that the low Binet mental age may be due to lack of linguistic development, which is not necessarily a sign of general deficiency. In cases where notification to the Mental Deficiency Authority is proposed, a low performance score should be taken to indicate a likelihood that the child will fail to look after himself or to work satisfactorily in a manual occupation.

* *See* Drever and Collins, 'Performance Tests of Intelligence', 1936, Edinburgh, Oliver & Boyd.

Reinforcing and underpinning these detailed instructions was the form mentioned, Form 306 M, on which the school Medical Officer was advised to make his report. This had begun life as Schedule F of the model arrangements for certifying a child under the 1913 Act and had asked the school medical officer to report under the following heads:

Family and personal conditions and history. . . .
Physical conditions　—　(a) general
　　　　　　　　　—　(b) stigmata
Mental conditions: N.B. in assessing mental conditions the tests
designed by Binet and Simon are recommended
　　　　　　　　　—　(a) motor mechanisms
　　　　　　　　　—　(b) reactions to sensory stimulation
　　　　　　　　　—　(c) emotional conditions
　　　　　　　　　—　(d) tests of intelligence
　　　　　　　　　—　(e) tests of will-power[44]

From 1924 to 1925, in a process surely not unconnected
with the activities of the Wood Committee, the form was reviewed and a new draft was circulated to selected school
medical officers, Drs Burt, Tredgold and Shrubsall and Miss
Fox for comment, before final revision and publication.[45]
This form, reproduced here in full, remained in use until
after the Second World War.[46]

Form 306 M

Suggested Form of Report on Child Examined for Mental Deficiency.

N.B.—　The Form should be signed by a Medical Officer approved by the
　　　　Board of Education under section 55 (3) of the Education Act,
　　　　1921, and under section 31 of the Mental Deficiency Act, 1913.
　　　　It should be filled up as fully as possible and all the information
　　　　available given under each heading. (See paragraph 3 of Circular
　　　　1359.) The actual conditions and achievements of the child
　　　　should be recorded and such general terms as "good," "fair," etc.,
　　　　avoided.

[44] Ed 50/113, proofs of schedule F, January 1914.
[45] Ed 50/113, Ed 50/123, Circular 1359 of 1935 and Form 306 M.
[46] See the discussion of the form's adequacy in 1939 after the Keasley case in
Ed 50/268.

Local Education Authority ....

I. Name of child (in full) ....

Address ....

Date of birth ......   Age (years and months) ....

School ....
(If the child is not in attendance at school, state the name of the last school attended (if any) and the date upon which the child left.)

II. Physical Examination :—

(a) General (results of routine medical inspection) ....

....

....

(b) Special :—

(1) Sight: blindness, total or partial, errors of refraction ....

....

(2) Hearing: deaf-mutism, partial deafness, partial mutism .....

....

(3) Speech: defective articulation, lalling, idioglossia, echolalia, etc.
....

(4) Nose and throat: enlarged tonsils, adenoids, mouth breathing, otorrhœa
....

(5) Motor Mechanism: posture, gait, paralysis, etc. ....

....

(6) Deformities ....

(7) Cleanly habits ....   Salivation. ....

(8) Stigmata ....

III.   Particulars of Environment, Home Conditions, etc.   . . . .

. . . .

Regularity of School Attendance . . . .

IV.   Family History (in regard to insanity or other mental or nervous
defect, criminality, epilepsy, alcoholism, illegitimacy, etc.)

. . . .

V.   Personal History :—

(a) Constitutional defects, injury at birth or subsequently, malnutrition, rickets, fits, congenital syphilis, encephalitis lethargica, infectious and other diseases, accidents, etc.

. . . .

(b) Commencement of

(1) Speech . . . .

(2) Walking . . . .

(3) Cleanly habits . . . .

VI.   Personal and Social Qualities :—

e.g., appearance, general bearing, habits, self-care, self-protection,
will power (initiative, concentration, purpose), co-operation
with others, special aptitudes

. . . .

. . . .

. . . .

. . . .

VII.   Temperamental Conditions :—

(a) Abnormal manifestations of affection, temper, fear, destruc-
tiveness, spitefulness, acquisitiveness, docility, curiosity,
aggressiveness, sullenness, excitability, solitariness, etc.

. . . .

. . . .

. . . .

(b) Night terrors, food neuroses, wandering, etc. . . . .

. . . .

. . . .

. . . .

(c) Abnormal manifestations of sex, stealing, cruelty, untruthfulness, etc. Amenability to discipline or punishment

. . . .

. . . .

. . . .

VIII. Response to School and Home Environment :—

(a) Information gained from interrogation of the child . . . .

. . . . ; . . . .

. . . .

(b) Information obtained from others; *e.g.*, parents, guardians, teachers, social agencies

. . . .

. . . .

IX. Response to School Instruction :—

The record should state precisely what the child can do under each heading, including the type of book (if any) the child can read, examples of the child's writing from copy and dictation and of sums worked and the forms of manual work it can undertake.

A report from the teacher should be appended and should indicate how far the child falls short in educational attainments of a normal child of similar age. If the child is old enough his attainments in reading, spelling, arithmetic, etc., should be expressed where possible in terms of a mental age, obtained by standardized scholastic tests.

(a) Expression by means of Speech . . . .

. . . .

. . . .

. . . .

(b) Letters, words, reading . . . .

. . . .

. . . .

(c) Counting, manipulation (both mental and on paper) of simple numbers, simple money values.

. . . .

. . . .

(d) Writing (1) from copy; (2) from dictation . . . .

. . . .

. . . .

(e) Manual Work . . . .

. . . .

. . . .

		Mental Age (m) ...	....
X. Response to Intelligence Tests.		Actual Age (a) ...	....
		Mental Ratio $\left(\frac{m}{a} \times 100\right)$	....

Specify the Tests used, *e.g.*, The Binet Simon, The Stanford Revision, recording the results in the table below. If Burt's or other revisions are used a separate table indicating the actual tests used at each age should be attached.

If in addition such Tests as Healy, Porteus, Word Association, etc., are used the results should be recorded on a separate sheet.

No. of Test.	AGE								Pass Failure	+ —
	III	IV	V	VI	VII	VIII	IX	X	XI	XII
1 - - -	....	....	....	....	....	....	....	....	....	....
2 - - -	....	....	....	....	....	....	....	....	....	....
3 - - -	....	....	....	....	....	....	....	....	....	....
4 - - -	....	....	....	....	....	....	....	....	....	....
5 - - -	....	....	....	....	....	....	....	....	....	....
6 - - -	....	....	....	....	....	....	....	....	....	....

XI.   General Observations,
          including the impression derived from the child's behaviour
          and response at the time of the examination.

XII.   Diagnosis (underline the appropriate heading or headings):—

     (a) Physically defective—stating defect.

     (b) Blind, or partially sighted.

     (c) Deaf-mute, or semi-mute or semi-deaf.
     (d) Epileptic.
     (e) Merely dull or backward.

     (f) Neurotic, or
         unstable.
     (g) Mentally defective
         (feeble-minded).
     (h) Moral defective.
     (i) Imbecile.
     (j) Idiot.

XIII. Treatment recommended :—

     (a)   An ordinary class in a Public Elementary School.   ....

     (b)   A special class for dull or backward children
               under the Public Elementary School Code.   ....

     (c)   A Special School for Physically Defective, Blind,
               Deaf or Mentally Defective children (state
               what type of school and also whether day or
               residential is recommended).   ....
           [By Special School is meant a school certified by
               the Board of Education under Section 52 (1)
               or Section 56 (1), as the case may be, of the
               Education Act, 1921. By Special School for
               Mentally Defective Children is meant a school
               so certified for educable Mentally Defective
               (feeble-minded) children only.]

(d)   Notification to the Local Authority under the
Mental Deficiency Act, 1913, as amended by
the Mental Deficiency Act, 1927. (State the
Article of the Mental Deficiency (Notification
Children) Regulations, 1928, under which it is
considered that the child's name should be
notified.)   ....

(e)   Other recommendation, if any.   ....

(Signed) ....
  Qualifications as
Medical Practitioner ....   Address ....

Official position (if any) under   Date ....
the Local Education Authority   ....

We have come some distance from Dr Francis Warner's
'Method of Examining Children in Schools as to their
Development and Brain Condition'.[47]

Even so, SMOs could not be relied upon to fill in the form
properly. The SMO for Stoke-on-Trent, who had made a
special study of mental defect and one of those to whom the
draft of 306M was sent, replied with a long letter which included several horror stories:

A number of MOs clearly do not use any revision of the Binet tests,
others who do, state the mental age so indefinitely that it gives one no
information at all. I often get this sort of thing . . . 'Mental age 6-9'!
. . . I met an ASMO of a large county . . . who has been engaged on the
work of 'Ascertainment' for some years and he staggered me by in-
forming me that he had never used the Binet tests or seen anyone else
use them.

He himself, he went on, preferred Burt's revision of Binet
to the Stanford one, since it had been standardized on
English children; and he concluded with an extended discussion of modes of calculating correlations.[48]

Here, in this one letter, were encapsulated the extremes of
the range of knowledge about mental testing among SMOs,
from considerable expertise to smug ignorance. This range
probably contributed at least as much as policy decisions

[47] See above, p. 10.
[48] Ed 50/123 SMO Stoke-on-Trent to Dr R.H. Crowley 1 July 1924.

about the provision of special-school places to the wildly varying estimates of the incidence of mental deficiency between one authority and another;[49] and 'M' Branch devoted much time and energy to raising the minimum standards. At one level, *The Health of the School Child* was an annual propaganda exercise, although it was no more possible to ensure that all SMOs read, marked and learned it than it was to get them to fill in forms properly. But there was some added incentive given in the encouragement to and full reporting of individual pieces of research undertaken by SMOs. Between 1921 and 1932 there were never less than four or five investigations of mentally defective, retarded or backward children going on and in most years there were as many as ten such projects. Between 1908 and 1932, 1,322 research projects had been undertaken altogether and mental defect was the second most frequently chosen area of investigation, outstripped only by rheumatism and heart disease.[50]

Much the most powerful weapon in educating SMOs, however, lay in the necessity for the SMO to secure the Board of Education's approval of his qualifications before any certificate of deficiency issued by him would stand up in law.[51] Initially and inevitably, the decision to grant or to withhold such approval had to be taken on an *ad hoc* basis. But from 1920 onwards, the Central Association for Mental Deficiency/Welfare, primarily in the person of the indefatigable Miss Fox, organized short, two-part courses annually for SMOs on the ascertainment and treatment of mental defectives. Thereafter the Board of Education normally treated attendance at Part I of the course as a necessary precondition of approval and took a beneficient view of attendance also at Part II, designed to follow after some experience in schools. It also succeeded in construing first Part II of the 1902 Education Act and then Part VI of the 1921 Education

---

[49] See above, p. 62.

[50] *The Health of the School Child, 1932* (London, 1933), Appendix A. The calculation for 1921–32 is mine, from figures in *The Health of the School Child* for those years. For an example of detailed reporting, see the account of Dr Newth of Nottingham's investigations into educational backwardness in *The Health of the School Child, 1924* (London, 1925), p. 140.

[51] 62 & 63 Vict., c. 32, s. 1(3); 3 & 4 Geo., V c. 28, s. 31; 11 & 12 Geo. V, c. 51, s. 55(3).

Act as enabling LEAs to pay the expenses incurred by SMOs in attending.[52]

Then in 1936 the Board was persuaded to approve an extension of the course and the provision of a second parallel one at the London School of Hygiene and Tropical Medicine. As Dr Tredgold, on behalf of the CAMW, explained,

We have observed that during the last four or five years an increasingly large percentage of very inexperienced Medical Officers with little or no knowledge of mental testing have attended the courses. They either do not know the standardised tests which are now generally in use, or even if they have used them, their knowledge of the scoring of results of the tests is so limited that their findings may be and often are, quite unreliable. In other circumstances they have themselves told us (and we have also observed it this year) that they are very much at sea in making the approach to the children whom they are about to test.

Henceforward the course would include a substantially increased component of lectures, demonstrations and practical classes on testing, and the additional course would follow the same pattern.[53]

There is no doubt, therefore, that mental measurement came to play a central role in the Board of Education's approach to mental defect in the inter-War years. But by some writers this has been seen as but one manifestation of the increasing influence of eugenists at the Board of Education. R.A. Lowe has contended for 'the increasing acquiescence of the Board of Education in an "hereditarian" view' in its approach to mental deficiency.[54] He deployed two principal pieces of evidence in support of this: the campaign for the legalization of sterilization triggered off by the Report of the Wood Committee, and the activities of the Board of Education's anthropometric committee. The latter can be disposed of first. Lowe presented this committee as being set

[52] Ed 50/118. See also Ed 50/267: in 1938 the MOH for the Cumberland tried — and failed — to persuade the Board to approve some lectures and general guidance from Dr Auden of Birmingham, now retired to the Lakes, as an alternative to attendance at the CAMW course.

The CAMW's short courses for teachers, 1918–22, were not so fortunate, being gradually strangled by Treasury objections — which caused A.H. Wood to expostulate at one point, 'we have subjected Miss Fox to treatment that would properly have been resented by a pickpocket' — Minute 24 May 1920, Ed 50/117.

[53] Ed 50/267, direct quotation from Tredgold's letter to the Secretary, 'M' branch, 23 July 1936.

[54] Lowe, 'Eugenists, Doctors and the Quest for National Efficiency', p. 306.

up in 1930, specifically in response to the post-Wood agitation.[55] A careful study of the Board of Education file which he himself cited, Ed 50/33, shows first, that the committee had been set up in 1924,[56] to provide

a reliable set of anthropometric measurements as a national standard with which to compare local figures. Problems of nutrition and standardization not infrequently confront [Government Departments] and require for their solution reference to a series of norms for height and weight and other similar data.[57]

Second, the eventual decision not to publish its report depended in part upon consideration of cost,[58] but also upon the view of the principal investigator, Major Greenwood, that the statistical work was not good enough.[59] Finally, the report, available in typescript to all interested parties, concluded as follows:

It cannot certainly be said that the combination of racial deterioration implied by a kakogenically selective birthrate and the environmental buffets of war and industrial distress following war, have left easily legible traces upon our anthropometric data ... the present generation of children compares favourably with that of its parents, . . . this sampling inquiry, in spite of its many faults and imperfections, is at least presumptive evidence that the alleged C3 population has not begotten a generation demonstrably inferior to its predecessors.[60]

Mr Lowe's treatment of reactions to the Wood Report entails not so much misrepresentation as a very selective and tendentious use of evidence. It has to be remembered that the Wood Committee considered the incidence of mental deficiency among the adult population as well as among children. The evidence about adults was, as the members themselves stressed, much more difficult to collect and to assess, and their calculations were correspondingly more tentative and less reliable.[61] They canvassed the possibility

[55] Ibid. p. 304.

[56] Ed 50/33 Minute Newman to Permanent Secretary 18 Mar. 1932.

[57] Ibid. undated printed Memorandum at the front of the file.

[58] Ibid. copy of the letter from the President of the Board, Donald MacLean, to all members of the committee, 26 May 1932.

[59] Ibid. Minutes 17 Dec. 1930 and letter Sir W. Fletcher, MRC to Newman 29 Jan. 1932.

[60] Ibid. typescript Report, p. 36.

[61] Wood Report, iii, ch. III, pp. 21, 28–36. See also the interesting and, on the whole, favourable comments of Lionel Penrose, *The Biology of Mental Defect* (London, 1949), pp. 20–1 *et seq.*, stressing the importance of breaking the Wood

of sterilization as part of their discussion of the treatment of adults, but they also challenged the essentially static nature of much custodial care — a mental deficiency institution should, they said, be 'not a stagnant pool but a flowing lake', doing its utmost to prepare patients for life in the community; and their detailed recommendations were concerned to a considerable extent with this.[62] Their report did indeed trigger off an extended public debate about sterilization, leading in 1932 to the establishment of a committee to consider the subject, under the chairmanship of Sir Laurence Brock. But when it reported, the committee was prepared to recommend only the legalization of *voluntary* sterilization; and no legislation in fact followed.[63]

Sir Laurence Brock was Chairman of the Board of Control and this whole question was very much a matter for the Board of Control, barely touching the Board of Education. Mr Lowe makes much of Lord Eustace Percy's reply to a letter from Lord Riddell, the committed eugenist proprietor of the *News of the World*;[64] but when read through carefully, the letter commits Percy to nothing, being a characteristic example of the politely neutral letter a minister has to write when the correspondent is too grand to receive the standard 'receiving attention/has taken note of' acknowledgement from his private secretary.

Other individuals and organizations with a more or less eugenist standpoint also lobbied the Board of Education — as no doubt they were also lobbying the Board of Control. But so did The Distributist League (President, G.K. Chesterton) who thought 'that the strain of malnutrition, insecurity and bad houses had been insufficiently considered as a

---

figures up by age group and remarking on the problems of ascertainment in the case of adults. Penrose was considerably further towards the 'environmentalist' end of the environmentalist/hereditarian continuum than Tredgold or Burt — see e.g. his Buckston Browne Prize Essay, *The Influence of Heredity on Disease* (London, 1934).

[62] Wood Report, ii, esp. ch. V.

[63] Report of the Departmental Committee on Sterilization (henceforward Brock Report) P.P. 1933–4 xv Cmd 4485, esp. ch. vi; Jones, *Mental Health Services*, pp. 223–5; G. R. Searle, 'Eugenics and Politics in Britain in the 1930s', *Annals of Science* xxxvi (1979), pp. 159–69.

[64] Lowe, 'Eugenists, Doctors and the Quest for National Efficiency', p. 303.

predisposing condition for mental deficiency'.[65] To convict a department on the basis of its post-bag is guilt by association indeed.

Mr Lowe's one clear-cut piece of evidence is a quotation from what he describes as 'a recorded public statement'[66] by Dr Ralph Crowley. This statement contains, among other things, the remark that 'the propagation of undesirables is a national menace'. I have been unable to find such a statement by Crowley in the file cited by Mr Lowe. However, the whole paragraph Mr Lowe quotes is identical with a paragraph in Lord Riddell's paper for the Medico-Legal Society on 'Sterilization for the Unfit', which Riddell enclosed with his letter of 1 May 1929 to Lord Eustace Percy.

These remarks of Dr Crowley's, if they exist, constitute a single instance. The surviving papers show no answering response inside the Board of Education. The officials, as has been said, went through the motions of examining the chances for legislation in the wake of the Wood Report; and having established that they were *nil*, let the subject drop.[67] Although Dr Crowley was a member of the Brock Committee, its inquiry and report appeared to touch the Board of Education as a department not at all. Although there was perhaps a special resonance about the passage in *The Health of the School Child, 1935*, discussing the proper use to be made of family history when a child is being examined for suspected mental defect:

It is sometimes not at all clear what use certifying officers make of the information they procure and record on family history. It is to be feared that where there is a history of mental deficiency in the family, the school medical officer may tend to approach the examination of the child with prejudice, on the hypothesis that the child is more likely to be mentally defective if parents or relatives have shown signs of mental instability or defect. It should be recognised that while the probability of a child of such parents being abnormal may be greater than that of a child of average parents, no child should be prejudiced merely by such a probability. On the other hand, a child whose intelligence is somewhat below average, but who is not defective, has had a very poor chance of developing the potentialities he possesses,

---

[65] Ed 50/124 Memorandum accompanying the letter from the Distributist League to the Ministry of Health, Sept. 1929, sent on to the Board of Education.

[66] Lowe, 'Eugenists, Doctors . . .', p. 304.

[67] See above, p. 67.

and so may even appear to be mentally defective. Where one, or both, of the parents therefore is unstable or defective, the school medical officer should count that as a point in the child's favour, not as one against him, and should demand proof that his retardation, intellectual, social, or educational, is due to mental defect and not to the bad environment of his home, or to lack of training by his parents.[68]

The evidence concerning the Wood Committee and the debate about sterilization is thus more complex and many-sided than Mr Lowe is inclined to allow. But a much more generalized and looser version of the argument that a commitment to the techniques of mental measurement reflects a basically hereditarian approach, has been put forward by Mr Lowe elsewhere, and seems to have acquired a more general currency.[69] The extent to which eugenist or hereditarian considerations form an identifiable context for the testing of normal children is explored below.[70] But it is relevant to consider here whether the developing commitment to mental measurement at the Board of Education entailed any kind of intellectual retreat from the position articulated by Newman between 1910 and 1914, namely that the majority of mentally defective children were educable and it was the Board's duty to educate them to the limits of their various abilities.

There is no evidence of such a retreat. While welcoming the new sensitivity and precision brought by mental measurement to the problem of classification, the officials of the Board tried hard not to treat its categories as new absolutes. The concept of mental age and the device of the IQ had made it possible to illustrate more plainly than ever before that 'mental defect' encompassed a wide spectrum of abilities. At the same time the Board showed itself sympathetic to a new focus on the problems of dull and backward children, and the emerging notion of maladjustment, i.e. awareness that factors other than physical or mental defect could significantly impair a child's performance socially and academically — often both. All of this pulled the Board of

[68] *The Health of the School Child, 1935* (London, 1936), pp. 121-2.

[69] Lowe, 'Eugenics and Education'; see also Bernard Norton, 'Psychologists and Class', in *Biology, Medicine and Society 1840–1940*, ed. Webster, pp. 289–314, and Joanna Ryan and Frank Thomas, 'Mental handicap: the historical background' in *The Practice of Special Education*, ed. Will Swann (Oxford, 1981), pp. 87–9.

[70] See chs. 5, 7 and 8.

Education further away from any static, custodial approach
to the mentally defective child.

Neither Newman nor Eichholz ever came to regard either
the mental test or the full panoply of the certification
examination as determining a child's fate once and for all.
When in 1923 Wood first began to float his ideas about
'changing the rules',[71] which *could* have led to a retreat,
Eichholz replied briefly but emphatically: 'it is not possible
to forecast the social future of a young, educable mentally
defective'. Newman was more prolix, but the burden was the
same. 'We are', he wrote,

in a transition period in regard to the diagnosis and treatment of these
children. The mental tests which were introduced 10 or 15 years ago
have not proved entirely satisfactory, and are still in need of a good
deal of maturation; even then, I am doubtful whether any particular
and specific tests will ever prove to be sufficiently simple, safe and
reliable to form a single criterion as to which child is and which is not
mentally defective.

There was also the phenomenon of growth: 'Many of these
children have a way of developing and changing almost
beyond recognition.'[72]

More generally, the build-up of knowledge in the Board of
Education did not lack a critical dimension. The lengthy
quotations from *The Health of the School Child, 1935*
above,[73] show full awareness of the literature of criticism of
tests, as for example in the discussion of the uses of non-
verbal tests, the consideration of the case for a sequence of
tests rather than a single test, the significance of uneven
score profiles and the heavy stress on the need to minimize
the child's fears and anxieties before any testing is attempted.

There are also some comments on the limitations and
possible 'culture-loading' of the Binet tests. And behind these
surely lay awareness of the pioneer study carried out by
Hugh Gordon, one of HM Inspectors of elementary schools,
in the early 1920s. In this study he had explored the extent
to which test performance was affected by schooling —
comparing the respective performances of physically defec-

[71] See above, p. 60.

[72] Ed 50/155 Minute Eichholz to Wood 17 July 1923, Minute Newman to
Wood 21 Aug. 1923.

[73] See above, pp. 73–7.

tive children, canal-boat children, gypsy children, and backward children attending ordinary elementary schools, over a period of several years — and finding that the differences were both significant and increased over time.[74]

This points us to the most important reason for the development of a critically alert expertise in the Board of Education: interest in mental measurement was not confined to 'M' Branch. 'E' Branch and the elementary education section of the Inspectorate were naturally very interested in the possibilities of mental measurement for the classification of normal children.[75] Moreover, they were responsible for dull and backward children, that category invented by Hugh Orange in 1899, in his efforts to persuade the Treasury that the 1899 Act would not cost much.

One of the most spectacular internal exchanges occurred in 1925, in the affair of Form 41D. This had been devised by 'M' branch for head teachers to complete as a preliminary to either certification of a child as mentally defective or transfer to a class for the dull and backward; and it contained some of Cyril Burt's tests of verbal abilities. It was shown to one of the women HMIs by a headmistress and the elementary education Inspectorate united to denounce it to 'M' branch as 'unsound educationally and likely to lead to serious misapprehension on the part of Head Teachers'. As they explained at a grand conference, their main objection was to the reading test:

Nowadays no children are taught to read at all until 5 or 6 years of age, they are now taught phonetically and . . . the suggestion that a child of 4 or 5 should be able to read the words indicated on 41D is in direct conflict with the Board's policy in regard to the education of infants. They further urged that these tests could not be regarded as affording any fair indication of educational retardation.

'M' branch beat a rapid retreat, removing most of the offending material and modifying the form.[76]

Fireworks like this, however, were not the norm. Since the appointment of Eichholz in 1900, there had been recurrent

---

[74] *Mental and Scholastic Tests Among Retarded Children* (London, 1923), Board of Education pamphlet no. 44.

[75] For further discussion, see below, ch. 5.

[76] Ed 50/132, direct quotations from the Inspectorate's Memorandum 2 Oct. 1925 and the Memorandum of the Conference 26 Nov. 1925.

efforts to involve the elementary education Inspectorate in the educational work of special schools and the medical Inspectorate in the medico-psychological aspects of the work of elementary schools; but like all such arrangements their smooth working rather depended upon the good relations of the particular individuals involved.[77] Special efforts were made to get a common approach to the treatment of dull and backward children, particularly when it emerged in 1920 that 'M' branch had been telling one LEA that such children should be housed in the same building as mentally defective children, while 'E' branch had told another that on no account should this be done. The inevitable conference eventually produced a procedural minute setting out the special provision that might be made for such children, but locating it firmly within the public elementary school.[78]

But the freeze on special-school provision made 'dull and backward' children an expanding and increasingly important category. Memorandum 224 to HM Inspectors urged them to encourage local authorities to develop provision for the dull and backward: 'the present financial stringency has made it clear that a uniform and comprehensive administration of the Defective and Epileptic Children Act of 1899 is quite impossible for many years to come.'[79] This was the context in which the row over Form 41D took place.

The Wood Committee Report made the reintegration of mentally defective children into the public elementary schools respectable and the position was consolidated in the 1930s. In 1933 a committee of the elementary education Inspectorate considered provision for dull and backward children and circulated a lengthy memorandum of guidance

[77] For the recurrent efforts, see Ed 50/22 H.P. Pooley's procedural Minute, 14 May 1900 (following Eichholz's appointment), Circular 478, 1903 and papers relating to inspection February–March 1907; Ed 22/6 Memorandum 5, 9 Mar. 1906; Ed 22/9 Memorandum 43, 22 Nov. 1909; Ed 50/27 Procedure Minute E 15/11, M No. 1 30 June 1911; Ed 50/109 papers relating to inspecting procedures August 1912–February 1914 and May–August 1920, culminating in Memorandum to the Inspectorate No. 193, Procedure Minute E 19/1920 M No. 84; Ed 22/19 Memorandum 169, 10 Sept. 1919; Ed 22/20 Memorandum 192, 20 July 1920 and Memorandum 193, August 1920; Ed 22/48 Memorandum 366, 1920; Ed 22/100 Memorandum 277, 20 May 1925.

[78] Ed 50/64 Minutes A.H. Wood to Sir E. Phipps 1920 and Sir G. Newman 9 July 1920, Procedure Minute E 22/20, M No. 82.

[79] Ed 22/97.

within the Inspectorate, supplemented in 1937 by a pamphlet for teachers and LEAs. Although both used the IQ as a classificatory device, both emphasized its limitations and argued that group and individual tests must be supplemented by extended observation of the child.[80] Meanwhile in 1934 'M' branch had acknowledged the trend by turning over the inspection of the educational work in day special schools entirely to the elementary education Inspectorate.[81]

Perhaps reflected in the process of reintegration too was the development of psychology as a specialism distinct from medicine. This was given some expression within the Board when John Lumsden, who was not medically qualified, became HMI for special schools. But the tensions between psychologists and doctors that marked the psychologists' struggle for professional recognition and status in the world at large[82] do not seem to have been significantly reflected within the Board at this time. If any change of attitude can be perceived at all, it is a generational shift. Working through the sequence of *The Health of the School Child*, one forms the impression — and it is no stronger than an impression — that the generation which succeeded Newman and Eichholz in 'M' branch was slightly more at home with mental measurement and its ramifications than those two pioneers ever became. This is hardly surprising: professionally Crowley, Maudslay, Bosworth-Smith and Lumsden had grown up with it, as it were. But yet again, it must be stressed that this greater familiarity with mental measurement and, by extension, the general field of the psychology of individual differences, brought neither narrowing of horizons nor increased emphasis on heredity — rather the reverse. For the other major development in the psychology of individual differences in this period was the emergence of the notion of maladjustment and the consequent beginnings of child guidance. The Board of Education responded sympathetically to the efforts of LEAs to support child guidance clinics and develop their

[80] Ed 22/108, Memorandum 336; *The Education of Backward Children* (London, Board of Education, 1937).

[81] Ed 50/131 Memorandum to Inspectorate E No. 343, M Instruction No. 47.

[82] See e.g. Cyril Burt, 'Conclusion' to Symposium on Psychologists and Psychiatrists in the Child Guidance Service, *British Journal of Education Psychology* xxiii (1953), pp. 8-28, and Sutherland and Sharp, '"The fust official psychologist ..." '.

own psychological services; and made valiant efforts to bend and break through the financial constraints. This seems to be a final proof that they remained as committed to a developmental approach in 1939 as they had been in 1914.

The literature on maladjustment, the reasons why a child's behaviour, either academically or socially, or both, does not match what is known of his ability, and on the child guidance movement, techniques developed to try to help the child fulfil his potential more effectively, is nearly as large as that on mental measurement, and cannot obviously be explored in comparable detail; although it is worth noting that both have their roots in that focus on children and their needs which began to intensify in the 1880s. Both are linked, too, through the much larger notion that ability is separable and separately identifiable from academic achievement. Suffice it to say here that discrepancies between high scores in mental tests and poor school performance and/or disruptive behaviour came to be seen as one of the more obvious indications of maladjustment.[83]

The first child guidance clinic in England has been financed by the Commonwealth Fund, in association with the LCC, and opened in 1929.[84] During 1930 the City of Oxford took the first steps to set up a clinic and actually got approval for the expenditure of £150 p.a. on it just before the economic blizzard descended. Thereafter, the Board of Education was prepared to sanction LEA use of private or charitably endowed clinics for advice about children, provided no public money was spent: refusing, for example, to allow the Swinton and Pendlebury Council to pay an annual subscription to the funds of the Manchester Guidance Committee, as token acknowledgement of the diagnostic help given.[85] Both Dr

[83] Gertrude Keir, 'A History of Child Guidance', Symposium on . . . the Child Guidance Service, *British Journal of Educational Psychology* xxii (1952), pp. 5–29; Catherine M. McCallum, 'Child Guidance in Scotland' ibid., pp. 79–88; M. Bridgeland, *Pioneer Work with Maladjusted Children* (London, 1971); and Olive Sampson, *Child Guidance, Its History, Provenance and Future* (British Psychological Society, Division of Educational and Child Psychology: Occasional Papers vol. 3, no. 3, 1980).

[84] 'Psychological Services for Children in London — from Burt to Underwood', Appendix B to *Report of the County Medical Officer of Health and Principal School Medical Officer to the London County Council, 1959*, pp. 137–8. I am grateful to Dr Patricia Potts for drawing my attention to this.

[85] Ed 50/102 survey of LEA usage of clinics to mid-1933.

Crowley and Maudslay felt this harsh; and in August 1933 Maudslay minuted Newman and the Permanent Secretary, stressing the 'valuable preventive work' and proposing 'recognising for grant small contributions by LEAs in respect of children referred by them to Child Guidance Clinics which we know to be satisfactorily conducted'. Newman was amenable but E. H. Pelham, the Permanent Secretary, was adamant: the embargo on new expenditure must hold at all points.[86] By 1935, however, things were easier and from then on the Board was prepared to consider sanctioning expenditure on a child guidance clinic under s.80 of the 1921 Education Act and to recognize as grant-earning any expenditure incurred by an LEA in sending a child to a recognized child guidance clinic.[87]

In the meantime, embargo or no embargo, psychologists had also been finding their way into local authority employ. Sometimes the LEAs presented them to the Board as lay members of the school medical services, sometimes as 'organizers' and thus members of the Director of Education or Chief Education Officer's support staff. Sometimes the LEAs did not bother to consult the Board at all. But when the Board finally took stock of the position nationally in 1938, it emerged that since 1930 at least fifteen LEAs had employed psychologists, sometimes on a part-time basis, who were advising on a whole range of problems, from mental defect through maladjustment, to the streaming of normal children. If they were counted as members of the medical staff, their salaries attracted a support grant of 50 per cent. But if they were members of the Director's staff, the support grant was only 20 per cent. A complex and characteristic argument between 'M' and 'E' branches as to the proper apportionment of a psychologist's time and responsibilities ensued. In the end it was agreed that the Inspectorate should draw up a schedule of duties and the LEA could choose which of them it wanted its psychologist to concentrate on. This choice would then determine the rate of support grant. What was never in dispute at all,

---

[86] Ibid. Interview Memorandum 27 July 1933, Minute Maudslay to Newman 5 Aug. 1933, Newman's annotation 11 Aug. 1933, Pelham's annotation 11 Aug. 1933.

[87] Ed 50/273, letter E.N. Strong to J.F. Henderson 13 Nov. 1935.

however, was the importance of the work — and as HMI Mr
Lumsden put it, in drawing up the schedule, 'care would
have to be taken not to cramp the development of the
service for the future'.[88]

To call this kind of activity and encouragement either
'eugenist' or 'hereditarian' is not illuminating. 'Eugenist'
has come to conceal more than it conveys; while between
the opposite poles of 'hereditarian' and 'environmentalist'
there are a multitude of possible positions; and a number of
those people deeply concerned about eugenic issues located
themselves at different places in this spectrum at different
points in time — and thought it no shame to do so.[89] In so
far as the Board of Education could not carry forward the
developmental approach articulated by Newman in the years
before 1914 — and defended by him stoutly until his retirement in 1935 — it was because of lack of money, not because
it had been infiltrated by hereditarians or 'eugenists'. The
refinements of mental measurement and the emergence of
the notion of maladjustment were perfectly compatible with
a developmental approach to the classification and treatment
of mental defect; and the latter, with its focus on discrepancies
between ability, achievement, and behaviour in the individual
child, led firmly away from any static, custodial approach.
The tale of policy for the subnormal child in the inter-War
years is essentially one of aspirations and ambitions frustrated
and sometimes rendered impotent by straitened resources.

[88] Ibid. 'Psychologists in the Service of the LEAs', Memorandum by J. Lumsden 27 June 1938; Minute Lumsden to Davidson and Ainsworth 2 July 1938;
'The rate of grant payable for the appointment of Psychologists, with particular
reference to the Somerset proposal', conference Memorandum 11 July 1938 —
from which the direct quotation comes. The fifteen authorities of whose doings
the Board knew a little were: Leicester, Birmingham, Bristol, Cardiff, Southampton, Sheffield, Nottingham, Hull, Northumberland, Jarrow, Dewsbury, Somerset,
Southend, Swansea, Tottenham. The last five appear initially to have availed
themselves of the part-time services of peripatetic psychologists employed by the
CAMW; but Southend, Jarrow and Swansea went on from this to make their own
appointments and it was a proposal by the Somerset authority to do likewise
which precipitated the review. Oxford does not figure in this list because, exceptionally, the LEA's child guidance clinic did not employ a psychologist.
[89] Searle, 'Eugenics and Politics in Britain in the 1930s', and, more generally,
Gary Werskey, The Visible College (London, 1978).

Chapter 4

Measuring Normality

The prerequisite of any discussion of subnormality is a notion of normality, however understated or ill-defined. While 'normal' and 'subnormal' are conceived of as distinct and clearly separable categories, it is possible to discuss their treatment separately. But once subnormality becomes generally accepted as an umbrella label for a variety of states, shading almost imperceptibly into the normal, such separation becomes increasingly artificial — as chapter 3 has shown. That discussion must now be complemented and extended with a consideration of notions about the capacities and achievements of the normal child, and attempts to classify and measure these, in the period up to 1914. This entails a discussion of formal examinations, the ideological framework in which they were embedded, their content and the dramatic developments in the technology of examining, or 'testing', as some of it was beginning to be called, at the end of the period. Ultimately, in later chapters, we have to address ourselves to the question of why it was that the measurement and classification of normal children became so closely linked with selective and competitive examinations in twentieth-century England. But first we must look at the roots of both processes and see how they begin to converge.

I The ideology of merit and the scholarship ladder

Payment by results, introduced into the elementary schools in the 1860s, was a sustained attempt to apply the principles of the free market to the education of the labouring poor. But it also signalled the invasion even of the lowly elementary school by the passion for formal examinations which had been steadily gaining ground in England since the end of the eighteenth century. The first signs of this passion are usually taken to be the Trinity Fellowship competition of 1786 and the Oxford Examination Statute of 1800. By 1880 not only did examinations loom large on the University scene, they determined entry into the Indian Civil Service and were beginning increasingly to be used for entry into the Home Civil Service. They were also seen as a prime instrument of reform for ancient but moribund grammar schools, and as ways of setting standards for the host of new proprietary schools – for girls as well as for boys – now appearing.[1]

A mechanism of such popularity was not, of course, without its accompanying ideological baggage. We can begin to explore this by looking at a passage from a speech of Macaulay's on the India Bill of 1833:

It is proposed that for every vacancy in the civil service four candidates shall be named, and the best candidate selected by examination. We conceive that, under this system, the persons sent out will be young men above par, young men superior either in talents or in diligence to the mass. It is said, I know, that examinations in Latin, in Greek, and in mathematics, are no tests of what men will prove to be in life. I am perfectly aware that they are not infallible tests: but that they are tests I confidently maintain. Look at every walk of life, at this House, at the other House, at the Bar, at the Bench, at the Church, and see whether it be not true that those who attain high distinction in the world were generally men who were distinguished in their academic career. Indeed, Sir, this objection would prove far too much even for those who use it. It would prove that there is no use at all in education. Why should we put boys out of their way? Why should we force a lad, who would much rather fly a kite or trundle a hoop, to learn his Latin Grammar? Why should we keep a young man to his Thucydides or his Laplace, when he would much rather be shooting? Education would be mere useless torture, if, at two or three and twenty, a man who had neglected his studies were exactly on a par with a man who had applied himself to them, exactly as likely to perform all the offices of public life with credit to himself and with advantage to society. Whether the English system of education be good or bad is not now the question. Perhaps I may think that too much time is given to the ancient languages and to the abstract sciences. But what then? Whatever be the languages, whatever be the sciences, which it is, in any age or country, the fashion to teach, the persons who will become the greatest proficients in those languages and those sciences will generally be the flower of the youth, the most acute, the most industrious, the most ambitious of honourable distinctions. If the Ptolemaic system were taught at Cambridge instead of the Newtonian, the senior wrangler would nevertheless be in general a superior man to the wooden spoon. If, instead of learning Greek, we learned the Cherokee, the man who understood the Cherokee best, who made the most correct and melodious Cherokee verses, who comprehended most accurately the effect

[1] On payment by results, see above, pp. 6–7. On examinations in general, see John Roach, *Public Examinations in England 1850–1900* (Cambridge, 1971).

of the Cherokee particles, would generally be a superior man to him who was destitute of these accomplishments. If astrology were taught at our Universities, the young man who cast nativities best would generally turn out a superior man. If alchymy were taught, the young man who showed most activity in the pursuit of the philosopher's stone would generally turn out a superior man.[2]

He is arguing that academic success and the intellectual stature and achievement represented thereby, should be the criterion for advancement in the public service. Underpinning this is the proposition that superior ability and superior character are closely related, almost interchangeable.

The India Bill of 1833 was lost and the principle for which Macaulay contended was secured only twenty years later, in the India Act of 1853 and the Report of a Committee which he headed, on the details of its implementation in recruitment to the Indian Civil Service, in 1854. But at the same time a committee consisting of Macaulay's brother-in-law, Sir Charles Trevelyan, and Sir Stafford Northcote was proposing the adoption of the same principle for recruitment and selection in the Home Civil Service. Implementation of it was begun under an Order in Council of 1870.[3]

In his 1833 speech, Macaulay had spoken of 'talents' and 'diligence'. Speaking on the 1853 Bill, he talked of men with 'superior powers' and the need for a test of 'ability'.[4] The 1854 Report discussed the form of new Indian Civil Service examinations, commenting, 'the object of the examiners should be rather to put to the test the candidate's powers of mind than to ascertain the extent of his metaphysical reading'.[5] In choosing these words to describe a kind of bedrock quality, reflected in but distinguishable from attainments, he was following a well-established usage, stretching

[2] *The Works of Lord Macaulay* (London, 1898), 12 vols., xi, pp. 571-3. This passage was also singled out for approving quotation by Sir George Otto Trevelyan, *The Life and Letters of Lord Macaulay* (London, 1908), pp. 585-6.

[3] Roach, *Examinations 1850-1900*, pp. 14, 23-4, chs. 8 and 9.

[4] *Hansard* 3rd ser. cxxviii cols. 739-59, esp. col. 756 (24 June 1853). See also the comments of Trevelyan, *Life and Letters of Macaulay*, pp. 586-92.

[5] *Report to the President of the Board of Control on the Examination of Candidates for the Indian Civil Service, November, 1854*, p. 56, printed as *Annexe A* to the *Report on the Selection and Training of Candidates for the Indian Civil Service, 1876*, P.P. 1876 iv ff. 300-6, f. 302.

back at least to David Hume.[6] Also part of this usage was another term, 'intelligence', which was, after 1900, to displace the others and to acquire some very powerful resonances. Macaulay used this term on at least one occasion;[7] although he seems to have preferred the other formulations. But some index of its general availability is provided by the flat statement of Northcote and Trevelyan that the examination for entry into the Home Civil Service 'may be so conducted as to test the intelligence, as well as the mere attainments, of the candidates'.[8]

Macaulay and his committee, and Northcote and Trevelyan, were thus proposing the equation of ability/talent/intelligence with merit; and the establishment of competitive examinations as the principal mode of selecting government servants in England in the second half of the nineteenth century, suggests some more generalized acceptance of this. Keith Hope has traced the emergence of this 'political conception of merit', as he so aptly characterizes it, in eighteenth-century Scotland and shown the parts played by *Edinburgh Review*-ers, Clapham sectaries and, above all, Macaulay, in grafting it on to essentially aristocratic, Whig notions of reform. But in this process the notion of merit lost some of its earlier, democratic overtones and came close to use as an instrument of exclusion. Eighteenth-century Scottish notions of meritocracy had tended to envisage selection [of able boys] at an early age, followed by repeated reselections at subsequent ages, all eligible boys being available for selection at each stage.[9] This approximates to the system described by twentieth-century sociologists as 'contest mobility'. The notions of meritocracy which came to prevail in mid- and late nineteenth-century England instead envisaged formal selection by examination as taking place at a rather later stage and not necessarily from the whole population, only

[6] Keith Hope, 'The Political Conception of Merit' (1977, to be published by Russell Sage), chs. 1 and 15. In this attempt to delineate the ideology of merit I owe a great debt to Dr Hope's important work.

[7] 1824, in 'On the Athenian Orators', *Knight's Quarterly*, quoted Hope, 'The Political Conception of Merit', p. 164.

[8] *Report on the Organisation of the Permanent Civil Service* P.P. 1854 xxvii, f. 11.

[9] Hope, 'The Political Conception of Merit', ch. 1. See also Hearnshaw, *Cyril Burt*, pp. 47–8.

from those with a particular educational experience. The competitions for both the Indian and Home Civil Services were intended for graduates.

This, in itself, may not be especially exclusive, if access to the educational system is relatively open. But in nineteenth-century England it was not. Educational provision was stratified not by age but horizontally, by class. Elementary education was defined as that provided for the labouring poor. Elementary schools could and did include children as old as fourteen. The teaching provided in Mechanics Institutes and night-schools for adult members of the working class was also described as elementary and earned grant under the government's Elementary Education Code until 1893.[10] Secondary schools, whether old endowed foundations, new proprietary or limited company enterprises, or wholly private ventures, were intended for the middle and upper classes and could and did take children of all ages between seven and twenty. And even within the category of secondary schools, there was further stratification, between those schools attracting children whose parents had crossed, or who wished their children to cross what has been called 'the great social divide' between Players and Gentlemen;[11] and schools for children whose parents were content with the lesser achievement of 'respectability'. The former group of schools were predominantly boarding-schools, retaining their pupils at least until sixteen, more often till eighteen or even twenty. Some of their pupils went on to the University; others, if they aimed at specific occupations at all, aimed at the ancient professions or the services. The latter group of schools met demand from parents who were not prepared, or could not afford, to make 'gentlemen' of their boys — or, in the second half of the century, 'ladies' of their girls — while nevertheless being unprepared to allow them to associate in school with the children of the labouring poor. Their children were far less likely to board; would leave schools at fourteen, or at the latest sixteen, aiming at commercial or white-collar clerical,

[10] *Special Reports on Educational Subjects in England and Wales*, vol. 1, P.P. 1897 xxv, pp. 54–5.

[11] D.C. Coleman, 'Gentlemen and Players', *Economic History Review*, 2nd ser., xxvi (1973), pp. 92–116.

sub-professional occupations, or, occasionally, skilled craft work.[12]

Class and wealth thus determined access to education other than that provided in the elementary school. Class and wealth therefore also functioned to preselect those from whom the formal examinations for University awards and degrees, for entry to the Indian and to the Home Civil Service, would make a final selection. It is a peculiarly *aristocratic* version of meritocracy.[13]

Examinations conducted under the Revised Code were not, of course, competitive and only in a very limited and special sense, qualifying: the child who passed, 'earned' his grant and moved up a Standard. And after 1890 the machinery of payment by results was gradually dismantled. The 'political conception of merit' and examination as its central instrument came to impinge more directly and significantly on the closed, dead-end world of the elementary school through the articulation of what became known as the 'scholarship ladder'. The idea emerged explicitly first, however — as one might expect — in a discussion of the principles to guide reform of the élite schools, the secondary schools, in the course of the 1860s.

In 1861 the Clarendon Commission was required to investigate the state of the nine ancient foundations, Eton, Winchester, Harrow, Rugby, Charterhouse, Westminster, St Paul's, Merchant Taylor's and Shrewsbury; the Taunton Commission's brief, between 1864 and 1867, covered all other educational provision between these nine and the elementary schools, 'to consider and report what Measures (if any) are required for the improvement of such Education, having especial regard to all Endowments applicable or which can rightly be made applicable thereto'.[14] One of the

[12] For a fuller discussion see Gillian Sutherland, 'Secondary Education: The Education of the Middle Classes' in Sutherland ed., *Government and Society in Nineteenth Century Britain: Commentaries on British Parliamentary Papers: Education* (Dublin, 1977), pp. 137–66. On girls' schools and their social stratification, see Sheila Fletcher, *Feminists and Bureaucrats. A study in the development of girls' education in the nineteenth century* (Cambridge, 1980), esp. ch. 6 and Appendices 1–4; and Carol Dyhouse, *Girls Growing Up in Late Victorian and Edwardian England* (London, 1981), chs. 2 and 3.

[13] For a more extended discussion, see Hope, 'The Political Conception of Merit', ch. 14.

[14] *Report of the Schools Inquiry Commission*, P.P. 1867–8, xxviii, p. iv.

problems perceived by both sets of Commissioners was the immobilization of substantial endowments, tied as the funds were to purposes which seemed to them wholly inappropriate. In the cases of Harrow and Rugby, for example, considerable funds were taken up with the provision of 'foundation privileges' for local boys. That is to say, boys living locally had the right to be educated free at the school; and it was by no means unknown for whole families to move to the area to take advantage of this – as the Trollopes had moved to Harrow in 1816.[15] Such families were known as 'sojourners'. The Clarendon Commission, reporting in 1864, recommended the replacement of foundation privileges at Harrow and Rugby by a two-tier arrangement: a local day-school for the sons of local tradesmen, and scholarships at the endowed boarding-school open to national competition. Proposals to this effect were embodied in a draft Bill.[16]

When the inhabitants of Harrow and Rugby challenged this Bill, before a Select Committee of the House of Lords in 1865, the reasoning behind the proposal was made quite explicit by another witness to the Committee, the Revd Frederick Temple, then the headmaster of Rugby School. He decisively rejected all local claims to special privileges in charitable endowments of this kind:

the founding of these schools very much partook of the character of a national movement, every man doing his best to educate his own bit of the country and . . . although his primary object was this general education, yet nobody thought of any way of giving it than by providing a good education just round his own spot.

In the plans for the reconstruction of the endowment, 'it appeared to me that the persons I was bound to consider were these:– First, the poorer foundationers and secondly the general public of England'. For those of the foundationers who really were local, he considered the appropriate provision to be a 'first-rate middle school [where] . . . the children of the tradesmen might receive an exceedingly good education, first-rate of its kind'. For the remainder,

[15] Anthony Trollope, *An Autobiography* (first published 1883), ch. I, 'My Education 1815-1834'.
[16] *Bill to make Further Provision for the Good Government and Extension of Public Schools* (No. 32), House of Lords Papers 1865 v, pp. 181-93.

Those sojourners who are on average two thirds of the foundationers I consider to represent the people of England generally . . . In dealing with this matter you have to consider that there is so much money to spend on free education which you cannot increase; and that the question is how best you shall select those who shall be the recipients of it . . . How are you to choose? As it is at present, we are making a sort of blind choice; that is, we give a free education to those who, for one reason or another are able to come and live in Rugby. There may be hundreds of others a great deal more deserving both on account of character and on account of talent, all of whom are not taken into consideration at all.

Instead of 'blind choice', therefore, he proposed scholarships to the boarding-school, open to national competition. This would be fairer to 'the general public of England' and give proper opportunities to those

to whom the want of high culitvation is the greatest loss. It is a comparatively slight loss to boys of a low scale of intellect if they do not get a very high kind of education. In fact I can see every now and then that there are boys who get very little benefit except the mere benefit of association with their fellows, from the teaching at the school. Their intellects will not take in any more, and though it is good for them, no doubt, to live among their fellows, I cannot say that the education as far as the books are concerned does really very much for them. But to a boy who has real ability it is the greatest possible loss to be unable to cultivate it; it is to him a real deprivation. Those are the boys, therefore, who have, it seems to me, the first claim — I may say that just as to them it is the greatest loss if they do not get it, so also to them is it the greatest boon if they do get it. They are the boys who afterwards are able to use it to advantage, and as they rise in the world, they find that every step only brings them more and more into the position that is natural to them.[17]

Like Macaulay, therefore, Temple — who was even more characteristically a product of Balliol than Macaulay of Trinity,[18] was concerned to find a boy of 'real ability'. And he proposed to provide mobility for him within the stratified world of secondary schools by means of scholarships.

---

[17] *Report of the Select Committee on the Public Schools Bill,* p. 155, q. 990, pp. 140-4, qq. 861-4, House of Lords Papers 1865, x, ff. 429, 414-8.
[18] On Temple, quintessentially the poor scholarship boy himself, see E.G. Sandford, ed., *Memoirs of Archbishop Temple by Seven Friends* (London, 1906), 2 vols. On the Balliol connection see Richard Johnson, 'Administrators in education before 1870: patronage, social position and role' in *Studies in the growth of nineteenth century government,* ed. Sutherland, pp. 126-9. On Macaulay and Trinity, see Trevelyan, *Life and Letters of Macaulay,* esp. ch. II.

The Select Committee's conclusions largely reflected Temple's views and the Bill went through.[19] Temple, meantime, was deeply involved in the activities of the other Royal Commission looking at secondary education, the Taunton Commission, which sat from 1864 to 1867. He was actually one of its members; he appeared before it as a witness; and he drafted a large part of its Report.[20] It is hardly surprising, therefore, to find the Taunton Report rehearsing similar themes.

The Taunton Commissioners dealt at much greater length with stratification within secondary education – as, in effect, their terms of reference required them to do. They proposed

to accept the distinction that we already find and to classify schools side by side, so that a parent, according to the destination for which he intends his son, may place him from the first in a school of the third grade, or of the second, or of the first. The three grades do not lead one into the other, but stand side by side, starting it may be said from the same point but leading to different ends.[21]

First-grade schools, 'generally classical schools' were for those leaving at eighteen. In urban areas they might be day-schools; elsewhere they were likely to be boarding-schools. Second-grade schools were for those leaving at sixteen and third-grade schools for those leaving at fourteen. Both of the latter were likely to be day-schools.[22]

The Commissioners took pains to stress that the schools of the various grades would perform different but equally valuable functions. There remained, however, the question of relations between grades. And since they had begun their discussion with praise for what they saw as the ancient function of endowed grammar schools – 'by giving precisely the same education to all classes to make it easy for talent in every class to rise to its natural level' – they had themselves raised the question of mobility. They continued, therefore:

We cannot think it well that the old glory of the grammar schools should be entirely lost, and that it should be henceforth impossible for

[19] *The Public Schools Bill as Amended by the Select Committee* (no. 202), House of Lords Papers 1865, v, ff. 194–205; 31 & 32 Vict., c. 118.
[20] Sandford, ed., *Memoirs Archbishop Temple*, i, pp. 135–7.
[21] *Report of the Schools Inquiry Commission* P.P. 1867–8, xxviii, pp. 94–5.
[22] Ibid., pp. 78–88.

ability to find aids to enable it to achieve distinction. Nor do we think it a necessary consequence of what we have proposed.

The schools of the third grade are not, and are not intended to be, preparatory to schools of the second; nor schools of the second to schools of the first. But provided only there be still maintained some one leading study as a link between the three, we still think it quite possible and even easy to arrange that real ability shall find its proper opening.

It is for this reason among others, that in all these schools we have suggested that Latin should generally hold a leading place. Even in schools of the third grade, where it would be impossible to make Latin the chief study, the elements of the language might receive sufficient attention to give the clever scholars a firm hold on it. These schools would keep the boys till 14, but of course boys of exceptional talent would often be near the head of such schools two or three years sooner, and by the time they were 13, and therefore of an age to enter an open competition, would have learnt a good deal more than boys who had only just reached the same class. Such boys picked out from the rest and sent to schools either of the first grade or the second, according to the talent that they showed and the professions for which they were destined would not be long at any disadvantage in the classes of the school to which they were thus promoted. . . .

It is plain that to pay for this passage from schools of a lower grade to those of a higher, the boys would usually need assistance. This assistance could best be given in the shape of exhibitions (i.e. scholarships), and as far as possible the endowments might be employed with advantage to provide the funds. Several of our witnesses spoke with great emphasis in favour of this proposal . . . With these views we entirely agree, and we are of opinion that exhibitions should be provided, open to merit and to merit only, and if possible, under such regulations as to make it tolerably certain, that talent, wherever it was, would be discovered and cherished and enabled to obtain whatever cultivation it required. These exhibitions would then do that work which the grammar schools once did and can now do no longer, and in our judgement there is no use to which endowments can be put more in accordance with the interests of the country and the original intentions of the founders.[23]

Legislation followed the Report of the Taunton Commission in the form of the Endowed Schools Act of 1869. This laid down a general framework, but left the detailed reconstruction of endowments to a body of Commissioners. Surprisingly little work has so far been done on the activities of these Endowed School Commissioners and their eventual successor, the Charity Commission. But all the signs are that the Taunton

[23] Ibid., pp. 95–6.

guide-lines were taken very seriously indeed.[24] And even as the Endowed Schools Commissioners began their work, the idea of a scholarship ladder was beginning to be canvassed among those involved in extending the provision of elementary schools to make a national system after the legislation of 1870. T.H. Huxley told his fellow members of the London School Board in February 1871:

> He should like to have an arrangement considered by which a passage could be secured for children of superior ability to schools in which they could obtain a higher instruction than in the ordinary ones. He believed that no educational system in the country would be worthy the name of a national system, or fulfil the great objects of education, unless it was one which established a great educational ladder, the bottom of which should be in the gutter and the top in the University and by which every child who had the strength to climb might, by using that strength, reach the place intended for him.[25]

The bottom rungs of a very rudimentary ladder had, in fact, been in existence for some time, in the form of the pupil-teacher system, established in 1846. In elementary schools approved of by the government Inspectorate, children of thirteen and over could be apprenticed, in effect, to the teacher for five years. During that time, they undertook some teaching and received additional instruction, on which they were examined each year. All pupil-teachers were eligible also to enter for national examinations conducted by the Inspectorate and the Principals of the Normal Schools (training colleges). Those who did best were awarded Queen's Scholarships, enabling them to attend a Normal School. Those of the rest who reached a certain standard were awarded Certificates of Merit. The effect of this had been to endow elementary teaching with a status, financial attraction and security which it had hitherto entirely lacked; and it enabled some working-class children to move to lower-middle-class white-collar respectability.[26]

To the limited opportunities provided by the pupil-teacher

---

[24] Sutherland, 'Secondary Education', pp. 157-8. A key exception to this dearth of secondary work, however, is Fletcher, *Feminists and Bureaucrats*, which maps the creation of girls' schools 1869-1902. Would that a study of boys' schools, of comparable quality, existed!

[25] Quoted in Hugh B. Philpott, *London at School. The Story of the School Board 1870-1904* (London, 1904), pp. 153-4.

[26] A. Tropp, *The School Teachers* (London, 1957), ch. II.

arrangements, Huxley and others of like mind now began to try to add scholarships to secondary schools, trying to mobilize new funds and endowments and pressing for some of the scholarships created by the remodelling of old endowments to be made accessible to, even in some cases restricted to, elementary-schoolchildren.[27] And the opportunities offered by both the pupil-teacher system and scholarships were underpinned and extended by the gradual development of more advanced work in those elementary schools known as Higher Grade Schools.

Higher Grade Schools were initially simply board schools which charged a higher fee than the others in the board's district. They thus attracted children who were not likely to leave at the earliest possible moment and these, in their turn, tended to attract good teachers. Such a combination enabled the schools to tackle the more advanced grant-earning work under the Elementary Education Code and also to try for grants from the Science and Art Department. Gradually boards began to realize that it might be sensible deliberately to concentrate resources in this way; and the Sheffield School Board was the first to take the logical step of establishing one Central Higher Grade School for the whole Board district, where the work began with Standard IV and which siphoned off all the children who wanted to stay on and do advanced work, whether as prospective pupil-teachers or with ambitions to try for a secondary school scholarship, from the surrounding board schools. Already by 1879 Barrow, Bradford and Nottingham School Boards had followed suit and in the 1880s other Boards, including London, joined them.[28]

Ladder building was thus becoming a feature of provision in elementary as well as in secondary education. And as pressure built up for systematic state intervention in the field of secondary education, the model of the ladder came to exert an even more powerful force. Temple, Huxley and their colleagues had presented the ladder as primarily of benefit to the individual — the boy — of talent and ability. The Royal Commission on Secondary Education, chaired by Lord Bryce between 1893 and 1895, struck a new note — as

---

[27] Philpott, *London at School,* pp. 154–5, 166–76.
[28] Ibid., pp. 155–67. Their legal status was always dubious; for more detail see Eric Eaglesham, *From School Board to Local Authority* (London, 1956).

befits the decade during which the images and metaphors of Social Darwinism first began to take a grip on the imagination of the public at large and the popular press. The Bryce Commissioners talked of a 'cultured class', comprehending

the so-called learned professions, the ministry, law, medicine, teaching of all kinds and at all stages, literature and the higher services, public life, the home and foreign civil service, and such like. This is the class whose school life continues till 18 or 19 and would naturally end in the universities. The more highly organised our civilisation becomes, the more imperative grows the need for men so educated and formed, the more generous ought their education to become and the greater the necessity for recruiting their ranks with the best blood and brains from all classes of society. And we conceive one of our functions to save this higher education from becoming the prerogative or preserve of any special order, and to make the way into it, and into all it leads to, more open and accessible to capable and promising minds from every social class.[29]

But when they descended to practicalities, their proposals had a very familiar ring. They were content to use the same threefold classification of secondary schools as Taunton, talking of second-grade schools as those 'whose special function, although it does not at all exclude an ideal of culture, is the education of men with a view to some form of commercial or industrial life'. The 'special function' of third-grade schools was 'the training of boys and girls for the higher handicrafts or the commerce of the shop and the town'.[30] They remarked on the lack of demand for second-grade schools and on the progressive extension of the elementary-school curriculum, especially through Higher Grade Schools. But the latter they interpreted as evidence of increasing demand for third-grade schools, and they did not see either phenomenon – or the combination of the two – as calling into question the whole horizontal stratification. 'Making the way into the cultured class more open and accessible' was still to be an affair of scholarships.[31]

A whole section of the Bryce recommendations was devoted to 'Scholarships and Exhibitions'. It began:

[29] *Report of the Royal Commission on Secondary Education* P.P. 1895, xliii, p. 138.
[30] Ibid., pp. 138–44.   [31] Ibid., pp. 52–5, 61–3, 66–70.

We have next to consider the means whereby the children of the less
well-to-do classes of our population may be enabled to obtain such
Secondary Education as may be suitable and needful for them. As we
have not recommended that Secondary Education shall be provided
free of cost to the whole community, we deem it all the more needful
that ample provision should be made by every Local Authority for
enabling selected children of the poorer parents to climb the educational ladder. Thus, for example, the promising child of an artisan or
small tradesman should have the opportunity of proceeding at the age
of 11 or 12 from the elementary to the secondary school and so pro-
longing his education, the cost of which prolongation might fairly be
borne wholly or to a large extent by endowments or other public funds.
Again, boys and girls of exceptional ability, whether belonging to the
wage-earning class or to the poorer families of the middle class, might
be enabled by public aid to proceed at the age of 16 or 17 from secondary school to the universities or to other places of higher literary,
scientific or technical education. The assistance we here contemplate
should be given by means of a carefully graduated system of scholarships (including in that term exhibitions), varying in value, in the age at
which they are awarded, and in the class of school or institution at
which they are tenable.

Later, in discussing the type of examination appropriate for
entry to secondary school, they recommended that it should
be 'restricted to a limited number of subjects, should include
a considerable amount of *viva voce* questioning, and should
be directed principally to ascertaining the general intelligence
of these candidates, rather than the extent of their acquired
knowledge'.[32]

The Education Act of 1902 created new local education
authorities in the form of county and county borough
councils, with powers to provide what came to be known as
maintained secondary schools. This enabled a significant
enlargement of secondary-school accommodation and scholarships. And in 1907 the Board of Education strengthened and
widened the ladder further, with its Free Place Regulations.
These increased grants to secondary schools but made it a
condition of the receipt of the full grant that a minimum of
25 per cent of the school's places should be free and open
only to children from public elementary schools, provided
they passed a simple qualifying test.[33] Simultaneously,

[32] Ibid., pp. 299, 301.
[33] *Annual Report of the Board of Education 1906-7*, p. 67, P.P. 1908, xxvi
Cd 3862. For more detail about the context, see also Olive Banks, *Parity and
Prestige in English Secondary Education* (London, 1953), pp. 61-7.

efforts were being made to discourage intending teachers from applying for articles as pupil-teachers and to encourage them to attend a secondary school and then go on to a training college.[34]

The effects of these developments were dramatic. In England in 1900 5,500 ex-elementary children were being supported by bursaries or scholarships from public funds at scondary schools. Already by 1912 49,120 children, or 32 per cent of the total population of maintained secondary schools, were former elementary-school pupils, who, having won a scholarship or passed a 'free-place examination', were receiving free tuition.[35]

But it is important not to overestimate the breadth and extent of this ladder. The total elementary-school population in 1912 was almost five and a half million children; and that same year, Albert Mansbridge told the Church Congress: 'There are, indeed, educational ladders *in some places*. In many parts of England they do not rest upon the earth; when they do, the rungs are not infrequently missing.'[36]

II The technology of testing

In his speech of 1833, quoted above, Macaulay had suggested that the content of competitive examinations was less important than their existence: provided they tested rigorously whatever was the principal study in the society, they would provide a rough but reliable guide to ability and character. But in practice the exercise was a more complicated one than that — and he acknowledged as much in the discussion of the detailed mechanisms for the Indian Civil Service examinations in the 1854 Report. Within a given curriculum some studies were likely to be thought more suitable than others in fitting men for the public service. Alternatively, one might want to compare and rank men — and women — from different educational backgrounds. The strategy appropriate for

[34] Tropp, *The School Teachers*, pp. 184–90.
[35] *Annual Report of the Board of Education 1911–12*, p. 4, ch. 1, para. 13, P.P. 1913, xx Cd 6707. The figure for 1900 does not include awards funded by endowments; that for 1912 does. See also for more details *Report of the Departmental Committee on Scholarships and Free Places* (Hilton Young Committee), pp. 2–5, paras. 5–15, P.P. 1920, xv Cd 968.
[36] *Authorised Report of the Proceedings of the Church Congress, 1912*, p. 250.

selecting from a small, already highly selected, homogeneous group might be different from that needed to rank a large, diverse population.

The first of these problems was easily solved: the Civil Service examinations faithfully reflected the continuing dominance of Classics and Mathematics at Oxford and Cambridge respectively. The second group of problems did not become substantial practical ones until much later. The Taunton Commissioners had plumped firmly for Latin as the common subject in their three grades of school and therefore the principal support of any scholarship ladder. But in 1907, drafting the Free Place Regulations, the Board of Education officials were much exercised by the need to make the qualifying examination for free places in secondary schools reflect the normal work being done in the upper Standards of the public elementary schools, and yet not let it fall significantly below the normal work being done by children of the same age already attending the secondary schools as fee-payers. And it was suggested that once the 'free-placers' arrived in the secondary school, it was most important that they 'should be kept together for the first year or two whilst they are learning the rudiments of a Secondary Education — e.g. Latin and French etc'.[37]

The full dimensions of this problem — very much what Albert Mansbridge meant when he talked of ladders 'not resting upon the earth' — were to be faced only after the War. In the mean time, between about 1870 and 1914, the technology of examinations had taken off into sustained, if somewhat higgledy-piggledy, growth. In this growth the key figure was Francis Galton. (And if one is to indulge at all in the game of weighing up the influence of eugenics, there is no doubt that the preoccupations of the first eugenist determined the direction of much of his work in mental measurement, playing a formative rather than a reinforcing role.)[38]

Galton did not concern himself in detail with scholarship

[37] Ed 24/372, direct quotation from the notes of a discussion between Bruce, Fletcher and Campbell 18 Apr. 1907.

[38] This theme has been admirably argued and documented by Donald A. Mackenzie, *Statistics in Britain 1865-1930. The Social Construction of Scientific Knowledge* (Edinburgh, 1981), ch. 3. As will become clear, my account of Galton's statistical work draws heavily upon Dr Mackenzie's discussion.

ladders; although he was entirely approving of the idea. In *Hereditary Genius* he observed

The best form of civilization in respect to the improvement of the race, would be one in which society was not costly; where incomes were chiefly derived from professional sources, and not much through inheritance; where every lad had a chance of showing his abilities, and, if highly gifted, was enabled to achieve a first-class education and entrance into professional life, by the liberal help of the exhibitions and scholarships which he had gained in his early youth.[39]

His primary focus was on these 'abilities' and their distribution. As we have seen, he had used 'genius' as a synonym for 'natural ability' in the title of *Hereditary Genius* and later regretted that he had not preferred the latter formulation.[40]

Like Macaulay, Galton posited a relationship between ability and character, but went rather further, defining natural ability to include character and using success in the world at large, not simply in its most prestigious examinations, as a criterion of ability. 'By natural ability', he wrote,

I mean those qualities of intellect and disposition, which urge and qualify a man to perform acts that lead to reputation. I do not mean capacity without zeal, nor zeal without capacity, nor even a combination of both of them, without an adequate power of doing a great deal of very laborious work. But I mean a nature which, when left to itself, will, urged by an inherent stimulus, climb the path that leads to eminence, and has strength to reach the summit — one which, if hindered or thwarted, will fret and strive until the hindrance is overcome, and it is again free to follow its labour-loving instinct. It is almost a contradiction in terms, to doubt that such men will generally become eminent. On the other hand there is plenty of evidence in this volume to show that few have won high reputations without possessing these peculiar gifts. It follows that men who achieve eminence, and those who are naturally capable, are, to a large extent, identical.[41]

By temperament, upbringing and — he himself would have argued, inheritance — he was an experimentalist. He was prepared to try to measure anything and everything, from the efficacy of prayer to the distribution of beauty in the British Isles. In his account of his travels in Southern Africa, he described an encounter with the handsomely proportioned wife of a Hottentot interpreter:

[39] *Hereditary Genius*, p. 362.
[40] See above, p. 35.
[41] *Hereditary Genius*, pp. 37–8.

I profess to be a scientific man, and was exceedingly anxious to obtain accurate measurements of her shape; but there was a difficulty in doing this. I did not know a word of Hottentot, and could never, therefore, have explained to the lady what the object of my footrule could be; and I really dared not ask my worthy missionary host to interpret for me. The object of my admiration stood under a tree, and was turning herself about to all points of the compass, as ladies who wish to be admired usually do. Of a sudden my eye fell upon my sextant; the bright throught struck me, and I took a series of observations upon her figure in every direction, up and down crossways, diagonally, and so forth, and I registered them carefully upon an outline drawing for fear of any mistake: this being done, I boldly pulled out my measuring tape, and measured the distance from where I was to the place where she stood, and having thus obtained both the base and the angles, I worked out the results by trigonometry and logarithms.[42]

It was hardly surprising, therefore, that after the first publication of *Hereditary Genius* he embarked on a series of attempts to devise adequate and uniformly applicable measures of natural ability. He tried hard to exploit boys' public schools as a source of data, commenting in a letter to *Nature* in 1880:

If a schoolmaster were now and then found capable and willing to codify in a scientific manner his large experiences of boys, to compare their various moral and intellectual abilities, to classify their natural temperaments, and generally to describe them as a naturalist would describe the fauna of some new land, what excellent psychological work might be accomplished? [43]

Then in 1884, at his own expense, he equipped and opened an anthropometric laboratory, as part of the International Health Exhibition then being held at South Kensington. Measurements were taken of weight, sitting and standing height, arm span, breathing capacity, strength of pull and of squeeze, force of blow, reaction time, keenness of sight and hearing, colour discrimination and judgement of length. When the Exhibition closed, in 1888, the laboratory was transferred to a more permanent site in the Museum and the collection of data continued until 1894.[44]

Collections of mixtures of precise physical measurements and sense data was also a feature of contemporary work on psychology in the United States and in Germany; and in

[42] Quoted in Forrest, *Francis Galton*, p. 45.
[43] Quoted ibid., p. 137.   [44] Ibid., pp. 180-2.

1890 the American, J.M. Cattell, published an article in *Mind*, 'Mental Tests and Measurements', in which he proposed a standard programme of sixty tests and measures for this type of work.[45] Galton, on the whole, was approving, although he commented tartly,

One of the most important objects of measurement is hardly, if at all, alluded to here and should be emphasized. It is to obtain a general knowledge of the capacities of a man by sinking shafts, as it were, at a few critical points.[46]

There is, of course, a strong family resemblance between these kinds of measures and the measures being proposed at that time to identify and grade mentally defective children.[47] Each activity encountered similar difficulties in achieving even a moderate degree of precision; and each activity rested upon the crucial assumption that there was a systematic relationship between physical characteristics, sensory perception and the higher mental processes. Galton made no contribution directly to the refinement of this conceptual framework. Given his assumption that success, not simply in whatever formal examinations there were, but more generally in the world at large, was a good criterion of ability, there can have seemed no particular need to concern himself especially with the *content* of tests and examinations. But his refinement of the mathematics of measurement eventually rubbed off on, brought a new authority — some would say, imparted a spurious sophistication — to concepts of mind and ability.

Galton's principal contributions to the mathematics of mental measurement were two: the application of the Gaussian or 'normal' curve of distribution to the distribution of human abilities, and correlation. The assumption that human abilities were unequally distributed was, of course, implicit in all schemes for competitive examination and in the political conception of merit as a theory. But few people had concerned themselves with the pattern or frequency of this distribution; although Macaulay had had some interesting comments to offer in the debate on the 1853 India Bill.

[45] *Mind* xv (1890), pp. 373–9.
[46] Ibid., pp. 380–1 'Remarks by Francis Galton F.R.S.'.
[47] See above, pp. 10, 15, 21–2.

Arguing the case for competitive examinations, he estimated that the Indian Civil Service employed about 800 men:

Among any 800 gentlemen whom you might select at random, there would be a certain number of men of very superior powers; the great majority might not be very much above nor very much below, the average of ability; but there must necessarily be, in every body of 800 men, not selected by some test of ability, a considerable number — say a tenth, or if you please, a twentieth — who fall decidedly below the average of ability.[48]

Galton again went much further. Confronting the question explicitly, in *Hereditary Genius*, he argued that there was no reason why the distribution of mental characteristics in a population should not, like the distribution of the physical characters of that population, follow a Gaussian distribution: 'there must be a fairly constant average mental capacity in the inhabitants of the British Isles, and that deviations from the average — upwards towards genius and downwards towards stupidity — must follow the law that governs deviations from all true averages.'[49] Thus, measurements of the abilities of a population, like those of their heights, or weights, ought to be distributed in a bell-shaped curve, and in a way which depended upon the mean (or 'true average') and the standard deviation (or probable error). Presented graphically, such measurements would appear as below.

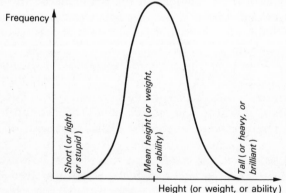

As Donald Mackenzie has pointed out, the mathematician Gauss's work had been done within the context of what was known as 'error theory'; and for error theorists, variability, or

[48] *Hansard* 3rd ser. cxxviii col. 756.   [49] *Hereditary Genius*, p. 32.

deviation from the mean, was something to be controlled, if not eliminated. For Galton, on the other hand, variability was of central interest. As Mackenzie so well puts it, 'was it really useful to think of an exceptionally able person as a large *error* by nature?'[50] In the detailed work which Galton began in the 1870s on the measurement of variance, he initiated a crucial shift of focus. Mackenzie summarizes the trend in the statistical literature of the next decade: 'there was a gradual transition from use of the term "probable error" to the term "standard deviation" . . . and from the term "law of error" to the term "normal distribution".'[51] The notion of normality began to acquire a new, apparently objective, precision; no longer was it to be seen only or primarily as the relativistic product of common sense and experience.

Galton also moved away from the error theorists in another important direction. They had been much concerned with distributions of single variables each considered in isolation. He, trying to chart and measure patterns of inheritance in the 1870s and early 1880s, was much more interested in the relationships between the distributions of groups of variables. This led him eventually to the concept of correlation and the calculation of correlation coefficients.[52] He explained the central idea to the Royal Society in 1888.

Two variable organs are said to be co-related when the variation of the one is accompanied on the average by more or less variation of the other, and in the same direction. Thus the length of the arm is said to be co-related with that of the leg, because a person with a long arm usually has a long leg, and conversely. . . . It is easy to see that co-relation must be the consequence of the variations of the two organs being partly due to common causes. If they were wholly due to common causes, the co-relation would be perfect, as is approximately the case with the symmetrically disposed parts of the body. If they were in no respect due to common causes, the co-relation would be *nil*. Between these two extremes are an endless number of intermediate cases, and it will be shown how the closeness of co-relation in any particular case admits of being expressed by a simple number.[53]

The actual mathematics of Galton's technique for calculating these 'simple numbers', or correlation coefficients, were not

[50] Mackenzie, *Statistics in Britain*, p. 58.   [51] Ibid., p. 59.
[52] For the stages of this in detail, ibid., pp. 59–66.
[53] Quoted in Forrest, *Francis Galton*, p. 197.

as sound or as elegant as they might have been; and they were subsequently refined and developed by his friend and disciple, Karl Pearson.[54] But as Pearson himself wrote:

Galton's very modest paper of ten pages, from which a revolution in our scientific ideas has spread, is in its permanent influence, perhaps, the most important of his writings. Formerly the quantitative scientist could only think in terms of causation, now he can think also in terms of correlation. This has not only enormously widened the field in which quantitative and therefore mathematical methods can be applied, but it has at the same time modified our philosophy of science and even of life itself.[55]

For mental testing specifically, here was a means of determining whether there was a significant relationship not only between the characteristics of parent and child, but also between one set of functions or abilities and another, exhibited by the same individual.

The uses of correlation in evaluating individual mental tests, those 'shafts, sunk at a few critical points, into the capacities of a man', as Galton had described them,[56] were soon perceived and developed by Charles Spearman, a retired army officer of independent means, who had taken himself to Leipzig, to work with the German psychologist, Wundt. During the Boer War he returned to the Army, being posted as deputy assistant Adjutant-General to Guernsey. The demands of the post — as one might guess — were not great and during this time, according to his own account,

inspired by Galton's *Human Faculty*, I started experimenting with a little village school nearby. The aim was to find out whether, as Galton had indicated, the abilities commonly taken to be "intellectual" had any correlation either with each other or with sensory discrimination. The intellectual abilities I measured by the children's school marks in various subjects; the sensory discrimination by a musical "dichord" of my own contrivance. The reply of the experiment was prompt and decisive; all the mental powers measured did obviously correlate with each other in considerable degree.

But hastily as I had embarked upon this investigation, I fell to brooding long over the results. Not satisfied with noting that the different abilities correlated considerably, I wanted to know *how much*. With great labor, I evolved an elaborate theory of "correlation coefficients" by which the degrees of correlation could be definitely

[54] Ibid., pp. 197–9.   [55] Pearson, *Life of Galton,* iiia, p. 56.
[56] See above, n. 46.

measured. Then too late, I began to search for previous literature on the subject and found that the greater part of my correlational theory had already been obtained — and much better — by other writers, especially by Galton and Udny Yule.[57]

This search of the literature also brought to light what, in Spearman's view, were weaknesses in Pearson's mode of calculating correlation coefficients, and J.M. Cattell's report of his failure to find correlations between the different abilities he had tested. Nothing daunted, Spearman ploughed on, correcting Cattell's mathematics, engaging in acrimonious dispute with Pearson, and continuing to experiment.[58] In 1904 he published in the *American Journal of Psychology* an article entitled ' "General Intelligence": Objectively Determined and Measured'.[59] In this article he not only set out his calculations of the correlation coefficients of different types of mental tests, he also proposed further refinements in the analysis of these, along with a justificatory theory of the nature of natural abilities or intelligence.

Spearman arranged his correlation coefficients in a table, or matrix, and engaged in a series of mathematical manipulations of this matrix, designed to elicit groupings of correlations. He described his objective as follows:

from any number of real series we can proceed on to dealing exclusively and precisely with any element that may be found common to these series; from ascertaining the inter-connections of, say, auditory discrimination, the capacity for learning Greek, and that for playing the piano, we can arrive at estimating the correspondence of whatever may be common to the first pair of faculties with whatever may be common to the second pair. By combining such correlations of higher order, it is feasible to execute any required amount of elimination and selection, so that eventually a dissociation and exactness may be introduced into psychology such as can only be compared with quantitative chemical analysis.[60]

These manipulations were the beginning of what has come to be known as factor analysis, a statistical technique for reducing a table of correlation coefficients to fewer and so more manageable dimensions, by replacing the variables with

---

[57] C. Spearman, *A History of Psychology in Autobiography*, i, p. 322.
[58] Ibid., pp. 322-3.
[59] *American Journal of Psychology* xv (1904), pp. 201-92.
[60] Ibid., pp. 258-9.

underlying factors, in a way which accounts for as much as possible of the variance in the original data.[61] This calculation — a very laborious proceeding in the days before the computer — produced for Spearman a single major underlying dimension running through all the correlation coefficients. On the basis of this, he moved on to theorize about the nature of mental abilities, making the great and perilous leap from the existence of correlations to propositions about causation.

The mere existence of positive correlations between different tests had always suggested that mental faculties were not wholly independent of each other and strictly compartmentalized. The questions then became ones concerning the nature and degree of interrelations: did human abilities cluster in several groups — an 'oligarchic' structure, as Spearman called it — or were they primarily manifestations of one underlying general ability — a 'monarchic' structure? His factor analysis led him unhesitatingly to plump for the latter. Its performance had enabled him to reduce his multitude of correlation coefficients to a manageable dimension; he proposed to treat the principal axis of the components thereby achieved as a real, deep structure. Human abilities, he argued, consisted essentially of two factors: general ability, which he preferred to call general intelligence or 'g'; and the residual 's' factor, specific and particular skills. Of these, 'g' was clearly the more important and of central interest to the examiner and would-be mental tester, since the less 's' and more 'g' revealed by any given test, the better general predictor it was likely to be. He summarized his conclusions resoundingly:

IV. The above and other analogous observed facts indicate *that all branches of intellectual activity have in common one fundamental function (or group of functions), whereas the remaining or specific elements of the activity seem in every case to be wholly different from that in all the others.* The relative influence of the general to the

---

[61] For a more detailed account, one of the most illuminating for the non-specialist which I have encountered, see Gould, *The Mismeasure of Man*, pp. 239–61; although see also the review by Harvey Goldstein forthcoming in *British Journal of Mathematical and Statistical Psychology*. Gould also provides, pp. 236–8, a convenient summary of the dispute about the 'invention' of factor analysis.

specific function varies in the ten departments here investigated from 15:1 to 1:4.

V. As an important practical consequence of the Universal Unity of the Intellectual Function, the various actual forms of mental activity constitute a stably interconnected Hierarchy according to their different degree of intellective saturation. Hence, the value of any method of examination as to intellectual fitness for any given post is capable of being precisely ascertained, since it depends upon :

(a) the accuracy with which it can be conducted;

(b) the hierarchical intellective rank of the test;

(c) the hierarchical intellective rank of the duties involved in the post.

Methods have been given whereby all these three points can be sufficiently ascertained.[62]

Spearman's primary concern had been the correlations between different tests and their significance. His methods, his findings and the central importance of 'g' were enthusiastically endorsed by the young Cyril Burt, in his first article, published in 1909, 'Experimental tests of general intelligence'.[63] Burt also addressed himself to the correlations which had interested Galton most, namely those between the abilities of child and parent. Here he reported a strong positive correlation, indicating that intelligence was, to a large extent, inherited. He concluded emphatically:

Parental intelligence, therefore, may be inherited, individual intelligence measured; and general intelligence analysed; and they can be analysed, measured and inherited to a degree which few psychologists have hitherto legitimately ventured to maintain.[64]

With the publication of these two articles, it could be said that mental measurement, or psychometrics, as it came to be called, had arrived. The immediate careers of the two authors give us a rough index of this. Spearman, the superannuated army officer who had attended neither a front-rank English public school, nor any English university, was made Reader in Experimental Psychology at University College, London in 1907 and in 1911 was elected Grote Professor of the Philosophy of Mind.[65] Burt, after reading Greats at Oxford, used the monies of the John Locke

---

[62] Spearman, 'General Intelligence', p. 284, his emphasis.

[63] *BJP* iii (1909), pp. 94–177.

[64] Ibid., p. 176.

[65] *DNB*.

Scholarship in Mental Philosophy to fund work in the psychology department at Würzburg in the summer of 1908; and in September of that year took up a post as Assistant Lecturer in Physiology and Lecturer in Psychology at the University of Liverpool. In 1913, strongly backed by Spearman, he was appointed to the newly created post of psychologist to the London County Council.[66]

More generally, the would-be deviser of tests and examinations now had some very sophisticated tools with which to work. Acceptance of the Gaussian or normal curve applied to the distribution of intelligence in a population, the calculation of correlation coefficients, and factor analysis, provided a framework for interpreting the results of tests administered to a large group; and methods for comparing and relating the results of different tests and examinations, and for comparing and relating the performances of different members of the same family. Associated with these tools was a theory of natural ability, or intelligence, as an essentially unitary quality, precisely quantifiable in the case of any given individual.

In the light of the statistical sophistication and the emphatic and explicit statements of theory, it comes as something of a shock to remind ourselves of the crude and subjective nature of some of the tests and experimental work, whose 'results' were being arranged, manipulated and 'explained' in these ways. By the time he prepared his 1904 article, Spearman had largely abandoned physical measurements and tests of sensory perception. He used four groups of measures: *'Present Efficiency'* — 'the ordinary classification according to school order (based here upon examinations)'; *'Native Capacity'* — 'the same school order but so modified as to exclude all influence of Age'; 'The third kind of Intelligence is that represented and measurable by the general impression produced on other people' (in practice, the teachers); 'The fourth and last sort of intelligence which has here been estimated is that known as *common sense*'.[67]

---

[66] Hearnshaw, *Cyril Burt*, pp. 13–15, 25–6; Sutherland and Sharp, ' "The fust official psychologist" '. See also Hearnshaw's general discussion of the intellectual and professional context at the beginning of ch. 2 and Dennis Doyle, 'Aspects of the Institutionalization of British Psychology: The National Institute of Industrial Psychology 1921–39' (unpublished Manchester Ph.D. thesis, 1979), pp. 9–11.

[67] Spearman, 'General Intelligence', pp. 250–1.

But if we look in more detail at the measures of '*common sense*' he used, it seems legitimate to wonder whether his results were any more precise than, say, Galton's efforts to estimate height in his anthropometric laboratory without being forced to ask his clients to take off their shoes. Spearman 'interviewed and interrogated' the eldest girl of a group of children he was studying, about the others'

sharpness and common sense out of school; and she seemed to have no great difficulty in forming her judgements concerning the others, having, indeed, known them all her life. As a check, and in order to eliminate undue partialities, it had been arranged that, as she left the house, the second oldest child should enter it and thus be able to give an as far as possible independent list, since neither had beforehand had any idea of what was wanted. Finally, a similar list was obtained from the rector's wife, who also had always lived in this village; but her graduation is unfortunately incomplete and therefore unusable, for she professed inability to pronounce verdict upon some few children who had not come much under her notice; as far as it went, it appeared perfectly homologous with the other two lists.[68]

Burt's mixture of tests included the normal school-attainments tests, some tests of sensory perception, teacher's rankings and boys' rankings of each other.[69] While 'the intelligence of the parents was assessed primarily on the basis of their actual jobs, checked by personal interviews; about a fifth were also tested to standardize the impressionistic assessments'.[70]

But in 1905 the Frenchmen, Binet and Simon, published their first series of tests; in 1908 came their first revision and the introduction of the age scale; and in 1911 their second

[68] Ibid., p. 251.

[69] Burt, 'Experimental Tests'.

[70] Hearnshaw, *Cyril Burt*, p. 29. This statement comes not from the article itself, in which no details were given — in itself a defect — but from a letter written long after by Burt, in response to a direct inquiry from Lionel Penrose. It has sometimes been argued in defence of Burt's very casual reporting of his experimental work — and, by extension, of the casual nature of some of that work — that standards were lower when he first began. This is not wholly unreasonable in the light of the preceding quotations from Spearman. It has to be said, however, first, that their contemporary, W.H. Winch, was consistently impeccable, even by the standards of the 1970s and 1980s, in reporting his experimental work; and second, that if standards in experimental work and its reporting rose in psychology as a whole in the course of the twentieth century, Burt's standards did not. If anything, they fell — see Sutherland and Sharp, ' "The fust official psychologist" ', esp. pp. 192-3 and Hearnshaw, *Cyril Burt, passim*.

revision. They had abandoned the idea that the higher mental processes could be measured indirectly and had attempted to devise a battery of tests which would engage them directly, yet not simply duplicate the normal school attainments tests.[71] The nature and carefully arranged variety of these tests can perhaps best be illustrated by quoting at length from the summary Dr George Newman made, for English School Medical Officers, in his Report to the Board of Education for 1911.

Tests of Binet and Simon, grouped according to Age

Three years.
1. Points to nose, eyes and mouth.
2. Repeats two numbers (7, 2).
3. Enumerates objects in a picture.
4. Knows name.
5. Repeats a sentence of six syllables.

Four Years.
1. Knows sex (boy or girl).
2. Recognises and names key, knife, penny.
3. Repeats three numbers (7, 4, 8).
4. Compares two straight lines [as to length].

Five Years.
1. Compares two weights [3 and 12 grams or 6 and 15 grams].
2. Copies a square (in pen and ink).
3. Repeats sentence of 10 syllables [*e.g.*, "His name is John. He is a very good boy"].
4. Counts four pennies.
5. Putting together pieces of a card [a visiting card is cut diagonally, and the child has to make a figure like the uncut card].

Six Years.
1. Distinguishes between morning and afternoon.
2. Defines in terms of use [*e.g.*, fork, table, chair, horse].
3. Copies outline of diamond shape.
4. Counts 13 pennies.
5. Makes aesthetic comparison of faces [from drawings and pictures].

Seven Years.
1. Shows right hand, left ear.
2. Describes a picture.
3. Executes three commissions correctly [*e.g.*, place key on chair; shut door; bring box].

[71] See above, pp. 53–4 for an initial discussion of these tests and a brief account of the context in which they were developed.

4. Counts nine sous (3 single, 3 double, *e.g.*, 1 1 1 2 2 2).*
5. Names four colours (red, blue, green, yellow).

Eight Years.
1. Compares two objects from memory.
2. Counts backwards, 20-0.
3. Sees picture lacks eyes, nose, mouth, and arms.
4. Gives day and date.
5. Repeats five figures.

Nine Years.
1. Gives change for sixpence or shilling.
2. Defines in terms superior to use [description of articles apart from use].
3. Names nine pieces of money.
4. Enumerates months of the year.
5. Understands simple questions ["What would you do if you missed a train? "].

Ten Years.
1. Arranges five weights in order.
2. Copies design from memory.
3. Criticises absurd statements [*e.g.*, "Is the snow red or black"].
4. Understands a difficult question [*e.g.*, "What would you do if you were delayed in going to school?"].
5. Uses three selected words in one sentence [London, money, river].

Twelve Years.
1. Resists suggestion [length of lines].
2. Uses three words in a simple sentence.
3. Gives 60 words in three minutes.
4. Defines three abstract words [charity, justice, goodness].
5. Puts dissected sentence together.

Fifteen Years.
1. Repeats seven figures.
2. Gives three rhymes.
3. Repeats a sentence of 26 syllables.
4. Interprets a picture.
5. Solves a problem from several facts.

*As these coins have no exact counterpart in English currency it is necessary to devise a comparable test in valuation.[72]

Binet and Simon had tried their tests out on hundreds of Parisian schoolchildren, revising, adjusting, discarding, adding,

[72] Report of the Chief Medical Officer, Board of Education 1911, Appendix E, pp. 313-5, P.P. 1912-13 xxi, Cd 6530.

on the basis of what they themselves observed and what teachers told them about patterns of performance. They also controlled systematically for age; and in proposing in 1908 the calculation of a 'mental age', which could be juxtaposed against a child's chronological age, they offered a measure of 'normality' and deviations from it, far more precise and rigorous than any hitherto available. Again, Newman's exposition of the details of calculating mental age is very clear.

The rules which Binet and Simon apply are two : (i) *A child has the intelligence of that age all the tests for which he succeeds in passing.* If a child succeeds in the tests of his age he is normal. If he can succeed only in those given for a child a year younger than himself he is in Goddard's [the American psychologist] view *backward* to the extent of one year, and similarly for two or three years. If he is more than three years backward he is *mentally defective.* To allow for unavoidable variation Binet found it accurate to consider that a child has the mental development of the highest age for which he has succeeded in all tests save one. For example, if he has succeeded in all but one test for nine years, and all but one for ten, he is still credited with the intelligence of a child of ten years old. (ii) *After fixing the age for which a child passes all the tests a year is added to the intelligence age if he has succeeded in passing five additional tests belonging to superior age groups, two years are added if he has passed ten such tests, three years if he has passed 15, and so on.* Thus a child passes five tests for the eighth year; he has the intelligence of eight years; in addition he passes three tests for nine years, and two for ten years. One year is added for the five tests, and he is credited with the intelligence of nine years. This seems at first sight to be artificial, but Binet has found it accurate.[73]

Newman's Report is part of the evidence that the response to these tests outside France was immediate and enthusiastic. As we have seen,[74] doctors and others concerned with the identification and education of mentally subnormal children were quick to perceive the help such tests could give them. But the Binet-Simon tests were as helpful as they were, because their measures of abnormality depended upon a notion of normality which attempted to synthesize and systematize the collective experience of psychologists, doctors and teachers, which was not simply the product of one physician's skill, empathy and experience.[75] And Binet's Anglo-Saxon audience was quick to see the possibilities of these kinds of

[73] Ibid., p. 313, his emphasis.　　　　　[74] See above, pp. 55-6.
[75] Cf. the comments of David Ferrier, above, pp. 21-2.

tests in assessing children over the whole ability range. In the United States, H.H. Goddard and Lewis Terman were amongst the earliest and most enthusiastic users of the Binet-Simon tests; and Terman's adaptation of the tests for use in California produced the 'Stanford-Binet', in successive versions of which the tests are most familiar to the twentieth-century English-speaking world.[76] In England, both Cyril Burt and the LCC inspector, W.H. Winch, published extensively between 1913 and 1915, on the uses of the Binet-Simon tests in assessing the abilities of normal children.[77]

Such an enthusiastic response — especially from Burt and Goddard, who were committed exponents of general intelligence — was profoundly ironic. Binet was deeply sceptical about 'g'; and in so far as he was prepared to commit himself at all, before his untimely death in 1911, he was inclined to stress the complexity of each individual's intellectual profile. His measure of normality was for him essentially a rough-and-ready device for identifying those children who might need special help, not a definitive judgement, not a tool to discriminate between one 'normal' child and another.[78] But the notion of mental age meshed all too well with the unilinear view of human abilities propounded by the supporters of 'g'. And the German psychologist, William Stern's, development from this of the device of the Intelligence Quotient, or IQ, in 1911, took the process a stage further. Stern divided mental age by chronological age, multiplied by 100 and rounded off to eliminate fractions, and described the abilities of a given child as a single number. It was just too easy to treat the child's IQ as his share of 'g', precisely quantified. In the years after the First World War, the combination of tests of the kind pioneered by Binet and Simon, a battery of items both carefully varied and carefully balanced, and adjusted for age, with theories of general intelligence and the associated sophisticated mathematical apparatus, was to be a potent one.

[76] Gould, *The Mismeasure of Man*, pp. 158–92.

[77] Cyril Burt, 'The measurement of intelligence by the Binet tests', *Eugenics Review* vi (1914), pp. 36–50 and 140–52. W.H. Winch, 'Binet's mental tests', *Child Study*, vi (1913), pp. 113–7; vii (1914), pp. 1–5, 19–20, 39–45, 55–62, 87–90, 98–104, 116–22, and 138–44; viii (1915), pp. 1–8, 21–7, 50–6, and 86–92.

[78] Wolf, *Alfred Binet*, chs. 4 and 5, esp. pp. 194–5, 204–5, 207, 209–10. Gould, *The Mismeasure of Man*, pp. 147–58.

Chapter 5

'Testing is like drug-taking'

By 1914 mental testing seemed poised for 'take-off'. In the inter-War years it achieved something looking respectably like sustained growth. It had an institutional base, a developing technical literature and ample publicity. 'General intelligence' came to be invoked almost as often in the educational press as 'national efficiency' had been in arguments about social policy before the War; and 'intelligence testing' came gradually to displace 'mental testing' in general usage.

I Institutional, theoretical and technical developments

In the years between the Wars, psychology as a whole firmly established itself as an academic subject, with the psychology of individual differences and thus mental measurement a prominent specialism within it. This process is a major topic for investigation in itself; and its outlines can only be crudely sketched here.[1] But already by 1914 there were eleven posts in psychology scattered among the English and Scottish universities and there was Burt's post at the LCC. After the War this institutional base was consolidated and extended. London, naturally enough, saw an increasing concentration of activity. In 1922 C.S. Myers left Cambridge to join H.J. Welch in founding the National Institute of Industrial Psychology; and from 1922 to 1924 Burt worked part-time there and part-time for the LCC. Then he became part-time Professor at the London Day Training College (forerunner of the Institute of Education), eventually, in 1933, succeeding Spearman in the Chair of Psychology at University College, London.

At least as important were developments in Scotland. In 1917 and 1918 a Bachelor of Education degree, with a

---

[1] Sources for, and a more extended discussion of, the developments sketched in this and the following paragraphs can be found in Doyle, 'The National Institute of Industrial Psychology 1921-1939', ch. 2. On Thomson and Moray House, see also below, pp. 139-40 and ch. 7.

substantial psychology component, was instituted at the four Scottish universities. In 1925 Godfrey Thomson came from the Chair of Education at Newcastle to the Chair of Education at Edinburgh, combining with it the Principalship of Moray House Training College and also bringing with him the consulting service on mental testing which he had begun to develop. Much more must be told of Thomson and the Moray House Tests, as they came to be known. For the moment, it is sufficient to point to the contribution that Edinburgh in particular and the Scottish universities in general made to the dissemination of information about the psychology of individual differences, and, indeed, to the academic succession within the subject itself. Of the 797 students who took B.Ed. degrees in the four Scottish universities 1918-61, 183 became university and training college teachers, another 168 educational psychologists and seventy-seven educational administrators, many of them pursuing their careers across the Border.

With this institutional infrastructure went the other standard manifestation of a burgeoning academic specialism, a technical literature. The *British Journal of Psychology* had been founded in 1904; in 1914 it became the official organ of the British Psychological Society (BPS), which itself had been founded in 1907. By 1921 the flow of contributions was sufficient to enable the establishment of a separate *British Journal of Medical Psychology*; and in 1930 the BPS took over responsibility for *Forum of Education* and renamed it the *British Journal of Educational Psychology*. Alongside journal articles came an increasing flow of monographs, launched by the LCC's publication of Burt's *The Distribution and Relation of Educational Abilities* in 1917 and *Mental and Scholastic Tests* in 1921.[2]

This expanding technical literature was naturally the arena in which contributions to all aspects of testing were made and discussed. Three questions dominated, the three which

[2] For a complete list of Burt's publications to 1940, see Appendix III to Sutherland and Sharp, '"The fust official psychologist"'. The discussion here has to be highly selective. For accounts of the development of the intellectual field as a whole, see J.C. Flugel and Donald J. West, *A Hundred Years of Psychology* (London, 1964), Parts IV and V; and L.S. Hearnshaw, *A Short History of British Psychology 1840-1940* (London, 1964), chs. xi-xv.

were identified by Burt at the start of his first paper in 1909:[3] does general ability exist, can it be measured and is it heritable? Burt had purported to find answers to all three in that article — 'yes' in each case — but that did not prevent them from becoming the subject of prolonged and sometimes heated debate in the following years. And, somewhat paradoxically, while the very existence of general ability was being questioned, the ways and means proposed and used to measure it grew ever more sophisticated.

Initially, the existence of general ability was not thought to be problematic. Charles Spearman in his 1904 paper had inferred from his empirical tables of correlation coefficients that the observed patterns were compatible with the existence of an underlying general factor of intelligence.[4] The resulting model of the intellect — simple, comprehensible and intuitively satisfying to the non-psychologist — looked set to become the overall framework within which the study of intelligence would develop. Indeed, this was the role which Spearman himself ascribed to the model.

But in 1916 the logic was challenged. Godfrey Thomson, still at this time a lecturer in education at Armstrong College, Newcastle, published in the *BJP* a paper arguing that while a theory positing a single general factor was able to account for the available data, it was not the only theory able to do so. He showed, using data gained from throwing dice, that a theory positing several factors, each common to several tests but none common to all, would predict the same pattern of correlations. He had no wish necessarily to deny the existence of 'g' but simply to show, as he put it, 'that Professor Spearman's calculations are incapable of discriminating between a General Factor and overlapping Group Factors'.[5]

This initiated a debate between Thomson and Spearman which was conducted vigorously until Spearman's retirement

---

[3] Burt, 'Experimental Tests of General Intelligence'.

[4] Spearman, 'General Intelligence Objectively Determined and Measured'.

[5] Godfrey H. Thomson, 'A Hierarchy without a General Factor', *BJP* viii (1916), pp. 271–81, direct quotation from p. 281. For a detailed analysis of the whole dispute, upon which the discussion which follows is based, see Stephen Sharp, ' "A Veritable Battle of the Giants"; Charles Spearman, Godfrey Thomson and the Factorial Study of Intelligence in Inter-War British Psychology', as yet unpublished.

from his Chair at University College, London in 1932 and
thereafter sporadically, until his death in 1945. Spearman
never wavered in his defence of general ability as a theory;
but he could find no real weakness in Thomson's mathematics. By 1935 Thomson had demonstrated formally that
a general factor theory and a group factor theory provided
interchangeable ways of looking at the same body of data.[6]
No resolution of the disagreement was achieved; perhaps no
resolution was possible. For at bottom it was a clash between
inductive and deductive logic. Spearman, the inductionist,
needed only the empirical evidence fulfilling the predictions
of the general factor model to make the concept of general
ability unassailable. Thomson, faced with this refusal to
accept the group factor theory as an alternative competing
on equal terms, could only assert repeatedly the deductive
basis on which he challenged the monopoly of 'g'.

At first reading, much of this debate about the proper uses
of factor analysis seems arcane and verging on the incestuous
— and it was one from which other British psychologists
rather carefully stood clear. But its implications are considerable. Thomson mounted a challenge to the theory of general
ability which could not easily be shrugged off. Before the
appearance of Thomson's first article, Spearman, showing a
tendency to reify theoretical constructs, had spoken of
general intelligence as if it were autonomous of the data from
which it had been inferred. He had then gone on to suggest
interpretations for it, settling on a notion of mental energy
which fitted well with his general view of the mind in 'out-
going', active terms.[7] Thomson's arguments acted to cut the
ground from under this by implying that 'g' was invented,
not discovered, and that it had no independent existence outside the equations embodying it. And although Thomson
was virtually alone among British psychologists in the inter-
War years in inclining towards a group factor view of intelligence, his position was shared by the increasingly influential
American school of psychometricians, led by E.L. Thorndike,

[6] Godfrey H. Thomson, 'On Complete Families of Correlation Coefficients
and their Tendency to Zero Tetrad-Differences, including a Statement of the
Sampling Theory of Abilities', *BJP* xxvi (1935), pp. 63-92.

[7] See B. Norton, 'Charles Spearman and the General Factor in Intelligence:
Genesis and Interpretation in the Light of Socio-Personal Considerations', *Journal
of the History of the Behavioral Sciences* xv (1979), pp. 142-54.

L.L. Thurstone and later J.P. Guilford. Their work demonstrated that factor analysis could be employed to extract a variety of theoretical structures, both single- and multifactorial, from the same set of data.

By the end of the inter-War years, therefore, the theory of general ability or 'g' had lost the copper-bottomed guarantees that factor analysis had been thought to provide. The theory continued to be a respectable way of interpreting the data derived from mental measurement, but it could no longer be presented as the *only* respectable way of doing so.

Yet while mounting this challenge to the central assumption of mental measurement as hitherto understood and practised, Thomson was simultaneously making major contributions to its technology. For while he was developing the case against general ability, he was also devising the Moray House Tests of Intelligence, English and Arithmetic. The aim of each of these tests was to represent the ability in question as a single number, amenable to the statistical manipulations such as standardization and the calculation of age allowance which, again, he himself had done so much to sophisticate.

Did all this activity not represent an implicit acceptance of the general factor view? Thomson drew a crucial distinction between description and explanation:

I simply do not believe in 'factors' of the mind, any more than I believe in faculties. This does not mean that I will not use the techniques devised by Professor Spearman and others for obtaining mathematical quantities which describe a mind. I have no objection whatever to that, provided it is recognised that they are no more than mathematical quantities. I do not think that g (general ability), for example, has any more real existence than a standard deviation or a correlation coefficient. I do not believe that it is mental energy, or any of the other things it has been guessed to be. It is nothing but an algebraic symbol.[8]

Rejecting the theory of general ability was no necessary bar to exploiting the associated technology. Thomson was prepared to work with 'g' as a *description* of intelligence, while doggedly refusing to accept it as an *explanation*.[9]

---

[8] Thomson, 'On Complete Families of Correlation Coefficients . . .', p. 90. See also Thomson in *History of Psychology in Autobiography* iv, p. 293.

[9] For a more extended discussion see Stephen Sharp, 'Godfrey Thomson and the Concept of Intelligence' in *The Meritocratic Intellect*, ed. Smith and Hamilton, pp. 67-78.

The single-factor view thus lost its position of monopoly. But as the work of Thomson shows, the utility of the testing methods derived from it could still be defended. Indeed, the steady development and increasing refinement of testing methods was a key feature of the literature of mental measurement in the inter-War years.

Two most important steps, the shift from individual to group mental tests and the development of parallel types of attainments tests, came right at the beginning of the period. As has been said, between 1911 and 1914 Burt and Lewis Terman both began to work not only on Anglo-Saxon versions of Binet and Simon's tests but also on group versions, that is, written versions which could be administered simultaneously to a large number of individuals and the answers scored by an unskilled person or even a machine. New-style tests of attainment followed hard on their heels. Mainly of English and Arithmetic, these followed a pattern similar to that of group tests of general intelligence: they allowed the examiner no subjective discretion in marking — thereby eliminating what was considered to be a major source of error — and they had been standardized on a population of suitable size and composition. New-style attainments tests thus offered the possibility of combining objective methods of examining, including new statistical techniques of item analysis in test construction, with more traditional and familiar subject matter.

In the United States, the American Army's Alpha and Beta Tests marked the launching of group mental and attainments tests. The British 'launch' was a much lower-key affair. In 1919, according to Burt, the Bradford County Borough Education Committee asked if they might use in their junior scholarship examination, some of the group tests with which he had experimented in Liverpool in 1911.[10] Revised versions of Burt's group tests were eventually published in 1921, in *Mental and Scholastic Tests*, along with his adaptation of the Binet-Simon individual tests and a series of educational attainments tests, all with critical commentary and a supporting bibliography, which included the most recent American tests.

[10] Burt, *Mental and Scholastic Tests* (1st edition, 1921), p. 221, n. 1.

The majority of Burt's group mental tests were verbal, asking children to provide opposites, analogies, synonyms and definitions, and to complete stories and arguments. The only one requiring some visual perceptions was the Graded Instructions Test, which he described as follows:

The various so-called "Instructions" or "Mixed Instructions" tests are based on the view that the measurement of a number of different mental activities provides a better test of intelligence than the measurement of only one mental activity. The questions here used have been roughly graded in order of increasing difficulty. Most of the questions indicate a type that might well be made the basis of a homogeneous series of questions, were it so desired. Since the material is graded and not uniform in difficulty, the test is best applied without a time-limit.

Test 25.—Instructions.

1.   Put a dot under this line:———————————

2.   Write a capital letter S in this square: ☐

3.   Cross out both A's in the word "ADA".

4.   Write ten (in figures) in the largest square:

    ☐   ☐   ☐   ☐

5.   Make a girl's name by adding one letter to "Mar ."

6.   If you have had your supper today, write Y for yes; if not, write N for no. . . . . .

7.   John has four big beads — white, red, green, and blue. He has given the green one to Tom; and the white and blue ones to Jane. Write down which he has kept? . . . .

8.   What do I need to light a fire beside matches, coal, and wood? Write the first letter of the word only. . . . . .

9.   Suppose it were Sunday to-day. What day would it have been the day before yesterday? . . . .

10.   What number follows next but one after 19? . . . . .

11.   If February comes after January, make two crosses here. . . . . .; but if not, make one cross here. . . . . .

12.   Suppose your mother were ill and sent you for the doctor, but you found it was raining. Think what you should do: (1) Wait until the rain has stopped? (2) Get a mackintosh or umbrella, and go at once through the rain? (3) Go to the post office and telegraph to him? (4) Ask your little sister to go instead? Write here the number of the correct answer. . . . . .

13. Draw a line under the word which contains the first letter of the alphabet more times than any other word does: cap, Adam, atlas, black, almanac, bluebottle.

14. Put a figure 1 in the space which is inside both the triangle and the square, but not inside the circle; put a figure 2 in the space which is inside the square, but outside both the circle and the triangle.

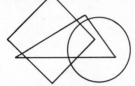

15. "It takes about . . . . . minutes to boil an egg." A number is missing from this sentence; if it is more than 10, write it here . . . . . ; if it is less, show the number by making strokes here. . . . .

16. Cross out the three wrong words in the following sentence: "Most motor-cars are driven by wind, steam, petrol, gas."

17. A wheel is part of a cart;
An foot is part of an inch?
   If one sentence only is correct, cross out the last word in the incorrect sentence; if both are true, write your name here: . . . . ; otherwise do nothing.

18. Fill in the missing word: "Daisies, tulips, lilies, and buttercups are all . . . ."

19. In the following sentence only one word out of the last five is needed. Put a ring round the word that is right: "Nights are longest in *June, summer, jellyfish, winter, Hampstead*."

20. Draw a line from the corner marked A, passing across the first square, between the second and sixth squares, between the sixth and seventh squares, under the seventh square, between the eleventh and twelfth squares, and across the sixteenth square to the corner marked B.

A
1	2	3	4
5	6	7	8
9	10	11	12
13	14	15	16
B

21. In the following words find one letter which is contained in only three of the words, and then cross out the remaining word which does not contain that letter:

heap, April, drake, lark

22-23. Write down four more words made up (like the first two words) out of three or four of the following letters: A, E, R, T.

(1) ate,   (2) tare,   (3) . . . . (4) . . . . ,
(5) . . . . ,   (6) . . . .

24.   Read these words; and think what their meaning would be if they were in the right order:

people church dance go to to

     If the sentence is untrue, put a line round the word which makes it wrong. But if the sentence is true, cross it all out.

25.   In the picture below you are looking at the reflection of a clock and some words in a mirror. What do the words say? . . . .
     What would be the actual time, if you could turn round and look at the clock itself?

COFFEE ROOM

Verbal skills were again at a premium in the seven tests of attainments, which included Reading, Spelling, Writing and Composition; but there were also tests of Arithmetic, Drawing and Handwork.[11]

In that same year, 1921, the *BJP* carried a full report from Godfrey Thomson on the group mental tests he had devised at the request of the Northumberland Education Committee, to assist in their junior county scholarship examination.[12] These were somewhat less elaborate than Burt's tests and specific provision was made to help the child over the initial unfamiliarity with an examination of this kind, through a practice test, the provision of illustrative examples and the division of the tests into two groups, A and B, identical in type and structure, but the second more difficult than the first. There was also a more substantial non-verbal component, as we can see if we look at the 'A' group of tests.

TEST A1

In the tests given below you have to cross out the extra word in each line. For example look at this first line:

[11] Burt, *Mental and Scholastic Tests*, pp. 230-3, 269-332, 339-69.
[12] 'The Northumberland Mental Tests', *BJP* xii (1921-2), pp. 201-22.

wood cork <u>stone</u> boat bladder

The extra word here is <u>stone</u>, because all the others float on water. Look at this second set:

chair table stool desk <u>roof</u>

The extra word there is <u>roof</u> because all the others are articles of furniture. Now try to cross out the extra word in each of the remaining lines:

grapes	oranges	wool	apple	banana
rifle	plough	sword	pistol	lance

TEST A2

You have to give the number that comes next in each of the following lines of numbers. The first three are answered for you to show what is meant:

1   2   3   4   5   6   (7)

Here the number that you have to write in the brackets is 7 because the first six numbers go up by steps of one at a time. The series below also have steps of different sizes but they do not always increase by adding the same number each time, but in other ways as well:

11   10   9   8   7   6   (5)

Here the numbers come down.

1   2   4   8   16   32   (64)

Here each number is twice as big as the one in front. Now try the others:

3	6	9	12	15	18	( )
2	4	6	8	10	12	( )
1	3	5	7	9	11	( )
1	2	3	4	3	2	( )

TEST A3

Read the following paragraph carefully and compare it with the diagram. The diagram gives the same facts as the paragraph.

PARAGRAPH

Mr and Mrs Adams had three children, (1) Ethel (the eldest), (2) Mabel and (3) James (the youngest). Ethel married Mr Thomas Hawthorn, and their son was named Timothy. James married Miss Bridget Mortimer, and they had two children (1) Edward and (2) Elizabeth.

DIAGRAM

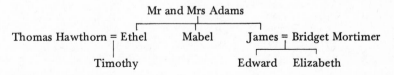

Now answer these questions (the first two are answered for you to show what is wanted):

	Answers
What relation is Timothy to Mabel?	Nephew
How many aunts has Edward?	Two
What is Timothy's surname?	
What is Elizabeth's surname?	
Who is Timothy's uncle?	

TEST A4

In your mind (without writing them down) you have to arrange the five words in each line below in their proper order, and then underline the middle word of this order. For example, consider

minute   second   year   <u>hour</u>   week

In their proper order these words would run thus: second, minute, hour, week, year. The middle word is hour and therefore hour is underlined above. Similarly shilling is the middle word of this next set

sixpence   penny   florin   sovereign   <u>shilling</u>

Now try to do the next tests in this way.

elephant	sheep	mouse	cow	puppy
forty	thirty	fifty	ten	twenty

TEST A5

You have to cross out the "extra" number on each of the following lines. For example, in

6   2   8   <u>7</u>   4   10

you cross out 7 because it is the only odd number, all the rest agree in being even numbers.

In this next case

4   7   8   6   <u>19</u>   3

you cross out 19 because it is the only number in double figures. Again in

<u>14</u>   3   15   9   6   12

you cross out 14 because all the rest are divisible by 3. Try to find and cross out plainly the "extra" number in each of the following lines:

18	16	4	8	20	12
5	9	3	4	1	7
75	62	20	10	15	25
17	49	4	24	13	18

TEST A6

The sentences below are in a foreign language, and their meanings are given in English. In each English sentence a word is underlined, and you have to underline the word which corresponds to it in the foreign sentence. You can do this by comparing the sentences with each other. For example, look at these.

1. Kuchh malai   <u>some</u> cream.
2. Kuchh puri leoge   will you take some <u>cake?</u>
3. Misri leoge   will you take sugar?

By comparing 1 and 2 you see that <u>kuchh</u> must mean <u>some</u> because it occurs in both sentences. Underline it in sentence 1 before you go any further. By comparing 2 and 3 you see that <u>leoge</u> means <u>will you take</u>. Underline it in 3. Then the only word you do not know in 2 is <u>puri</u> which must mean <u>cake</u>, so underline it in 2. You have now underlined in each foreign sentence the word corresponding to the underlined part of the English sentence.

Notice that the foreign words are not always in the same order as the English words.

Underline your words plainly.

You do not have to write anything, only to underline the proper words.

Now try these:

Ek piyala chae	A cup of <u>tea</u>.
Yih chae bahut achchhi hai	This <u>is</u> very good tea.
Chae bilkull taiyar hai	Tea is <u>quite</u> ready.
Kab taiyar karoge?	When <u>shall</u> you make <u>ready</u>?
Main bahut pyasa hun	I am <u>very</u> thirsty.
Bahut achchhi hai	It is <u>very</u> <u>good</u>.
Yih mera rumal nahin hai	<u>This</u> is not my handkerchief.

We shall come back later to the motives and objectives of the Bradford and Northumberland Education Committees. Now we need to note that their initiatives complemented Burt's work, to ensure that both group mental tests and standardized attainments tests entered the repertoire of mental measurement. *Mental and Scholastic Tests* went into three impressions in the 1920s; a second edition was published in 1933 and reprinted again in 1939. The test material itself was extracted as a separate *Handbook of Tests for Use in Schools* in 1923. (It reached a second edition in 1948.)

Thomson put the fees paid him by Northumberland and other authorities who began to copy them, into a trust fund to finance the development and publication of further tests;[13] and after his move to Edinburgh in 1925, the tests supported by this fund, including not only mental tests but also standardized tests of English and Arithmetic, became

---

[13] *History of Psychology in Autobiography* iv, p. 286.

familiar as the Moray House Tests. From time to time, technical problems encountered in test development were fed back by Thomson into the academic literature, most notably in the case of a major article in 1932, on the problems of calculating age allowances as part of the standardization of tests.[14]

The literature of mental measurement in the inter-War years also reflected continued interest in the third of the themes mentioned at the start of this survey, the heritability of intelligence. This had been Galton's central preoccupation; and Burt had enthusiastically proclaimed the importance of the inherited component in his 1909 article. In his commentary on the implications of the results of the Binet-Simon tests for 'Differences in General Ability due to Social Status' in 1921, he was rather more restrained, remarking:

That children of better social status succeed better with the Binet-Simon scale is not necessarily an objection to that scale; nor is it necessarily a ground for constructing separate norms: for by birth as well as by home training, children who are superior in social status may be equally superior in general ability. Conversely, if a child proves defective according to a scale that is otherwise authentic, the mere fact that his family is poor and his dwelling a hovel does not of itself condone his deficiency. His parents' home may be mean because their hereditary intelligence is mean. Whether poverty and its accompaniments affect the child's performances in any direct fashion — whether, for example, in the Binet-Simon Tests a child that inherits an abundance of natural ability may be handicapped through a lack of cultural opportunities — is a further and a separate issue. It is a recurrent problem which we cannot hope to solve until we have also analysed the differing effect of social status upon the individual tests, considered one by one.[15]

Burt's most extreme utterances on the subject, asserting that of the order of 80 per cent of intelligence was heritable, came only much later, in what, as one historian has remarked, is acknowledged to be his 'fraudulent period'.[16] But in general he took the view that the higher mental test scores usually achieved by the children of middle- and upper-class parents,

---

[14] 'The Standardization of Group Tests and the Scatter of Intelligence Quotients: A Contribution to the Theory of Examining', *BJEP* ii (1932), pp. 92–112, 125–37. See also below, pp. 216–17.

[15] *Mental and Scholastic Tests* (1st edition, London, 1921), p. 192.

[16] Norton, 'Psychologists and Class', p. 308 and *passim*.

represented real differences in innate ability between them and the low-scoring children of working- and lower-middle-class parents, differences which could only be ascribed to differences in heredity. Thus the distribution of ability as exemplified by mental-test scores constituted no challenge to the existing social structure; rather, it tended to endorse it.

Spearman and Thomson did not fundamentally disagree with this position; although they laid their emphases very differently. Spearman had contributed on 'Heredity of abilities' to the *Eugenics Review* in 1914; although his central preoccupation in the early twenties was an account of the principles of cognition which would embody his two-factor theory of intelligence.[17]

Thomson was very much more concerned with heritability, its measurement and consequences, reflecting in the auto-biographical essay written at the end of his life,

I have spent a considerable part of my life in trying, for the sake of my own philosophy of education, to decide whether heredity or environment has more to do with the scatter of intelligence among children, and even now all I can venture as a scientist to say is that both are certainly concerned, but in what proportion I do not know.[18]

Initially, in Northumberland in the early 1920s, he and James Duff, later Vice-Chancellor of Durham University, investigated the connection between the measured intelligence of children tested for purposes of secondary-school selection, and the occupations of their fathers. 'We found a steady drop of average IQ among the children as we proceeded from the families of the professional classes through the ranks of first skilled and then semi-skilled classes, to the unskilled and casual labourers. . . .it is difficult to know which is cause and which is effect.'[19]

One clear feature, however, was a negative relation between intelligence and family size. Set not simply against a declining birth-rate overall, but also against the very clear class differentials in this decline — that is, the drop in

---

[17] *Eugenics Review* vi (1914), pp. 219-37; *The Nature of 'Intelligence' and the Principles of Cognition* (London, 1923).

[18] Thomson, *History of Psychology in Autobiography* iv, p. 288.

[19] Ibid., p. 289 and James F. Duff and Godfrey H. Thomson, 'The Social and Geographical Distribution of Intelligence in Northumberland', *BJP* xiv (1923-4), pp. 192-8.

completed family size had been much more marked among the middle and upper classes — this might have very serious implications nationally. If the principal cause of the negative correlation between intelligence and family size was heredity, this could mean a progressive decline in the level of national intelligence.

Hereitability thus concerned Thomson just as much as questions about the existence of intelligence and the possibility of measuring it. It was a carefully examined theme in his two general surveys, *Instinct, Intelligence and Character* (1924) and *A Modern Philosophy of Education* (1929).[20] It generated a number of research projects;[21] and it was an important part of the context for two of the largest surveys of intelligence ever undertaken. For Thomson, as one might expect, was a key figure in the Scottish Council for Research in Education, founded in 1930; and its first enterprise was the Mental Survey of 1932, the testing by a group intelligence test of a complete age group of Scottish children, all the eleven-year-olds, numbering about 90,000.[22] The intention to repeat such a survey after an appropriate interval was present from the beginning; and in 1945 'Professor Godfrey Thomson brought to the attention of the Research Council a suggestion. . .that in view of the presumed decline of national intelligence by reason of the differential birth-rate the Research Council should undertake a repetition of the 1932 mental survey.' The second survey was to show, however, that the national intelligence, as measured, had actually increased; and the implications of this were still being worked through when Thomson died in 1955.[23]

While the first Scottish Mental Survey was being carried

[20] *Instinct, Intelligence and Character* (London, 1924, based upon lectures delivered at Columbia University in New York the previous year), pp. 170, 215; *A Modern Philosophy of Education* (London, 1929), p. 26 and ch. VII.

[21] Thomson, *History of Psychology in Autobiography* iv, p. 289.

[22] *The Intelligence of Scottish Children*, Scottish Council for Research in Education Publications V (London, 1933).

[23] *The Trend of Scottish Intelligence* SCRE Publ. XXX (London, 1949), direct quotation from p. 2; *Social Implications of the 1947 Scottish Mental Survey* SCRE Publ. XXXV (London, 1953); *Educational and Other Aspects of the 1947 Scottish Mental Survey* SCRE Publ. XLI (London, 1958); *Eleven-Year-Olds Growing Up* SCRE Publ. XLII (London, 1958); *The Level and Trend of National Intelligence* SCRE Publ. XLVI (London, 1961). See also Thomson, *History of Psychology in Autobiography* iv, pp. 290-2.

out, in 1932, a series of large-scale surveys, involving about 10,000 children and including the first attempt in England to see what light might be thrown on heritability by a study of twins, were also under way in London schools. These were carried out by the newly founded Social Biology Unit at the London School of Economics under the direction of Lancelot Hogben.[24] Hogben, as Gary Werskey has pointed out, was practically the only major English biologist of the inter-War period consistently to steer clear of any versions, strong or weak, of eugenic arguments. It is not, therefore, surprising to find the workers of the Social Biology Unit challenging the heavy emphasis on the genetic component in measured ability, characteristic of much of the mental measurement literature of the day.

In 'Ability and Educational Opportunity in relation to Parental Occupation', published in 1935, Gray and Moshinsky wrote:

The existence in the general school population of a small but positive correlation between the intelligence of children and the socio-economic status of their parents is now a generally accepted fact. Duff and Thomson obtained a value of r=0.28 for public elementary and secondary school children in the County of Northumberland. For our entire data the corresponding figure is 0.25±0.008 . . .

The magnitude of this correlation is only one quarter of the maximum possible value which would denote that each individual occupied the same ordinal rank in both series, i.e. intelligence and socio-economic ratings. Its usefulness for diagnostic purposes is slight. Because a group of individuals has a high average I.Q. we are not entitled to assert with

---

[24] On the Unit and Hogben, see José Harris, *William Beveridge: A Biography* (Oxford, 1977), pp. 288-90 and Werskey, *The Visible College passim* but esp. pp. 101-15. Their inquiries were written up as follows: L. Herrman and L. Hogben, 'The intellectual resemblance of twins', *Proc. Roy. Soc. Edinburgh* liii (1932-3), part ii, pp. 105-29; J.L. Gray and Pearl Moshinsky, 'Studies in genetic psychology: the intellectual resemblance of collateral relatives', ibid., pp. 188-207; Gray and Moshinsky, 'Ability and Opportunity in English Education', *Sociological Review* xxvii (1935), pp. 113-62, and 'Ability and Educational Opportunity in Relation to Parental Occupation', ibid., pp. 281-327. These two articles were subsequently reprinted in *Political Arithmetic*, ed. L. Hogben (London, 1938). For a discussion of the material in the LCC files relating to the Unit's work, see Sutherland and Sharp, ' "The fust official psychologist" '. Burt is supposed to have collected *his* twin data while working for the LCC. Unfortunately the sources cited by Professor Hearnshaw (*Cyril Burt* p. 229 notes 12 and 13) do not provide adequate evidence for this claim; for a more detailed discussion see Sutherland and Sharp, Appendix I.

any great degree of confidence that it must therefore be composed of children of high socio-economic status. The significant discrepancies between the mean intelligence of different social groups are compatible with the existence of a considerable proportion of able children within groups with a low mean.

For these reasons it would be quite unwarranted to assert that intelligence is *determined* by socio-economic status, a view which is widely held by those unaccustomed to the proper interpretation of correlation technique. We are equally unjustified in making dogmatic statements about the nature of the agencies associated with differences in socio-economic status which assist in producing differences in performance on intelligence tests. These remarks apply equally whether we are disposed to ascribe intellectual differences mainly to environmental inequalities, or, as is more often asserted, to differences in the genetic composition of various social classes.

Their eventual, very cautious, conclusion was that 'neither an extreme autogenic nor an extreme environmentalist hypothesis accords with the observed data in this and similar studies. Nor, without further evidence concerning the respective roles of differences due to nature and nurture in performance on intelligence tests, do they give the slightest indication that one hypothesis is less wide of the mark than the other.'[25]

From this discussion they moved on to examine the educational opportunities available to different socio-economic groups; and concluded:

The major part of these inequalities in educational opportunity remains after account has been taken of the relative ability of each social class. We are therefore dealing with disparities due to differences in social institutions, rather than to genetic inequalities. In other words, the ratios set forth in Table XI are a measure of nurtural as contrasted with natural differences in an important domain of social organization. Even so, they probably minimize the contribution of institutional agencies to differences in opportunity, since the inferior mean ability of the less prosperous social classes may itself arise partly from their educational disadvantages.[26]

In the inter-War years, clearly, mental measurement not only received institutional support but also exhibited a considerable degree of intellectual vitality and technical development. We need now to begin to look at the extent to which and the ways in which this was disseminated beyond the charmed circle of university teachers and students, and the readers of the *BJP*.

[25] pp. 296–9.   [26] p. 324.

II A Wider Public

Psychologists, concerned to establish not only the academic respectability but also the social utility of their subject, took communication and the presentation of intellectual self very seriously in this period. At the end of the First World War, the founding fathers of the British Psychological Society thought long and hard about opening their ranks to all interested persons, no longer confining membership to accredited research workers; and the decision to do so in 1919 brought an immediate and most satisfying quadrupling of membership, to 427.[27]

To survive at all, the National Institute of Industrial Psychology had to sell itself vigorously, since it depended for most of its income on outside research contracts from firms, government departments and, occasionally, trade unions.[28]

As far as mental measurement was concerned, the educational journals regularly reviewed books and reported discussions. In 1919, 'in response to a number of inquiries', *The Times Educational Supplement* provided a reading list on the subject. In 1920 it gave a very long and careful — although very belated — review to Burt's *The Distribution of Mental Abilities.* The following year it reviewed recent American group tests, pointing out that many of them were really attainments tests.[29]

Typical of the many lengthy reported conference discussions was the session on 'Psychological Tests' at the Imperial Education Conference in 1927, at which

Dr Ballard said that too often 'intelligence' means 'interested in the things that interest me'. The psychologist applies a different interpretation: to him intelligence is independent of training, of knowledge, of culture, even of interest. He is looking, not for performance but for promise. The usual verbal tests need to be supplemented by

[27] Doyle, 'The National Institute of Industrial Psychology 1921–39', pp. 22–4.
[28] Ibid., ch. 3.
[29] *The Times Educational Supplement* 24 July 1919, p. 375, 'Tests of Intelligence'; 30 Sept. 1920, p. 521, 'Local Authorities as Innovators'; 24 Dec. 1921, p. 575, 'National Intelligence Tests'. Cf. also ibid., 26 June 1919, p. 319, review of Stanford-Binet Tests; 3 July 1919, p. 333. 'Intelligence Tests in Practice'; 7 Apr. 1921, p. 157, review of Brown and Thomson, *The Essentials of Mental Measurement*; 28 Jan. 1922, p. 37, 'New Work in Mental Tests'; 23 Dec. 1922, p. 557, P.B. Ballard, 'The New Examiner'; *Education* 20 Nov. 1925, p. 501, comments on use of intelligence tests in British Columbia.

other tests in order to test intelligence in the true psychological sense.[30]

P.B. Ballard matched Burt as one of the most popular, or at least, most frequently encountered lecturers and writers on the technology of testing. Like W.H. Winch, an inspector of schools for the LCC, Ballard had become interested in mental measurement as a way of reporting with accuracy and objectivity on schools' work. 'Testing', he wrote,

is like drug-taking. It grows on one. I soon found myself in the thick of the mental-test movement. I began to realize the value of the new mode of testing, not merely as a means of gauging the children's native capacity to learn; but as a means of estimating progress in the ordinary branches of the study.[31]

Ballard's little book *Mental Tests*, published in 1920, was actually the popularization preceding the monograph, in the form of Burt's *Mental and Scholastic Tests* of 1921;[32] and in *The New Examiner*, first published in 1923 and reprinted no fewer than eight times before 1940, he set out the implications of mental measurement, as he saw them, for the conduct of examinations in general. In the early 1930s he and Burt, along with Spearman, Sir Michael Sadler and Sir Philip Hartog, were the leading members of the International Institute Examinations Enquiry, an enterprise concerned with exposing the subjectivity of much contemporary examining and spreading awareness of more scientific and objective methods.[33]

[30] Ibid., 22 July 1927 p. 92. Cf. also *The Times Educational Supplement* 2 Sept. 1920, p. 480, report of British Association meeting, Section L; *Education* 24 June 1921, pp. 460-1, report of the AGM of the Association of Headmistresses; ibid., 16 Sept. 1921, pp. 169-70 and *The Times Educational Supplement* 17 Sept. 1921, p. 415, reports of British Association meetings; ibid., 31 Dec. 1921, p. 582, report of a public debate between Ballard and a member of the British Phrenological Society; ibid., 14 Jan. 1922, p. 21, report of a meeting of the Child Study Society. *Education* 11 Jan. 1924, p. 23, report of the North of England Education Conference; 11 Sept. 1925, p. 244, report of British Association meetings; 10 Jan. 1930, pp. 50 and 52, report of the North of England Education Conference.

[31] P.B. Ballard, *Things I Cannot Forget* (London, 1937), pp. 198-202, direct quotation from p. 202.

[32] See Ballard's preface to *Mental Tests* (London, 1920).

[33] Mabel Hartog, *P.J. Hartog. A Memoir by His Wife* (London, 1949), pp. 130-40, Ballard, *Things I Cannot Forget,* pp. 205-10, Sir Philip Hartog and E.C. Rhodes, *An Examination of Examinations* (London, 1935) and *The Marks of Examiners* (London, 1936); Sir Philip Hartog and Gladys Roberts, *A Conspectus*

There was, however, one area of communication in which Ballard appears not to have joined Burt — broadcasting. In 1930 Burt made a whole series of broadcasts under the general title of 'The study of the mind', among which there were individual broadcasts on 'Educational tests', 'Intelligence tests', and 'Measurements in psychology'.[34]

The debate and discussion in the educational press were not wholly one-sided. Ballard and Winch's colleague in the LCC inspectorate, F.H. Hayward, the licensed clown of the educational world in the early 1920s, barracked constantly from the sidelines, stigmatizing intelligence tests as merely 'tests of cleverness'.[35] Others, such as Professor John Adams of University College, London, Professor J.A. Green of Sheffield, Frank Watts, Lecturer in Psychology at Manchester, Professor T.H. Pear of Manchester and Professor E.H. Campagnac of Liverpool, took and developed more seriously Hayward's basic point, the difficulty of isolating intelligence from the universe in which it had to operate, the problems with which it had to deal. They discussed questions of motivation, of particular aptitudes and the whole issue of culture loading, made the more obvious, dramatized even, by the substantial verbal elements in many tests.[36]

of Examinations in Great Britain and Northern Ireland (London, 1937); Sir Michael Sadler *et al.*, *Essays on Examinations* (London, 1936). See also John Roach, 'Examinations and the Secondary Schools 1900-1945', *History of Education* viii (1979), pp. 54-5.

[34] Sutherland and Sharp, ' "The fust official psychologist" ' Appendix III, item 52. See also the variety of the periodicals in which Burt published set out here. On Burt and Ballard's lecturing see, in addition to the references set out in note 30 above, *The Times Educational Supplement* 27 Aug. 1921, p. 388, report of lecture programmes in West Riding and in London; ibid., 15 Oct. 1921, p. 458, report of the programme of the Notts and District Education Study Society; *Education* 28 Oct. 1921, p. 242, report of lecture to the Education Guild; *The Times Educational Supplement* 12 Aug. 1922, p. 376, report of the programme of the Bingley Summer School for Teachers; ibid., 19 Aug. 1922, report of the proceedings of the Brighton Summer School in Psychology; *Education* 9 Sept. 1927, p. 243, report of British Association meetings. Also, by 1926 the National Institute of Industrial Psychology was advertising a set of five lecture-demonstrations for teachers on intelligence tests, which could be hired by any local education authority in the country — *Education* 12 Feb. 1926, p. 180.

[35] Ibid., 3 Nov. 1922, p. 260, 'Dr Hayward and Intelligence Tests'; also *The Times Educational Supplement* 28 Oct. 1922, p. 474 and 25 Nov. 1922, p. 511. On Hayward in general, see his extraordinary autobiography, F.H. Hayward, *An Educational Failure* (London, 1938), also *A First Book of School Celebrations* and *A Second Book of School Celebrations* (both London, 1920).

[36] *Education* 30 Jan. 1920, pp. 82-3 (Adams); *The Times Educational Supple-*

The wider discussion about heritability also found its publicists in the course of the 1930s. J.L. Gray, of the Social Biology Unit at the LSE, published *The Nation's Intelligence* in 1936, in the *Changing World Library* edited by Hyman Levy, which, as the jacket blurb had it, 'challenges the view that we are an intellectually decadent nation'. The following year brought an aggressive statement of the hereditarian view, in Raymond B. Cattell's *The Fight for Our National Intelligence*. Statements like these were part of a much wider debate about the possibility of national decline and the implications such a decline would have for social policy in the widest senses, all of which had a eugenic dimension. There is not space to do more than allude to this debate here.[37] More to the point, the possibility of a decline in the level of national intelligence did not appear to concern or to weigh with the educational world in this period to anything like the same degree as the *idea* and the *technology* of mental measurement. Although the larger question began to evoke some generalized concern in the years immediately before the Second World War, such concern had yet to find its way through into discussions of educational policy.

By contrast, mental measurement and the mechanics thereof had become a staple of educational policy discussions. As early as the mid-twenties 'general intelligence' had become almost a catch-phrase. In June 1926 the President, Alderman George Cadbury, explained to the Annual Conference of the Association for Education in Industry and Commerce the problems of balancing quantitative and qualitative considerations in chocolate making, and he summed up, 'General intelligence is of the utmost value in promoting efficiency.'[38]

---

ment 24 Mar. 1921, p. 132 (Watts); ibid., 19 Nov. 1921, p. 518 (Green); ibid., 7 Jan. 1922, p. 10 (Pear); Education 14 Jan. 1927, pp. 38-40 (Campagnac).

[37] A more restrained and probably more representative statement of the preoccupation with heredity is to be found in Olive Maguiness, *Environment and Heredity* (London, 1940). For the debate in general, see e.g. Searle, 'Eugenics and Politics in Britain in the 1930s', Jones, *Social Darwinism and English Thought*, pp. 167-71, Brian Evans and Bernard Waites, *IQ and Mental Testing. An Unnatural Science and its Social History* (London, 1981), pp. 61-73, and John Macnicol, *The Movement for Family Allowances 1918-45: A Study in Social Policy Development* (London, 1980), esp. ch. 4.

[38] *Education* 25 June 1926, p. 677. Cf. also ibid., 8 July 1927, p. 38, Sir D. Milne Watson to the same body.

In June 1927 an advertisement for the Singer Sewing Machine in the weekly journal *Education* quoted an unnamed head-mistress as declaring ' "The Needlework Lesson now seems to develop general intelligence too!" '.[39]

More important than such invocations, although not wholly unconnected, was the impact the protagonists of mental measurement succeeded in making on some parts of the bureaucracy of central government, notably the Board of Education's Consultative Committee and HM Inspectorate.

Strictly speaking, the Consultative Committee was not part of the bureaucracy. It had been created at the same time as the Board itself, under the legislation of 1900, 'consisting as to not less than two-thirds of persons qualified to represent the views of universities and other bodies interested in education', who normally served for six years at a time, nominated by the President. Its principal function was to advise the Board on any matter which the President chose to refer to it; and successive Presidents, in nominating the great and good, as usual tried to steer a course between the inclusion and placation of major vested interests and the exclusion of those who might make politically embarrassing recommendations.[40] However, an internal but unsigned Board memorandum, recommending the Committee's revival at the end of the War, noted:

No administrative inconvenience has been experienced in connection with the Committee's work except that of finding constant employment for it, and except that on one occasion the Board's action had to be deferred till the Committee had reported on a matter which had been referred to it.[41]

Choice of reference of course needed as much care as choice of members; and in May 1919 the Permanent Secretary, Selby-Bigge, canvassed the senior officials of the Board for suggestions. Five were forthcoming, including, from E.K. Chambers, the Shakespearian scholar, then Principal Assistant Secretary and in 1921 to become Second Secretary, 'What

[39] Ibid., 10 June 1927, p. 679.

[40] P.H.J.H. Gosden, *The Development of Educational Administration in England and Wales* (Oxford, 1966), p. 116; Ed 24/221, Ed 24/1224 papers 1912–1914; Ed 24/1228 Minute Permanent Secretary to President 5 Dec. 1918, Minute same to same 11 Feb. 1920.

[41] Ed 24/1227 unsigned Memorandum 23 July 1918.

use can be made in the public system of education of psychological tests of educable capacity'; and this was one of the two — the other being the question of differentiating secondary school curricula according to the sex of the pupils — which finally went forward to Fisher.[42]

Fisher accepted both of these topics and the psychologists responded to the first with enthusiasm. Among the members of the Consultative Committee at that time was Dr J.G. Adami, the distinguished pathologist and since 1919 Vice-Chancellor of Liverpool University. He chaired the subcommittee initially formed to deal with the reference on psychological tests and promptly brought about the co-option of Ballard, Myers, and Spearman. Burt also functioned in an advisory capacity; and evidence and memoranda were invited from everyone who had ever displayed any expertise and/or interest, including Winch, Godfrey Thomson, Professor T.H. Pear, Professor J.A. Green, the Northumberland Education Committee and Drs Eichholz and E.O. Lewis, whom we encountered in discussing mental handicap.

The subcommittee reported in 1922 and using this report as a brief, the full Committee heard further evidence before reporting itself finally in 1924.[43] Large sections of this 1924 Report resembled a textbook on mental measurement. Burt contributed an elegant historical survey which constituted the first chapter, along with Appendices IV, V, VII and VIII — 'Notes on Standardization and Norms', 'Correlation', 'Recent Publications on Psychology and Psychological Tests', and 'Examples of Tests, Individual and Group'. Appendix II was a short account of 'Some experiments recently conducted in England in the use of Group Tests and Individual Tests in Free Place Examinations and in Schools of different types'. Appendices III and VI dealt with foreign experiments and experiences, and Appendix IX presented 'The view of various psychologists' on '(a) The factors involved in

---

[42] Ed 24/1228 Permanent Secretary's Minute 15 May 1919, List 6 Aug. 1919 and Permanent Secretary's Minute to President 5 Dec. 1919. These four files Ed 24/1224, 1226, 1227 and 1228 are in a considerable jumble; but material scattered through them suggests that the political problems associated with choice of both personnel and topic, bulked larger and larger in the inter-War years.

[43] For the conduct of the inquiry see Ed 24/1226 papers July 1920–end 1923, Ed 24/1224 papers 1922–4 and the account in the published Report.

"general" ability' and '(b) The need for testing for "special" and "group" abilities'.

When the Consultative Committee got down to recommendations, it acknowledged and not unnaturally endorsed the part already played by individual tests in the identification and assessment of mental handicap.[44] The newer and more controversial field was the use of tests to differentiate between normal children and adolescents in educational classification and selection and in vocational guidance. Here, too, almost inevitably, the Committee pronounced in favour. The members considered group tests could help in classifying children by ability, for teaching in separate groups, on entry both to junior schools (at about age seven) and to secondary schools. In conjunction with the usual written papers and with interviews, both group and individual tests could help in the actual selection for secondary school places, particularly in arriving at decisions on borderline cases. They looked forward to further experiment on standardized attainment tests and tests for use in vocational guidance, both of which they thought could be helpful.[45]

Psychological testing thus received the Consultative Committee stamp of approval; and successive Consultative Committee reports in the inter-War years regularly referred back to this 1924 Report. The 1926 Report on the Education of the Adolescent, usually known as the Hadow Report after the then Chairman, Sir Henry Hadow, proposed that a 'written psychological test might also be employed [in secondary-school selection] in dealing with borderline cases, or where a discrepancy between the result of the written examination and the teacher's estimate of proficiency has been observed'.[46]

The Report on the Primary School in 1931 discussed the uses of intelligence tests both in classifying children at the point of transition from the infant to the junior school — 'this is one of the stages at which teachers may usefully apply intelligence tests' — and in secondary-school selection:

---

[44] Board of Education Consultative Committee, *Psychological Tests of Educable Capacity* (London, 1924), Part V, recommendations 13-17.

[45] Ibid., paras. 77, 78, 81, 85-7.

[46] Board of Education Consultative Committee, *The Education of the Adolescent* (London, 1926, henceforward Hadow Report), para. 157.

Since the primary purpose of the examination should be to test general capacity and ability to profit by continued education. . . , it is clearly important that attempts should be made to gauge these qualities apart from general attainment in English and Arithmetic. The evidence shews that in recent years much trouble has been taken in many areas to include a certain number of questions designed primarily to discover and assess intelligence. In addition to this incidental method of discovering intelligence, some authorities have added a group intelligence test. In our opinion, *carefully devised group intelligence tests may be a useful factor in selection, but it would be inadvisable to rely on such tests alone*. . . . On the other hand, if questions in external examinations for children at the age of eleven were always set with due regard to the peculiarities of the child mind, both in the form and matter of the questions and in their arrangement in the written paper, and if the same scientific methods were employed as in intelligence tests and standardized scholastic tests, such examinations would prove a more efficient means of discovering ability in young children than those now in use.[47]

The Report on Secondary and Technical Schools in 1938, again usually known after the then Chairman as the Spens Report, simply referred back to all these comments and reiterated a general endorsement.[48]

One shift, however, must be noted. In 1924 the Consultative Committee was clear about the likely practical utility of mental tests but it also registered the existence of some disagreement about the qualities being measured and particularly about the dominance of 'g'. Summarizing the main lines of debate, the Committee members suggested rather tentatively,

Most psychologists would probably agree that 'intelligence' is a general mental ability operating in many different ways, given as part of the child's natural endowment, as distinct from knowledge or skill acquired through teaching or experience, and more concerned with analysing and coordinating the data of experience than with mere passive reception of them.[49]

But they also provided Appendix IX — 'The views of various psychologists on (a) The factors involved in "general" ability,

[47] Board of Education Consultative Committee *The Primary School* (London, 1931), paras. 102 and 107, Report's emphasis.

[48] Board of Education Consultative Committee, *Secondary Education with Special reference to Grammar Schools and Technical High Schools* (London, 1938, henceforward Spens Report), ch. IX, para. 38.

[49] *Psychological Tests*, para. 54.

and (b) The need for testing for "special" and "group" abilities'. The 1931 Report on the Primary School referred back to this, but then went on confidently:

> The general result of recent investigations is that all intellectual activities seem to be closely correlated with one another in children between the ages of seven and eleven, though towards puberty these intercorrelations tend to diminish. Thus, during the period between the ages of seven and eleven, one central underlying factor tends to determine the general level of the child's ability.[50]

The Spens Report in 1938 again made the ritual reference back, but then went on to make even more positive and specific claims:

> *Intellectual development during childhood appears to progress as if it were governed by a single central factor, usually known as 'general intelligence', which may be broadly described as innate all-round intellectual ability. It appears to enter into everything which the child attempts to think, or say, or do, and seems on the whole to be the most important factor in determining his work in the classroom. Our psychological witnesses assured us that it can be measured approximately by means of intelligence tests. . . .*
>
> *We were informed that, with few exceptions, it is possible at a very early age to predict with some degree of accuracy the ultimate level of a child's intellectual powers, but this is true only of general intelligence and does not hold good in respect of specific aptitudes and interests. The average child is said to attain the effective limit of development in general intelligence between the ages of 16 and 18.[51]*

Behind this almost certainly lay the fact that the figure among 'our psychological witnesses' on whom successive Committees chose to rely, was Cyril Burt. His 'Memorandum on the mental development of children up to the age of 11' was published as Appendix III to the 1931 Report on the Primary School; and the section of the Spens Report dealing with the mental development of children between the ages of eleven and sixteen was 'based on a Memorandum prepared for the Committee by Professor Burt'.[52]

---

[50] *The Primary School*, para. 35.

[51] Spens Report ch. III, part II, para. 12, Report's emphasis.

[52] Ibid., note prefacing part II of ch. III. The dependence on Burt is the more interesting and perhaps says something about the force of his personality and his undoubted gifts as a communicator, in view of the fact that the Committee trawled quite widely for evidence — though not, however, going to the trouble of fetching Thomson from Edinburgh — see Ed 10/151 and 152.

*

The Consultative Committee was, as we have said, not the Board of Education proper. But the suggestion that it should look at psychological tests had come from within the office; and Adami's subcommittee 1920-2 had found an apt pupil in the official who was its secretary, R.F. Young, formally applauding 'the way in which he has grasped the technicalities equally with the basal principles of a new and most complex subject'.[53]

In addition, among the expert witnesses appearing before the Committee 1922-4 were two present members and one former member of HM Inspectorate of schools. The former HMI was Hugh Gordon, to whose study of the extent to which performance in individual Binet tests was affected by exposure to systematic schooling, reference has already been made.[54] This study had been published by the Board in 1923 and rapidly became a *locus classicus* in debates about the culture loading of tests and the particular vulnerability to this of tests in which the verbal component predominated.[55]

The two current HMIs were Frank Watts and C.A. Richardson. Watts, when he was lecturer in psychology at Manchester, had gone on record as critical of some of the grander claims made for mental testing.[56] Richardson, on the other hand, had been heavily involved in the experiments in Northumberland, to the extent of preparing a mental test for use as a supplement to attainments tests, in the selection of fee-paying pupils for entry to secondary schools in 1921 and adapting the 'Simplex' tests for use in the selection of intending teachers in 1923. And he continued his interest and developed his expertise throughout his career in the Inspectorate.[57]

As has already been said, the elementary education Inspectorate had shown itself ready to discuss critically and, indeed,

[53] Ed 24/1224, report of the subcommittee 25 May 1922.
[54] Above, ch. 3, p. 90.
[55] See not only the extract from *The Health of the School Child* quoted above but also e.g. Ballard, *The New Examiner,* pp. 119-21, Thomson, *Instinct, Intelligence and Character*, p. 217 and Burt, *Mental and Scholastic Tests* (3rd edition, 1947), p. 283.   [56] Above, p. 147, n. 36.
[57] *Psychological Tests* Appendix II (4) (b), p. 154; below, pp. 159-60; also personal information from G.F. Peaker HMI 1933-64 in an interview with Stephen Sharp on 6 Jan. 1978.

to challenge the use of mental testing by the medical Inspectorate in the diagnosis and measurement of backwardness and mental handicap — it had criticized Burt's reading
test as out of touch with current practice in the schools.[58]
Of wider impact were the efforts of both elementary and
secondary Inspectors to spread best practice, as they monitored LEAs' conduct of examinations for entry to grant-
aided secondary schools throughout the period. Best practice, in the Inspectorate's view, came to include the use of
group mental tests, not uncritically and in isolation, but as
one element in a battery of forms of assessment; and, even
more important, the application to the conduct of examinations as a whole, of the lessons learned from mental testing
about the need for and mechanics of standardization.

The Inspectorate's monitoring began in 1921 and continued until the outbreak of War. It had its roots, almost
certainly, in the conviction of the officials of the Board
that since places in grant-aided secondary schools were so
few, selection for them had better be done — and seen to
be done — as equitably as possible.[59] We shall see something of their activities and arguments when we come to
discuss the procedures of individual LEAs in chapters 7 and
8. But the general outlines emerge plainly enough from the
internal memoranda of the Inspectorate, which were, of
course, designed to pool available information and specialist
knowledge and ensure a common pattern of approach.

The first five investigations — into examining practices in
Leeds, Durham, Wiltshire, Surrey and Plymouth — produced
four major memoranda in April 1923.[60] Straightway, five
themes emerged which were to continue to exercise Inspectors throughout. The first was the inclusion and conduct
of an oral examination; the second was the weight, if any, to
be attached to the child's previous school record; the third
was the general sloppiness of setting and marking procedures;
the fourth was the use of an age allowance; and the fifth was
the size of the group examined. This last was a major point
and integrally connected with the two preceding ones: equity

[58] Above, p. 91.
[59] See the context provided by the discussions on the redrafting of the regulations for grant-aided secondary schools in Ed 12/348.
[60] Ed 22/127 Memoranda 426 A-D.

was best ensured and perceived to be so, when the entire elementary school population of a particular age was examined – as the Chief HMI for Secondary Schools, W.C. Fletcher, put it, 'the results must approach more nearly to the theoretically "best" selection'.[61] Moreover, this would give a group and spread of marks large enough for the calculation of some form of age allowances and standardization of different examiners' mark distributions. As a body, therefore, the Inspectorate came firmly down in favour of compelling the entire age group to sit the examination – as Durham, Wiltshire and Plymouth did, but Leeds and Surrey did not.[62]

On the other issues the Inspectors were, at this stage, rather more tentative, still feeling their way and gathering information. But in discussing both the use of an oral examination and the proper assessment of the child who did brilliantly on one test and appallingly on another, they were inclined to think that individual and/or group intelligence tests could help. The Chief HMI commented:

before we accept the favourable evidence of an interview against the result of a written examination, the machinery of intelligence tests might perhaps be used. For such cases an oral intelligence test would seem to be most valuable, but the position of a child in a group intelligence test taken by all the candidates (or all those with a chance of success) might be a sufficient check.[63]

And the Inspectors who had conducted the inquiry in Leeds, reported that 'the results of the Group Intelligence Test. . . correlated well with the final results of the examination'.[64]

Fifteen months later, the Chief HMI produced a further digest of the inquiries carried out so far.[65] Again, the same themes dominated. The case for compelling all public elementary schoolchildren to be examined remained clear: the examination provided a way of taking stock of the work of the public elementary school; no child lost a chance through parents' or teachers' negligence; and the examination itself drew attention to the secondary-school provision. In the Parts of Kesteven, in Lincolnshire, where compulsion had

---

[61] Memo A, para. 13.
[63] Memo A, paras. 4 and 5.
[65] Ed 22/128, Memorandum 455, 19 Aug. 1924.

[62] Memo C, para. 4.
[64] Memo B.

recently been introduced, 'Children are now being drawn from parts of the county not previously reached by Secondary Education.' Some of these children were not getting much home support and encouragement, but this would take a generation or so to sort itself out — 'it may rather prove to be an illustration of the principle that schools have to educate the parents as well as the children'.[66]

Again there was extended criticism of sloppy marking procedures, the English Essay papers universally producing the most bunched and idiosyncratic marking.[67] Two authorities, Exeter and Durham, had been advised to use properly standardized group intelligence tests as a check on their marking procedures in attainments tests, in the first stage of their examination. Wallasey, on the other hand, had been advised that its so-called 'General Intelligence' paper was in fact a second English paper, and encouraged to drop it.[68] 'General intelligence' was also being rather loosely used to label some lines of questioning in oral tests.[69] Finally, the only authority which appeared to be seriously concerned about age allowances, was the LCC, which now ran its examinations twice a year, thereby ensuring that the oldest and youngest candidates were separated by no more than six months.[70]

In the latter half of 1927, Fletcher's successor as Chief Inspector with special responsibility for secondary schools, F.B. Stead, felt that enough experience and information had now been accumulated to enable the Inspectorate to go public, as it were. In 1928 the Board published as pamphlet 63, a *Memorandum on Examinations for Scholarships and Free Places at Secondary Schools*. This discussed at length the material thrown up by the seventy-five investigations so far conducted, the level of detail including examples of well-set and badly set English and Arithmetic papers.

The *Memorandum* gave a cautious welcome to intelligence tests:

The use of these tests, which has increased in recent years, has probably originated in a belief that they measure with reasonable reliability and

---

[66] s. III.   [67] ss. V and VI.
[68] ss. VI and VIII.   [69] s. IX.
[70] s. VIII; see also Fletcher's circulation of a paper by HMI Carson discussing this, Ed 22/129 Memorandum 468, 27 Jan. 1925.

consistency capacity rather than attainment and in a desire to discover a test which, to a greater degree than the ordinary papers in Arithmetic and English, shall be independent of the chance effects of home circumstances, teaching deficiency, fortunate promotion, luck in questions and the like. Opinion is nevertheless deeply divided upon the question of the value and suitability of the tests themselves, and upon the relevance of the usual arguments for and against them. Only in a very few cases has a comparison been made of the relative efficiency of intelligence tests on the one hand, and of ordinary Arithmetic and English papers on the other for the purpose of predicting the degree of success of the candidates in their subsequent Secondary School course. Any such investigations carried out by Local Education Authorities, or Secondary Schools, would be of great value. . . .

It is evident that these investigations could only be carried out in relation to small groups of pupils since, in general, the relative progress of the pupils can only be compared with a batch which entered together upon the same course of study in the same school. Although the evidence of a few investigations might easily prove fallacious, the evidence of a large number of enquiries carried out by many Authorities and Schools might possibly point to a definite answer. What is needed is a widespread rather than an intensive study of the facts; on this alone can a final judgement be formed. A general use of these tests in making awards would be premature. Meanwhile whatever views may be held regarding the larger claims that have been made on behalf of properly constructed intelligence tests, the ease with which they can be used makes a valuable addition to the armoury of weapons, which includes school records and oral tests, for discovering children who have not done themselves justice in the examination in English and Arithmetic and for discriminating between candidates near the border-line.[71]

The *Memorandum* expressed considerable unhappiness about oral tests, remarking that, 'in general they are so variable and ill-defined in nature as to be at least of very doubtful value and so unstandardised and inconsistent in operation as to introduce a degree of error which is manifestly unfair'.[72] Likewise, it was lukewarm about the effective use of school records.[73]

The main thrust of the pamphlet was an attempt to improve examining techniques and practice in general. An age allowance was presented as essential, best achieved by trial and error during the marking, adding or subtracting marks to 'equalize approximately the number of awards in the several age groups'.[74] Earlier, a strong preference had been expressed for the compulsory examination of all eligible children.[75]

[71] Para. 56.   [72] Para. 62.   [73] Ch. VIII.
[74] Ch. IX, quotation from para. 71.   [75] Para. 20.

Two chapters were devoted to 'The Order of Merit' and 'The Analysis of Marks', the first pointing out that an examination which produced a closely bunched set of marks was not doing its job very well. Such bunching, particularly common in the marking of English papers, also affected the weighting of one paper against another. 'The influence of a subject on the order of merit is, in fact, determined by the "effective" spread of marks in that subject and not by the maximum or the average mark.' English and Arithmetic scores should also 'correlate well'; 'an examination in which this did not happen should on that ground alone be regarded with suspicion'.

Finally,

If use is to be made of oral tests (and of school records and intelligence tests) as factors determining the order of merit, it is suggested that a procedure somewhat of the following kind might be adopted.

Let the oral test, school record and intelligence test each divide the candidates into, say, five classes, A, B, C, D, and E. Then from a wide borderline constructed by the written test exclude in succession:—

  all candidates having three Es
  all candidates having two Es and a D
  all candidates having one E and two Ds

and so on until the ground is thinned so that the final order can properly be determined on the written marks of the residue.[76]

The chapter 'The Analysis of Marks' correspondingly provided specimen examples of adequately detailed mark sheets and distribution tables, to show spreads of marks and, if necessary, highlight the peculiarities of individual examiners, so as to make it possible to adjust for these.

As monitoring continued, so did the flow of information and examples of practice, good and bad. Between 1928 and 1936 seventeen LEAs' examining practices were investigated a second time and forty-nine more a first time.[77] And between 1931 and 1934 additional material was provided by the activities of a special committee of the Inspectorate. This committee circularized all Inspectors to see if they could produce any examples of school records which could be or were being used effectively in the selection process. A paper by C.A. Richardson to an Inspectors' conference at Malvern

[76] Ch. X, direct quotations from paras. 75-7.
[77] *Special Places, Supplementary Memorandum to the Board of Education Pamphlet on Free Place Examinations* (London, 1936), p. 3.

in July 1933, on the most sophisticated method for the calculation of age allowances, was subsequently circulated and the procedure decreed to be one to be recommended to LEAs.[78] Most important, the committee ran its own 'field trials', involving 10,000 children and using tests in English (no essay) and Arithmetic, and Moray House Group Intelligence Test no. 11.[79]

In March 1934 HMIs were advised that parts of pamphlet no. 63 needed updating and some sections would probably have to be rewritten. Among these was the rather tentative welcome given to intelligence tests, although

one thing is certain — that if Intelligence Tests are to be of any use they must be set and marked by persons having both knowledge and experience. For instance a test which has not been standardized will do more harm than good.

On the very difficult question of the relationship between scores in group and scores in individual tests, Inspectors were referred to Godfrey Thomson's article in the *BJEP* in 1932. Also due for rewriting was the section on the use of school records, as the recent investigations 'suggest that teachers' rankings are more reliable than had been supposed'.[80]

In 1936 there duly appeared a *Memorandum* supplementing pamphlet no. 63 of 1928. 'The purpose of the examination', declared its Introduction,

is the selection at the age of 11+, of children fit to profit by secondary education. The importance of accurate selection is vital and the main business is to get the right children. At the same time the free development of the Junior School must not be jeopardized and the taking of the examination must not be looked on as the aim and end of the education given there.

This last point was an oblique reference to the sustained opposition of the NUT to attempts to use the examination as a way of reviewing the performance of public elementary

[78] Ed 22/109 Memorandum E351, 1 Oct. 1934; see also duplicate in Ed 22/138 Memorandum S, 583.

[79] Ed 12/261 R.S. Wood to Secretary, Treasury 10 June 1933, R.S. Wood to E.W. Liddington 16 June 1933. For the activities of the committee as a whole, see Ed 10/151, V5(53), Memorandum for the Consultative Committee by the Chief HMI for Secondary Schools, F.R.G. Duckworth, October 1935.

[80] Ed 22/138 Memorandum 578 26 March 1934. For Thomson's article, see above, n. 14.

schools.[81] As a result, it was clearly not thought politically possible to insist on the examination of the whole age group; and the paragraph on age allowances tailed off rather lamely:

9. An age allowance should always be given. Its amount should be determined by the results of the examination and not laid down arbitrarily in advance. For calculating on a strictly equitable basis it would be necessary that the complete age group should be examined, either over the whole of the geographical area concerned or in some representative part of it. More general considerations bearing upon the development of Junior School work may however lead Local Education Authorities and teachers to hesitate to submit the whole of an age group to the same test and it is not therefore suggested that examination of the whole age group should be made compulsory.

Oral tests and interviews were again condemned (para. 4); but increased use of school records was urged (para. 3). And on the conduct of the written examinations the *Memorandum* was crisp and authoritative.

1. A two-stage examination is not necessarily more efficient than a one-stage examination.*
2. It is generally agreed that no tests of attainment should be set except in English and Arithmetic.
Evidence has accumulated which suggests that the value of what are known as intelligence tests is higher than had been supposed, provided that such tests are constructed, and their results used, under expert guidance. It is therefore recommended that such a test be included in every examination. . . .
4. The range of the syllabus examined, especially in arithmetic, should not be greater than the average child who takes the examination may fairly be expected to cover. . . .
5. The proposed examination questions should be tried out in advance in some other area. This practice has been adopted by a number of examining bodies in the past. The proposed questions may be set, in another area, either as a school exercise or as part of the internal examinations in several schools and the results are communicated in confidence. Thus ambiguities can be removed, and the relative difficulty of the questions and the 'weight' of the papers can be adjusted approximately as required.
For children of this age it is better to use a large number of short questions rather than a few relatively long ones. Such questions, which

*A one-stage examination is an examination which occupies as a rule one or two days and decides the final award of places in the Secondary school or Schools. A two-stage examination consists of a preliminary examination designed to sift out those candidates who may be considered as wholly unfit for Secondary education. It is followed by the final examination which determines the awards.

[81] See below, pp. 247–8, for further discussion of this.

enable a wide field to be covered in a relatively short time, both facilitate objective marking (i.e. marking that is independent of the examiner's personal judgement) and reduce the strain of examination on the children. No one doubts the value of instruction in composition as part of the school curriculum in English but in view of the evidence as to the unreliability of essay questions as part of the examination, hesitation is felt in recommending the inclusion of such questions.

7. The questions should be graded in difficulty, as determined by the preliminary try-out. A few very easy and a few very hard questions should be included.

8. In assigning the relative weight to be attached to the separate papers and to the school records, the examiners should ultimately be guided by the 'follow up'*. It is suggested that, provisionally, the intelligence test and each of the attainment tests be assigned equal weight.

*The 'follow up' means the investigation of results which manifest themselves at a subsequent stage in the educational careers of the pupils.[82]

By the mid-1930s, therefore, HM Inspectorate was thoroughly well versed in what the Introduction to the *Supplementary Memorandum* called, 'modern examination technique'. The HMIs had looked very carefully at the uses — and abuses — of contemporary intelligence tests and they had come to the conclusion that, properly devised and administered, such tests had a part to play in selection processes. Perhaps even more important, they had also taken very seriously the implications of mental-test procedures for examining practices in general: the importance of the size of the group examined, the case for trials and the whole issue of standardization; and the case for trying to eliminate, or at least reduce as far as possible, the subjective element in marking.

The *Memorandum*'s publication in 1936 coincided, as it happened, with some of the publicity attracted by the International Institute Examinations Enquiry's activities.[83] The Board of Education felt confident that it could stand entirely clear of this: its officers reckoned that they already knew what could and could not be expected of examinations, how

[82] *Supplementary Memorandum* 1936, pp. 6-7.
[83] For the International Institute Examinations Enquiry, see above, p. 146. For examples of the publicity, see *Education* 13 Dec. 1935, pp. 574-5, 20 Dec. 1935, pp. 608-9, 27 Dec. 1935, pp. 625-6, 3 Jan. 1936, pp. 6-9, 10 Jan. 1936, p. 25, 17 Jan. 1936, p. 82, 24 Jan. 1936, p. 111, 31 Jan. 1936, p. 142, 10 July 1936, p. 31 and 31 July 1936, pp. 103-4.

well and how badly they might be conducted.[84] As the 1928 *Memorandum* had explained:

Whether the free place examinations are in themselves desirable or whether other and perhaps better methods of selecting pupils for admission to Secondary Schools could be devised — these are questions which are often asked but they are not here discussed. . . The memorandum is concerned not with these wider questions of educational policy on which so much is said and written, but with the practical problem which every Local Education Authority is called upon to face:— given a system of selection by examination, how can that system best be worked?[85]

By the mid-1930s the Board and the Inspectorate felt that they were equipped to give LEAs very clear advice on how that system could best be worked.

[84] Ed 12/261 papers relating to the publication of the 1936 *Supplementary Memorandum*.

[85] Introduction, para. 2.

Chapter 6

The Rise of the Eleven-Plus Examination

In its *Memoranda* on examinations for entry to secondary school, the Board of Education had carefully avoided 'wider questions of policy': 'given a system of selection by examination, how best can that system be worked?' But these wider questions must now be faced. Why was it that the main field of application for mental measurement and the techniques associated with it in dealing with normal children, was this process of selection for secondary education? We must now try to unravel the ways in which competitive examinations came to dominate not only secondary school entry but also the relationship between elementary and the other forms of post-elementary education beginning to be developed.

On the face of it, this trend did indeed provide a marvellous opportunity for the advocates of mental measurement to bring their notions of a unitary general intelligence, their techniques and their claims to objectivity to bear. As the previous chapter has shown, they found an informed and on the whole sympathetic hearing in central government; and it has been assumed that by the outbreak of the Second World War mental testing had achieved a position of unparalleled dominance in the public education system. The reality at the grass roots, in individual LEA areas, was a great deal less tidy, more complex and uneven than this. The chapters following this one will be devoted to an attempt to chart exactly who did — and did not — do what and why. First, however, it is necessary to examine the nature and extent of new provision for post-elementary education and its relation to the elementary schools, and to see how it was that a competitive examination at the age of eleven-plus came to loom so large in this.

*

At the beginning of the twentieth century in England, state education had meant elementary education, education for the working classes, and, in the main, for the children of the working classes, as the fixing of the minimum school-leaving age at twelve years in 1899 emphasized. But the years up to the First World War saw the beginnings, very tentative and partial, of government involvement in the education of adolescents, middle-class as well as working-class.

The Education Act of 1902 can be seen as a first gesture, in that it brought rate and state aid to existing secondary schools and allowed the county and county borough councils, the new LEAs, to create additional secondary schools. The 1907 Free Place Regulations took the process a stage further, in earmarking a minimum proportion − 25 per cent − of places at secondary schools on the grant list, specifically for pupils from public elementary schools.[1]

Examinations for free places were thus added to the examinations already existing for the scholarships and bursaries to secondary schools provided from charitable and other funds; and often the same examination was used to select for both. As the Board of Education Report for 1923–4 put it, in a survey chapter on the development of secondary education, 'a first result, therefore, of the system was to extend and strengthen the existing scholarship schemes, in fact if not in name'.[2] The mechanism of these examinations represented a first attempt to relate the hitherto wholly separate systems of education: as the same Board of Education Report had it, it began to break down 'the middle wall of partition' between elementary and secondary schools.[3] But this mechanism could not − and was not expected to − provide for more than a tiny minority of young adolescents. Secondary schools were for the élite. Sir John Gorst, formerly Vice-President of the Committee of Council on Education, had told a British Association meeting in 1901,

while primary instruction should be provided for, and even enforced upon all, advanced instruction is for the few. It is the interest of the commonwealth at large that every boy and girl showing capacities above the average should be caught and given the best opportunities for developing these capacities. It is not in its interest to scatter broadcast a huge system of higher instruction for anyone who chooses to take advantage of it, however unfit to receive it.[4]

---

[1] See above, p. 110.
[2] P.P. 1924–5 xii Cmd 2443, para. 26.   [3] Ibid.
[4] Quoted in Banks, *Parity and Prestige*, p. 51. See also the remainder of ch. 4.

And many shared this view, without necessarily choosing to present it as 'in the interest of the commonwealth at large'.

But popular demand for 'advanced instruction' appeared steadily to expand. Manifested initially in the development of the Higher Grade schools, it was rapidly to transform what had initially been conceived as a qualifying examination for free places, into a fierce competition.[5] And although the school-leaving age had been raised to twelve only in 1899, a further increase was almost immediately canvassed.[6] Some more systematic provision for young adolescents who could not — or ought not to — find places in secondary schools appeared to be needed. Indeed, there were those, like Sir William Anson, Parliamentary Secretary to the Board of Education, who saw such provision as essential to the effective functioning of secondary schools as élite institutions. In 1905 he told the House of Commons:

If no intermediate type of school between the elementary and the secondary is created, I fear it will lead to the lowering of the standards of the secondary schools.[7]

and the Board's regulations of that year provided for the creation of new 'higher elementary schools'.

Many LEAs found these new regulations unduly restrictive. By 1917 there were only thirty-one such schools in England and a further fourteen in Wales. The more enterprising authorities sought to meet what they perceived to be the need in other ways. Exploiting the existing elementary-school regulations, the London County Council pioneered what they called 'central schools', aimed at children intended to leave at fifteen or sixteen and designed to 'give their pupils a definite bias towards some kind of industrial work while ensuring that their intelligence shall be fully developed'. Already by 1912 they had opened thirty-one central schools. Manchester followed suit, with four central schools. London and a cluster of LEAs in the North of England also developed

---

[5] See above, p. 108.
[6] Sherington, *Education 1911-20*, pp. 5-6.
[7] Quoted in Banks, *Parity and Prestige*, pp. 54-5. The paragraphs that follow, on higher elementary schools, central and junior technical schools, are based in the main on Professor Banks's discussion in chapters 4 and 8. The other direct quotation is taken from p. 98.

'junior technical schools', again intended for those staying to fifteen or sixteen, with courses in which manual instruction played an important part, and in some cases directly linked to particular apprenticeships and trades.

*

Despite all this activity, it would be difficult to argue that the essentially horizontal stratification of the educational system into elementary and secondary was either seriously eroded or directly challenged by 1914. Indeed, the limited, carefully controlled mobility probably reinforced the stratification, giving some flexibility and a new respectability. The War, however, greatly enhanced concern about the education of adolescents; and for a time, in the immediate post-War period, it looked as though this basic structure and stratification might, for the first time, be substantially undermined and directly challenged.

The sources of potential change were two: the reconstruction plans of the coalition governments of 1916-22 and the advisers of the Labour Party, now strong enough to bid for electoral power. Education figured substantially in the discussions of reconstruction initiated by Lloyd George's wartime coalition, and H.A.L. Fisher was offered a reforming brief when invited to become President of the Board of Education in December 1916. He introduced his first bill in 1917 and the 1918 Education Act received the Royal Assent three months before the end of the War.[8]

This Act raised the minimum school-leaving age to fourteen and gave individual LEAs power to raise it a further year, to fifteen, if they saw fit. LEAs were given a general instruction to plan for the extension, reorganization and overall integration of educational provision in the areas for which they were responsible. Such extension and reorganization were expected to include central and junior technical schools, as well as higher elementary schools and also 'continuation

---

[8] Sherington, *Education 1911-20,* chs. iv and v. I take the force of Dr Sherington's argument that Fisher brought no new ideas to the Board of Education; rather, he availed himself of thinking and planning already well advanced within the Board. But it seems to me still possible to contend that these ideas would not have reached the statute book when they did, and to the extent that they did, without the impetus of reconstruction.

schools', schools for the further part-time education of those who had left full-time education at the minimum age.[9]

The extent of the free-place system and the detailed organization of secondary schools were matters for circulars and regulations rather than legislation. In 1919 Fisher appointed a Departmental Committee to review the existing provision of local authority free places and scholarships tenable at secondary schools and institutions other than universities or training colleges, and to recommend improvements, 'thereby rendering facilities for higher education more generally accessible and advantageous to all classes of the population'.[10]

The Committee was chaired by Edward Hilton Young, MP, who had lost his right arm in the raid on Zeebrugge, a friend both of E.M. Forster and of G.M. Trevelyan, and, like Trevelyan and Fisher, a Liberal who threw in his lot rather hesitantly with that of Lloyd George.[11] It also included the usual selection of interested parties, among them Miss E.R. Conway and Captain F.W. Goldstone of the NUT, C.J. Phillips HMI, and E.K. Chambers, the Shakespearian scholar, but also Principal Assistant Secretary at the Board of Education.[12]

They appear, however, to have functioned reasonably harmoniously. They chose to take their cue from the general instructions at the beginning of the 1918 Act, commenting:

Section 4(4) of the Act effects a revolution and looks forward to a new order. . .
The wording of the Act suggests that the free place arrangements can no longer be based on a limited percentage of school places but should be based on the number of children capable of profiting.

---

[9] 8 & 9 Geo. V, c. 39.

[10] P.P. 1920 xv Cmd 968 – Hilton Young Report. In my account of the Report and in the discussion that follows, I have not dealt at all with the question of maintenance allowances and only briefly with debates about the abolition of all fees in secondary schools. Both, of course, have important parts to play in improving access to secondary education; but neither is central to my main theme, a consideration of the processes of classification at eleven-plus.

[11] *DNB*; Mary Moorman, *George Macaulay Trevelyan: a memoir by his daughter* (London, 1980).

[12] For Chambers, see also above pp. 149–50, and F.P. Wilson and John Dover Wilson 'Sir Edward Kerchever Chambers', *Proceedings of the British Academy* xlii (1956), pp. 267–85.

'Capable of profiting' they defined as follows: the child

must be capable intellectually both as to attainments at the appropriate age and as to promise and capacity. His previous education must have been such as to enable him to take his place without difficulty in the new school and his natural capacity must be of a kind to ensure that he will develop normally as he grows up in his school.[13]

But it was when they got down to the *numbers* of children so capable that they had a flight of quite striking radicalism: 'practically all children except the subnormal are capable in this limited sense', i.e. three-quarters of the child population, or about 2.75 million children. The current population of grant-aided secondary schools was, as they noted, some 300,000. Then they slid back down to earth with a bump. A realistic medium-term target would, they thought, be twenty secondary-school places for every thousand persons in the population, which, calculated on the basis of the existing population, would give a target of about 720,000 places. As for free places, 'perhaps we cannot say more than that the present percentage must be increased' and they suggested a minimum of '40% as an arbitrary and experimental figure' with which to begin.[14] The ultimate objective ought, however, to be the abolition of all fees for secondary education.[15]

They also addressed themselves to the age of transfer from elementary to secondary school and to methods of selection. Their witnesses were unanimous that eleven-plus was the appropriate age for transfer:

This conclusion, and we agree with it, is reached mainly on practical grounds but is not controverted by any evidence we have heard based on the nature of child development. Indeed, it has been put to us that the age of 11 does mark a definite stage in the development of most children, and that from 11 to 13 the changes taking place are as a rule so critical that a boy [*sic*] of 13 is not only two years older than he was at 11 but even a different boy. On practical grounds of school organisation, however, there seems to us to be little doubt that 11 plus is the right age for transfer.[16]

As far as methods of selection were concerned, they considered 'some kind of formal test' necessary and recommended that there be both a written and an oral test. The written test

---

[13] Hilton Young Report, paras. 24, 26, and 27.
[14] Ibid., para. 32. See also their comments later, in paras. 101–3.
[15] Ibid., ch. v, esp. para. 44.   [16] Para. 57.

should be confined to English and Arithmetic:

The reasons for confining the written examination to English and Arithmetic are clear. We have been told by a psychologist who has made a special study of the problem [Cyril Burt was the only psychologist among their witnesses] that at the age of 11 or 12 these are the subjects that correlate most closely with general capacity. Common sense suggests that the limitation of the test to these two subjects minimises the risk of special preparation and prevents the examination from dominating the syllabus and methods of the primary school. English should always be understood to include composition, and the papers should be framed so as to test power of thought as well as of expression. In Arithmetic the questions should mainly, but not wholly, take the form of problems. If these conditions are observed we believe that the object of the test, to discover capacity rather than attainment, will be better fulfilled than by any other form of written test.[17]

The Committee's immediate practical proposal — raise the minimum percentage of free places from 25 to 40 — was distinctly conservative. But the potential of the report as a whole was less so. Its assertion that 'practically all children except the subnormal are capable' of profiting in some degree from a secondary education came closer than any official, or semi-official, statement had before to the view that elementary and secondary education were not parallel and separate tracks with different starting-points, but sequential phases of one process. Its focus on eleven-plus as the appropriate age for transfer was of particular importance here. By saying that '11+ seems the right age to end elementary education and begin secondary education', the Committee was doing much to erode the notion of secondary education as a self-contained track, entered, more often than not, via the preparatory school at about age seven. If the ages at which elementary education was expected to end and secondary education to begin, were the same, then it became both conceptually and practically much easier to treat them as sequential phases of one process.

As the Hilton Young Committee had noted, there were good practical reasons for treating eleven-plus as the age of transfer, i.e. that was when it was tending to happen anyway. And in 1924, in its survey of the development of secondary education, the Board of Education explained exactly how

[17] Paras. 62–4.

this had come about and how vital the free-place system had proved to be in the process. Initially, in the early 1900s, elementary schools had tended to hang on to their able pupils as long as possible; also

children would not enter [secondary schools] as fee-payers till their last chance of a free place was gone, so that old free place pupils were accompanied by older pupils who had competed but failed... Hence a rule fixing the age for scholarships or free places which it was within the power of an Authority to make had a far-reaching influence on the whole entry.

In the years before 1914, London and Lancashire had been the trend-setters, in fixing the age at eleven-plus; but schools, especially the newer ones, with weak or no preparatory departments, and other authorities, had rapidly come to appreciate the advantages both of a uniform age of entry and a school life of reasonable extent. In 1910–11 as many as 36 per cent of the pupils entering grant-aided secondary schools had been aged thirteen or more. By October 1924 only 14 per cent of the entry was aged thirteen or over and by then 54 per cent of children entered between the ages of eleven and twelve, and the remaining 32 per cent between the ages of twelve and thirteen.[18] Subsequently, far more elaborate justifications for eleven-plus as the appropriate age for transfer, in terms of the physical growth and developmental psychology of the child, were to be offered.[19] But from Hilton Young onwards, it was axiomatic that eleven-plus was the appropriate age for change.

This point and many others in the Hilton Young Report were picked up and developed into a much more emphatic and aggressive public statement of the 'one-process' view in 1922. In that year, the Labour Party Executive approved and published a long memorandum, written for its education advisory committee by R.H. Tawney, with the title *Secondary Education for All.* This stated categorically that primary and secondary education should be the first and second stages of

[18] *Board of Education Report for 1923–4*, P.P. 1924–5 xii Cmd 2443, para. 29. The Board's Regulations for Secondary Schools from 1922 on positively discouraged entry later than the age of twelve and younger than ten - see *Board of Education Report for 1921–2*, P.P. 1923 x Cmd 1896, paras. 68–70.
[19] Hadow Report, paras. 87–8; *The Primary School*, chs. II–IV; Spens Report, ch. III.

a single educational process, through both of which all normal children ought to proceed. The memorandum transformed the Hilton Young medium-term target of twenty secondary school places per thousand of population into an immediate target and its long-term target of secondary-school places for 75 per cent of the elementary-school population into a medium-term target. Likewise, the abolition of all fees in grant-aided secondary schools was proposed as a medium-term target.[20]

The enthusiasts for reconstruction had thus contemplated a considerable enlargement of the state's responsibilities for the education of adolescents and the Labour Party had translated this into the slogan 'Secondary Education for All'. But neither group, in the years before 1939, succeeded in radically reconstructing the relationship between secondary and elementary – or primary, as some people were now beginning to call it[21] – education. Even as the Hilton Young Committee reported in 1920, the winds of the 'anti-waste' campaign were beginning to blow.[22] The modest proposal for increasing the minimum percentage of free places to forty was ignored. In January 1921 the Board of Education issued Circular 1190, suspending all schemes of development and re-organization under the first sections of the 1918 Act; and by the end of that year, battle had been joined over the proposals of the Geddes Committee to reduce the Education Estimates by £18m. Fisher eventually succeeded in whittling down the projected cuts by almost two-thirds, to £6.5m.[23] When the Coalition finally collapsed in October 1922 there was little to show for the great plans for the education of adolescents.

[20] *Secondary Education for All: A Policy for Labour*, ed. R.H. Tawney for the Education Advisory Committee of the Labour Party (London, 1922); on targets, see pp. 9 and 28.

[21] e.g. Tawney. More generally, people moved somewhat uneasily back and forth between these two terms throughout the period. Even the Consultative Committee's Report on *The Primary School* oscillated between the two; and it would not be entirely unfair to treat this as a classical Freudian slip, revealing the continuing power of nineteenth-century notions of education. But the importance of the term 'primary' to any serious attempt to view education as one process is self-evident, and is illustrated by the Hadow Report's determined preference for this term in the magnificently convoluted discussion of the meanings of 'primary' and 'secondary' quoted below, pp. 175–6.

[22] Morgan, *Consensus and Disunity*, pp. 241–6.

[23] Simon, *Educational Reform 1920–1940*, pp. 33–58. See also Morgan, *Consensus and Disunity*, pp. 288–95 and Sherington, *Education 1911–20*, ch. VII.

Children were now staying in school a year longer; although even the implementation of this had been delayed.[24] But it had been made clear to LEAs that the further increase in the leaving age, to fifteen, permitted by the 1918 Act, could not at this stage be implemented. LEAs which had begun to respond to the invitations, explicit in the 1918 Act and implicit in the Hilton Young Committee's discussion of the free-place system and the age of transfer, to plan for more extended post-primary provision, were stopped in their tracks. And continuation schools were officially abandoned, with only the ones at Rugby, which had succeeded in attracting the support of local industry, surviving.[25]

The situation of extreme financial constraint now taking shape, involving a necessity to battle even to maintain the status quo, let alone attempt any new development, was, as we have already seen from the discussion of special education, to prevail through this decade and the next, to the outbreak of war in 1939. Such constraint was, perhaps, less of a problem for the Conservatives, since their policies for post-primary education were less ambitious than either those of the Labour Party or those of the Lloyd George Liberals who had made the running in the coalition governments of 1916-22. Both Edward Wood, later Lord Halifax, President of the Board of Education 1922-4 and again 1932-5, and Lord Eustace Percy, President 1924-9, saw as their first priority the preservation of the élite position of secondary schools within any developing system of post-primary education.[26]

---

[24] Simon, *Educational Reform 1920-40*, p. 32.

[25] Sherington, *Education 1911-20*, pp. 161-3.

[26] See Percy's remarks in *Some Memories*, p. 101. It is one of Brian Simon's major themes in *Educational Reform 1920-40* that these two Conservative ministers had no policy as such, but simply reflected the Treasury view. For a more balanced interpretation, see Kevin Jefferys, 'Edward Wood at the Board of Education 1922-4', forthcoming in the *Journal of Educational Administration and History*, 'Lord Eustace Percy and "Higher Education for All", 1924-29', a draft chapter of his doctoral dissertation, and 'Sources for Conservative Party Education Policy 1902-1944', *History of Education Society Bulletin* xxx (Autumn 1982). Sherington has also argued (pp. 137-8) that this was basically Fisher's position, suggesting that behind statements about 'educational opportunities for all lay a view of secondary schools confined to the few'. Although, therefore, financial considerations came to displace all else in 1920-2, he was by no means sorry to see some of the more radical of the Hilton Young proposals shelved.

In general the Labour Party attached higher priority than the Conservatives to education in the allocation of limited resources. But Labour, too, accepted the overall limitations and the financial orthodoxy of the balanced budget. In addition, the challenge of 'Secondary Education for All' was less radical than it sounded. Burdened with hindsight, we translate this as meaning a common — or comprehensive — school for all adolescents. But this interpretation began seriously to be canvassed and to gain ground within the party only towards the end of the 1930s. For much of the period under discussion few Labour Party supporters who proclaimed 'secondary education for all' meant 'expand the existing system of secondary schools so that every child can move on there from the elementary school'. They were far more likely to mean 'expand the provision at existing secondary schools for children with an academic bent, and make new provision in schools such as central schools and junior technical schools, for those children of different aptitudes who are at present stagnating in the "higher tops" (as they were known) of un-reconstructed elementary schools'. There are real distinctions to be drawn between 'secondary education for all' and 'post-primary — or post-elementary — education for all'.

We can perceive the nature and force of these distinctions and the very gradual and partial nature of the shift within Labour Party attitudes and policy more plainly, if we look at the Labour Party's involvement with and response to the Board of Education Consultative Committee's discussions of post-primary and secondary education between 1924 and 1926, and 1933 and 1938. This involvement was continuous and real, since Tawney was a full member of the Consultative Committee from 1912 to 1931; while his fellow member of the Labour Party education advisory committee, Professor Percy Nunn, was co-opted to the special drafting sub-committee for the 1926 Report. The members of the Consultative Committee between 1933 and 1938 likewise included Albert Mansbridge, the founder of the WEA, the Labour Alderman E.G. Rowlinson, from Sheffield, and the Labour peeress, Lady Simon of Wythenshawe, whom Tawney advised and encouraged.[27]

[27] See the lists of Committee members prefacing the Hadow and Spens Reports;

The reference to the Consultative Committee in 1924 invited its members to consider the organization and curricula 'suitable for children who will remain in full-time attendance at schools, other than secondary schools, up to the age of 15'. Their report in 1926, known after their chairman, Sir Henry Hadow, as the Hadow Report, endeavoured to grasp various nettles. 'Primary education', they declared,

should be regarded as ending at about the age of 11+. At that age a second stage, which for the moment may be given the colourless name 'post-primary' should begin; and this stage which, for many pupils would end at 16+, for some at 18 or 19, but for the majority at 14+ or 15+, should be envisaged so far as possible as a single whole, within which there will be a variety in the types of education supplied, but which will be marked by the common characteristic that its aim is to provide for the needs of children who are entering and passing through the stage of adolescence.

And 'Primary' was footnoted as follows:

The peculiarities of English educational terminology are chiefly to be explained by its history, of which some account is given in Chapter I, and in the Notes on Nomenclature in Appendix II. The term 'secondary education' is at present employed in two senses; first, in the more general sense in which we hope that it may come to be used, to indicate the second or post-primary stage in education, in all schools of a secondary or post-primary type; and in the second place in a more restricted sense (in which it is ordinarily used today) as meaning the education given in schools recognised under the Board's Regulations for Secondary Schools. In Part iii of the present chapter we have suggested that it is desirable that education up to the age of 11+ should be known by the general name of 'primary education', and education after the age of 11+ by the general name of 'secondary education', the new post-primary schools which we desire to see developed being thus regarded as a particular form of secondary education. When we use the expression in the narrower sense (in which it is most commonly used today) we have placed it in inverted commas, except where the context excludes any ambiguity and in quotations from evidence where witnesses employ the phrase in their own sense.[28]

They went on to distinguish the different types of school giving secondary education by the following names: 'Grammar School', 'Modern School', and 'Senior Classes'.

Hadow Report, p. xvii; Simon, *Educational Reform 1920–40*, pp. 260, 263–4. On the Consultative Committee see also pp. 149–50 above.

[28] Hadow Report, para. 87.

The first is intended to be applied to schools of the existing "secondary" type which pursue in the main a predominantly literary or scientific curriculum, the second to schools analogous to the existing selective and non-selective central schools, the third to departments or classes within Public Elementary Schools, designed for pupils who do not pass to either of the above types of schools.[29]

In 1926 the Consultative Committee thus rejected an 'educational ladder' in the sense that a few children were selected to go on to secondary schools, while for the majority, the educational process then tailed more or less rapidly off. But this rejection did not entail also the rejection of classification and differentiation. At the end of their primary school careers children were to be grouped by aptitude, some to proceed to secondary 'grammar' schools, others to proceed to secondary 'modern' schools, and yet others to remain in 'Senior classes'. The report summed it up: 'all go forward, though along different paths. Selection by differentiation takes the place of selection by elimination.'[30]

The brief to the Consultative Committee in 1933 asked it to look at 'the organisation and interrelation of schools, other than those administered under the Elementary Code, which provide education for pupils beyond the age of 11+; regard being had in particular to the framework and content of the education of pupils who do not remain at school beyond the age of about 16'. Technically, therefore, it was supposed to look at secondary/grammar and junior technical schools only. In practice, the Committee found it impossible to exclude from its discussion the central schools and 'Senior classes' of the Hadow Report; these schools and classes might be conducted under the Elementary Code of regulations, but they actually educated a larger proportion of the post eleven-plus age group than the other two put together, and the Committee made no real attempt to exclude them from consideration.[31]

The eventual recommendations were in many ways a re-vamped version of Hadow, expanded to take account of technical schools. The 1938 Consultative Committee, under the chairmanship of Sir Will Spens, also argued for selection by differentiation at the age of eleven; the alternative post-primary routes the members now saw as three: the secondary/

---

[29] Para. 101.   [30] Para. 89.   [31] Spens Report, p. xix.

grammar school, the technical high school, and the modern school — central schools and 'Senior classes' collapsed into one. They continued to see these alternatives as best offered by distinct institutions; but they did at least consider the possibility of combining the three routes within a multilateral or common school and suggest that this might be tried on an experimental basis in sparsely populated rural areas.[32]

The majority of Labour Party members had greeted the Hadow Report with enthusiasm; and reorganization along Hadow lines was a central plank of party policy for the next ten years.[33] But by early 1938 the Party's new education advisory committee was taking an increasing interest in the idea of the multilateral school. At first it was suggested that there should be experimental schemes, as the Consultative Committee was to propose at the end of the year. But by the time the Spens Report was actually published, some enthusiasts had moved beyond this, to demand systematic multilateralism and to attack the Spens Report for its conservatism. The position has been admirably summed up by Rodney Barker:

The Labour Party was not perhaps publicly committed to the introduction of multilateral schools by the beginning of 1939; but it was publicly associated with the idea, and one of its policy committees was examining the implications of the various ways in which the new type of school might be developed. The party was to continue the examination, on and off, for the next twelve years, and was not to come to any firm conclusion until 1951.[34]

For all practical purposes, therefore, Labour policy on

---

[32] pp. xix–xxii, chs. IX and XI.

[33] Barker, *Education and Politics* chs. iii and iv, esp. pp. 57–8; Simon, *Educational Reform 1920–40*, ch. 3.

[34] Barker, *Education and Politics*, p. 74. As will be clear, I have relied heavily on Barker's discussion of Labour attitudes. Brian Simon's attempt to argue that the Spens Report contained 'On the one hand . . . recommendations which could easily be used to reinforce . . . differentiation at the post-primary stage and retention of the grammar school as sole road to the university. On the other hand . . . uncompromising advocacy of the substantive reforms required to introduce secondary education for all, concentrated together in Chapter 9. . .' (p. 263) cannot be sustained either by a careful reading of the Report or in face of the evidence offered by Barker. Simon's interpretation is more appropriately seen as a continuation of the arguments he, with others, was conducting within the Labour Party from 1938 onwards, in the effort to get the Party to commit itself to multilateralism and the common secondary school.

post-primary education in the inter-War years was that of the Hadow Report.

Party policies, Labour as well as Conservative, thus interacted with the financial constraints significantly to narrow the range of effective choice in policy for the education of adolescents and, one might say, brought it back to ground already familiar to us. The real areas for debate, disagreement and possible government action from the fall of the Lloyd George Coalition to the outbreak of the Second World War were two: the extent of the free-place system, with the linked question of the total size of the secondary/grammar sector; and the amount of money available for other forms of post-primary school, again with a linked question, that of raising the school-leaving age to fifteen. And the policies of successive administrations, despite much sound and fury, were essentially a series of see-saw variations on these themes. As Rodney Barker has put it, 'the major differences were over the speed and extent of reform, rather than over its direction'.[35] Although only Conservative politicians would cheerfully have accepted the description, policy-makers were still engaged in a species of ladder building not that different from the ladder building of the later nineteenth century.

The Hilton Young recommendations, as we have seen, had not been implemented; and financial problems from 1919 onwards had actually led to a decline in the total number of admissions and also of free-place holders, to secondary schools in receipt of government grant.[36] Edward Wood, the Conservative President of the Board 1922-4, secured Treasury agreement to begin to reverse this process, but the government fell before any action was taken.[37] In 1924 his Labour successor, Sir Charles Trevelyan, formally withdrew Circular 1190, inviting LEAs now to proceed with plans for reorganization. There was also some small financial encouragement to expand the number of secondary-school places in

[35] Barker, *Education and Politics*, p. 49. I am grateful to Kevin Jefferys for reminding me of this comment; and also for pointing out that the 'see-saw' effect was much sharper here than in the field of special education — see for example the issue of Circular 1341 in 1924 (above, p. 62) at a time when Labour was supposed to be 'reversing the engine'. Generosity in the field of special education was, of course, much less likely to pay any electoral dividend.

[36] See Appendix I, Table 1.1 below.

[37] Jefferys, 'Edward Wood'.

general and free places in particular; while the President
declared his willingness to receive plans from LEAs who
wished altogether to abolish fees in those secondary schools
for which they were entirely responsible.[38]

With the return of a Conservative government in November
1924 the pendulum swung back. The extra grant for free
places above the 25 per cent minimum was cancelled at the
beginning of 1925.[39] Then in November 1925 came Circular
1371, calling for a complete standstill in educational provision for the three years 1926-9 and replacement of the
percentage grant system by block grants. An unprecedented
public uproar led to the eventual withdrawal of this Circular.[40]
But under relentless Treasury pressure to hold down, if he
could not cut back, the Education Estimates, it is small
wonder that Lord Eustace Percy, the Conservative President,
barely responded to the Consultative Committee's urgings to
accelerate the process of reorganizing post-eleven-plus provision and firmly rejected its recommendation to implement
the raising of the school-leaving age to fifteen nationally,
within the next six years.[41]

The reappearance of Charles Trevelyan at the Board, with
the Labour government of 1929, brought another brief
period of 'go'. LEAs were once again encouraged to increase
the percentage of free places provided and to dust off their
plans for reorganization. The leaving age Trevelyan attempted
to settle once and for all by legislation, introducing no less
than three successive bills. But his Cabinet colleagues were increasingly preoccupied with the economic situation; while
the parliamentary supporters of the voluntary schools, in
particular the Roman Catholics, with whom, of course, it
suited the Conservatives to align themselves, defended their
vested interests with the maximum of obstruction. Eventually
in February 1931, in despair not only about his bill but also
about the performance of the government as a whole, Trevelyan resigned; and the third bill itself was lost in the general
crisis in August.[42]

[38] Barker, *Education and Politics*, pp. 49-55.   [39] Ibid., p. 56.
[40] Simon, *Educational Reform 1920-40*, pp. 84-115. For percentage and
block grants, see above, pp. 67-8.
[41] Ibid., pp. 132-41.
[42] Ibid., pp. 151-67; Barker, *Education and Politics*, pp. 60-3.

The crisis of 1931 brought about the severest pressure yet; and, as has been mentioned, the May Committee succeeded where Geddes and Lord Eustace Percy had failed, namely in putting an end to the percentage grant system.[43] Following another May recommendation, in September 1932 the President, Wood, now Lord Irwin, announced the abolition of free places as such. Instead, grant-aided secondary schools might offer a comparable proportion of 'special places': the parents of children successful in the competition for these would be subjected to a means test and could be required to pay part or even full fees. The schools were also required to raise the general level of their fees.[44]

A first gesture towards easement was made in 1933, with the reference to the Consultative Committee already discussed.[45] But, as we have seen, it took its members until November 1938 to produce their report. The first real sign of reduced pressure came only in 1936: the Education Act of that year provided for the raising of the school-leaving age to fifteen throughout the country in three years' time – on 1 September 1939.[46]

*

Mercifully for children and their parents, these oscillations of policy were mediated through the LEAs, most of whom could see more clearly than the centre appeared to be able to see the electoral, if not the educational, case for a measure of consistency.[47] Even so, 'stop-go' made its mark, as we can see if we look at the figures for the total annual intake and for the admission of free-place holders to secondary schools on the grant list over the period, set out below in Appendix I, Table 1.1.

[43] See above, pp. 68.
[44] Simon, *Educational Reform, 1920–40*, pp. 180–7 and Appendix I.
[45] See above, pp. 176–7.
[46] Not, in the event, implemented. By the beginning of 1936 only thirteen LEAs had exercised their right to do this under the permissive clause of the 1918 Act, repeated in the consolidatory Education Act of 1921 – Simon, *Educational Reform 1920–1940*, p. 219, n. 2.
[47] A theme worthy of a great deal more investigation. But see the mentions of feedback from Labour local authorities scattered throughout Barker's and Simon's studies; also the particular role of the Duchess of Atholl in conveying grass-roots and LEA opinions to Eustace Percy and to Baldwin – Simon, *Educational Reform 1920–1940*, pp. 90, 101-2 and 112.

Likewise the process of reorganizing all-age elementary schools into primary schools or departments and central or modern schools or departments, or into primary classes and senior classes, if the location of existing buildings and demographic patterns would not allow physical separations, was a slow and halting one. (Although it should be said that denominational vested interests interacted with financial constraints to play a part here.) Table 2 in Appendix I below summarizes the progress of 'reorganization' in the years after Hadow.

The difficulties faced by LEAs in trying to steer a steady course were not as great as they might have been, owing to the fall in the annual number of births during the War years and again from 1921 to 1933. The fall in the child population of school age in the inter-War years is set out below, in Fig. 1, of Appendix I; and its contribution in improving children's chances of access to secondary education can be seen in Appendix I, Table 1.2 and the commentary that accompanies it.

Even so, by 1938 only 13.2 per cent of children over thirteen and under fourteen in England and Wales were to be found in grant-aided secondary schools. In addition, against the relief afforded by the prolonged fall in the annual number of births must be set a continuing and apparently inexorable rise in expectations and, in particular, in the demand for secondary and other forms of post-primary education, on the part of the population at large. Such a rise is unquantifiable in any precise sense; but it seems likely that the first signs were there even before the end of the nineteenth century – the development of Higher Grade schools, the immediate transformation of the free place qualifying examination into a competition, and the first central and technical schools.

Despite the War, the pressure continued and, if anything, became more intense. In its survey chapter on secondary education, the Board of Education's Report for 1923-4 noted: 'after a few months' hesitation and perplexity at the beginning of the War, a new phenomenon became apparent – a real demand for education, or, at least a demand for places in schools, for which there was no precedent.'[48]

---

[48] P.P. 1924-5 xii Cmd 2443, para. 31. There was a similar increase in demand during the Second World War, linked with the increased prosperity resulting from

Table 1 in Appendix I below appears to confirm this. The Hilton Young Committee in 1920 acknowledged the pressure of demand; and on its tentative estimate, between nine thousand and eleven thousand children who had reached an acceptable standard, could not be found free places in 1919-20 — aside from the would-be fee payers who were also turned away.[49]

Government policies from 1922 onwards constituted a much more serious interference with the market than anything that had gone before; but contemporaries were in no doubt that the pressure of demand remained. Noting, in the Report for 1922-3, that the increase in secondary school admissions seemed now to have peaked and levelled off, the Board of Education ascribed this to a mixture of causes: lack of accommodation, fee increases, restrictions on the award of free places and more stringent entry requirements; but concluded, 'it would be unsafe to assume that the enthusiasm for secondary education which was so striking a feature of the years immediately following the War has been in any serious degree diminished'.[50] Eustace Percy had no grounds, either at the time or subsequently, for inflating this phenomenon. Yet, reflecting on the inter-War period in his memoirs, he wrote:

meanwhile, something was happening in the country which had hardly yet penetrated to the mind of any politician in Whitehall or Westminster. The demand for real 'equality of opportunity' in education was becoming nothing less than the main popular motive for political action. In many minds, this demand was, no doubt, a very crude form of idolatry, or, at any rate, a gross exaggeration of the advantages which the old 'governing classes' could be imagined to have derived from mere schooling. At its worst, it could become a rather repulsive design to use the State schools as instruments for propagating a revolutionary philosophy, as the 'public' schools were supposed to have inculcated a philosophy of oligarchy. But in the mind of the average elector, the demand proceeded from a much simpler appetite for the best available

the full employment of war time — see P.H.J.H. Gosden, *Education in the Second World War, a Study in Policy and Administration* (London, 1976), pp. 87-92. Increased prosperity probably contributed to increased demand during the First World War also.

[49] Hilton Young Report, para. 104 and Table D. See also the heavy reliance on this by Tawney in *Secondary Education for All*, esp. pp. 36-8.

[50] P.P. 1924 ix Cmd 2179, paras. 144-5.

standards of excellence in thought and manners and a not ignoble desire for access to the means of attaining such standards. And if those means were often conceived also as the means to power in the State for a new popular governing class, that did not necessarily render the desire less admirable.[51]

In reflecting thus, Percy was not intending to suggest that demand was evenly spread for all forms of post-primary education. His principal concern and interest was with the greatly enhanced demand for the élite education of the secondary/grammar school. And the sense that the educational ladder was still a reality in inter-War England is strengthened by the realization that 'selection by differentiation', as it developed, was very much a ranking exercise. Both *Secondary Education for All* and the Hadow Report had argued that the newer types of post-primary schools should enjoy 'parity of esteem' with the already established secondary schools; and at the end of the period the Spens Report reiterated this.[52] But the very words in which the Consultative Committee discussed its choice of nomenclature for the various types of secondary school in 1926, point to the unreality of such a proposition. As we have already seen, it proposed to talk of Grammar Schools, Modern Schools and Senior Classes.[53] It went on to explain:

The extension of the name Grammar School to cover not only the old foundation to which it is usually applied, but the larger number of County and Municipal Secondary Schools which have been founded since 1902, involves a new departure. But the name seems to us to have several advantages. It suggests a predominantly academic curriculum, in which languages and literature along with mathematics and natural science play a considerable part. It links the newer developments of secondary education to an ancient and dignified tradition of culture. Its associations are valued by the public; and we are informed that in some cases secondary schools established quite recently by Local Education Authorities have been called Grammar Schools for that reason.

For the second and third type of school [i.e. selective and non-selective central schools] a name is needed which indicates that their curriculum, as compared with that of the Grammar School, will be more realistic, in the sense of being more closely related to practical

---

[51] Percy, *Some Memories*, p. 94.
[52] Tawney, *Secondary Education for All*, pp. 109–13; Hadow Report, paras. 112, 142; Spens Report, pp. xxxv–vi and Ch. XI, para. 132.
[53] Above, pp. 175–6.

interests. The German name for such schools — *Realschulen* — does not seem to have any complete analogue in English. But we think that the word 'Modern' expresses adequately what we mean, and that it will convey to the public the right suggestion — that the education which these schools offer, without being primarily vocational, gives a prominent place to studies whose bearing on practical life is obvious and immediate. The term 'Senior Classes' proposed for the fourth type of school is not free from objection. We suggest it because it gives a general and simple description of arrangements, which, while varying largely in their form, are marked by the common characteristic that they are designed for the older pupils who have not been transferred to any of the three types of schools referred to above.[54]

The secondary/grammar schools were not only first in the field, they were also clearly established as élite institutions, both socially and intellectually, and the only route to university education. As Carr-Saunders and Caradog Jones remarked, in the second edition of *The Social Structure of England and Wales*, describing the fortunes of the elementary school leavers of 1935: 'of the various types of full-time educational institutions to which these children go, the secondary school is the most important in the sense that it is an almost indispensable step in the ladder leading to most of the better-paid vocations.'[55] It would have taken a massive transfer of resources and major changes in attitudes to higher education as well, to enable any new type of post-primary school to mount an effective challenge to this position; and neither of these was treated as a practical proposition.

Even if, therefore, selection by differentiation was a caucus race, in which everybody got prizes, some prizes were distinctly more attractive than others; and the development of both central schools and junior technical schools, in their different ways, made this very plain. The two pioneers of the central-school system, London and Manchester, had from the beginning conceived of such schools as selective institutions; and a number of other authorities followed them in this. Such selective central schools recruited at the same age as the secondary/grammar schools and by means of the examination competition already in existence for the award of council and

[54] Hadow Report, para. 101.
[55] A.M. Carr-Saunders and D. Caradog Jones, *A Survey of the Social Structure of England and Wales as illustrated by statistics* (second edition, Oxford, 1937), p. 119.

other scholarships and free places. The parents of children at the very top of the list in these competitions were, in theory, given a choice between central- and grammar-school places; and from time to time a central-school place was preferred to a grammar-school place. But the usual pattern was for the topmost tranche to fill the grammar-school places, leaving the central-school places for those just below them on the list.[56]

Judged by the criterion of external examination successes, the selective central schools were extremely successful. Yet by the beginning of the 1930s their popularity was on the wane and the actual number of such schools was being reduced. They had, as Olive Banks puts it, provided 'a cheap secondary education at a time when the demands for such an education far outstripped the power of the local authorities to supply it'. But increasingly LEAs — and parents — were coming to feel that the resources involved would be put to better use either in the pursuit of the real thing, or in the development of non-selective modern schools.

Junior technical schools, by contrast, were increasingly popular — a popularity to some degree reflected in the reference to the Consultative Committee in 1933. But this popularity was in part a function of scarcity — by 1936 there were still only 136 such schools in the country — and in part a function of their very clear vocational role and pay-off, increasingly prized as the depression deepened. On the other hand, the advocates of such schools consistently complained that under the Board of Education's regulations they were only allowed to recruit thirteen-year-olds. Exclusion from the selection process or processes that went on at eleven-plus meant, they argued, that the abler children were creamed off by grammar schools and central schools. And the Consultative Committee in some sense acknowledged the force of this argument by recommending in the Spens Report that the expanded system of technical schools, 'technical high schools'

[56] The fullest account of central and junior technical schools is that given by Professor Banks, *Parity and Prestige*, ch. 8, and in the main I have relied on this account in this paragraph and the two that follow. Professor Banks, however, claims that a majority of central schools were non-selective; whereas all the material concerning central schools which I have come across in investigating LEA eleven-plus selection and examining practices indicates that they were selective.

which they proposed, should recruit at eleven-plus, using the same examination as that for entry to the grammar schools.[57]

*

The inter-War years thus saw a gradual extension of state responsibility for the education of adolescents, involving thereby an attempt to bring elementary and secondary education into a sequential relationship. Integral to such an attempt was the establishment of a single age of transfer — the age of eleven. But the *process* of transfer, if not selective in the old absolute sense, was not simply a process of descriptive classification, it was essentially a process of ranking, reflecting a clear hierarchy among post-primary or 'secondary' schools. Selection for the secondary/grammar school was a very real phenomenon; and in this sense the old scholarship ladder lived on. Rising expectations and financial constraints enhanced the selective aspects of the classification process, creating something like a bottle-neck, which the oscillations of 'stop-go' only dramatized further.

The principal instrument in the process of selection/ classification, as practised by almost all LEAs, was of course a formal examination, which, taking place at the age of transfer, came to be known as 'the eleven-plus examination' or simply 'the 11+'. As we have seen, the Hilton Young Committee had firmly recommended a formal examination for the award of free places and secondary-school scholarships in 1920.[58] This was echoed and developed by the Hadow Report in 1926:

while we think all children should enter some type of post-primary school at the age of 11+, it will be necessary to discover in each case the type most suitable to a child's abilities and interests, and for this purpose a written examination should be held, and also, wherever possible, an oral examination.

and taken for granted in the Spens Report in 1938.[59]

As we have seen, the examinations for charitable and LEA awards were linked with and usually integrated with the free-place examinations.[60] Where there were selective central

[57] Spens Report, ch. XI, paras. 109–10.   [58] Above, pp. 169–70.
[59] Hadow Report, para. 157; Spens Report, ch. XI, paras. 110 and 140.
[60] Above, p. 165.

schools, the same examination was used to select for them, too. The Board of Education's *Memorandum* on the conduct of free-place examinations in 1928 noted that of the seventy-five areas so far monitored by the Inspectorate, in twenty-two a single examination sufficed for the award of all free places and the admission of all pupils to all secondary and central schools. In a further eleven areas the only other examinations were for the admission of fee-paying pupils to secondary schools.[61]

The transformation of free places into special places further dramatized and enhanced the role of this examination. The council scholarship/free-place examination was not, as the 1928 *Memorandum* reminds us, the only mode of entry into a grant-aided secondary school. Children whose parents were willing to pay the full secondary-school fees, might be required to take the free-place examination, or a scaled-down version of it, or an entirely separate test — all being closer to qualifying than to competitive exercises and thus of a lower standard. The replacement of free by special places in 1933, under which arrangement a special-place holder could, in theory at least, be required to pay the full fee, underlined the duality of standard as never before. Gradually a number of LEAs took the logical course and declared all their secondary-school places special places, recruiting by a single examination with a single standard, led, naturally enough, by those LEAs which had earlier, despite the opposition of successive Conservative administrations, declared all their secondary-school places free places. By 1938 this was the firm policy recommendation of the Executive of the Association of Education Committees; and it was also endorsed by the Spens Report. Finally, in 1938 the Spens Report recommended too that the eleven-plus examination be used also to select for places at technical schools.[62]

The eleven-plus examination thus became the pivot between primary and post-primary education; and a strong performance in it might alter, even determine the course of a child's life. Given what we know of straitened resources and rising expectation, it seems not unreasonable to expect it to have become the cynosure of all eyes, to expect to find

[61] Para. 6.
[62] *Education* 18 Mar. 1938, pp. 332–4; Spens Report, ch. XI, para. 139.

among policy-makers at all levels a steadily developing concern to make its operation as accurate and equitable as possible, making them, thus, an increasingly attentive audience to the arguments of the mental testers.

The discussion of the information available to, and the attitudes of, the Consultative Committee and Inspectorate in the preceding chapter conforms with and encourages this expectation. Against this background it is hardly surprising to find Brian Simon writing of 'the general use of group test results as the key to programmes of classification'. Much of his discussion of classification in the period 1920–40 is concerned with 'streaming', classification within the school; but in a section beginning, 'This was the climate in which the doctrine of mental testing was brought to perfection', he goes on,

> if children did not get to secondary school it was because they had 'failed' in selection tests, objective measures of whether the children had the capacity to profit from secondary education. The qualifying examination was imperceptibly replaced during these years by a system designed to ensure that only the right number of children did qualify, while the rest were eliminated. Nothing could have been simpler, once 'objective' tests were introduced, since all that was involved was the drawing of a line at the requisite point, decided by the number of secondary school places actually available, and declaring that children below that line had failed to qualify.[63]

The author of another major secondary work covering the inter-War period, Olive Banks, is both less pejorative and more direct. In claiming a 'greater attention to the selective process at eleven plus' during the late 1920s and early 1930s, she writes,

---

[63] Simon, *Educational Reform 1920–1940*, ch. 6, direct quotations from pp. 245, 248–9. 'Streaming' or 'setting' within a school does, of course, involve classification just as much as does the use of examinations to determine which schools children should attend from the age of eleven onwards. I have chosen to concentrate on the latter rather than on the former because it seems to me the more important version of classification, with all its consequences for the child's future. Streaming within the school was very often a consequence of the existence of 'selection by differentiation' at eleven-plus and derived much of its force and importance from the latter. In addition, information about the incidence and timetable of streaming is even more difficult to come by than information about the exact nature and conduct of eleven-plus examinations — see Appendix II — and there is not much precise detail either in Professor Simon's discussion or the sources he cites.

By the outbreak of war in 1939 the use of intelligence tests and standardised tests of English and Arithmetic with appropriate age allowances
had been adopted by almost every local authority, in an attempt to
ensure the maximum efficiency in the selection of children for the
places available.[64]

Neither author gives sources for these general statements;
and they are simply not true. Attention *was* increasingly
focused on the selective process at eleven-plus, but this did
not invariably lead to the adoption of mental tests. What,
then, did happen? Discovering how LEAs actually conducted
their eleven-plus examinations in 1919–39, and which of
them used mental tests and when and how and why, turned
out to be far from easy. The evidential problems are discussed
in detail in Appendix II below; and as this makes plain, the
generalizations that follow are not based on perfect knowledge. Whether perfect knowledge is attainable is another
matter; but it does seem possible now to attempt some
generalizations about orders of magnitude that are better
founded than those of Professors Simon and Banks.

There were in the period under discussion 146 LEAs in
England and Wales with responsibility for secondary education.[65] At least eighty-one of these, at some point, used
something they called an intelligence test in their eleven-plus
selection process. It is possible that as many as twenty-seven
more authorities also did so, although it is unlikely that, if
perfect information could be secured, the total would be as
high as 108.[66] Thus over half but under three-quarters of the
LEAs with responsibility for secondary education in England
and Wales in 1919–39 made use of mental testing. Moreover
the use could be intermittent; having tried a test or tests,
they did not invariably go on using it, or necessarily try any
other. Nor was this use always technically respectable; some of
the processes LEA officers dignified by the label 'intelligence

[64] Banks, *Parity and Prestige*, p. 129.
[65] This excludes the 'Part III authorities', so called because Part III of the
1902 Education Act gave them responsibility for elementary but not for secondary
education in their areas — see Gosden, *Educational Administration* pp. 179,
191–8.
[66] See Appendix II. These are final figures and supersede those given in the
earlier interim reports on the work represented by 'The Magic of Measurement',
'Measuring Intelligence', and SSRC Reports HR4204/2. 'Test use' is, however,
defined in its loosest and most all-embracing sense — see chapters 7 and 8 below.

test' would not have been — often were not — acceptable to contemporary specialists. As for standardized English and Arithmetic tests, fewer authorities still appear to have used these. Indeed, when their use can be identified, it seems often to have been a function of the decision to use Moray House intelligence tests and the subsequent discovery that, conveniently, Moray House could supply English and Arithmetic tests as well.

Thus, although the eleven-plus examination had come to dominate the transition from primary to post-primary education, the examination process itself could not be said to be dominated — so far — by mental testing and its associated techniques. Despite the increasingly clear and specific guidance being offered by the centre, a substantial number of LEAs took no notice. Chapters 7 and 8 explore the variety of local practice, providing the detail that underpins the generalizations of the preceding paragraph; and they try to make some sense of the activities both of authorities who appeared to take notice and of those who did not.

Chapter 7

The Clients of Moray House

The sequence of events between the first Northumberland Test in 1921 and the inauguration of the Moray House series of tests in 1925 is best described in Godfrey Thomson's own words:

Those Northumberland tests of mine were the beginning of a life-long task, which I have felt bound to persevere in for the sake of intelligent children. I began at once to receive requests from other counties and towns in England to make tests for them for their selective problems. For these they paid me fees such as they had been in the habit of paying to the examiners who previously had set questions for them in English, history and what not. Soon after I went to Edinburgh in 1925 I decided that I would safeguard myself from the temptation to make money out of this activity, and I devised a committee to receive all these fees, and the University of London Press royalties from the publication of my tests (after 1925 called Moray House Tests), and apply them to research in education, particularly research into the making and standardizing of tests. After a few years I took legal advice and had a regular trust deed made and trustees appointed by the University of London.[1]

Which these 'other counties and towns in England' from 1921 to 1924 were, it has not proved possible to discover. But the creation first of the committee and then of the trust, and the related expansion of activity, including the use of some of the material to train students in the Education Department in some of the techniques involved, brought more systematic record keeping; and some of this information can be checked against LEA records and HM Inspectorate's reports.

Before we begin to look at this in detail, however, two caveats must be entered. First, the Moray House Papers, now on deposit in the Library of Edinburgh University, although full and of vital importance, are not complete. Only gradually, as test use spread, did Thomson and his associates feel it necessary to keep a strict record of who was using which test, when. Thus although such records were kept for the

[1] Thomson, *History of Psychology in Autobiography*, IV, p. 286.

standardized Arithmetic and English tests — MHA and MHE — from their first devising, a similar record was begun for the intelligence tests — MHT — only with MHT 14. Users of MHT 1-13 have to be hunted out from the correspondence and analyses of raw data; and these papers are plainly incomplete. The three lists — contained in exercise books — have the occasional, apparently accidental, omission; but their coverage is more systematic than that of any other single source and on a handful of occasions in this chapter when no other source for test used is cited, these lists are the only source.

A second and much more serious problem is the poverty of the local authority sources. They are poor in two senses: much has been destroyed, or for other reasons not found its way into local archive offices. In addition, what does survive is very often disappointingly cryptic — minutes recording simply a decision taken, rehearsing none of the arguments or issues.[2] Thus the lists of the English — and the solitary Welsh — clients of Moray House up to 1940, and the years in which they used Moray House Tests, which follow, are probably reasonably complete and accurate. But when we move on from these to consider motive and intention, speculation will all too often have to take the place of hard information.

Table 7.1: *English and Welsh LEAs using Moray House Tests (MHTs, the 'intelligence tests') 1925-1940**

Authorities	Years in which MHTs used	
	1925-30	1931-40
(a) County Boroughs		
Halifax	1927-30	1931-40
Darlington	1928-30	1931-5 (?)
Preston	1928-30	1931-40
Barrow-in-Furness		1931-40
Newcastle-upon-Tyne		1931-2, 1936-9
Wakefield		1932-4
Doncaster		1934-40
Birmingham		1934-40
East Ham		1934-6
Norwich		1934
Huddersfield		1934, 1936-7
Dewsbury		1936-40
Liverpool		1936-9

[2] For a fuller discussion of these problems, see below, Appendix II.

Authorities	Years in which MHTs used	
Newport, Mon.		1936–40 (?)
Gateshead		1937–9
Salford		1937–40
Wolverhampton		1937–40
Croydon		1938–40
Southport		1938–40
St Helen's		1938–40
Stoke-on-Trent		1938–40
Tynemouth		1938–40
Smethwick		1938–40
Wigan		1938–40
Bradford		1938
Bolton		1939
Brighton		1940
Reading		1940
Oldham		1940
(b) Counties		
W. Riding of Yorkshire	1925–30	1931–40
Isle of Wight	1925–6	1931–40
Northumberland	1926–30	1931–40
Lancashire	1929–30	1931–40
Oxfordshire		1934–8
Warwickshire		1935–40
Leicestershire		1936–40
Cambridgeshire		1938–40
Devon		1938
Cheshire		1940

*1940 is of course my arbitrarily imposed date. Moray House continued to provide tests and to expand its clientele throughout the War and immediate post-War period.

Table 7.2: *English and Welsh LEAs using Moray House Standardized Arithmetic Tests (MHAs) and Moray House Standardized English Tests (MHEs) 1930–40*

Authorities	Years in which MHA and MHE used
(a) County Boroughs	
Darlington	1930–5
Preston	1932–9
Doncaster	1934–40
Leicester	1936–7
Newcastle-upon-Tyne	1936–8
Dewsbury	1937–40
Wolverhampton	1937–40
Huddersfield	1937

Authorities	Years in which MHA and MHE used
Croydon	1938–40
Bradford	1938
Reading	1938
Salford	1939
Tynemouth	1939–40
Brighton	1940
Gloucester	1940
(b) Counties	
Northumberland	1931–40
West Riding Yorkshire	1937
Devon	1938

One thing is immediately plain from these two tables: Moray House Tests become really big business only after about 1930-1. If we translate the lists into a series of maps — Figs. 7.1-3 — the point is dramatized and we see also that the pioneer users, with the single exception of the Isle of Wight, were wholly concentrated in the North. Even as late as 1940, use of Moray House Tests was still predominantly a Northern phenomenon.[3]

Amongst the considerations which appeared to weigh heavily with those pioneer Northern authorities in the conduct of their free-place and junior scholarship examinations, was equity. In 1920, Thomson, as the newly appointed Professor of Education at Newcastle, gave two Saturday evening public lectures on intelligence tests, 'in which I had become very interested'.

These led to an invitation from the education authority of the County of Northumberland to confer with them on a problem in which Dr Andrew Messer, chairman of one of their committees, thought intelligence tests might help. This problem was how with most justice to select 11-year-old children in the primary schools for the privilege of free secondary school education. It was a problem which had a personal interest for me for, as I said earlier, I would myself have had no education beyond the primary school, had I not won a free place in a secondary school in a competitive examination.

Northumberland had for some years held such competitive examinations at age eleven or a little younger, in the ordinary primary school

---

[3] In this context it should be remembered that Moray House also had a substantial clientele in Scotland. Their activities and preoccuptions lie beyond the scope of this book and would be well worth separate study.

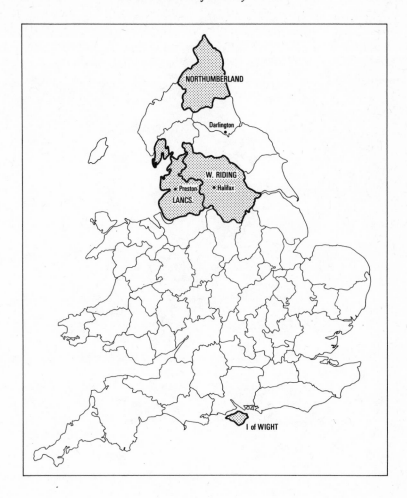

Fig. 7.1 MHT users 1925–30 in England and Wales

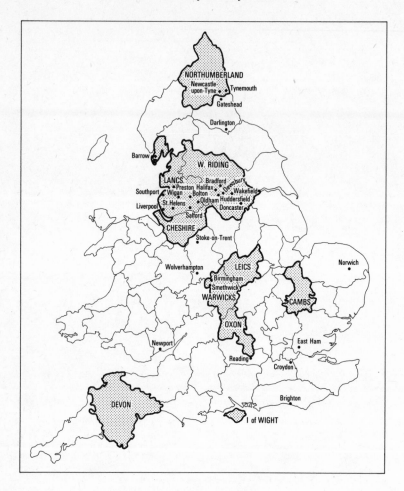

Fig. 7.2 MHT users 1931–40 in England and Wales

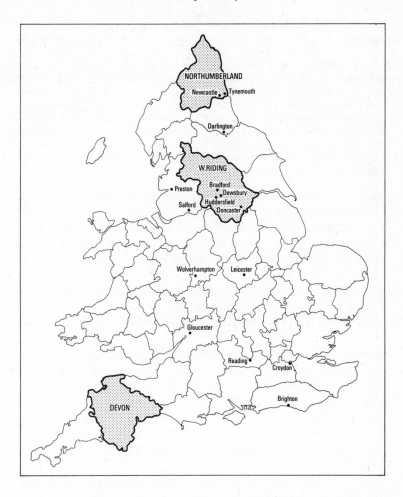

Fig. 7.3 MHA and MHE users 1930–40 in England and Wales

subjects. They had found, however, that a large number, indeed a large majority of the primary schools of the county never put forward any candidates, and that nearly all the free secondary school places were won by pupils from a few schools near Newcastle. Primary schools in the mining villages and in the remote valleys of the Cheviots did not supply candidates and this, it was feared, was because these schools could not compete with the better staffed and more lavishly equipped suburban schools in preparing pupils for such an examination. But intelligence tests, it was hoped, might discover in those schools some children of potential secondary school ability even if their environment and their poorer primary schooling had handicapped them in the existing kind of examination.[4]

This first experiment did draw 'a satisfactory number' of children from the small rural schools into the competition; and the next year Thomson was allowed to test the whole eligible age group, 'thus beginning a practice which I have since steadily recommended. The complete age group avoids sampling error, and socially it has the advantage that one is sure that if any intelligent children are missed, it will at least not be because they were not tested.'[5]

By June 1923 a special subcommittee reviewing the part played by the intelligence test was recommending both that it be given greater weight than the English and Arithmetic tests and that the free-place examination should also be used for the selection of fee payers at the grant-aided secondary schools. In 1924 and 1925, when Thomson was away in the United States, as Visiting Professor at Columbia, the authority, on his advice, engaged Cyril Burt to devise group tests for them.[6] Thereafter, they employed Moray House Tests consistently.

The problem of dealing fairly with children from widely differing backgrounds had also exercised the Lancashire County Council Education Committee for a considerable time. Not only did the Committee have urban/rural disparities of an extreme kind, it was also responsible for

---

[4] Thomson, *History of Psychology in Autobiography*, IV, pp. 284–5. See also Northumberland CC Papers, Minutes of the Scholarships and Exhibitions Sub-Committee 27 Jan. 1921. Details of the current locations of local authority archives are set out below in the Bibliography.

[5] Ibid., Report of the SESC 28 July 1921; Thomson, *History of Psychology in Autobiography*, IV, p. 285.

[6] Ibid., p. 286; Northumberland CC Papers, Minutes SESC 21 June 1923 and 31 Jan. 1924, and Report of SESC 24 Apr. 1924.

providing secondary education for the children from a number of Part III authorities, over whose elementary schools it had no control. Initially, it experimented with various schemes of allocating awards by districts and the use of an oral examination.[7] Then in 1923 a scheme was introduced whereby all elementary-school heads reviewed all eligible children and compiled two lists, the first of those they considered secondary-school material and the second of those they considered central-school material; the parents of all children on the first list were then invited by the authority to allow them to sit the free-place and county scholarship examination.

These adjustments by no means solved all problems. When the government Inspectorate reported on the Lancashire examination in 1927, it commented upon the subjectivity of elementary heads' conduct of the primary review — 'it is difficult to believe the cause of the variations lies entirely in the quality of the children reviewed' — and of the oral examinations, conducted by both secondary and elementary heads. When the HMIs met the Director of Education and LEA representatives in November 1927, discussion focused almost entirely on the problems of trying to achieve objective standards; and the Director of Education mentioned a plan to try an intelligence test in the next year's examination: 'the marks would not be included and at first at all costs (*sic*) the inclusion of the test would be merely experimental.'[8]

Actual practice was rather more constructive than this suggested. The Scholarships Sub-Committee reported to the Education Committee in May 1928:

The introduction of the Intelligence Test for the first time this year was intended to provide a supplementary means of detecting ability. No candidate who had reached the before-mentioned standards on the Written Papers was penalised by reason of a poor score on the Intelligence Test. On the other hand, however, certain candidates who had not scored the requisite marks on the ordinary written papers were found to have done very well on the Intelligence Test. After taking into account their ages, 184 such candidates were admitted to the Oral

---

[7] Lancashire CC Papers, Scholarships Sub-Committee of the Education Committee, Memorandum Sept. 1918, Minutes of 2 Dec. 1918. Report of the Conference 4 Nov. 1918, and Minutes of 2 Feb. 1920.

[8] Ed 77/54.

Examination, all of whom had written marks which were not more than 20 below the normal figure of 47.5 per cent. The Examining Board have recommended that such candidates should receive Scholarships if they secured 60 per cent of the marks at the Oral Examination; 93 out of 184 candidates complied with this condition.

There were also 62 other candidates who had satisfied all these conditions, but whose total marks on the Examination as a whole did not quite reach the standard which it has been customary to adopt for the award of Scholarships. It is clear they are equally entitled to Scholarships, and it therefore follows that as a result of the Intelligence Test 155 candidates have obtained Scholarships.[9]

By 1930 the Sub-Committee was prepared to go further:

as it stands, the arrangement limits the advantage of a high intelligence quotient to those whose written mark is relatively low, giving no such advantage to candidates whose written work places them in the upper part of the list summoned for Oral Examination, but whose Oral mark is not sufficiently high to gain a Scholarship. Stated in another way, the effect of the Intelligence Test in the past has been to compensate for a deficiency of Oral marks when the marks in the Written Test were relatively high. Now that the Intelligence Test has established its utility for candidates with lower marks in the Written Test, it seems reasonable and indeed logical to extend its influence to the candidates higher on the Written list. It is, therefore, suggested that those with the Intelligence Quotient already accepted as high enough to secure special treatment should be given a graduated bonus of 10 to 12 marks, so that a high Intelligence quotient may give an advantage to all candidates whose success is doubtful. This bonus will bring into the list 47 candidates who would not otherwise gain scholarships.[10]

The Sub-Committee was thus trying to use the Intelligence Test not only to compensate for difference in elementary schools' capacity to prepare their pupils for attainments tests in Arithmetic and English, but also to iron out some of the idiosyncrasies of oral examinations. The Sub-Committee was not, however, prepared to go as far as Thomson would have liked, and test the whole age group. The primary review was still left to the elementary heads.[11]

One of the further uses of an intelligence test, implicit — almost taken for granted — in these Lancashire discussions, was to help spread out the great cluster of candidates at the

[9] Lancashire CC Papers, SSC Minutes 7 May 1928.
[10] Ibid., SSC Minutes 5 May 1930.
[11] See the entry for Lancashire in Hartog and Roberts, *A Conspectus of Examinations* and the Moray House Report on the Lancashire Examination in 1934, printed as an appendix to this chapter.

borderline. This was a consideration which seemed to weigh very heavily with the West Riding of Yorkshire Education Committee when it introduced a group intelligence test (MHT3) in 1925. The Committee reported that the test

made it possible to select the borderline cases to be further tested by oral examination, not merely on the ground of their having come within an arbitrary distance of the qualifying standard in the Written Test, but also on the result of their work in another test requiring a minimum of acquired information and differing widely in character from the Written Test itself. The marks scored by a candidate in the Intelligence Test did not count towards the aggregate mark determining his success or failure in the Examination; they only served to decide, if he happened to be among the more doubtful of the borderline cases, whether he was worth testing orally. It is found that the introduction of an Intelligence Test has had the effect of awarding Scholarships to 165 candidates who otherwise would not have obtained admission to the Oral Test; on the other hand, it has excluded from the Oral Test 200 candidates who would otherwise have obtained admission to it.[12]

Thomson himself pointed out that the pattern of performance in the whole range of tests also underlined the wide differences between the criteria used by individual elementary-school heads in recommending children for entry into the examination; and he suggested that the intelligence test could in future best be used as part of this preliminary review and administered to the whole age group.[13] But this seems to have been consistently resisted; and Thomson's part in the examination was carefully limited by the authority to ordering the 'borderline' candidates — in 1933 alone, numbering 1,375.[14]

Discriminating fairly at the borderline also worried the only West Riding county borough to employ Moray House Tests before 1930, Halifax. The HMIs, discussing the problem with the LEA's Examinations Board in 1924, suggested that an intelligence test might be of greater help than an oral examination; but action was taken only two years later. The

[12] Moray House Papers, I, f. 10, Draft Report for the Education Committee of the West Riding of Yorkshire County Council, p. 5.

[13] Ibid., p. 22.

[14] Moray House Papers II, f. 26 Report on the West Riding Examination 1932; III, f. 71, Report on the West Riding Examination 1933; VII f. 9, Minutes of meeting of West Riding Central Examinations Council 28 May 1935; II, f. 26 Thomson to Hallam 13 May 1932; III, f. 67 Hallam to Thomson 27 May 1933; III, f. 69 Thomson to Hallam 30 May 1933.

first use of Moray House Tests, in 1927 and 1928, coincided also with a 'follow-up' investigation, which suggested that the form of examination the Examinations Board had been using had proved in a number of cases to be a very poor predictor of potential. By 1932 all attainments tests had been abandoned; and school record cards, kept from the age of seven, 'and the results of a qualifying Intelligence Test form the basis of an Order of Merit List of candidates for free places from each school'. By 1936 the intelligence test was being used also in the selection processes for fee payers at grant-aided secondary schools, entrants to central schools and entrants to junior technical schools. Conferring with HM Inspectors, 'the Chairman and several members of the [Education] Committee wished to be assured that the present method of selection was picking out the right people for advanced education. R[egional] I[nspector] thought there could be no doubt as to the general efficiency of the system' and with his colleagues, devoted energy instead to trying to reduce further the part played in the process by the last remaining vestige of the old arrangements, interviews by secondary-school heads.[15]

Perhaps similar considerations influenced Preston County Borough Council Education Committee; perhaps it simply followed where Lancashire led. Anyway, in 1928 Preston reorganized its procedures and instituted a compulsory first examination for all elementary schoolchildren aged between eleven and twelve, consisting of standardized tests of English and Arithmetic and a group intelligence test. In the view of the Inspectors, led by C.A. Richardson, who reported in 1935, 'the machinery and question papers are so near perfection' that most of the second examination which followed could be dispensed with.[16]

We are likewise in the dark about the context of the decision to employ a Moray House Test at Darlington in 1928. But the hint in subsequent minutes of some opposition

---

[15] Ed 77/126; Halifax CBC Papers, Minutes of the School Management Sub-Committee 17 May 1926; Ed 77/127; Ed 77/128 (the direct quotations come from these two files); Ed 110/84.

[16] Ed 110/103. There is no information as to whose standardized tests were used. The Moray House Papers suggest that use of MHA and MHE began in 1932. They also show MHT in use in Preston by 1930-1 — I, ff. 17-19.

to tests, the nature of the correspondence that developed between the Chief Education Officer and Thomson and then the disappearance of Darlington from the Moray House records after 1935, combine to suggest that the initiative was very much the personal one of Whalley, the Chief Education Officer.[17]

The only southern LEA, very much the odd one out amongst the pioneer users of Moray House Tests was, of course, the Isle of Wight. Thomson was invited to provide tests for the LEA in 1925 and 1926, each time at very short notice, giving him insufficient time to carry out what he considered adequate standardization.[18] Then he was dropped, only to be invited to contribute tests again from 1931 on. The minutes of the Higher Education Sub-Committee and the Examinations Board are not explicit about the reasons for either the invitation or the decision in 1926. But the Isle of Wight and the West Riding of Yorkshire were the two areas where Thomson collected data for comparison with his Northumberland data on the correlation between family size and intelligence.[19] In addition, the minutes of the Isle of Wight Examinations Board for the inter-War period as a whole indicate that the local teachers, both elementary and secondary, were very active in the affairs of the Board and that the use of an intelligence test was the subject of considerable dispute among them.[20]

The hand of the Isle of Wight teachers wishing to include an intelligence test in their selection procedures for secondary

[17] Darlington CBC Papers, Higher Education Sub-Committee Minutes 9 Feb. 1928, 15 Mar. 1928, 12 July 1928. The year 1935 is the last in which Darlington is recorded in the Moray House Papers as using MHT, MHE, and MHA; but an 'intelligence test' and a 'group test', type unspecified, are mentioned in the HESC Minutes 16 Sept. 1937. For Whalley's correspondence with Thomson, see below, pp. 215-17.

[18] Moray House Papers, I, f. 2, 'Moray House Tests 1-5: summary of their histories and formulae' — the tests used in IOW were MHT4 and in its earliest form, MHT2; also I, ff. 5-7 — the discussion of the Ready Reckoners for use with these. Isle of Wight CC Papers, Minutes of the Higher Education Sub-Committee 19 Dec. 1924.

[19] Thomson, *History of Psychology in Autobiography* IV, p. 288; above pp. 141-2; and Isle of Wight CC Papers, Minutes HESC 25 June 1926.

[20] Ibid., Minutes HESC 19 Dec. 1924, 24 Sept. 1926, 25 Feb. 1927, 16 Dec. 1927, 26 Oct. 1928, 28 Mar. 1930, 18 Mar. 1932, 26 Oct. 1932, and 23 Nov. 1932; also the Minutes of the Examinations Board 7 May 1932 and 29 Apr. 1939. See also the description of the Board and its composition in Ed 77/50.

schools was almost certainly strengthened by a rather critical report on those procedures by HM Inspectorate in 1927. The question papers were thought in general to be too difficult, including the question on the English II paper, described as a test of general intelligence, 'If a boy or girl whose home is in a tropical country came here to live with an English family, what customs would appear strange to him and what questions would he be likely to ask?'[21]

The main recommendation of the report was that the entire age group should be examined; and when at last, in 1931, this was acted upon, the examination consisted solely of a Moray House Test. Those children with an IQ of 110 or more (raised to 115 in 1934) then underwent attainments and oral tests.[22]

Wrangling continued, however, about the use of the IQ in calculating the eventual order of merit of those children who had gone through stage II of the examination. HM Inspectors, in the second report, advised that it should not be treated as if it were just another mark. This, however, was ignored; and interestingly, although the Board corresponded with Thomson over a challenge from a headmaster to some of the IQs assigned to individual children in his school, it did not, apparently, occur to members to consult him on this.[23]

*

The Isle of Wight may appear the odd one out, juxtaposed against the Northern pioneer users of Moray House Tests. But two aspects of its proceedings point to more general trends in the use of Moray House Tests in the 1930s: the key role of local teachers and the importance of the increasingly clear-cut guidance about the proper conduct of the examination coming from the government Inspectorate. Local teachers, of course, were important throughout; and any viable examination scheme needed their support as well as

[21] Ibid. This was cited in the section of the HMIs' report marked 'not for communication to the LEA', but no doubt the point was conveyed informally.

[22] Ed 110/19; Isle of Wight CC Papers, Minutes HESC 31 Oct. 1930, 28 Nov. 1930.

[23] Ed 110/19; Isle of Wright CC Papers, Minutes of HESC 23 Nov. 1932, 25 Oct. 1933; Minutes of Examinations Board 6 May 1933, 17 June 1933, 21 Oct. 1934, 12 Jan. 1935, 7 Nov. 1936, and 9 Oct. 1937.

that of the LEA's officers. The resistance to testing the whole age group in the West Riding of Yorkshire may well have come from the teachers;[24] and in 1922 the Northumberland branch of the NUT had protested — in vain — about the plan to test the whole age group.[25] But the Halifax teachers had had no complaints; and the teachers' panels advising the Dewsbury and Newport, Monmouthshire County Borough Council Education Committees respectively, seem to have played substantial parts in the decisions of both committees in 1936 to employ Moray House Tests in their special-place and junior scholarship examinations.[26]

Just as increasing teacher acceptance of test use was a feature of the 1930s, so was the increasingly sharp profile of the Board of Education and its Inspectors. C.A. Richardson, then the local divisional HMI, had had a hand in the original Northumberland experiment in 1921; and one of the Examinations Officers recollected the trio of Richardson, Thomson, and Dr Andrew Messer as sweeping all — including, presumably, the Northumberland NUT — before them.[27] But between 1928 and 1936, as we saw in chapter 5, the Inspectorate as a whole nailed its colours firmly to the mast in respect of standardized testing, through pamphlet 63 and its supplement, and its own experiments — using MHT 11 — in the early 1930s.

The tone of the confidential reports on the individual authorities also sharpened noticeably. In some areas this plainly had an effect. Oxfordshire County Council chose to interpret the Board of Education as *requiring* the junior scholarship examination to consist of 'papers in English (not "English Subjects") and Arithmetic and a written "Intelligence Test" '.[28] In five other authorities, Croydon, Liverpool,

[24] See the comments of the oral examiners on MHT in the draft West Riding Report of 1925, Moray House Papers I, f. 10, pp. 23-4.

[25] Northumberland CC Papers, SESC Minutes 28 Sept. 1922.

[26] Above, n. 15. Dewsbury CBC Papers, Minutes of the Higher Education Sub-Committee 23 June 1932, 13 Feb. 1933, 15 Jan. 1936, 22 Feb. 1936, 13 Nov. 1936, and 26 Nov. 1936. Newport (Mon.) CBC Papers, Minutes of the Examinations Board 21 Jan. 1935, 29 Jan. 1936, and 23 Mar. 1937. The information that the tests used are Moray House Tests comes from the HMIs' report Ed 77/136 in October 1938.

[27] Information from Mr G. Bosomworth, in response to GSQ 1975.

[28] Oxfordshire CC Papers, Education Committee Report on the Examination for County Junior Scholarships 12 Jan. 1938. The comment quoted is a retro-

Salford, Birmingham and Doncaster, changes in the conduct of the examination followed hard on the heels of critical reports. In Croydon the Inspectors waited until the re-organization of elementary schools was complete and a new Education Officer in post before making a second visit; but in 1937 a group of six, including Richardson, criticized an over-elaborate two-stage examination, recommending instead a single examination with an intelligence test and standardized English and Arithmetic papers.[29] In 1938 the authority went over to Moray House tests – MHT, MHE and MHA – lock, stock and barrel.[30]

Birmingham is a much more puzzling case. The authority appeared to be exceptionally well informed about the developing study of the psychology of individual differences. In 1919 C.W. Valentine, later to become Professor of Psychology at Birmingham University and active in the International Institute Examinations Enquiry in the 1930s, had become chairman of the Higher Education Sub-Committee; in 1920 the authority had commissioned Cyril Burt to investigate the incidence of mental defect in its schools.[31] Yet in 1926 it instituted what sound like distinctly home-made intelligence tests, to be marked by the clerical staff of the Education Office, in an exceedingly elaborate examination with six papers.[32] The authority's chief examiner at this stage was an outsider, B.C. Wallis, also employed at various times by other authorities;[33] and he rather vigorously resisted the criticisms levelled at the tests – that they were primarily

spective one. Characteristically the Appendix to the Report of the Higher Education Sub-Committee 18 Oct. 1933, reporting the decision to introduce a test in 1934, gives no reasons.

[29] Ed 77/109, Ed 110/71.

[30] The source for this is Moray House's own lists. The papers of the Croydon CBC Higher and Technical Education Sub-Committee throw no light on it; and the Education Officer's Report on the examination in 1940 simply refers to 'objective papers in English and Arithmetic, along with an Intelligence Paper'.

[31] Birmingham CBC Papers, Higher Education Sub-Committee Minutes 28 Nov. 1919 and Elementary Education Sub-Committee Minutes 21 May 1920.

[32] Ibid., Higher Education Sub-Committee Minutes 26 Feb. 1926; see also Minutes 25 Feb. 1927.

[33] For Wallis's appointment, see ibid., Higher Education Sub-Committee Minutes 23 Dec. 1925. He also worked for Brighton, Brighton CBC Papers, Secondary Schools Sub-Committee Minutes 22 Dec. 1925; for Liverpool and for the London County Council – see below, pp. 207, 261–2.

exercises in very careful and precise reading and far too easily coached for — by Inspectors in 1928. However, in 1934 a Moray House Test was used for the first time; and in October 1935 Wallis was replaced by E.O. Cutter.[34]

Wallis, ironically, turned up at Liverpool, as the new chief examiner in 1936, this time part of a reform package. The Inspectorate reported three times on the Liverpool examination, in 1923, 1932 and again in 1934, finding a great deal to criticize in the excessive difficulty of some of the papers and the enormous discretions allowed to the heads of the secondary schools involved: the whole enterprise seemed highly subjective, while the difficult papers exerted a damaging effect on the pattern of work in the elementary schools of the city. It was not easy, however, to change things: 'experience has shown that it is difficult to make Mr Mott [C.F. Mott, the Director of Education] take any official communication seriously'; and elaborate negotiations with the Chairman of the Education Committee ensued. Eventually in January 1936 the Board of Education was informed that Liverpool would appoint outside examiners, headed by B.C. Wallis, and borrow also the intelligence test so conveniently being set for Lancashire County Council by Godfrey Thomson. Inspectors debated the pros and cons of yet another inquiry, to follow this up; the Chief HMI for secondary schools remarking that they 'must proceed the more carefully because we have already had considerable trouble with Mr B.C. Wallis who is a bellicose individual'. Eventually in 1938 they again looked at the effect of the examination on the elementary schools of the city.[35]

Salford, too, proved sticky. The first HMIs' report in 1926 criticized the papers, set by the LEA's inspectors, as very poor discriminators, bunching marks badly and with no age allowance; but they noted gloomily the apathy and ignorance not only among the local inspectors but also in the Education Committee as a whole. By 1933 the authority had a standing Examinations Board, had made one experiment in 1932 with home-made intelligence tests, had introduced a very simple

[34] Ed 77/113; Birmingham Higher Education Sub-Committee Minutes 25 Oct. 1935.
[35] Ed 77/61 and Ed 110/92, direct quotations from minutes dated 1 Dec. 1934 and 28 Feb. 1936 in the latter file.

age allowance, but had still not faced the issues of standardization of questions and marking procedures. Very moderately
couched criticisms were, however, met with a cheeky response from yet another of the stage army of external
examiners, E.O. Cutter, who had replaced Wallis at Birmingham. 'He said he knew intimately the Examination arrangements of another LEA [i.e. Birmingham] which had all the
refinements which had been discussed and he doubted
whether their results were any better than those of Salford.'[36]
However, in 1937 the authority went over completely to
Moray House Tests.

The case of Doncaster is interesting because one of the
most scathing reports ever to come from the government
Inspectorate, in 1929, failed on its own to move the authority. Every aspect of the examination, from the home-
made, unstandardized, unclear, and badly balanced intelligence test, through the difficult Arithmetic papers, to the
essay questions on the uses of iron and the days of Robin
Hood, was criticized. The Inspectors concluded, 'it is impossible to speak with any confidence of the order of merit
as being a correct interpretation of the relative performances
of the candidates'. The Chairman of the Education Committee
instituted 'a full investigation', reporting in due course that
'there were no grounds for the allegations made'. But by the
time free places had been replaced by special places, 'the
Education Committee considered the report on the "Special
Places examination 1933" and discussed proposals regarding
future examinations: *Recommended* that for the 1934
examination Professor Godfrey Thomson of Edinburgh
University be invited to set questions for the Examination
for "Special Places" '.[37]

There are similar hints that the replacement of free by
special places made at least two other authorities look again
at the adequacy and equity of their secondary-school selection
procedures. In Bolton in January 1935 a special subcommittee
of the Higher Education Sub-Committee 'considered in detail

[36] Ed 77/67; Salford CBC Papers, Annual Report of the Education Committee for 1932, p. 67, 'Scholarships'; Ed 110/108, direct quotation from report
of the conference with LEA representatives.

[37] Ed 77/125; Doncaster CBC Papers, Education Committee Minutes 18 Mar.
1929, and 12 Oct. 1933. The three direct quotations come from these three sources
respectively.

the report of the Director of Education on the Special Place System and its effect on general entry to Secondary Schools'; and among other things, resolved 'to broaden the basis of the Scholarship Examination'. Examination arrangements for 1936 and 1937 included a 'Standardized Intelligence Test' unfortunately of a type unspecified. In July 1938 the 'examination supervisor' was packed off to a short course on the administration of intelligence tests at the LSE; and in December of that year the Higher Education Sub-Committee decided that the examination for 1939 would consist of a standardized intelligence test for all children in the appropriate age group, followed by a further intelligence test and standardized tests in English and Arithmetic for selected candidates.[38] One at least of these intelligence tests was from Moray House.

In Devon in 1935 pressure from one of the secondary schools for the use of an intelligence test seems to have coincided with the Higher Education Sub-Committee's review of the consequences of special places. The experimental test for 1936 was set by a Professor Watkins, for 1937 by a Mr R.K. Robertson, and in 1938 they tried all three Moray House Tests.[39]

As will already be plain, specially devised *ad hoc* 'intelligence tests', used by authorities before turning to Moray House, were by no means uncommon. These ranged through an enormous spectrum, from exceedingly sophisticated procedures in Leicestershire, through the do-it-yourself efforts of the Director of Education at Wigan, to the efforts of A.W. Wolters at Reading to argue that *his* attainments tests obviated the need for a separate test. Leicestershire, under its Director of Education, William Brockington, was one of the pacemaking authorities of the period.[40] It instituted a review of

[38] Bolton CBC Papers, Higher Education Sub-Committee Minutes 21 Jan. 1935; 21 Dec. 1936; 20 Dec. 1937; 18 July 1938; 12 Dec. 1938. The Inspectorate's report in 1929 had concentrated on the need for an age allowance and standardization of marking procedures — Ed 77/58 and Bolton HESC Minutes 17 Mar. 1930.

[39] Devon CC Papers, Education Committee Minutes 27 June 1935. Item 402; 24 Oct. 1935 item 856, 23 Jan. 1936, report of the Higher Education Sub-Committee; 21 Jan. 1937, HESC report; 22 July 1937, HESC report.

[40] Malcolm Seaborne, 'William Brockington, Director of Education for Leicestershire 1903–1947' in *Education in Leicestershire 1540–1940* ed. Brian Simon (Leicester, 1968), pp. 195–224.

its examination procedures as early as 1924-5, in the light of the 1924 Consultative Committee report on psychological tests of educable capacity. A subcommittee of teachers and administrators experimented, and recommended both a standard procedure for oral examinations, derived from individual tests, and a group test for inclusion in the written examination. It would, they thought, allow children from poor rural schools to show promise and help to spread out candidates at the borderline. The Central Examinations Board appears to have continued to compile its own 'group test' until Leicestershire went over to using MHT in 1936.[41]

Cambridgeshire, likewise, made a sustained effort to model its oral examination on an individual test: in 1925 'a passage and ten questions for use in the Oral Test were prepared; marks were assigned to each question and to the reading test, and the method of marking was standardised'. But only in 1938, guided by Eric Farmer of the Psychological Laboratory, University of Cambridge, did the authority resolve upon the inclusion of a group intelligence test; and in 1939, at the urging of Godfrey Thomson, for the first time tested the whole age group.[42]

The nature of the 'intelligence test' introduced in Barrow-in-Furness in 1924 is not specified;[43] but other enterprises seem to have been distinctly more Heath Robinson. The Director of Education in Wigan made up his own test, rather politely described by the government Inspectors as 'of an experimental nature'.[44] The test, author unknown, with which Norwich experimented in 1932 was, however, stigmatized as a test of 'information rather than intelligence'.[45] The tests of Dr Hoskin, an assistant master at the Junior Technical School, used by the Smethwick Education

[41] Leicestershire CBC Papers, QR 92 (1926-7) Appendix C, Report on Oral Examinations and Intelligence Tests, February 1926; Scholarships Sub-Committee Minutes 14 Jan. 1927, 11 Jan. 1929, 20 June 1931.

[42] Cambridgeshire CC Papers, Education Committee Minutes 30 June 1925, adopting the Higher Education Sub-Committee Minutes of 16 June 1925; 5 Apr. 1938, adopting the HESC Minutes of 1 Feb. 1938; 20 Dec. 1938, adopting the report of the HESC of 29 Nov. 1938.

[43] Barrow-in-Furness CBC Papers, Minutes of the Higher Education Sub-Committee 18 Feb. 1924, 28 Feb. 1927.

[44] Ed 77/70.

[45] Ed 77/85. Norwich is recorded in the list of users of MHT as using it once in 1934 — see below. But Moray House Papers III f. 20 shows Norwich trying MHT10 on a specimen group of children in 1932.

Committee in 1927, appear to have been abandoned by the time HMIs reported in 1934.[46] The Huddersfield Education Committee Examining Board chopped and changed, first devising its own tests, 'but the results failed to command general approval'. Then it gave standardized tests, nature unspecified, to borderline candidates; and finally, in 1935, to the undisguised relief of the government Inspectorate, it decided to administer a Moray House Test to the whole age group.[47] This was done in 1936 and 1937; but then Huddersfield disappeared again from the Moray House lists of users — as did Norwich after trying one Moray House Test in 1934.

Finally, at the other extreme of the spectrum from Leicestershire was Reading, where the chief examiner from 1912 to 1941 was A.W. Wolters. Over the years his approach to marking and age allowances got steadily more sophisticated, and all eligible children were required to sit the first stage of the examination.[48] But throughout, he took the view that 'intelligence' could perfectly well be tested within the compass of an ordinary attainments paper. This, however, presented problems both with setting and marking. As HM Inspectorate commented in 1928:

the tendency to regard the questions mainly as Intelligence Tests is reflected to some extent in the marking. In Question 6 for instance (I multiplied £3.15s.4 1/2d by 14 and then divided the answer by 7, what was the answer to this division sum?) correct answers obtained by a long method received only 20 per cent of the full marks for the question. A far better method is to have the paper of such a length that a candidate who wastes too much time on one question necessarily prevents himself from doing justice to the whole. The difficulty of marking equitably this particular type of question (the Intelligence Test question) is shown also in Question 8 (How many times can 3.05 be taken from 21.3805?) which is so worded as to suggest that a whole number answer is required; though in fact such an answer was not accepted and in most cases obtained no marks.[49]

In 1938 Reading tried Moray House English and Arithmetic

[46] Smethwick CBC Papers, Minutes of the Higher Education Sub-Committee 18 Oct. 1926, 2 Mar. 1927. The Inspectorate's report Ed 110/110 (1934) is, however, a curiously limp production for this date; and the Report on the Examination for admission to the Junior Technical School in 1936 shows Dr Hoskin's tests still in use for this.

[47] Ed 77/130; Ed 110/86.

[48] See e.g. Reading CBC Papers, Examiner's Reports to the Education Committee 1929, 1930 and 1937.   [49] Ed 77/18.

Tests. Then in 1940 it began to use Moray House group intelligence tests; and the following year Wolters resigned.[50]

Why Reading made the move to Moray House Tests, the minutes do not indicate; and we are equally in the dark about the context of the decisions first to begin testing and then to switch to Moray House at Barrow, Wigan, Smethwick and Huddersfield. Likewise, it has proved impossible to discover anything of significance about the circumstances in which decisions to use Moray House Tests — and in some cases then to drop them again — were made at Newcastle-upon-Tyne (1931-2, 1936-9), Wakefield (1932-4), East Ham (1934-6), Warwickshire (1935-40), Gateshead (1937-9), Wolverhampton (1937-40), Southport, St Helens, Tynemouth, Stoke-on-Trent (all 1938-40), Cheshire, Oldham and Brighton (all 1940) — and Bradford (1938). In Brighton the exceedingly professional external examiner in 1938 and 1939 had been William, later Sir William, now Lord, Alexander, the general of the Association of Education Committees in the 1950s.[51] Perhaps it was his recommendation? But Bradford is the most frustrating case. It had used Burt's group test in 1920.[52] In 1923 HM Inspectorate reported that,

The whole business of setting and marking *Intelligence Tests*, as in previous years, was carried out and a Report issued by the Intelligence Tests Committee, an unofficial body of persons interested in such tests and willing to cooperate in investigating their possibilities in Bradford. . . .
As in previous years the results were used in borderline cases only.[53]

Thereafter there is mystery. The minutes of the Scholarships Sub-Committee contain no reference at all to intelligence tests.[54] The authority responded to the survey conducted by Sir Philip Hartog and Gladys Roberts for the International Institute Examinations Enquiry between 1933 and 1935, by stating that it used an intelligence test;[55] but the Moray House Lists record only the use of a single MHT by Bradford in 1938.

[50] Reading Higher Education Sub-Committee Minutes 2 Jan. 1941.
[51] William Alexander, *The Educational Needs of Democracy* (London, 1940), p. 72. I owe this reference to Deborah Thom.
[52] See above, p. 133.   [53] Ed 77/123.
[54] Bradford CBC Papers, Scholarships Sub-Committee Minutes.
[55] *A Conspectus of Examinations*, s. 1. Wolverhampton replied likewise.

But it seems not implausible to suggest that by the 1930s two other related factors were at work, in addition to those tentatively sketched out above: a simple imitation effect, reinforced by personal links and contacts, and spreading awareness of the quality of the service provided. Barrow-in-Furness, in 1931, like Liverpool in 1936, found it very convenient to use the tests that Lancashire County Council was using.[56] Looking at the map once again — Fig. 7.2. above — it seems a possibility than an 'imitation effect' played some part in the decisions at Gateshead, Wigan, Southport, Warwickshire, St Helen's, Oldham, Newcastle-upon-Tyne, Tynemouth, Wakefield, Stoke-on-Trent and Wolverhampton.

Quality of service can be viewed in a number of ways. Employing Moray House could remove much, even all of the process of examining from the hothouse arena of local politics and vested interests. It was also relatively cheap. The 10,000 copies of MHT 11 required for HM Inspectorate's trials in 1933-4 cost the Treasury only £25.[57] Thomson's marking key meant that the marking could be done very quickly and cheaply — literally by the clerks in the office, if that was what the authority wanted. And the Moray House fee for the analysis of raw scores from all three tests MHA, MHE and MHT was a mere 18 guineas.[58] Birmingham, which did have the papers marked by the office clerks, estimated the total cost of examining the whole age group with a Moray House Test in 1936 to be within £100.[59] Because it was using the Lancashire MHT, Liverpool paid Thomson a fee of only 7 guineas in 1936 and 1937, plus the printing costs — in 1936 £10.5s.3d. By contrast, B.C. Wallis was costing 60 guineas plus his fare and a subsistence allowance of £1.11s.6d a day as Chief Examiner in English and Arithmetic.[60]

But the service provided by Moray House was also a service of quality in a more absolute sense: in the sense that the

---

[56] Ed 77/55.

[57] Ed 12/261 R.S. Wood to Secretary, Treasury 10 June 1933, Wood to Liddington (HMSO) 16 June 1933.

[58] See the reports on the Doncaster tests of 1934 and 1935, Moray House Papers II, f. 90 and III, f. 109.

[59] Birmingham Higher Education Sub-Committee Minutes 29 Mar. 1935; for the use of clerks to mark, see HESC Minutes 25 Feb. 1927 and 20 Dec. 1935.

[60] There were also nineteen assistant examiners for these papers, paid at piece rates — Liverpool CBC Papers, Education Committee Minutes, entries relating to Junior City Scholarship Examination 1936 and 1937.

most rigorous and sophisticated examining techniques then available were consistently and often informatively brought to bear on the problems of selection faced by individual LEAs. Thomson and his associates took infinite pains at every level: with the public relations and exposition of their activities, with the details of the conduct of examinations, with the analysis of the raw scores and with the constant reviewing and updating of tests.

The Moray House Papers for this period carry a series of notes on the history of groups of tests, their construction, initial use and standardization.[61] A major review of test structure was undertaken at the end of the 1920s and as a result, MHT 16 inaugurated a new, and in Thomson's view a more sensitive, test pattern. The Note on MHT 16 shows well what kind of care was taken:

Note on Moray House Intelligence Test 16.

MHT 16 was made according to the 'recipe' recommended by Sampson (See volume 2, inside front cover); namely,

Instructions 13 items	Reasoning 13 items
Same-opposite 12 items	Arithmetic 12 points
Analogies 11 items	Classification and Difference 11 items
Proverbs 8 items	Completion 7 items
Number series 7 items	Cipher 6 points

    TOTAL   100 points

The essential differences from earlier M.H. tests are:— a new form of introduction to the analogies items, thus:—
Look at this example:—

    (1) 'Finger' is connected with 'hand' in a certain way.
        With what is 'toe' connected in the same way?
        ...   .   (<u>foot</u>, knee, arm, shoe, nail)
    The correct answer has been underlined in the bracket.
Now look at example (2):—

    (2) 'Clothes' have a certain purpose for man. For what has 'fur' the same purpose?
        ...   .   (coat, <u>animal</u>, bird, skin, cloth)
You see clothes keep a man warm, and fur keeps an animal warm, so 'animal' is the answer to the question, and it is underlined in the bracket.

Now do these in the same way:—
'Wise' bears a certain relation to 'foolish'. What bears the same relation to 'love'?

        (stupidity, hate, liking, noble, great)

[61] See for example the notes on MHT 1-5 and on MHT 6, to the end of 1931 in Moray House Papers, I, ff. 2 and 14.

Introduction of a 'COMPLETION' passage (items 89 to 95), not used in M.H.T. 2.

Introduction (as 'classification') of questions involving underlining pairs of corresponding words:—

In the following lists of words there are two alike in some way. All the others are quite different. Underline in each case the two which are alike.

72.   cat, train, man, dog, fish
73.   elephant, satin, shoes, silk, butter
74.   merry, grotesque, happy, stupid, warm
75.   shilling, money, penny, sixpence, spend

The test was tried out in stencil form in Milton House School on 39 children average ages 11 yrs. 4 months. The resulting average score was 68.2 points, obviously too high.

A more difficult version was printed and tried out on 50 boys at James Gillespie's boys' school, on 7th November 1932. The average age in this case was 11 yrs. 9 months and the average score was 56.8. This was regarded as satisfactory, and with a few minor alterations, the test was prepared for use in England.

Standardization at Darlington. December 1932.
1275 cases in an 11 yr. old group, and a background school of 310 pupils between the ages of 8 and 12 yrs.
For results see pages 53, 54. For I.Q. statistics, page 55.[62]

In analysing the results of tests great pains were always taken; and Thomson took very seriously points raised by the officers of individual authorities who sent the raw scores to him and then had the job of conveying his analysis back to their colleagues, doing his best to ensure that they understood what was being done and why. In this way J.H. Hallam of the West Riding and J.G. Collier of Northumberland received a considerable education in mental measurement.[63]

But perhaps the most striking example of this was Thomson's correspondence with H. Whalley of Darlington. Whalley seems to have been already well grounded in the subject; and when in 1929 Darlington used NIIP standardized tests of English and Arithmetic alongside MHT 7, he straightway invited Thomson to advise on the proper relationship to be established between the three scores — which Thomson duly

[62] Moray House Papers III f. 57. Part of the preparation for this was Mrs Sampson's item by item analysis of MHT 12 and 13 in Moray House Papers II, f. 6.
[63] See the correspondence with Collier and Hallam scattered throughout Moray House Papers I, II, and III.

did.[64] Later in the year, reviewing the data provided by the 1928 and 1929 examinations, Whalley became concerned that 'the method of converting raw scores into an intelligence quotient seems to give an undue advantage to the very young candidate' and they engaged in a long technical correspondence before he was reassured on this point.[65]

Darlington children appeared to do exceptionally well in intelligence tests; and this seems to have been one element leading to the complete review of test structure in 1930-1.[66] It also fed Thomson's preoccupation with appropriate methods for standardizing group as distinct from individual tests; and in a long letter to Whalley of 6 April 1931, he foreshadowed some of the arguments to be set out in full in his *BJEP* article later that year. He began:

Your letter . . . raises a problem which, in a wider form than you give it, has been troubling me for some years. I fear I must write at some length about it.

No doubt the figures which you quote from memory from Burt are what he gave — 12% or 15% at and over IQ 115. In the group of very nearly 1000 Californian children upon whom Terman carefully standardized the Stanford Revision of the Binet Test, the standard deviation of IQ was almost exactly 13 points, which corresponds, with normal distribution, to about 13% of the candidates attaining or exceeding IQ 115, which falls between Burt's two figures.

The reasons for the departure from this at Darlington are to be found in one or more of the following. The phenomenon is not peculiar to Darlington, but I find it more marked there than almost anywhere:—

(1) Darlington children, as I have frequently told you, do very well in the group tests, often beating the expectation based on trials at other places.

(2) The Intelligence Quotients meant by Burt, and also those obtained by Terman are Binet IQs, obtained by individual testing. Group test IQs seem to show a wider scatter.

(3) There is a connection between the scatter of IQs and the age-allowance which the IQ procedure carries with it, and the endeavour to give the correct age-allowance implies permitting the scatter of the IQs to rise if there is to be consistency in the conversion of raw score into IQ.

[64] Darlington HESC Minutes 26 Feb. 1929; Moray House Papers I, f. 16, undated letter from Thomson to Whalley.

[65] Ibid., Whalley to Thomson 21 Nov. 1929, Thomson to Whalley 23 Nov. 1929, same to same 29 Dec. 1929, with postscript and tables.

[66] Ibid., I and II *passim*.

(4) The conditions of testing are different, at an examination upon which very much depends, and for which the schools have been preparing, from the conditions of testing envisaged by Burt; and the results therefore artificial and distorted from his point of view, though perhaps correct from that of the educational administrator.
(5) It is possible that the scatter of intelligence is actually, and not merely apparently, wider than Burt and Terman think.

I shall deal with these points in what follows, though as they are interconnected, I have not found it possible to take them one by one . . .[67]

Not all authorities, as we have seen, gave Thomson the scope that these three pioneer authorities had done. But when the Isle of Wight headmaster Mr Haddock complained about the IQ assigned to four of his pupils by the 1933 test, Thomson offered to embark on a series of further tests, free of charge, not only of these four but of a whole school. In 1939 he dealt patiently with lengthy questions about the precise instructions to be given to test invigilators.[68]

This kind of thing perhaps comes under the head of public relations; as perhaps also does the visit of his assistant, Mowat, to Dewsbury in 1937, to discuss trials of MHE and MHA as well as MHT.[69] But the invariable courtesy and care with which Thomson and his associates dealt with *every* point, however trivial, raised by an authority surely helped him in his efforts to improve more important aspects of its examining practice. In 1934 and 1935 Birmingham used Moray House Tests only on those children who chose to present themselves as candidates for the special-place examination. In his report on 1934 Thomson explained at length why it was much better to test a complete population. By the time he was ready to report on the 1935 examination, he was able to say:

we need not press in the report for the testing of a complete year group, as already Birmingham has decided to follow this plan in the new session. . . . and we welcome the steps which Birmingham is taking next year to avoid the difficulties and possible injustices which were inevitable in the systems of 1934 and 1935 and which were discussed at length in last year's report.[70]

[67] Ibid., I, f. 44. This letter replies to Whalley's letter of 1 Apr. 1931.
[68] Isle of Wight Examinations Board Minutes 21 Oct. 1934 s.v; 12 Jan. 1935 s. iv; 23 Sept. 1939 s. viii.
[69] Dewsbury HESC Minutes 26 Nov. 1936, 24 June 1937, 20 Oct. 1937.
[70] Moray House Papers VI, f. 62 Birmingham report, 27 Aug. 1935 — see also Birmingham HESC Minutes 29 Mar. 1935.

The classical report, however, was written for Lancashire in 1934; and it is so full and characteristic a statement of Moray House practice and objectives, that it is set out in its entirety as an appendix to this chapter.

*

Godfrey Thomson was not, did not choose to be, a publicist for his subject, a charismatic figure in the manner of Cyril Burt. But his gift for lucid exposition and what he himself admitted to be 'rather a flair for inspiring and conducting big surveys'[71] did much to disseminate information about and knowledge of mental measurement. It seems deeply ironic that the man who had effectively challenged the dominance of the idea of 'general intelligence' in the theory of mental measurement, who was on record as considering the multilateral or comprehensive school to be the most desirable form of post-primary school,[72] should have done so much to sophisticate selection processes for the élite secondary schools. But he was also a realist. Jennie Lee, who had been his student in 1925-6, recalled long afterwards, how he had compromised gracefully with all those timid students in his first Edinburgh lecture class, who demanded dictated notes instead of the reading and seminar work he had planned for them.[73] He could have done nothing to undermine the bedrock of assumptions, political, economic and social, on which the eleven-plus examination was erected. If selection, then, was the order of the day, let that selection be conducted as equitably, as carefully, as fairly as he knew how. He had been, as he pointed out, a scholarship boy himself, working his way up to university from the elementary school; and there was a particular resonance in his remark, 'Those Northumberland tests of mine were the beginning of a lifelong task, which I have felt bound to persevere in for the sake of intelligent children.'[74]

[71] Thomson, *History of Psychology in Autobiography*, IV, p. 294.
[72] On general intelligence and the factors of the mind, see above pp. 130-3. On his preference for the multilateral school, see *A Modern Philosophy of Education*, p. 209.   [73] Jennie Lee, *This Great Journey* (London, 1963), p. 69.
[74] Above, p. 191.

Appendix (from Moray House Papers III, f. 62)

COUNTY OF LANCASHIRE EDUCATION COMMITTEE
Report on the use of Intelligence Test 1934

We are informed that the Education Committee of Lancashire would welcome an explanatory report from us concerning the uses of an Intelligence Test in the Junior Scholarship Examination. For this reason we propose, in the present report, to give not only an account of the actual work we have done in Lancashire in 1934 with some discussion of the results obtained, but also a general statement concerning the importance of Intelligence Tests in County Scholarship Examinations.

Examinations in school subjects (say in English and Arithmetic) show which children have profited most by their schooling so far, but they do not always give a reliable indication of a pupil's ability to profit by secondary schooling. It sometimes happens that pupils of not great ability master the relatively easy and mechanical work of the primary school thoroughly as a result of hard work but their ability is insufficient, in spite of their industry, to enable them to achieve success in the more difficult and less mechanical work of the secondary school. It is also true that some teachers cram their pupils for a set examination more efficiently (if this is real educational efficiency) than others, so that results in an examination which tests schooling only may be misleading. Some children clever enough to profit by secondary schooling may not do themselves justice in examinations of school work as a result of having been absent when this work was taught. It is a pity if a disability which their inherent intelligence will overcome will prevent such children from gaining scholarships. The intelligence test makes a minimum demand on school knowledge. The questions set are upon a number of subjects which may be trivial in themselves but which serve their purpose in giving the child opportunity of displaying clear and accurate thinking on new and untaught problems. The more trivial or the more novel the questions are the less likely is it that schooling will influence the results and hence the more likely it is that the test is testing inherent ability.

A pupil's success in a secondary school depends very largely on two things, (1) the mastery which he has over the processes taught in the primary school and (2) his ability to master new work. The first of these is measured well by examinations in school subjects (but more scientifically by standardised attainments' tests) and the second by intelligence tests, so that the use of examinations or attainments' tests plus intelligence tests constitutes a very thorough test of fitness for secondary schools.

In an intelligence test there are very easy questions near the beginning. These have the effect of giving the children confidence. They also help to differentiate among very dull children where such differentiation is required. Intelligence tests also include very difficult questions as these provide the means of discriminating amongst the clever children. It sometimes happens that teachers or others criticise the very easy or very difficult questions of a test saying that these questions are too easy or difficult for children of the age in question, but when this assertion is made it is forgotten that the test is not constructed solely as a measure of more or less average children; it is meant to measure adequately children of all levels of ability. Children of age eleven or thereabout differ in intelligence to such a marked degree that the dullest will find difficult the easiest questions that one can devise and the cleverest will make a very creditable attempt to answer extremely hard questions.

So far this report has concerned itself with the nature of the questions comprising intelligence tests. The other virtues which such tests possess reside in their standardisation.

To standardise a test properly it is necessary to give the test in a given area to all the children of some particular age-range. This age-range may be quite wide but should not be less than a year. Suppose for definiteness that the test is given in an area to all children without exception who are over eleven years of age and under twelve. The intelligence test contains a large number of small questions. Each child's score is found by counting the number of questions he has done correctly. After each child's score is found (this score is called the raw score) the scores are arranged in monthly groups; that is, the scores made by children of eleven years 0 months are considered separately from the scores made by children of 11y.1m. and so on. The *average* scores made by the children month by month are calculated and it is always found that these averages mount fairly steadily.

Irregularities in the steps-up from month to month arise because the children born in one month may accidentally happen to be on the average slightly better or worse than those born in some other month. It has been found that the larger the area the less irregular are the monthly increments because the children of each month are then so numerous that accidental variations disappear in the averages. Since it is certain that apart from *accidental* variations the monthly averages would rise steadily the experimentally determined averages are adjusted until they do give equal increments from month to month. This adjustment is made by the mathematical method of Least Squares. This increment per month is obviously a scientifically determined age-allowance. It is the amount by which children of any month exceed in performance the children who are one month younger. Children of different ages can all be given the same chance at an examination if there are added to or subtracted from their score so many monthly increments according whether their age is so many months less or more than the basic central age of the candidates.

Unfortunately, except by good fortune, age-allowances do not turn out to be the same at all levels of ability. It frequently happens in an intelligence test or other examination that *very* clever children of 11y.0m. do so well that they could not possibly do very much better were they a year older. Unless the examination or test contains many difficult questions there is this lack of headroom which prevents clever children from 'expanding' so much in a year as do the average children. It accordingly follows that the age-allowance at high levels of ability may have, from the nature of the test (lack of headroom), to be less than it is for average children. The actual determination of these different age allowances is a technical matter which was first described by Professor Godfrey H. Thomson in the *Brit. Journ. Educ. Psychol.* Feb. and June, 1932. Unless age-allowances are scientifically determined it is very unlikely that they can be accurate.

A child whose raw score is the same as the average score made by children of precisely his own age is of course an average child and he is given the standard score of 100. It is clear that all average children, whatever their age, will have a standard score of 100. Standard scores are spread up and down from 100 in such a way that their spread, as measured by their standard deviation, is 15. These figures of standard score — average 100, standard deviation 15 — are the figures for Binet Intelligence Quotients so that standard scores are really Intelligence Quotients. The whole statistical procedure of determining for any test the ready reckoner by which to convert raw scores into standard scores is known as the process of standardisation.

The following facts stand out from the above:—

(1) To standardise a test it is necessary to test all the children of an age-group. If the dull children are omitted the average of the others will not be the average of the population and so could not correspond to standard score 100. This is the case in Lancashire. Only selected candidates are presented to the Junior Scholarship Examination and hence it is impossible to standardise a test on the candidates. For this reason in 1934 the test was given (a) to a group of 681 representative children of age 11-12, and (b) to a group of 182 representative children of age-range 8-13. It was on these representative groups of children that the test was standardised for Lancashire.

(2) The standard scores of different intelligence tests standardised on the same area are strictly comparable. This follows because the average ability and the spread of ability within the complete year-group of children will be the same from year to year. It is unreasonable to expect that the children of a large administrative area, when considered in the mass, should vary from year to year, and so the average standard score is made 100 and the standard deviation of scores is made 15 each year. The two tests remain absolutely comparable even if they are of quite different difficulty. If in the second year the test is more difficult the average score made by the children will be less and this less score will qualify for the standard score 100. There are obvious advantages in having scores that are comparable from year to year.

If tests are standardised on different areas the results are not necessarily comparable as the average mental ability in one area is not necessarily the average mental ability in the other. An area through the nature of its industries may have attracted a population which is more or less able than the population of the country as a whole. It is thus that areas differ in intelligence.

(3) An intelligence test when properly standardised makes exact and proper correction for age-differences.

The test used in Lancashire in 1934 was Moray House Test 16

(M.H.T.16). Just before this test was constructed in 1933 there was conducted in the Education Department, Moray House, University of Edinburgh, a careful research which made a critical examination of the earlier Moray House Tests. This research yielded most valuable results and has since served as a guide in the construction of our tests. M.H.T. 16 was made in the full light of this knowledge. We are accordingly satisfied that the test used in Lancashire in 1934 is very satisfactory as a test of intelligence.

The test was given on Saturday, 3rd March, 1934, and it was preceded by a preliminary practice test which was given solely for its psychological effect of preparing the children for the test proper. These practice tests give the children some practice in answering in the ways which tests demand. The test was taken by 5599 scholarship candidates whose official ages ranged from 11y.0m.–11y.11m. The test was given to (a) 681 unselected i.e. representative children (including candidates) of age 11y.0m.–11y.11m, and to (b) 182 children of a representative school, the children varying in age from 8 years to 13 years. It was from results (a) and (b) that we standardised the tests. We took care that the standardization was not out of line with the figures attained by the large group of candidates. As a result of our standardisation ready reckoners were made and sent to the County Office. From these ready reckoners the raw scores made by the children could be converted into standard scores (or I.Q.). An analysis of the figures shows that the average I.Q. of the scholarship candidates was about 100, whilst the best quarter of the candidates had I.Q.s of 116 or more, whilst the poorest quarter had I.Q.s lower than 105. I.Q.s less than 95 were very exceptional. This shows that the method by which Lancashire selects its candidates, whatever it may be, is quite effective in preventing pupils of really inferior ability from taking the scholarship examination. We do notice, however, that the preliminary selection of the candidates is not quite just to the younger children. In the six younger months of the year-group there were 2719 candidates whilst there were 2880 candidates in the older half of the year-group. The quarter year totals were 1343, 1376, 1400, and 1480. The differences in these figures are not nearly so serious as we have observed in some other areas, but nevertheless there is sufficient discrepancy to show that children born in some months find it a little more difficult to become candidates than children born in some other months of the year.

In 1934 for the first time the intelligence test occupied 45 minutes. The other authorities to which we give intelligence tests allow us 45 minutes, so that in 1934 it is possible for the first time to make just comparison between Lancashire and our other English districts. The 1934 results show us that Lancashire is neither ahead nor behind the general level of the country in intelligence. Lancashire is such a big county that in it there is demand for labour of all sorts, very skilled, somewhat skilled, and unskilled. We should therefore expect that to Lancashire there will have been attracted a very diversified population. For this reason it has been quite according to our expectations that we have found that the children of Lancashire are typical of England as a whole. To say that the children are neither better nor worse than the children of England generally implies neither praise nor blame of the County's educational efficiency. The intelligence test seeks to measure inherent ability and obviously if the ability which it actually does measure is inherent it is not dependent upon the school system.

Chapter 8

'On lines suggested by Monsieur Biné (*sic*)

We must now look at the pattern of test use elsewhere in the country. As the discussion of the clients of Moray House makes plain, the use of tests is not what is known as a 'dichotomous variable'. That is to say, the statement that a particular LEA used an intelligence test in its eleven-plus examination does not tell you whether the test was technically respectable or very much home-made. It does not tell you whether the authority examined the whole age group eligible or only some children in that group. It does not tell you how the test was marked and interpreted, what relationship was established between the test scores and marks in other parts of the examination. Nor does that statement convey anything about frequency of use; authorities might use a test once, regularly for fifteen years, for several years and then abandon it, or switch to another test. Conversely, the statement that an authority did *not* use an intelligence test tells you nothing about the examination procedures which *were* in use in its area.

Test use is thus simultaneously a very artificial and a very loose category. Attitudes to testing do not even resemble a continuum, more a series of intersecting planes. For this reason alone, the maps and lists which follow must not be treated as statements of great precision: they are rough guides to orders of magnitude and regional variations. In addition, as I have said so many times and shall have to go on saying, the information available so far is so patchy. In a number of ways this chapter and the preceding one are and ought to be sitting targets for the criticism and corrections of other research workers, perhaps with a local or regional focus, using local newspapers and individual school records, cajoling more papers out of education authorities' back files and basement dumps.

For all these reasons, the identification of motives for and objectives in the adoption of a particular mode of examining is near-impossible. It is very difficult even to discern any recurring patterns of activity among local authorities. Efforts to correlate the use of an intelligence test with a variety of geographic, demographic and economic variables yielded little that was illuminating.[1] What follows is thus essentially a rough descriptive classification of activity, with occasional glimpses of motives.

*

Altogether, thirty-nine LEAs are known to have used MHTs, an additional two authorities using MHE and MHA but not MHT.[2] A further forty-two also described themselves as, or were described as, using intelligence tests in their secondary-school selection procedures at some point or another between 1920 and 1940. Some of these LEAs may, in fact, have been using Moray House tests. It looks as though all the LEAs named in chapter 7 not only purchased Moray House tests and had them printed as part of their examination papers, but also made some use of the services of Moray House in the analysis of the test scores.[3] However, back numbers of Moray House Tests and scoring keys could be purchased on the open market — as the Board of Education had explained to the Treasury;[4] and it is possible that some of the authorities discussed below, described as using standardized intelligence tests of an unspecified kind, were using Moray House tests.[5] Anyway, crypto-clients of Moray House and all, they are listed below in Table 8.1 and mapped in Figs. 8.1 and 8.2.

Table 8.1: *English and Welsh LEAs using intelligence tests other than Moray House Tests in eleven-plus selection 1920–40**

Authorities	Years in which tests used	
	1920–30	1931–40
(a) County Boroughs		
Bournemouth	1922–5	
Burnley	1922–30 (?)	1930s
Leeds	1922– (?)	
Sunderland	1922 (?)–30	1931–40

[1] For a detailed report on these efforts, see Appendix II to SSRC Final Report HR 4204/2.   [2] Above, pp. 192–4, Tables 7.1 and 7.2.

[3] This is not absolutely certain, since the surviving Moray House Papers do not contain correspondence with every LEA named in their chronological lists of users.

[4] Above, p. 160 n. 79.   [5] I owe this point to Deborah Thom.

Authorities	Years in which tests used	
Wallasey	1922	
Barnsley	1923-6 (?)	1930s
Northampton	1924-30	1931-40
Oxford	1926-30	1931-40 (?)
Cardiff	1926	
Coventry	1929-(?)	
Southampton		1931
Bury	(occasional 1920s)	
West Bromwich		1931 (?)
Manchester		1932-40
Birkenhead		1932-40
Ipswich		1934-40
Portsmouth		1937-40
Nottingham		1930s
Bath		(occasional 1930s)
Derby		1930s (?)
Gt Yarmouth		1930s
Walsall		1930s

(b) County Councils

Northants	1921-30	1931-40
Surrey	1922-(?)	
E. Riding Yorks	1922/5 (?)	
Notts	1923-30	1931-40
Lindsey (Lincs)	1924 (?)-30	1931-40
E. Sussex	1924(?)-(?)	
Kent	1925-30	1931-40
Monmouthshire	1925-30	1931-40
Bucks	1925/6-30	1931-40
Westmorland	1925-6	1938-40
W. Suffolk	1926(?)-30	1931-40
E. Suffolk	1923, 1926-30	1931-40 (?)
Huntingdonshire	1926(?)-	
Gloucestershire	1928(?)-30	1931-40 (?)
Dorset	(1920s)	1933-40
N. Riding Yorks		1931(?)-40
Wiltshire		1932/3-40
Isle of Ely		1937-40
Worcestershire		1930s (?)
Kesteven (Lincs)		1930s

*The presence of a question mark and/or brackets denotes some degree of uncertainty, elaborated in the discussion of each individual authority below.

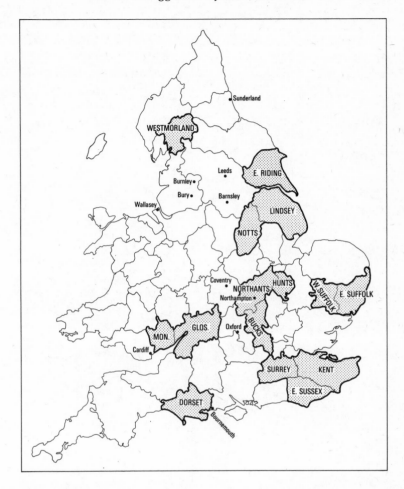

Fig. 8.1 LEAs using intelligence tests other than Moray House Tests 1920–30

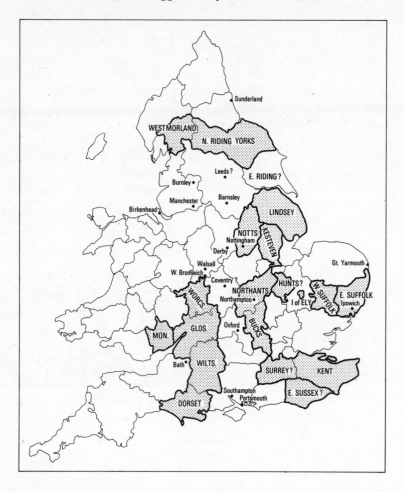

Fig. 8.2 LEAs using intelligence tests other than Moray House Tests 1931–40

Two points seem immediately worth noting about Table 8.1 and the maps in Figs. 8.1 and 8.2: markedly more authorities took initiatives in the 1920s than in the 1930s; and these early initiatives seem to have been randomly distributed around the country. The contrast with the pattern of use of Moray House Tests, initially concentrated in the North and having its most rapid phase of expansion in the 1930s, is plain. Taking a closer look, two intersecting principles of classification suggest themselves: choice of test — was it a recognized, standardized test, was it devised by an outside examiner, or was it very firmly home-made; and marking and interpretation of test — was it marked by an outsider, did he have any share in interpreting the scores and relating them to other marks in the examination, or were both marking and interpretation firmly an inside job?

In practice these give us four rough groupings of authorities: those where setting, marking and interpretation were all done by the authority's own teachers and officers; those where an outside examiner — or examiners — was brought in to set and usually to mark and have some say in the interpretation; those authorities where recognized tests were marked and interpreted by insiders; and, inevitably, those authorities where both provenance and interpretation of the test are unknown. There were also occasional instances when recognized and already published tests were set and marked by outside examiners, but they are not enough to constitute a significant grouping. In addition, as authorities' examining practices varied so markedly over time, these rough groupings must not be treated as mutually exclusive. I have discussed particular authorities' practices within one group rather than another because they spent more time on that particular mode of examining than any other, and/or because their conduct of that mode makes some more general point about the mode.

The unknowns, the cases where it has not so far proved possible to discover anything about the provenance or interpretation of the intelligence tests used, had best be got out of the way first. They are the county boroughs of Derby, Burnley and Walsall and the county of Worcestershire. All four responded either to the initial survey carried out by Sir Philip Hartog and Gladys Roberts for the International

Examinations Enquiry in 1933 or to its follow-up in 1935, with the information that they used intelligence tests.[6] In Derby the introduction of testing *may* have been part of the response to a highly critical Inspectors' report in 1929.[7] Burnley appeared to be experimenting with a 'General Intelligence Paper' as early as 1922.[8] But no more can be said than this.

The three groupings of authorities about whose activities we do know a little more, are similar in size. It is easier to deal first with the two sorts of 'inside jobs', authorities where recognized tests were marked and interpreted by the authority's own employees, and authorities where employees did the setting as well, before moving on to the near-un-classifiable activities of 'outsiders'.

Inside jobs — I

Twelve authorities can be discussed in the group of those where insiders used published, recognized tests: Birkenhead, Sunderland, Gloucestershire, Bury, Bath, Bournemouth, Ipswich, Nottingham, Parts of Kesteven, Dorset, Northamptonshire and Great Yarmouth. If there were crypto-clients of Moray House around, as I suggested earlier, this is the most likely group in which to find them. Only two, however, can be identified with certainty, Nottingham and Ipswich. The Nottingham records are quite infuriatingly cryptic: the first mention of the use of an intelligence test comes in 1936 when the Director of Education's Report on the Board of Education's Supplementary Memorandum requires no action, as 'local practice coincides with the recommendations'. Then in 1938 the decision to *cease* to use Moray House Tests is recorded, because the authority considers the children's performance in them can be improved by coaching.[9]

The Ipswich records are rather more informative. Having

[6] Hartog and Roberts, *Conspectus of Examinations*. All authorities named supplied returns to this survey, but this is not mentioned or cited as a source unless it is the only one for any given statement.   [7] Ed 77/32.

[8] Burnley CBC Papers, Higher Education Sub-Committee Minutes 9 Mar. 1922; see also Scholarships Sub-Committee Minutes 25 Feb. 1925.

[9] Nottingham CBC Papers, Secondary Schools Sub-Committee Minutes and Papers, Report of the Director of Education September 1936, Minutes 4 Feb. 1938.

begun with a two-stage, voluntary examination in the 1920s, its Examinations Board had moved by degrees to a first-stage compulsory eliminating examination, sat and marked in the elementary schools. Concern was then expressed, however, about the problems of standardizing such decentralized marking, and in 1934 it was decided to add 'a simple intelligence test (100 marks)'. The following year, it was decided that the intelligence test 'be obtained from Moray House'. The year after the authority went several steps further, in deciding not to include the intelligence test score in the aggregate marks; and to allow children near the borderline in the attainments tests but with a high IQ, to proceed to stage two of the examination.

In reaching these decisions the Ipswich Examinations Board was fully alive to the necessity of involving 'someone suitably qualified'; but it appeared confident that two of the women members of the Board, Miss Debenham and Mrs Morris, were equipped to do the work. In this and subsequent years Moray House Tests were used — there is reference in the minutes concerning the arrangements for 1937 and 1938 to an 'unpublished Moray House Test'; but in both years Mrs Morris undertook the checking of marking and made the decisions about the borderline candidates with high IQs. There is no hint of any Moray House involvement with the conversion of the raw scores or with any other aspect of the analysis.[10]

In only two other instances are the sources of the test named. The Inspectorate's report on procedures at Great Yarmouth in 1937/8 grumbled, among other things, about 'an Intelligence Test obtained from the Institute of Education but used as an examination exactly like the other papers and separately marked for boys and girls'.[11] Sunderland, where the test in use was named as the Otis, is discussed below.[12] More often, the Inspectorate remarks simply on 'a standardised test of the usual kind'; or Examination Board accounts record fees paid for marking but not for setting the intelligence test.

[10] Ipswich CBC Papers, Examinations Board Minutes 3 Oct. 1927, 7 May 1928, 1 May 1930, 7 Nov. 1933 (source of direct quotation), 20 Feb. 1934, 6 Nov. 1934, 12 Nov. 1935 (source of direct quotation), 10 Nov. 1936, 9 Nov. 1937; Ed 110/87 (draft HMIs' Report, 1934).

[11] Ed 77/83; see also draft in Ed 110/82.   [12] See below, p. 233.

Much the most common pattern of usage seems to be the inclusion of a test, usually written, but occasionally administered orally, in stage two of an examination; and some of the secondary-school heads involved seemed to have welcomed them as providing an alternative to or an extension of the standard interview. Bournemouth used a written test in stage two of its examination, replacing the oral, from 1922 until 1925.[13] The Northamptonshire examination from 1921 to 1935 involved a 'Mental Test', distinguished from both the Written and the Oral Tests, but apparently conducted by the oral examiner, as part of stage two.[14] Dorset likewise began with 'tests of general intelligence' included in the oral examination in 1923. But in 1934 it was arranged:

(i) That a standardized uniform intelligence test be given to all children who reach 40% of the marks in the Competitive Examination. ...
(ii) That the standardized intelligence test to be given be selected by a Small Committee of Headmasters and Headmistresses of Dorset Secondary Schools.

'Standardized' the test may have been, but Dorset allocated it a mark like the other papers and in subsequent years juggled with the totals.[15]

Secondary-school heads were in general much in evidence. In Gloucestershire, Kesteven, Bury, Bath and Sunderland, where the secondary heads effectively conducted stage two, they quite frequently used tests. The Inspectorate's report on Gloucestershire in 1928 commented that while the examining practices of individual heads varied quite a bit,

the commonest tests have been a written intelligence test, mental arithmetic, the reading of a passage aloud followed by questions on it, and an interview from which an impression is formed of the personality and general alertness of the child.[16]

[13] Bournemouth CBC Higher Education Sub-Committee Minutes 12 June 1922; 2 Feb. 1925, recommendation (g) of the special sub-committee on Junior Scholarships.
[14] Northamptonshire CC Papers, Higher Education Sub-Committee Minutes 12 Feb. 1921 Appendix A, 14 June 1930, 13 June 1931 and 11 June 1932. From about 1935 there seems to have been a written test paper, which everyone sat — see HESC Minutes 20 July 1935 minute 1139, 5 Oct. 1935 minute 1249 and 5 June 1939 minute 1890.
[15] Dorset CC Papers, Higher Education Sub-Committee Minutes 10 Jan. 1923, 19 Apr. 1934 item 69(c), 12 Oct. 1936 item 128(d).
[16] Ed 77/45; cf. also the report on Bury in 1928, Ed 77/60.

In the Parts of Kesteven one of the secondary schools involved regularly 'gives a short intelligence test and a general paper'.[17]

In Bath, as in Sunderland, an intelligence test was more the favoured ploy in the examination of the girls than in the examination of the boys. But in Sunderland in 1927, the Inspectorate was very critical of the way in which the Otis test administered to the girl candidates was marked: 'the score was counted as an examination mark, the Intelligence Quotient being worked out merely as a matter of interest'. Twenty per cent of the candidates turned out, however, to have an IQ of less than 100 — 'the bearing of this fact upon the system of entry for the examination is important.' In face of this, the Sunderland Higher Education Sub-Committee changed the next year to a system of compulsory examination with an intelligence test 'used as a check' on the attainments tests.[18]

Birkenhead, by contrast, earned the equivalent of a 'rave review' from the Inspectorate team — E.F.G. McCutcheon, G.R. Owst, C.A. Richardson, and M.P. Roseveare — in 1934. 'In their most recent development of a system of Intelligence Tests in connection with elementary school records for every individual pupil', the report began, 'they show themselves to be in the van of progress.' At the time Birkenhead still made use of attainments tests:

great attention is paid, however, to the preliminary data supplied by the Head Teachers of the Elementary Schools, showing their candidates in order of merit, according to their past school record and the results of Intelligence Tests applied to them in the schools. The case of every child placed high on those lists who has proved unsuccessful in the Examination is carefully scrutinized in the Office. For such children and those generally who figure just below the borderline of final awards, a further opportunity of proceeding to a secondary school is provided later in the shape of Deferred Scholarships from the Central School.

In the use and development of Elementary School Records the Authority is about to take a still more important and progressive step. A new School Record Card has been drawn up and, in future, it is intended that every child in the area shall be given an Intelligence Test at the ages of 5+, 7 or 8+ and 11+. These three independent estimates of the children's capacities should afford adequate material for the

[17] Ed 77/75 (HMIs' Report September 1934); see also draft in Ed 110/25.
[18] Ed 77/40 (source of direct quotation); Sunderland CBC Papers Higher Education Sub-Committee Minutes 18 Oct. 1927. For Bath in 1932 see Ed 77/98.

award of Special Places; and any investigation at 11+ of attainment in Arithmetic and English might then well be of a qualifying nature only, and not in any sense competitive.[19]

Birkenhead is the only clearly documented case of an authority beginning to use intelligence tests as the backbone of the school record in the 1930s, although Wiltshire and Kent, discussed below,[20] appear to have been moving in the same direction. But if this were to become a trend — as it seems to have done after 1940 — it might represent a more sophisticated use of intelligence tests than in the single sudden-death examination at eleven-plus, but it would also make a nonsense of any accompanying claims to treat the school record as an independent variable in the selection process.[21]

Inside jobs — II

There were thirteen authorities where the devising as well as the marking of intelligence tests seems to have been an inside job: Wallasey, Leeds, Barnsley, the Isle of Ely, Southampton, Manchester, Surrey, Nottinghamshire, Lindsey, East Suffolk, the North Riding of Yorkshire, East Sussex and Huntingdonshire. In the cases of Leeds, Surrey, Wallasey, Huntingdonshire, East Sussex and the North Riding, the available information is so thin that we can say little more than that.

The intelligence test being used by the East Sussex Examinations Board to discriminate between candidates at the borderline evoked no comment, positive or negative, from HM Inspectorate in 1929 — probably a good sign.[22] The Inspectorate's report on examination procedures in the North Riding in 1929 seems to have disappeared; and although the introduction of an intelligence test followed soon after, all we know from the Higher Education Sub-Committee Minutes are the names of the organizing committee of teachers who set and marked the papers.[23]

[19] Ed 77/25; see also draft in Ed 110/54.   [20] See below, pp. 239–41.
[21] Discussions with Deborah Thom first alerted me to the importance of this point.   [22] Ed 77/110.
[23] North Yorkshire CC Papers, Higher Education Sub-Committee Minutes 10 Dec. 1929, 9 June 1931, 10 May 1932, 9 May 1933, 10 Apr. 1934, 9 Apr. 1935, 10 Mar. 1936.

Leeds, Wallasey and Surrey were all visited by HM Inspectors in the first round of investigations 1922-3, when their comments were both less detailed and more tentative than they were subsequently to become. The test administered at Leeds *sounds* home-made, although clearly better devised than that used in Surrey, 'which might more properly be described as a *general knowledge* [*sic*] paper'.[24] Rather similar criticism was levelled at the 'General Intelligence' paper tried at Wallasey in 1922, which 'in effect amounted to a second paper on "English" and it has been decided to drop it in future — just as a miscellaneous paper on History, Geography, Nature Study and Science set in 1921 has already been dropped'.[25] And it looks as though the papers set for Huntingdonshire children after the Inspectors' visit in 1925 were also of this hybrid general kind:[26] the authority informed Hartog and Roberts ten years later that its examination consisted of 'Arith. Eng. and Gen. Information'.

Test design and content were likewise the subject of critical comment from the Inspectorate at Barnsley in 1926, Southampton in 1932, Manchester in 1933 and the Isle of Ely in 1939.[27] The variety of response from these four authorities is striking. The Isle of Ely simply ignored the comments.[28] Southampton and Manchester had both embarked on experiments with tests because of worries about discriminating fairly at the borderline. Southampton Scholarships Examination Board abandoned it after the single botched effort.[29] Manchester Education Committee, by contrast, worried away at the problem, Lady Simon of Wythenshawe asking HMI Miss T. Smith if *more* use should be made of intelligence tests. By 1938 Manchester had switched to using 'tests published by the University of London Press Ltd.' — Moray House? — although the marking and interpretation

[24] Ed 77/107 (Surrey); Ed 77/131 (Leeds).   [25] Ed 77/27.
[26] Ed 77/52; Huntingdonshire CC Papers, Education Committee Minutes and Papers, Report of the Joint Advisory Committee 6 June 1925, presented to the Education Committee 22 July 1925, agenda item (3).
[27] Ed 77/122 (Barnsley); Ed 77/49 (Southampton); Ed 110/93 (Manchester); Ed 77/22 (Isle of Ely).
[28] Isle of Ely CC Papers, Higher Education Sub-Committee Minutes 19 Mar. 1940 minute 555.
[29] Southampton CBC Papers, Education Committee Minutes 2 Feb. 1931 minute 6(c)(ii)(3); Ed 77/49.

were still done by its own Board of Examiners and the intelligence test was marked out of 100 like any other examination paper.[30]

The intelligence test devised in Barnsley by the Director of Education from 1923 disappeared soon after the HMIs' report in 1926. But by the mid-1930s some sort of intelligence test was again being used in the special-place examination, to select for both secondary and central schools. It is possible that like Manchester, the Barnsley Education Committee eventually turned to published tests.[31]

But not all LEA officers and teachers had failed fully to grasp the principles on which multiple-choice questions are constructed — as the Director of Education had done at Barnsley in the early 1920s — or — like the Isle of Ely authority in the late 1930s — cheerfully composed their tests by selecting the questions they fancied from a mass of published tests.

The home-made tests developed in Lindsey and in Nottinghamshire were thought to have their idiosyncrasies, but nevertheless to be quite serviceable as cross-checks on the attainments tests used in the examinations.[32] Nottinghamshire officers and teachers seem to have been particularly assiduous in monitoring their examination, beginning to experiment with an age allowance from 1928 on, scrutinizing question papers item by item; and in 1933-4 bad 'bunching' of the marks allotted for the intelligence test paper led to major rethinking.[33]

The activities of the East Suffolk authority received only a brief scrutiny from the Inspectorate in 1924.[34] But if the Education Committee's own reports are anything to go by, it too, like Nottinghamshire, worked to some purpose to

[30] Ed 110/93; reply by the Chief Education Officer Mr D.A. Fiske, to GSQ 1975, 19 May 1975 (source of direct quotation); Manchester CBC Papers, Manchester City Education Committee Prospectus on Scholarship awards, 1940, para. 2.

[31] Ed 77/122; Barnsley CBC Education Committee Minutes and Papers, Scheme for the Annual Examination of Pupils for admission to Secondary and Central Schools 1928, Triennial Report of the Education Committee 1936-9, s. II, Senior Schools.

[32] Ed 77/76 (Lindsey, 1927), Ed 77/92 (Nottinghamshire 1928).

[33] Nottinghamshire CC Papers, Higher Education Sub-Committee Minutes and Papers, Reports on the Examination for County Junior, Naval and Intending Teacher Scholarships 1924, 1925, and 1931-34, Minutes 1 Dec. 1925, 13 June 1926 and 10 Dec. 1935.   [34] Ed 77/103.

develop an effective test. From 1920 to 1922 the written papers in English and Arithmetic, which formed the first stage of the East Suffolk examination, were set and marked by an outside body, the Joint Scholarships Board,[35] and 'general intelligence' was examined in the oral which followed for selected candidates. But in 1923 a first effort was made by a small committee of elementary and secondary teachers, chaired by the Secretary to the Education Committee, to systematize the conduct of the oral examination; and 'a modified Mental Test' was set and marked by Mr Eldridge, the Headmaster of the Eye Grammar School, 'on lines suggested by Monsieur Biné' (sic).

By 1926 the local teachers were running a single examination with attainments tests and a mental test, and Mr Eldridge's contribution to the report suggests that he was now really getting into his stride, despite the office typist's continuing troubles with psychologists' names.

The tests used were group tests of the type now becoming fairly familiar in this connection; the first five groups of tests belonging to the classes called respectively Similars and Opposites, Best Meaning, Odd Word, Analogies, Best Reason. The last group was a series of five simple inferences from a test devised by Prof. Shearman [sic] for the use of which his consent was given. Of these tests the 2nd and 4th groups seemed to provide the greatest difficulty; there was no case in which all the tests of 4 were correctly answered. It may be that as no tests of this type had previously been set in the County Series of Mental Tests, the new form provided an extra difficulty. The average being the distinctly urban ones of Lowestoft, Ipswich, Bungay, Felixstowe, with East Bergholt in addition. The lowest average was at Yoxford, but the number of candidates there was small and its average therefore may be subject to special conditions. It is to be noted that if the Lowestoft totals are removed the County average would be distinctly lowered. The results raise interesting questions as to the distribution of mental power in the County, but there are not sufficient data from these results to answer such questions. The time allotted for the tests was, I think, too long and the averages may be vitiated by this. The time should be so arranged that only the best candidates can finish. This was obviously not the case, as the majority of the candidates attempted the last section. If a Mental Test is to become a standard part of the Minor Scholarship Examination, I should suggest either a shortening of the time allotted, or a distinct lengthening of the paper; the latter being the preferable course.

[35] For the Joint Scholarships Board, see below, p. 242.

In 1927 the examiners' report set out for the East Suffolk Higher Education Sub-Committee the precise function of the 'Mental or Intelligence test',

as a check on the results from the other papers worked and as a guide to the intelligence factor generally of the examinees.

The mental test paper was not standardized and therefore it is not possible to state with any certainty what mental age or IQ the particular scores indicate. But as a guide and a rough check it did good service and points out significantly that it is possible for a child to have good intelligence without equally good scholastic attainment. Modern Research goes to show that this type (the clever, high IQ child) suffers no harm from being called upon to exert its powers — indeed, it is the better for it.

Unfortunately, the sequence of reports seems to cease in 1927, so it is impossible to judge whether the momentum of development, as distinct from the use of tests, was sustained into the 1930s.[36]

Outsiders

Thirteen LEAs used intelligence tests devised, marked and to a greater or lesser degree, interpreted by 'outsiders'. They were Monmouthshire, Buckinghamshire, Portsmouth, Cardiff, West Bromwich, Coventry, Oxford, Northampton, Westmorland, West Suffolk, the East Riding of Yorkshire, Wiltshire and Kent. 'Outsider', however, is a blanket label covering everything from local amateurs to individuals and organisations with some pretensions to national reputation. At one extreme there was West Bromwich, where the single external examiner who conducted the entire examination was an outsider in the sense that he was not a regular employee of the authority; but in most other respects he resembled those Directors of Education and secondary-school heads with a passionate interest in testing, whom we have already encountered. His 'Intelligence Test, English' and 'Intelligence

[36] Reply by Mr F.J. Hill, Chief Education Officer of Suffolk to GSQ 1975, 18 June 1975; East Suffolk CC Papers, Higher Education Sub-Committee Minutes and Papers, 17 July 1923 Report for item 3 of agenda, 29 June 1926 Report for item 3(a) of agenda, 28 June 1927 Report for item 3 of agenda (these are the sources of the direct quotations). Reports on the 1934 and 1935 examinations in East Suffolk are filed with the HESC Minutes of 15 Jan. 1935 and 17 Dec. 1935, but they are not informative about the details of the intelligence test.

Test, Arithmetic' were definitely not orthodox; but HM Inspectors found them quite effective. However, his method of 'scoring' marks was like nothing they had ever seen before and they wished to know a great deal more before they could be convinced of the uses of this.[37]

Probably belonging here, in spite of her occupation, was Dr M.E. Bickersteth — 'a lady on the staff of the Education Department in Edinburgh University' — who conducted the oral examination of borderline candidates for the East Riding of Yorkshire authority in 1925. The examination included 'reading aloud, a short conversation (to discover interests, alertness etc.) and the answering, mainly on paper, of "Intelligence Test" questions'.[38] The oral survived in the East Riding until 1932; then in 1941 representations were made to the Higher Education Sub-Committee advocating the inclusion of an intelligence test.[39]

At the other end of the spectrum were authorities consciously looking for recognized expertise, notably Wiltshire, Portsmouth and Kent. Portsmouth came to testing late in the day, in response to the Board of Education's Supplementary Memorandum of 1936. The authority redesigned its whole examination in accordance with the Memorandum's recommendations, with a decision 'That the Intelligence Test be set by a recognized authority on the subject such as Dr P.B. Ballard or Dr Spencer.'[40]

The review of examination procedures in Wiltshire was prompted by the replacement of free by special places in 1932-3. The external examiner, responsible to the new Examinations Board, was initially Mr A.E. Chapman of Birmingham University, who was then succeeded in 1937 by Dr F.J. Schonell — famous to generations of post-Second World War teachers and children as the deviser of standardized reading tests.

[37] Ed 77/101 (1931).   [38] Ed 77/118.
[39] East Riding of Yorkshire CC Papers, Higher Education Sub-Committee Minutes and Papers, Minutes 1 Apr. 1924, 31 Mar. 1925, 9 Jan. 1933. Report of special subcommittee 14 Jan. 1941, item (6) Examination for East Riding County Minor Scholarships.
[40] Portsmouth CBC Papers, Minutes of the Examinations Board 30 June 1937, minute 546. The information as to whom they eventually employed seems to be missing. The Dr Spencer mentioned may have been F.H. Spencer, the recently retired Chief Inspector for the London County Council — see F.H. Spencer, *An Inspector's Testament* (London, 1938).

How expert Chapman was, when he first began work as an examiner, is uncertain: HM Inspectors had been somewhat critical of the General Paper he set at Coventry in 1929.[41] And it is not clear whether he introduced an intelligence test in Wiltshire straight away. But intelligence tests were certainly in use there by 1935. At the same time, the Pupils' Records Sub-Committee of the Wiltshire Teachers' Advisory Committee had invited Professor H.R. Hamley and Dr Field, and later Dr Susan Isaacs, all then at the Institute of Education in London, to advise them on developing pupils' record cards and measures of special aptitudes and personality traits as well as of intelligence. Between February and July 1935 over 800 children took part in field trials of the scheme devised.[42]

The Kent authority committed itself to mental measurement and all its works even more comprehensively than Wiltshire; and it is perhaps more than a coincidence that the Director of Education in Wiltshire, Keith Innes, was a protégé of the Director in Kent, Salter Davies.[43] The Kent Scholarships Examination Committee had, in fact, begun with homemade tests. But at the end of 1927 HM Inspectors had raised the question of whether the test scores were being used less as a cross-check on the English and Arithmetic papers and more as just another mark to be added to the total. In addition, the difficulties experienced by the Kent authority in trying to deal even-handedly with pupils from elementary schools in a number of Part III authorities as well as from its own elementary schools, were at least as great as those experienced by Lancashire.[44] The discussions generated by all this led, among other things, to a recommendation in 1930 that the intelligence test in the examination of 1931 should

---

[41] Ed 77/114. Chapman continued in Coventry, as in Wiltshire, until 1937, but it is not clear whether his intelligence test did — Coventry CBC Papers, Minutes of the Secondary Schools Sub-Committee October 1928, December 1932 and 6 Dec. 1937.

[42] Reply by Mr I.M. Slocombe, Deputy Education Officer of Wiltshire, to GSQ 1975 12 May 1975, accompanied by transcripts of Notes of Pupils Records Sub-Committee of the Teachers' Advisory Committee meeting of 28 Apr. 1934 and their interim Report, 1935. Wiltshire CC Papers, Education Committee Minutes 25 Nov. 1932 minute 809, 28 July 1933 minute 365, 29 Nov. 1935, 30 Oct. 1936, and 26 Nov. 1937.

[43] Toby Weaver, 'Education: retrospect and prospect: an administrator's testimony', *Cambridge Journal of Education* ix (1979), p. 6.

[44] Ed 77/53. For Lancashire, see above, pp. 198-200.

'be set by a psychologist to be specially appointed by the Kent Education Committee for the purpose'. Dr A.G. Hughes of the London County Council was duly appointed and acted in 1931 and 1932. In 1933 he was succeeded by Dr S.J.F. Philpott.

The replacement of free by special places brought further complications, in the view of a special subcommittee of the Scholarships Examination Committee; and it recommended that from 1933 English and Arithmetic should also be dealt with by external examiners. At the same time the sub-committee recommended a standard record form for use in schools, one of the questions on which was 'General ability and Terman mental ratio (if known) giving date taken'. Philpott's colleague as examiner in 1933 was P.B. Ballard and then in 1934 Professor H.R. Hamley; and all three wrote at length in the *Kent Education Gazette*, the official monthly journal of the Kent LEA, on the tests they had devised, their rationale and the patterns of performance. In addition, in June 1933 Ballard appealed in the *Gazette* for head teachers to volunteer to assist in the standardization of his Group Test of Intelligence for juniors 'in order that the test could be available for use in connexion with the Record Card'.[45] Both Kent and Wiltshire were, in effect, providing considerable in-service training in mental measurement and associated techniques for their teachers in the mid-1930s.

A similar educative function was probably performed by the Revd A. Donald Amos, Master of Method in the Education School at University College, Cardiff, who devised intelligence tests for Monmouthshire Education Committee from 1925 to 1946. The pamphlet of guidance he produced for Monmouthshire teachers in 1937 referred to an initial period of experiment 1925–31 with different forms of tests, on which many teachers had commented; and one of the objectives of the pamphlet was to indicate 'how the children may best be made familiar with tests of this kind'.

Although Amos advised no other authority, apart from

[45] Ed 77/53; Kent CC Papers, CC/MC 15/12 Minutes of the Scholarship Examinations Sub-Committee 2 Feb. 1927, 14 Dec. 1927, 9 July 1930, 12 Nov. 1930 (source of direct quotation), 4 Mar. 1931, 3 Oct. 1931, 29 June 1932 and 30 Sept. 1932; C/E 10/14 *Kent Education Gazette* January 1934, February 1934, March 1934 (source of direct quotation), December 1934 and January 1935.

setting a single experimental test for the Cardiff Education Committee in 1926, his standing was sufficient for him to publish in the very first number of the *BJEP* (February 1931) on 'Examination and Intelligence — Test Forecasts of School Achievement'. And surviving examination papers 1936-40 show a familiar sequence of Instructions and Simple Reasoning Tests, Completion Tests, Absurdities Tests, Tests of Classification and Analogies. Almost all are verbal tests; there are very few numerical or spatial tests. Even so, it cannot have been too great a shock for the local children when the authority went over to using Moray House Tests in 1947.[46]

The other two remaining groups of 'outsiders' are much more difficult to categorize than either the enthusiastic amateurs or the proselytizing professional psychologists; nor can they be comfortably placed in a continuum between these two poles. They were in certain senses professional and their approach to attainments tests was usually technically quite sophisticated, but their approach to intelligence tests was rather less so. The two bodies concerned are the Joint Scholarships Board and the NUT Examinations Board. The Joint Scholarships Board is not much more than a name from the early 1920s. It seems to have been a free-lance examining body, but in so far as it assumes flesh at all, it took the person of its chief examiners, first Mr Evan Small and then Dr Grace Perrie Williams. By about 1927 no more is heard of the Board and Dr Perrie Williams is functioning in her own right. Though neither was 'a bellicose individual', they seem most to resemble Mr B.C. Wallis, who was employed at different times by Liverpool, Birmingham, Brighton, and London;[47] and like him, they worked both for authorities who used intelligence tests and those who did not. Thus, representing the Joint Scholarships Board, they examined for East Suffolk 1920-3, before the teachers took over all the examination.[48]

[46] Reply by Mr T.M. Morgan, Director of Education for Gwent, to GSQ 1975, 6 May 1975; Monmouthshire CC Papers, A. Donald Amos, *A Preparatory Guide to the Gwent Intelligence Tests* (Monmouthshire, 1937), Examination Papers 1936-40, General Intelligence Tests. For the Cardiff experiment, see Cardiff CBC Papers, Minutes of the Secondary Schools Sub-Committee 9 Apr. 1925 and 11 Mar. 1926.

[47] See above, pp. 206-7 and below, pp. 261-2.

[48] East Suffolk CC Papers, Report of the Chief Examiner on the Minor Scholarships 1922, with minutes HESC 14 June 1922, ditto 1923, with minutes HESC 24 Mar. 1923. See also above, pp. 236-7.

Similarly, from 1933 Dr Perrie Williams was Chief Examiner for the Worcester City authority, which appears to have made no use of tests;[49] and from 1927 to 1938 she examined for the Bournemouth City authority, which had abandoned intelligence tests in 1925.[50]

At one stage or another Dr Perrie Williams was also employed by the counties of Oxfordshire, Gloucestershire and Lindsey, and by the City of Oxford. In the case of the three counties we know no more than that.[51] The records of the Oxford City Examinations Board, up to the end of 1936 at least, tell us more and enable us to form some picture of her work. Her first reports for East Suffolk in 1922 and 1923 had been detailed and careful, concerned with the levels of difficulty of questions and the spread of marks. She produced similar annual reports for Oxford, averaging twenty pages, and showing increasing statistical sophistication.[52]

The authority was at this point operating a two-stage examination. Entrance was voluntary and about 600 children attempted it. In stage one attainments were tested; about 200 children were expected to emerge from this to go forward to stage two. Stage two entailed a written group intelligence test, a 'reading test' and interviews with the Examinations Board and secondary-school heads. Dr Perrie Williams struggled hard with this 'Reading Test', explaining that the marking scheme for *any* test used must be uniform and clearly agreed — 'it obviates the great variations inevitable when there are several examiners testing separately'. Eventually in the spring of 1936

[49] Worcester CBC Higher Education Sub-Committee Minutes 10 Mar. 1933.

[50] Bournemouth CBC HESC Minutes 3 Oct. 1927 and annually until 1938. For Bournemouth 1922-5, see above, p. 232.

[51] The Oxford City Examinations Board Minutes refer to her work for the county and for Gloucestershire when they appoint her — Minutes 22 Jan. 1926, but the records of those two authorities throw no further light on this. For other information about them, see above, pp. 205, 232. Lindsey had done quite respectably with a home-made intelligence test in the 1920s — see above, p. 236; and it is not clear what led to the appointment of an external examiner in 1936 or what intelligence tests all children of the appropriate age group were required to take, as the first stage in the selection process — Lindsey CC Higher Education Sub-Committee Minutes 30 Oct. 1936 and 29 Oct. 1937.

[52] e.g. her report on the 1929 examination for the first time sets out the frequency distribution of the marks — Oxford Examinations Board Minutes, 14 Jan. 1930. See also Minutes 11 Dec. 1930, 8 Dec. 1931, 1 Nov. 1932, 11 Apr. 1933, 13 June 1933, 4 Dec. 1934, 2 Dec. 1935 and 8 Dec. 1936.

it was scrapped.[53] She also battled hard, but unavailingly, for an age allowance.[54]

Dr Perrie Williams seems to have been somewhat less sure-footed in her approach to the group test part of stage two. The Oxford Examinations Board picked a different published test each year. In 1926 the test used was the 'National Intelligence Tests Scale A, Form II'. In 1927 the boys were given NIIP Test no. 34, while the girls were given a Simplex Test. In 1928 the 'Revised Edition Dearborn Group Tests' were used. Then in 1929 Dr Perrie Williams offered her own test, which was duly tried. But it is by no means clear that she went on doing so. In 1935, at least, a Moray House Test was used.[55]

For the Oxford authority the Board of Education's 1936 Memorandum coincided with a major protest from the local branch of the NUT about the length and nature of the examination; and in December 1936 the Chief Education Officer reviewed all Oxford's procedures. His recommendations included the proposal that the first stage of a new examination should be an intelligence test administered to the entire eligible age group in the elementary schools — although the words he chose to elaborate on this were a somewhat curious mixture. 'It is vital', he wrote, 'that the test for the present purpose should be what is known as a "performance test", non-verbal, requiring as little literary and arithmetical knowledge as possible.'[56] If the Examination Board Minutes from 1937 on had survived, we might know what the Board actually ended up doing and what part, if any, Dr Perrie Williams played in it.

Examining seems to have been Dr Perrie Williams's livelihood. By contrast, the NUT Examinations Board found itself conducting eleven-plus examinations for LEAs almost by accident and was never really comfortable or confident with the role. When the Board was finally wound up at the end of 1935, the NUT Executive explained:

[53] Chief Examiner's Memorandum annexed to Examination Board Minutes 16 Mar. 1927.
[54] Examinations Board Minutes 11 May 1929.
[55] Ibid., 3 June 1926, 4 May 1927, 24 Jan. 1928, 17 Apr. 1929, 16 Apr. 1935.
[56] Ibid., 8 Dec. 1936 and the CEO's Memorandum annexed to them.

It was set up by Conference in 1895 with the idea that if at some future time the object of the Union to secure the recognition of the teaching profession as a diploma-granting authority were achieved, the Union would have suitable machinery in being to carry out that object. In its early years its chief work consisted of the conduct of tutorial examinations for pupil teachers. To this were added commercial and handicraft examinations for the award of certificates of proficiency to part-time students. The Board also conducted a number of examinations for the award of diplomas to specialist teachers, but these were gradually abandoned as it was found impossible to obtain recognition for them by the Board of Education. Since the War the Board's work has been chiefly concerned with the part-time students' examinations and with special examinations for the award of free places in secondary schools.[57]

It was indeed plain that the Teachers' Registration Council and associated wider schemes for the profession, in the person of the Union, to control its own recruitment and entry would come to nothing by the middle of the War; and the Board only narrowly escaped being wound up in 1917.[58]

Up to this point no more than four LEAs in any one year had used the NUT Examinations Board to help them in selecting children for various types of post-elementary education.[59] But during the 1920s the number of LEAs using the Board gradually swelled. In 1932, the peak year, the Board set eighteen examinations for thirteen authorities. Some of these authorities were Part III authorities, selecting for central schools, others had special scholarship trusts to administer. But the NUT Examinations Board had at that time some part in the selection processes conducted by ten LEAs with full responsibility for secondary education: Rochdale, Bootle, Westmorland, South Shields, Buckinghamshire, East Ham, West Ham, Grimsby, West Suffolk and Holland (Lincs.).[60] In the early 1920s the Board had also been

[57] *NUT Annual Report for 1935* (London, 1936), Executive's Report, p. lxi.
[58] *NUT Annual Report for 1916* (London, 1917), pp. xl–xli; *NUT Annual Report for 1917* (London, 1918), p. liii; *NUT Annual Report for 1918* (London, 1919), pp. lvii–lviii.
[59] See *NUT Annual Reports* for years 1900–18.
[60] There is some difficulty in reconciling the summary totals given in the published *NUT Annual Reports*, with the details scattered through the MS Minute Books of the Examinations Board. The latter in its turn, is not always as accurate as it might be. For example, the detailed lists for 1932 and 1933 set out on p. 291 of Minute Book IV (11 Nov. 1933) do not include West Suffolk, yet the minutes of the West Suffolk HESC (see below) make recurrent references to the provision of examination papers by the NUT – e.g. minutes 15 June 1932 and 14 June 1933.

involved for a time with the free-place examinations in the county borough of Northampton.[61]

This business alone could not make the NUT Examinations Board financially viable.[62] It was, nevertheless, a sizeable group of local authorities; and the experience of working with this group might have equipped the NUT, or at least the Examining Board, to come to speak with some authority on questions of examining policy and technique, and possibly to do something to spread best practice. But the complexities of educational politics and perhaps the looseness of the federation of local associations that was the NUT meant that such a positive role was firmly eschewed. When HM Inspectorate was critical of the inclusion of papers in History and Geography in the Northampton examination in 1924, the NUT Examinations Board retorted that the responsibility lay with the LEA.[63] And this sums up the Board's stance. With one significant exception, to which we will come, it followed where its clients led, however idiosyncratic the client.

In general the NUT Examinations Board's conduct of attainments tests in English and Arithmetic seems to have been competent; although the Inspectorate adopted a distinctly wary tone in commenting on examinations in which the NUT was involved.[64] The HMIs did, however, criticize the absence of an effective age allowance in the Buckinghamshire examination in 1927; and the NUT Examinations Board's response reveals all the delicacies of its position – at least as the members saw it. They agreed that they should consider the question of age allowances,

although this does not directly concern the Board as an examining Body [!] . . . It was pointed out that the Executive had stated that it was not desirable that marks allowances or deductions should be made, but the Board thought that as an examining Body it should go into the matter as advice on the question was sometimes sought by education authorities.

When they next met, they had before them the aforementioned Executive statement and an

---

[61] Ed 77/87 (HMIs' Report 1924); NUT Examinations Board Minutes IV, 10 Oct. 1925, p. 197.
[62] Ibid., 10 Mar. 1934, pp. 299–302, Memorandum on the Board's position.
[63] Ed 77/87; NUT Examinations Board Minutes IV, 10 Oct. 1925, p. 197.
[64] See all the Inspectors' reports cited in this section of the discussion.

article by an official of the Northumberland Authority on a suggested method of an age allowance, based on 'standard deviation'. It was decided that although this question does not directly concern the examining Body, the Board were in agreement with the policy of the Executive that it was not desirable that marks allowances should be made in respect of the younger children nor should the older be handicapped by a deduction from marks.[65]

A similar conflict between a possible role as examination technologists and more general considerations of union policy, was reflected in the one issue on which the NUT Examinations Board did firmly resist the client's demands, the provision of what came to be known as a 'general efficiency examination'. As we have seen, the effectiveness and equity of a selective examination depends in part on the presence of a sufficiently large and representative population of candidates. By 1924 the Middlesex Education Committee — like Northumberland — had determined to subject all its elementary schools to what it called 'efficiency tests', 'designed to determine the number of their pupils likely to profit by a secondary school course'.

Payment by results was still a very real memory, however, and the Middlesex Education Committee was promptly denounced by the NUT, whose Conference in 1925 deplored 'any reversion to the individual examination system' and protested 'emphatically against the tendency observable in some areas to use the examination for scholarships to secondary schools as a test of the efficiency of primary schools, instead of what it should be, — a test of the child's natural ability'. The Association of Education Committees, the LEA trade union, fanned the flames by defending the rights of its member authorities to assess the efficiency of the schools for which they were responsible. Indeed, the AEC encouraged them to do so and a major slanging match ensued. Eventually both sides nominated representatives to a specially formed committee, which then spent another four years producing a report so diplomatic as to give no clear lead at all.[66]

[65] NUT Examinations Board Minutes IV, 10 Mar. 1928, p. 235 and 27 Oct. 1929, p. 243.
[66] *Education* 15 Feb. 1924, p. 103, 24 Apr. 1925, p. 380, 18 June 1926, pp. 650, 652, 654 and 656 AEC debate 'Examinations in Public Elementary Schools', 25 June 1926, pp. 671-2 'Authorities — the Schools — and the Children', 3 Sept. 1926, pp. 199-200 'An Individual Examination', 22 Apr. 1925, p. 450 NUT

As we have also seen, the introduction of special places caused some authorities to consider once more the equity of their selection procedures. In 1933, as a result of such a reconsideration, the Buckinghamshire Education Committee decided to examine the whole eligible age group in its elementary schools and invited the NUT Examinations Board to conduct this examination. Hitherto, Buckinghamshire teachers had carried out their own preliminary review and the NUT Examinations Board had set and marked the papers of those children selected by the review for stage two. The Examinations Board Secretary replied:

I am asked to express regret that the policy of the Union prevents our cooperation in an external and compulsory examination of the type suggested for the award of Special Places. Moreover, the candidates vary so widely in their attainments and the curricula of the schools are so differentiated, as recognised in your letter, that the difficulties of a satisfactory standardisation are almost insuperable. We feel that such an examination cannot even approximately ensure that the best selection will be made.

The consensus of opinion is that in such circumstances it is preferable to have a preliminary review of the candidates, and that this review should take the form of an internal examination in which the teachers and the administrative staff are associated. An internal preliminary test of this kind is used by many of the largest Authorities for the elimination of those clearly unfitted for transference, leaving the more capable to be submitted to a final selective examination in which the numbers are much smaller, though still high in comparison with the limited number of possible awards.

If your Committee could see its way to adopt some such procedure as this, we should be pleased to cooperate with your Central Examinations Board in the conduct of the Final Examination as we have been privileged to do during so many past years.

The Buckinghamshire Committee did not 'see its way' and ceased to employ the NUT Examinations Board.[67]

Conference Presidential Address, 28 Jan. 1927, pp. 116-19 F.F. Potter's speech to the Association of Directors and Secretaries of Education, 2 Mar. 1928, p. 237 'School Examination: A More Hopeful Outlook', 18 July 1930, pp. 59-69 'Examinations in Public Elementary Schools', 12 Dec. 1930, pp. 555-6, 'Examinations: Their Uses and Abuses'; NUT Examinations Board Minutes IV, pp. 279-82 (12 Feb. 1932), report of the NUT EB subcommittee on the report of the joint committee of the NUT and AEC. See also above, pp. 160-1 for the Board of Education's efforts to avoid confrontation on this issue. Even in 1939 the whole thing seemed to be flaring up again over a proposal in Leamington to examine all elementary-school leavers — Education 10 Feb. 1939, p. 179.

[67] NUT Examinations Board Minutes IV, pp. 291-2 (11 Nov. 1933).

'General efficiency tests' apart, however, the NUT Examinations Board did provide what the clients asked for — including, on occasion, intelligence or quasi-intelligence tests.

As has been said, the NUT Examinations Board was employed at one time or another to conduct examinations for secondary-school entry, by eleven LEAs. Four of these, Westmorland, Buckinghamshire, West Suffolk and Northampton, asked the Board to devise intelligence tests and, indeed, seem to have taken quite a sustained insterest in the subject.[68] However, the very variety of its experience with such tests once more shows the NUT Examinations Board avoiding a positive role, behaving in an even more amateur and uncertain fashion than it had done on the subject of age allowances. The Board neither provided the four authorities with clear guidance nor equipped them with expectations about the nature of a properly constructed intelligence test and its analysis.

Not very much information is available about the test the NUT Examinations Board supplied at Northampton in 1924;[69] and Northampton ceased to use the Board's services some time in the later twenties. But when the authority's Director of Education reviewed arrangements at the end of 1934 — offering information about the practices of other authorities for comparative purposes, a surprisingly rare occurrence — the use of an intelligence test for all candidates was one of the issues he raised. The local Examinations Board decided to go ahead on this and one 'Dr W.S. Flack Ph.D., M.Sc., Headmaster of Aston Commercial School, Birmingham' was asked to devise and mark the test; an arrangement which continued at least until the War. The surviving tests and minutes of discussions suggest strongly that Dr Flack and the Northampton Examinations Board were all amateurs together. Elements in Dr Flack's tests imitated early Moray House Tests; but they were over-long, with no great attention to balance. On at least one occasion the Board cut out sections and there were prolonged discussions about the marks to be allocated and how these should be related to marks for

---

[68] For the other seven see Ed 77/43 (East Ham 1924), also above, p. 212; Ed 77/44 (West Ham 1924); Ed 77/39 (South Shields 1926); Ed 77/66 (Rochdale 1928); Ed 77/77 (Grimsby 1929); Ed 110/83 (draft report Grimsby 1936); Ed 77/59 (Bootle, incomplete, n.d.); Ed 77/73 (Holland 1928).

[69] Ed 77/87 — the report is incomplete.

attainments papers. As far as can be seen, there were no trials of questions elsewhere and very little concern with standardization.[70] For the Westmorland Minor Scholarships Examination in 1925 the NUT Examinations Board provided a 'General Paper', with questions on Scripture, Geography, History, Science or Nature Study, and General Knowledge, the latter 'usually of the nature of intelligence tests'.[71] But in the separate 'general examination' which the authority ran itself (and which was also used as stage one of a separate free-place examination, conducted by the secondary schools) an intelligence test, of an unspecified type, though described as yielding an IQ rather than a mark, was administered. By the mid-1930s and the disappearance of the NUT Examinations Board, Westmorland was at last beginning to integrate its various examinations. In 1931 it experimented with an intelligence test in stage two. In 1938 the intelligence test was included in stage one. There is no hard information about the tests used or the background of the examiner, a Mrs Craig. But the minute on arrangements for 1939 suggests that the local Examinations Board chose from a selection of published tests submitted to it; and that year the worked and marked papers were subsequently posted off to the NIIP, 'where experts were obtaining from these papers useful data for future tests'.[72]

Westmorland had thus made contact with a source of recognized expertise by the end of the period. Buckinghamshire got there sooner, although not with any help from the NUT Examinations Board. In the 1920s the NUT Examinations Board had contributed to the second stage of the Buckinghamshire free-place and scholarship examination a short 'intelligence test', carrying a small number of marks — in 1928, for example, lasting fifteen minutes and carrying thirty marks out of a possible total of 210 marks for the

[70] Northampton CBC Papers (ML1801) Examinations Board Minutes and Papers especially Memorandum on Schools Examination 8 Dec. 1934 annexed to Minutes of 3 Feb. 1935, Minutes 3 Feb. 1935, 15 Mar. 1935, 13 May 1935, 7 Nov. 1935, 24 Jan. 1936, 1 Feb. 1937, 14 Mar. 1938, 10 Mar. 1939, 13 Mar. 1940 and Dr Flack's test for 1936.   [71] Ed 77/115.

[72] Ibid.; Westmorland CC Papers, HESC Minutes 19 Sept. 1921 'Minor Scholarships', School Management Committee Minutes 9 July 1928 'General Examination', ibid. 11 Jan. 1932, Education Committee Annual Reports, 1936, pp. 4–7, Examinations Board Minutes 11 Apr. 1938, 3 Apr. 1939 and 8 Apr. 1940 (source of direct quotation).

whole examination. The questions tended to involve mental arithmetic and grammar. But when at the end of 1932 the Buckinghamshire Scholarships and General Purposes Committee decided to invite the NUT Examinations Board to conduct a general examination in English and Arithmetic, it also decided simultaneously and independently 'to communicate with Dr Cyril Burt, inviting him to devise a standardized intelligence test'. Dr Cyril Burt presumably declined but made helpful suggestions; for the arrangements for 1933 included provision for Dr S.J. Philpott — also this year working for Kent — to devise and administer an intelligence test.[73]

In considerable contrast, West Suffolk had a sustained encounter with the best then available in the technology of mental measurement at the beginning of the 1920s — and the experience was as water off the proverbial duck's back. While it seems fair to comment on the NUT Examinations Board's general lack of grip on the new technology, the saga of the West Suffolk eleven-plus examinations in the inter-War years does serve to remind us that some of the NUT's clients could be very idiosyncratic indeed.

In 1922 and 1923 some members of the West Suffolk authority had become concerned at the fact that some elementary schools entered no children at all for either the free-place examination or the separate county junior scholarship examination. The upshot was not only an externally administered attainments test for all children between ten and twelve in the elementary schools in 1924, but also, in 1925, the administration to the same age group of Northumberland Test number 1. This second year, all children with an IQ of over 115, plus those nominated by head teachers, plus those whose parents insisted — totalling 300 — then went on to take Ballard's English and Arithmetic tests, as set out in *The New Examiner*, in competition for the sixty-five free places available. The architect of all this was HMI J.B. Russell, with assistance from C.A. Richardson, Ballard and Godfrey Thomson; and he considered the exercise thoroughly vindicated standardized tests, administered to the whole eligible age group.[74]

[73] Ed 77/19 (HMIs' Report 1928); Buckinghamshire CC Papers, Scholarships and General Purposes Sub-Committee Minutes 19 Nov. 1925, 15 Nov. 1928, 15 Dec. 1932 (source of direct quotation) and 19 Jan. 1933.

[74] Ed 77/224, Report printed as a pamphlet for use of Office and Inspec-

Perhaps the cost of examining everyone — estimated at
£150 for just over 2,000 children — or the pressure on places
which might thereby be generated, or both together frightened
the West Suffolk Education Committee. Anyway, whatever
the reasons, Russell's report, with all its implications, sank
without trace. In 1926 the authority once more held two
separate competitions, one for free places and one for junior
scholarships, entrance to both of which was voluntary. The
only change was the use of papers set by the NUT Examinations Board but marked locally. Then in 1928 an intelligence test was added to the junior scholarship examination
but not to the free-place examination, only to be abandoned
again when the separate junior scholarship examination was
abandoned again at the end of 1933. This last intelligence
test paper deserves quotation in full:[75]

WEST SUFFOLK COUNTY EDUCATION COMMITTEE
JUNIOR SCHOLARSHIP EXAMINATION
INTELLIGENCE TEST   *Time: 20 minutes*
You may answer all the questions

1. From the words in each bracket below, copy the word having a
   meaning similar to that of the word outside the bracket:—
   Purchased (shared, paid, used, bought, took)
   Marvellous (great, pleasant, wonderful, awful, unusual)
   Conceal (defend, consent, contain, state, hide)
   Conflagration (fight, confusion, riot, fire, onslaught)
   Valour (justice, courage, loyalty, mercy, faith)
   Dearth (liberty, scarcity, dying, dulness, sorrow)
2. A is north of B, and B is west of C. The distance from B to A equals
   the distance from B to C. A motor-car travels on a straight road
   from C to A. In what direction is it moving?
3. If 9 X 6 is not greater than 5 X 8 draw a circle and print the word
   'square' inside it; otherwise write all the odd numbers between 4 and
   24 and underline all the numbers less than 17 and greater than 7.
4. (a) What relation is my sister's mother to my brother's daughter?
   (b) It was stated that a man who had had an accident walked to a
   hospital where a doctor attended to his broken limb. Say as nearly as
   possible which limb was broken.

torate only. West Suffolk CC Papers, Secondary and Higher Education Sub-
Committee Minutes 8 Aug. 1923 (items 2 and 3), 14 Nov. 1923 (item 21), 9
July 1924 (item 11), 17 Dec. 1924 (item 1), 11 Mar. 1925 (item 2) and 1 July
1925.

[75] Ed 77/105 (HMIs' Report 1928); West Suffolk S&HESC Minutes 18 Aug.
1926 (items 7 and 8), 4 Apr. 1928, 15 June 1932, 1 Feb. 1933 (item 5), 5 Apr.
1933 (item 18) and 14 June 1933, with annexed examination paper.

5. Jack owes Jim 10d., and has a half-crown and sixpence. Jim has four pennies, a two-shilling piece and a half-crown. How can they settle?

It should be pointed out that the West Suffolk Examinations Board on occasion amended draft papers supplied by the NUT Examinations Board,[76] and this 1933 intelligence test may owe more to its own efforts than to those of the NUT Examinations Board. But either way, questions 3 and 4 are sitting targets for one of those periodic angry exchanges in the correspondence columns of educational journals, about the sillinesses and sheer trickery of so-called intelligence tests.[77]

The demise of the NUT Examinations Board in 1935 left the West Suffolk Examinations Board to fend for itself. In 1936 its members tried 'a paper based on General Knowledge and General Intelligence tests' in the special-place examination. In their report they reverted once more to 'the question of the child who does not enter'. The 1937 examination therefore began with a compulsory preliminary test for all pupils in elementary schools eligible by age, another home-made intelligence test and, for good measure, they put a 'General Intelligence' paper in stage two as well.

They were sufficiently pleased with this combination to continue it is 1938 and 1939. The new style of intelligence test papers suggests that someone had been doing quite a lot of reading in the area and is not dissimilar from the style developed by Dr Flack at Northampton. But as HM Inspectors commented in 1939, the preliminary examination 'is in no sense a standardized test and . . . it carries with it no allowance for age. Its efficacy is very limited and its reliability as a diagnostic agent is very questionable.'

The stage two paper,

apart from being in many respects a repetition of the preliminary test, tended to test knowledge other than English and Arithmetic — a proceeding of doubtful propriety, if not, indeed, quite at variance with the regulations of the Board of Education.

[76] e.g. West Suffolk Examinations Board Minutes 14 Mar. 1931.
[77] e.g. the correspondence launched in *The Times Educational Supplement* by 'Secondary Headmaster' in 1921: *The Times Educational Supplement* 28 May 1921, p. 240, 4 June 1921, p. 252, 11 June 1921, p. 264 and 18 June 1921, p. 280.

They summed up: 'the arrangements at present in force in West Suffolk are hardly in keeping with modern theory and practice.' In October 1939 the West Suffolk Secondary and Higher Education Sub-Committee threw in the towel altogether, recommending that the examination for 1940 should have one stage, consisting of only two papers, English and Arithmetic, each to be provided by Moray House.[78]

*

The examining procedures reviewed so far most resemble a kaleidoscope. The diversity is staggering, as is the frequency of change over time, both points epitomized, surely, by the sharply contrasting doings of those three neighbouring East Anglian authorities, West Suffolk, East Suffolk and Ipswich. LEAs usually took in each other's washing, to the extent of providing a free place for a child who moved in from an area where he/she already held one; but how did children fare whose parents moved house during or just before the examination year?

This review also yields glimpses of objectives and intentions. Some of the considerations which played a part in leading some authorities to employ the services of Moray House recur: the impact of particularly critical Inspectors' reports and the Board Memorandum of 1936; reappraisal brought about by the substitution of special for free places; difficult decisions at borderlines; and marked disparities between elementary schools. But these are glimpses, not organizing themes. All too often, even when we know what an authority did in the way of examination procedures, we do not know why it did so.

It is now, I hope, plain why the firm generalizations offered by Brian Simon and Olive Banks about the dominance of mental measurement in England and Wales by the end of the 1930s do not hold up. The reception of mental measurement was far more complex and much less tidy than they suggest; and the difficulties of describing and characterizing *what* was done loom as large as, if not larger then, the difficulties of

[78] Ed 77/106 (HMIs' Report 1939); draft of this also in Ed 110/40. West Suffolk Secondary and Higher Eduation Sub-Committee Minutes 27 Jan. 1936 (item 5), Reports of the Examinations Board for 1936, 1937 and 1938 and Minutes 11 Oct. 1939, item 4(b).

explaining *why* it was done. These two activities, description and explanation, can be distinguished, but are not in practice entirely separate. If we could manage to characterize the complexity, diversity and untidiness with some degree of generality, we could get at least part of the way towards some hypotheses about intentions and objectives.

The table and maps at the beginning of this chapter suggested, and the subsequent discussion has confirmed, that there was a striking amount of interest in and experiment with intelligence tests in the early 1920s. Much of this, however, was ill informed and ill designed. Many of the most technically respectable schemes were products of the 1930s, developed by authorities which had not succumbed to the initial craze. The pattern of use of Moray House Tests, explored in chapter 7, is on the surface a different one, but in fact it is complementary. The Moray House clients of the late 1920s were a handful of authorities in the North-East, quite possibly a number of them with particular personal links with Thomson/Newcastle/Edinburgh. The widespread use of Moray House Tests was very much a feature of the 1930s, when they were among the most technically respectable tests — if not *the* most respectable tests — on the market. It looks as though we could usefully distinguish between an initial unfocused, often superficial, enthusiasm, which made 'general intelligence' a fashionable catch-phrase, and a much slower-growing awareness of the possible uses of mental measurement in highly competitive examination conditions. What little we know about the secondary-school selection procedures of authorities which did not use intelligence tests, seems to bear out these distinctions and make it possible to refine them a little further.

'Non-users' are listed in Table 8.2 and mapped in Fig. 8.3 below. Among them there were indeed authorities who knew little and cared less about examining techniques. But there were others who paid lip-service to the idea of general intelligence; and yet others who were well informed but wary. Finally, the peculiar case of the Welsh authorities points the way to more general considerations about the nature of English secondary-school selection processes in this period.

Prejudiced ignorance characterized the behaviour of the Stockport authority in the late 1920s. The report on the

Table 8.2: *LEAs not known to have used intelligence tests in selection for secondary education 1920-40*

(a) County Councils

Anglesey
Bedfordshire
Berkshire
Breconshire
Caernarvonshire
Cardiganshire   Rutland
Carmarthenshire   Staffordshire
Cornwall   Shropshire
Cumberland   Somerset
Denbighshire   Soke of Peterborough
Derbyshire   W. Sussex
Durham
Essex
Flintshire
Glamorganshire
Hampshire
Herefordshire
Hertfordshire
Holland (Lincs.)
Isle of Man
London
Merionethshire
Middlesex
Montgomeryshire
Norfolk
Pembrokeshire
Radnorshire

(b) County Borough Councils

Blackburn   Merthyr Tydfil
Blackpool   Middlesbrough
Bootle   Plymouth
Bristol   Rochdale
Burton-on-Trent   Rotherham
Carlisle   Sheffield
Chester   Stockport
Dudley   South Shields
Eastbourne   Southend
Exeter   Swansea
Hastings   Warrington
Hull   West Hartlepool
Gloucester   West Ham
Grimsby   Worcester
Lincoln   York
Leicester

Fig. 8.3 LEAs not known to have used intelligence tests in secondary-school selection 1920–40

Inspectorate's visitation in 1928 concluded: 'as it stands, the Examination has almost every possible fault.' Nor was the informal conference with the secretary and chairman of the LEA encouraging. The chairman displayed complete ignorance, while the secretary described a suggestion that they might examine all eleven-year-olds as 'socialistic' and leading to a 'nation on the dole'. 'The position is that at Stockport there is a reactionary authority with a secretary who spends most of his energies in "trimming" to the varying views of the dominant faction.'[79]

There was considerable ignorance in Carlisle also. But the Conference following the Inspectors' visitation in 1933 was altogether more encouraging. HMI C.B. Joyner

went into considerable detail about the technique of conducting an Examination such as this. The Committee, who were profoundly ignorant on the subject, were very interested and asked a number of questions.

I made it clear to them that while this particular Examination was being conducted with great care and trouble by those responsible for it, it was being done in a very amateurish way, and though it was successful in picking out the best candidates and rejecting the worst, the discrimination between the closely bunched candidates in the middle was largely fortuitous. I suggested to them that as they seemed to have no-one who was familiar with [the] modern highly specialised technique of examination work, they would be well advised to get some expert from outside to come and help them. This suggestion seemed to appeal to them, and the Director had already told me privately beforehand that he would welcome such an arrangement.[80]

Whether, in the end, they did this, we do not know. The examination described in the authority's return to the Hartog and Roberts inquiry between 1933 and 1935 was unchanged.

Elsewhere, however, profound ignorance was tempered by — or perhaps sometimes concealed by — lip-service to the phrase 'general intelligence'. Such lip-service, invocation almost, extended well beyond authorities who actually tried some sort of test. It is in fact very difficult to draw any clear line between those authorities, discussed above, where

---

[79] Ed 77/26. It should be said, however, that when the Inspectors returned in 1934 they found no changes in the structure of the examination but a great improvement in the quality of the marking, and the informal conference seems to have been altogether a more friendly affair — Ed 110/115.

[80] Ed 110/68.

published tests, or some questions from them, were used as part of a second-stage and/or oral examination, and those authorities, like Norfolk and Worcester, where orals were simply described as 'a *viva voce* test of general intelligence'.[81] The position in Lincoln was not dissimilar, although expounded rather more elaborately by the Director of Education. In 1925 he informed his Education Committee:

Leading Educational and Medical experts are finding each year new problems of intelligence and psychology, and already the idea is promulgated that there exists in each child of whatever class of society, an 'Intellectual Quotient' which is practically equal in capacity at birth, and which rapidly develops or depreciates in early years, according to the nature of its education and environment. If neglected in early years it breaks out later to express itself in all that is wild and extravagant in later life. Hence the vital necessity of suitable training in early life.

He congratulated himself, however, that the Lincoln two-stage examination, with attainments tests and oral, was successful in discovering the talented children.[82] This was one of the more extraordinary accounts of the activities of 'Leading Educational and Medical Experts'! But remarks like this do make it plausible to suggest that the fashionable label 'tests of general intelligence' was quite often used to dress up general papers, oral examinations and other procedures that an authority was already using.

There was plainly a very considerable gap between the 'dressing-up' exercises and the kind of careful scrutiny given to the question of intelligence tests by authorities like Kent — or, indeed, Darlington, under the guidance of Whalley. But careful scrutiny did not always lead to the adoption of intelligence tests. In some cases, it could lead to a considered decision to do without them. One such authority seems to have been Hull, whose Higher Education Sub-Committee resolved in July 1935: 'That, as an experiment for one year only, an Intelligence Test be set to the candidates taking the

[81] Norfolk Education Committee Papers, Education Committee Minutes 14 Jan. 1922 item 13(c), Higher Education Sub-Committee Minutes 13 Jan. 1940 item 10(b) and 15 June 1940, Minutes Examinations Board 15 Feb. 1940; also Ed 77/80 (HMIs' Report 1927) and Ed 110/29 (HMIs' draft report 1938). Cf. also Ed 77/117 (HMIs' Report Worcester 1929) and Ed 77/119 (HMIs' Report Hull 1924).

[82] Lincoln CBC Papers, Education Committee Minutes 30 June 1925, item 1.

second part of the 1936 Examination, subject to the marks not being taken into account for examination purposes.'[83] Apparently the authority was not impressed, for nothing more was heard about a test.

The most striking instance of an authority whose careful scrutiny led to a considered rejection of tests, however, is that of the London County Council. The absence of the LCC from the list of test users is at first sight startling: it was the pace-making authority in so many ways — including the use of individual tests in the identification and assessment of mentally handicapped children; and it was the employer, part-time, from 1913 to 1932, of Cyril Burt. But as I have argued elsewhere, Burt's interest in the technology of testing for secondary-school selection seems to have been on the wane in the 1920s.[84] The interest in testing that there was came from elsewhere among the LCC staff; and the whole issue was treated in a way which was in keeping with their standing as pace-makers and opinion formers.

A first initiative was taken in 1917 by D.R. Daniell, the Chief Examiner. In company with P.B. Ballard he administered tests orally to all eleven-year-olds in six schools in Ballard's district, as a cross-check on the current scholarship examination. In three schools the results matched well; in the others they did not.[85] Small surveys of this kind seem to have been repeated from time to time;[86] and in 1924 group attainments tests were used to supplement the more traditional pattern of examination in English and Arithmetic.[87]

[83] Hull CBC Higher Education Sub-Committee Minutes 9 July 1935.
[84] Sutherland and Sharp, ' "The fust official psychologist" '. This discusses in detail the extent of Burt's involvement in these LCC experiments.
[85] LCC Papers, EO/PS/3/36 form letter from Education Officer to selected head teachers 10 Jan. 1917 and accompanying MS notes.
[86] Ibid., first paragraph of the confidential memorandum by the Chief Education Officer, G.H. Gater, 9 Oct. 1925.
[87] The surviving papers are a source of some confusion on this. Dr Allen's Minute to the Chief Education Officer of 1 Oct. 1924, EO/PS/3/36, talks of 'mental tests' and 'a series of tests on the lines of those which Dr Ballard and others have introduced into the schools'. But in view of the prolonged experiments with 'intelligence tests' discussed below and a letter from the Assistant Education Officer to the Director of Education for West Bromwich, 26 Mar. 1926 EO/PS/3/36, sending specimens of recent LCC papers — 'prepared on lines resulting in their being analogous to intelligence tests, while retaining their character as questions in English. This type of paper has been adopted because it is more examinable than either essays or more orthodox English questions.
The Council has not officially conducted experiments in the use of intelligence

That same autumn, Daniell's successor as Chief Examiner, the excitable Mr B.C. Wallis, proposed a large-scale experiment, supplementing both stages of the existing examination with group intelligence tests. Neither officials nor head teachers were in principle opposed; but discussion of the detailed arrangements was brought to a halt by economic pressures and resumed only in May 1927, when the LCC Education Committee began to consider its response to the Hadow Report.[88] A subcommittee consisting of Burt, Ballard, Wallis and F.H. Spencer, the LCC Chief Inspector, was authorized to devise a special series of tests, which were administered to 800 children in Ballard's division (Chelsea), the week after they had sat the Junior County Scholarship Examination in November 1927. Eight tests were devised: Understanding Instructions, Opposites, Likeness, Mixed Sentences, Completing Sentences, Numbers, Orientation and Simple Reasoning. There were no trials as such, although Burt did try out one set of draft questions 'on a number of rather bright children of my acquaintance'; and after the event, the worried secretary of the committee got Ballard to send the tests round for comment to Spearman, Godfrey Thomson, William Brown and W.H. Winch.[89]

The results of the intelligence test and the scholarship examination agreed fairly well at the extremes, but much less well in the middle. After a very detailed analysis of individual scores, Wallis reported that this was in part, at least, because the intelligence test 'was a verbal or linguistic test' and did not 'test capacity in Arithmetic'. He concluded, therefore, that 'An intelligence test of this character will not serve as a measure of Intelligence sufficiently good to satisfy the requirements laid down by the Council for the award of Junior County Scholarships.'[90]

tests in the schools, and their use for testing pupils whether in competition for scholarships or for other purposes, has not been sanctioned' — it seems reasonable to conclude that the tests in use were attainments tests.

[88] Those papers remaining — i.e. other than those already cited — in EO/PS/3/ 36; and draft agenda item May 1926 and the paper for the Education Committee and its subcommittees by G.H. Gater 13 May 1927 in EO/PS/3/37.

[89] Ibid., especially Minutes of the HESC 7 July 1927, letter Assistant EO J. Brown to Burt 21 July 1927, letter Burt to Brown 27 Oct. 1927, the draft question paper itself, letters from Wallis to Brown 8 Jan. and 11 Jan. 1928, and the minutes of the subcommittee's meetings 26 Sept., 3 Oct. and 28 Oct. 1927.

[90] Ibid., 'Some Notes on the Results by Mr Wallis. The Intelligence Test. Pre-

The rest of the committee demurred at this emphatic conclusion and Ballard was asked to follow up in the fullest possible detail thirty cases where the discrepancy was extreme.[91] He admitted the force of Wallis's points, if one were in the position of having to choose between an intelligence test and an attainments test as a selector, but contended still 'that an I [intelligence test] examination reveals promise which is not brought out by an attainments examination'.[92] The subcommittee's eventual report to the LCC Higher Education Sub-Committee was thus a compromise, presenting the results of the experiments as insufficiently conclusive and recommending a further, bigger trial in 1929.[93]

This second trial, in November 1929, involved over 2,000 children; although details of the tests which were administered are missing. Again, there were quite significant discrepancies between test scores and marks secured in the Junior County Scholarship Examination; and Dr A.G. Hughes, who had succeeded Ballard (and who was to devise tests for Kent in 1931 and 1932) investigated in depth 120 of these, collecting information about the children's health and home conditions, and about the pattern of their work and behaviour in elementary, secondary and central schools. He reported as follows:

If one of the two methods is to be used alone, there is no doubt that the scholarship examination is to be preferred. No method, which is reasonably simple administratively, can do more than rough justice to the candidates, and it may be assumed that for the majority, the scholarship examination gives a fair measure of 'scholarship ability' — an ability which, though largely dependent upon a good degree of innate intelligence, is also compounded of such worthy character qualities as perseverance and ambition. 'Scholarship ability', as thus described, must by the age of 11 produce some definite measurable attainments, and it is reasonable that a test of these attainments should be used as a method of selection.

An intelligence test alone would select some intelligent children who, by reason of permanent extraneous handicaps, could not profit to a reasonable extent by a secondary school education. As several of

liminary Report to the Special Committee', 27 Jan. 1928; see also his Memorandum for the subcommittee 17 July 1928.

[91] Ibid., minutes of the subcommittee meeting 28 Mar. 1928.

[92] Ibid., Ballard's memorandum for the subcommittee meeting 17 July 1928.

[93] Ibid., minutes of the subcommittee meeting 17 July 1928, Brown's draft for the HESC October 1928.

the head teachers remarked, a central school is often a better type of school for some of the intelligent pupils. There must, however, be many intelligent children suffering in small degrees from temporary extraneous handicaps — illnesses at critical times, changes of school, changes of teacher — and for these children selection by means of an intelligence test plus a scholarship examination would appear to be fairer than by examination alone.

The investigation has furthermore shown that the scholarship examination selects some children of only ordinary intelligence — children who have enjoyed special advantages, among which may be mentioned good homes, ambitious parents, specially good teaching. This result also suggests that selection by means of an intelligence test plus a scholarship examination would be a fairer method than by examination alone.

A child who is on the borderline because of handicaps suffered is more worthy of a scholarship than a child who is on the borderline because of advantages enjoyed. The evidence obtained in this investigation seems to indicate that, while the scholarship examination tends to favour the child who has enjoyed special advantages, the intelligence test tends to compensate the child who has suffered special handicaps. If these premises are accepted, it follows that, good as the scholarship examination is for its purpose, it would be even better if it were combined with an intelligence test. The attainments of the children who just win scholarships are not appreciably different from the attainments of those who just miss winning them, and if additional weight were given to intelligence in making the awards, the change would be in the direction of equalising opportunities for children of equal innate ability.[94]

The subcommittee was still not entirely content with this and in the course of 1931 involved the heads of appropriate central schools in surveying the performance of all of those of their pupils who had taken part in the experiments of 1927-8 and 1929-30.[95] But this exercise added nothing of substance; and the recommendations that eventually went forward to the LCC Higher Education Sub-Committee in the spring of 1933 were essentially those offered by Hughes.[96]

Perhaps the sheer judiciousness of the subcommittee proved its undoing. Its report was presented by the Chief Education Officer, G.H. Gater, who had not himself been a

[94] EO/PS/3/38 'Intelligence Tests and the Junior County Scholarship Examination — 1930 Experiment', paper by A.G. Hughes 16 Apr. 1931.

[95] Ibid., preliminary paper for conference 18 May 1931 by E.P. Bennett, 14 May 1931; minutes of conference 18 May 1931.

[96] Ibid., report on behalf of the subcommittee by G.H. Gater, Chief Education Officer, 24 Jan. 1933.

member of the subcommittee. And in his presentation of it
to the LCC Elementary and Higher Education Sub-Com-
mittees, he made it plain that he was even less convinced
than the members of the special subcommittee, for he added
a rider:

> the work of the chief examiner will be taken over by two district in-
> spectors from June of this year. I am reluctant to consider changes in
> the form of the scholarship examinations until these officers have had
> some experience of these examinations, especially since the report does
> not question the fundamental suitability of the present junior county
> scholarship examination for its purpose, and I feel that the consider-
> ation of the carrying out of the proposal of the investigating committee
> should be postponed until the two inspectors have had a year's ex-
> perience of acting as chief examiner.

The Committees duly postponed consideration and nothing
more was heard of the proposal, either in 1934 or subsequent
years.[97]

Questions about political structures and processes of
decision making raised by the London episode are ones to
which we shall return in the next chapter. The episode also
suggests that those authorities with a sophisticated approach
to attainments testing, well-informed about the implications
of mental measurement for this, 'New Examiners' on the
Ballard model, were rather less likely to be seduced by the
cruder forms of 'intelligence tests' and the grandiose claims
made for them. It sounds so obvious a point; but it is nevertheless one worth labouring, because it does mean that
being well informed about the whole field of mental testing
and examination techniques did not automatically lead to
the use of an intelligence test. It could equally well be the
context in which the authority decided that the extra refinement of the selection process which the inclusion of an intelligence test might bring, was *not* worth the labour and
expense, and perhaps delicate negotiations, which it would
entail.

It looks as though this was the pattern of thinking in both

---

[97] Minutes of the LCC HESC meeting 9 Mar. 1933, item 22, and LCC Elementary Education Sub-Committee meeting 21 Mar. 1933, item 9. There is no
reference to a revival of the proposal in the index to the minutes of these subcommittees for 1934 and 1935; nor is there any mention of an intelligence test
in the entry for the LCC in Hartog and Roberts — specially checked just before
they went to press in 1937.

Blackpool and Sheffield, as well as in London and Hull. The Director of Education for Blackpool in the early 1920s, Dr A.E. Ikin, was one of the early publicists for mental measurement, writing and speaking quite extensively on the subject;[98] and between 1920 and 1926 the authority's Examinations Board developed a two-stage examination in English and Arithmetic, the first part of which was compulsory for all public elementary schoolchildren of the appropriate age, and which determined whether children went to secondary schools, central schools, or stayed in the 'higher tops' of the elementary schools. It was also adopted as the entrance examination for would-be fee payers at the secondary schools and thus taken by some children from local private schools also. The team of Inspectors who visited the authority in 1927, J.J.R. Bridge, A.J. Smith and C.A. Richardson, ended their visit, as usual, with a conference with the Examinations Board. Discussion focused first on the problems of bunched marks in the English papers, then

Mr Bridge proceeded to discuss the question of the inclusion of an Intelligence Test in the examinations. He thought the value of these had been proved. Miss Dunn said she had given intelligence tests to the girls already admitted on the results of the examinations. Mr Bridge spoke highly of the results of Intelligence Tests in Northumberland, and said he thought a general Intelligence Test in the preliminary examination would be a good idea. It might, among other advantages, help the classification in the Elementary schools. Mr Richardson said that if an intelligence test were set in the preliminary examination, it would not be necessary to set another one in the second examination, for one such test should serve the purpose of both examinations.[99]

The Blackpool authorities presumably held back, however; for they described their examination to the Hartog and Roberts inquiry between 1933 and 1935, as consisting simply of English and Arithmetic tests.

Sheffield, by contrast, had exceptionally well-set and marked English papers; and their efforts to standardize the marking of the essay were the most successful that the Inspectors who visited in 1933, A.J. Margetson, W. Newbold, E.S. Snelling and H.M. Thurston, had seen. The major problem

[98] See e.g. his article 'Educable Capacity, Statistical Results of an Inquiry' in *The Times Educational Supplement* 26 Sept. 1918, p. 413 and the correspondence that followed in subsequent weeks.
[99] Ed 77/57.

here was the absence of an age allowance. But the question
of intelligence tests was surely also discussed at the concluding conference, for the draft Inspectors' report read:

> There is a growing tendency on the part of Local Authorities to recog-
> nize the discrimination [*sic*] value of Intelligence Tests in the selection
> of candidates for entrance into Secondary Schools and it appeared that
> in Sheffield, while the Examiners were rightly suspicious of such tests
> when compiled by non-experts, there might be no strong opposition to
> the use of some well-standardised tests of known reputation. There is
> probably at the moment insufficient evidence in favour of Intelligence
> Tests to justify their superseding the traditional type of examination
> when the latter is well-conducted, as it is in Sheffield. It is suggested,
> however, that it would contribute materially to the improvement of
> methods of examining both here and elsewhere if the Examiners
> could keep in close touch with experiments conducted by other
> Authorities.[100]

But Sheffield, too, held back — at least in the short run. For
that authority also described its examination to the Hartog
and Roberts inquiry 1933-5 as consisting simply of papers
in English and Arithmetic.

The existence of a well-established pattern of attainments
tests, generally agreed to be an efficient selector, might,
therefore, encourage an authority to be rather wary of the
introduction of a new test; a wariness perhaps reinforced, as
the Sheffield report suggests, by an acquaintance with some
of the sillier activities perpetrated in the name of intelligence
testing. It was a position Inspectors recognized and they
acknowledged its strength. The tone of the conference
summary and the report quoted above are markedly different
from, for example, the draft reports on procedures at
Durham in 1935 and Grimsby in 1936. In both the latter
cases the HMIs concerned thought the attainments tests
which constituted the existing examinations exceedingly
badly handled — a point of particular interest in the case of
Grimsby, since the authority's 1936 examination was set by
teachers, acting in a private capacity, who had previously
acted for the NUT Examinations Board. In both cases the
HMIs unequivocally recommended the adoption of what we
may call the 1936 Memorandum package, standardized tests

[100] Ed 110/109.

of English, Arithmetic and Intelligence, with a properly calculated age allowance.[101]

The last remaining group of 'non-testers', not belonging with any of those so far discussed, comprises the Welsh authorities. As has been said, the two border authorities, Monmouthshire and Newport, used tests and their neighbour, Cardiff, conducted a single experiment in 1926.[102] The other fourteen authorities appear not to have concerned themselves with mental measurement at all; although HM Inspectors were suggesting the use of intelligence tests to the Anglesey and Brecon authorities in 1938 and 1939.[103]

It would be dangerous simply to ascribe this to ignorance and/or a general lack of concern for education. Welsh authorities were in the van of those pressing for an extension of the free- and special-place system. By 1938 78 per cent of the children in Welsh secondary schools had partial or total exemption from fees, as compared with 56 per cent of the children in English secondary schools. Eleven of the Welsh authorities filled their schools entirely with holders of special places.[104] More generally, a significantly higher proportion of Welsh children went on to secondary schools. By 1938 the number of boys and girls in secondary education in Wales was 18.4 per 1,000 of total population of all ages, as against 10.9 per 1,000 in England as a whole — and 8.4 per 1,000 in London.[105]

---

[101] Only the draft reports have survived in Ed 110/11 (Durham) and Ed 110/83 (Grimsby); but in both cases it seems that the critical tone and emphatic nature of the recommendations were softened inside the Office before a version was sent to the authority — see the note RHC to Savage 11 Dec. 1936 in the Grimsby file and the comments on the Durham draft by the Inspectorate's own committee on free-place examinations. The tone of the Grimsby draft is also worth comparing with that of the Inspectorate's report on the Grimsby examination in 1929, Ed 77/77, on which the NUT Examinations Board had rather prided itself — NUT Examinations Board Minute Book IV, pp. 253-4, 23 Nov. 1929.   [102] See above, pp. 241-2.

[103] Ed 110/130 (Anglesey, January 1939); Ed 110/131 (Brecon 1938).

[104] *Board of Education Report for 1938* P.P. 1938-9 x, Cmd 6013, ch. II, para. 9, ch. X, para. 16. See also the material on special place negotiations in Ed 110/130 (Anglesey), Ed 110/131 (Brecon), Ed 110/132 (Caernarvonshire), Ed 110/33 (Cardinganshire), Ed 110/134 (Carmarthenshire), Ed 110/135 (Denbighshire), Ed 110/136 (Flintshire), Ed 110/140 (Montgomeryshire), Ed 110/141 (Pembrokeshire), Ed 110/142 (Radnorshire), Ed 110/147 (Swansea), Ed 110/144 (Merthyr Tydfil), Ed 110/137 (Glamorganshire), Ed 110/143 (Cardiff) and Ed 110/146 (Rhondda Valley).

[105] Annual Statistics for 1938, Appendix to *Board of Education Report for 1938*, P.P. 1938-9 x, Cmd 6013. Table 41.

Historically, the Welsh counties had been committed to a system of secondary education much less highly selective than that in England. Welsh County Councils acquired powers to set up post-elementary schools under the Welsh Intermediate Education Act of 1889, thirteen years before English counties acquired comparable powers; and their jealous protection of 'their' schools was acknowledged and reflected in separate treatment by the Board of Education from 1907 onwards.[106] The Welsh attitude is admirably conveyed by a comment in the memorandum of the interview between Anglesey representatives and representatives of the Board of Education on the vexed question of special places in 1933, that the authority 'had adopted the policy of concentrating all forms of post-primary education in their secondary schools'.[107]

We do not know what the Welsh authorities thought about mental measurement, if they thought about it at all; but it is possible they considered it of little relevance when their primary concern was to sustain and develop secondary schools with a broad social base, fiercely resisting schemes likely to make them more exclusive. Perhaps even more important, they had to conduct their attainments tests in Welsh, as well as in English and Arithmetic; and I know of no efforts in this period to develop a verbal reasoning test in Welsh.

*

The activities of the 'non-testers' thus confirm that attitudes to mental measurement in general and intelligence testing in particular do not fit tidily into one or other of the categories of acceptance or rejection. The flurry of interest in the idea of tests and the extent to which 'general intelligence' became a fashionable catch-phrase in the early and mid-1920s is striking. But it is doubtful whether this had a substantial and lasting effect upon actual examining practice and the

[106] Leslie Wynne Evans, 'The Evolution of Welsh Educational Administration 1881–1921' in *Studies in the Government and Control of Education since 1860* (London, History of Education Society, 1970); also Sir Wynn Wheldon and Sir Ben Bowen Thomas, 'The Welsh Department, Ministry of Education 1907–1957', *Transactions of the Honourable Society of Cymmrodorion* session 1957, pp. 18–36.
[107] Ed 110/130, memorandum of interview 10 Mar. 1933.

impression conveyed by Fig. 8.1 above, the map of test 'users' 1920-30, is almost certainly an overstatement of the extent of informed interest in mental measurement up to 1930. Likewise the impressions produced by Figs. 8.2 and 8.3 above, 'users' 1931-40 and 'non-users' 1920-40, almost certainly understate the extent to which information about the techniques of mental measurement had been disseminated and had affected examining practice by the end of the 1930s.

Chapter 9

'The public service of education in this country is decentralized'

The variety and sheer unpredictability of the reception of mental measurement in England and Wales in the inter-War years was surely enhanced, perhaps in part caused by the marked decentralization of the decision-making process. Some consideration of this decentralization and of the principal participants in the local government of education complements the characterization of responses to mental measurement attempted in the two preceding chapters. It also provides further groundwork for an attempt in the final chapter to sketch an hypothesis which might explain the variety and complexity of these responses.

*

The Education Act of 1902 had given LEAs very considerable powers and discretions. Fisher's 'Act of 1918, if implemented in full, would have extended these; and in its truncated version did nothing to impair them.[1] Financial and economic constraints pressed heavily on local as on central government, but paradoxically these constraints increased the local authorities' room 'for manœuvre *vis-à-vis* the centre. Since the inter-War Board of Education had no financial carrots to offer for the adoption of what it saw as best practice in any given area, it was very often powerless to intervene, unless an authority was flagrantly breaking the law. As we saw when discussing provision for mentally handicapped children and the employment of psychologists, some authorities used their room for manœuvre, others did not.[2] And differences of policy and practice were throughout accentuated by the inequities of the rating system.

Some contemporaries applauded the decentralization,

---

[1] Above, pp. 167–8, 172–3.; for further detail, see Selby-Bigge, *The Board of Education*, esp. chs. I and VIII. The quotation which forms the title of the chapter is taken from p. 175.   [2] Above, pp. 95–6.

others did not. Lord Eustace Percy reflected that 'something like this indirect rule is the necessary pattern of all social service administration'.[3] Selby-Bigge, the Permanent Secretary 1911–25, however, commented that it made it particularly difficult to reduce inequalities in basic provision.[4] One of the objectives of Board officials in planning what was to become the 1944 Education Act was to regain the initiative in policy-making for the centre.[5]

Decisions about access to secondary education in the inter-War years, about the nature and conduct of the 'eleven-plus examination', thus rested in a very real sense with the 146 county and county borough councils in England and Wales. Within each authority the taking of such decisions involved not only the local councillors but also the local education officials and local teachers, elementary and secondary.

The tendency to fragmentation was not infinite, in that all four groups had national organizations, on some issues of policy at least, expressing collective views. In expatiating on the advantages of 'indirect rule', Eustace Percy commented that it had one major danger,

that educational policy might in practice be worked out, not by per-sonal touch with a diversity of local authorities, but by negotiations with a national Association of Education Committees managed by a small group of experienced Councillors and Directors of Education, with its own weekly journal, its own members of Parliament, and its own alliances or feuds with an even more highly-centralized National Union of Teachers. The densest screen that can shut out Whitehall from real tactical control of a social service — far denser than any general Staff of civil servants — is a screen composed of persons elected by elected persons, for the graces of representative government cannot be transmitted at second-hand.

I say this was the danger; but when I tried to get behind that screen, I found it easy, for the local Nestors of education who composed it — with the exception, perhaps, of one or two of the harder-bitten Directors of Education — were as much on their guard as I could be against the temptation to play at caucus politics.[6]

It sounds improbably cosy; and a systematic reading of the two weekly journals, *Education* for the AEC and *The School-master*, subsequently *The Teacher*, for the NUT, underlines

---

[3] Percy, *Some Memories*, p. 123.
[4] Selby-Bigge, *The Board of Education*, pp. 199–202.
[5] Gosden, *Education during the Second World War*, pp. 238–41.
[6] Percy, *Some Memories*, p. 121.

the improbability. As we have seen, the prolonged disagreement over the appropriateness of examining all eleven-year-olds made it impossible for the Board of Education to press for this on grounds of equity.[7] But this was the one aspect of examining on which there were strongly held and fiercely defended collective views. On other aspects and on mental measurement and its technology, the Board of Education was indeed dealing with 'a diversity of local authorities'. Views there were; after all, questions of examining and mental measurement bore directly upon the professional concerns of teachers and local education authority officers; but there was little in the way of a collective view amongst any one group.

The group whose work and professional lives were most nearly affected by mental measurement and the associated questions of examination technology were the elementary-school teachers. As we have seen, the legacy of payment by results had brought the NUT out firmly against 'general efficiency examinations' in the mid-1920s. But neither the union nor the would-be specialist body, the NUT Examinations Board, moved on from this to develop clear positions, positive or negative, on other aspects of examining and selection processes.

A strongly negative position would not have been wholly unexpected. The teacher formed his view of the child after prolonged observation and tested it by familiar attainments tests: this was his expertise. What was he to make of a group test, devised perhaps by someone who had never seen his school or the child? It was easy to administer a group test; but in marking the answers the key allowed him no discretion. To turn raw scores into IQs he had to use a set of mysterious tables. There were also the difficulties of reconciling this IQ with the results of observation and attainments tests. Not only were there practical problems, but the immutability attaching to the notion of intelligence could be seen as reducing, if not challenging outright, the teacher's role and power as the cultivator and moulder of the child's abilities. The introduction of group tests into eleven-plus examinations could present teachers with problems in maintaining a hard-won but still precarious authority.

[7] Above, pp. 160–1, 247–8.

Some part of teachers' insistence on finding a place in the selection process for the child's school record was surely rooted in feelings like this.

At the same time, it is equally possible and even plausible to see how a positive stance might have been developed. The new technology could have been appropriated and exploited to buttress and reinforce elementary teachers' claims to professional status. The doctors, after all, had been quick to add individual mental tests to their army of diagnostic tools for the identification of subnormality. Brian Simon has argued that 'psychometrists were completely in the ascendant and statements of their beliefs, couched in a form suggesting that the findings were the result of basic research into the human mind, figured in every textbook for teachers in training, in almost every tract by educationists for educationists', mentioning in support two popular texts, published respectively in 1936 and 1937.[8]

But as chapters 7 and 8 have shown, the reality was betwixt and between, some local teachers being deeply suspicious of mental testing, others co-operating apparently happily. Much depended, I suspect, on whose idea it was to experiment with a mental test and how it was presented to the teachers who would be involved. More generally, in making his large-scale claims, Professor Simon neglects the whole question of time-lag. Students bred on textbooks published in 1936 and 1937 were likely to be taking their first teaching jobs in 1939 and 1940. It would take them rather longer to reach headships and deputy headships. True, there were the Scottish graduates with B.Ed. degrees migrating southwards from 1920 onwards, some of them to training-college lectureships; and there were no doubt also student purchasers of *Mental and Scholastic Tests* and *The New Examiner*.[9] But even students trained at the beginning of the 1920s took time to climb the elementary-school career ladder; and before we pronounce on the content and balance of training-college curricula, we need to look at these curricula a great deal more carefully.

Work to organize, catalogue and make available training-college archives has only recently begun; and the *Checklist*

[8] Simon, *Educational Reform 1920–40*, p. 243.
[9] Above, pp. 129, 145–6.

prepared by a working party of the History of Education Society appeared too late for me to take proper advantage of it.[10] But a study of one exceptionally well-preserved set of archives, those of the colleges at Ripon and at York, now the College of Ripon and York, St. John, was both illuminating and suggestive. Psychology had a place in the curriculum at both colleges; although the HMI's report on York in 1931-2 commented that neither of the two members of staff who taught it had specialist qualifications.[11] At Ripon in 1934, HMI Miss Skillicorn suggested that,

more attention might profitably be devoted to the modern psychology of intelligence and temperament, with especial reference to the nature and degree of the differences between individual children, and the bearing of these on such questions as classification, preparation of syllabuses, examinations and the most effective methods of teaching the different types of children.[12]

A psychology practical notebook for the years 1930-2, prepared by a student who subsequently went on to become Principal of Ripon, shows that the class covered sixteen topics over the period, the last of which was 'Mental testing', entailing one piece of work on test marking and a second on 'IQs and correlations between Estimates, Tests and Age'; although earlier in the course the students had covered a number of basic statistical techniques as separate items.[13]

It seems as though interested students could make the acquaintance of mental measurement, but it was not rammed down their throats. This impression is strengthened by a study of the examination papers set for all the Yorkshire Training Colleges over the period. The Final Examination Paper for the General Course in the Principles of Teaching regularly contained about twenty questions, two or at most three of which could be answered with reference to mental measurement. The 1925 paper asked:

[10] History of Education Society, *Colleges of Education: A Checklist of Archives*, Leicester, n.d. [1981].

[11] Archives of the College of Ripon and York St. John, SJC/EP/11, item 9, HMI's Report 1931-2, para. 6. I am deeply indebted to Dr John Addy, the Archivist, for drawing my attention to these very full and well-ordered archives and for facilitating my work upon them.

[12] Ibid., RTC/Misc/23, item 2, HMI's Report 1933-4, para. 7 (1).

[13] Ibid., RTC/CW.

5.   What effects, good or bad, on teaching and classification have followed from the assumption that there is an 'average child'?

18. Why does a teacher examine his class at the end of a term or periodically at other times? Indicate the possible uses to which such examinations may be put.

The 1939 paper asked:

13(b)   Mental Tests arise out of practical needs of education. Discuss the use of these tests in school.

17.   What is the value of school records of individual children? Describe the kind of records you would keep of the children under your care, and how you would cooperate with the rest of the staff in compiling them.[14]

Perhaps Yorkshire was special; but psychometrists do not seem to have been completely in the ascendant there.

Whatever went on in training colleges, it might still be argued that the NUT, the largest elementary teachers' union, with all its pretensions to professional status, *ought* to have formed a view on mental measurement. But this is cloud-cuckoo-land. Given the diversity of opinion and attitude among its members and local branches, it could not have made a collective view stick. For the whole period 1920–40 the union was battling to protect its members' salaries, the recurrent target of successive governments' economy drives.[15] There was absolutely no incentive to render itself vulnerable on yet another front.

Questions of mental measurement and examination technology affected elementary-school teachers most closely; but they were not the only teachers affected by it. There were the secondary-school teachers, too. They must be treated as a group distinct from the elementary-school teachers, of higher and more assured social status, even when the latter were secondary-school- and college-educated and had not begun their careers as pupil-teachers. For the most part, secondary-school teachers were graduates and securely part of the local professional élite. If their schools were direct-grant schools and perhaps members of the Headmasters' Conference, they could lay claim to membership of a national élite group.

[14] Ibid., SJC/Ex/1, item 7 and SJC/Ex/2, item 8.
[15] Tropp, *The School Teachers*, ch. xii — a rather cosy account of what were actually some bitter conflicts.

Secondary-school teachers were, therefore, less likely to feel threatened by mental measurement but also less likely to have had even the brief formal encounter with it which a psychology component in a 'Principles of Teaching' course could give. Attitudes ranged all the way from lofty disdain to enthusiastic, if sometimes strikingly amateur, experiment. The summit of disdain was occupied, perhaps appropriately, by J.L. Paton, High Master of Manchester Grammar School. He explained to the North of England Education Conference in 1920 that he considered the extended interviews which he himself conducted infinitely superior to any intelligence test. He described types of questions which ranged from asking for a summary of passages from Addison and Macaulay, to sums about the accommodation of motor cars in garages; and he ended:

> while you are discussing this . . . and whatever may arise out of it, you are gauging from that boy's replies, and specially from the way he speaks and the set of his lips, what his will power is. This is, perhaps, the most important thing of all. What has this boy set himself to be? That more than anything else will determine his future. . . . This is where Simon-Binet fails us. Your boy may have a first-rate capacity for knowledge, but all he may want to know is all about the Carpentier-Beckett fight. The all-important thing about him is what sort of knowledge does he hunger for? And is his desire for it steadfast? Is it what economists call 'effective demand'? Will it be strong enough to resist the infection of the street with its posters and its newspaper placards? Will he have a soul that refuses to be fed on these things? Will he know the higher from the lower? The temporary from the abiding? And will he choose the better and eschew the worse? Has he his soul, as Plato would say, turned towards the light? If so, he is the lad your school was meant to help and he will help it as much as it helps him.[16]

Other secondary heads and teachers plainly felt differently. Those, like Mr Eldridge of West Suffolk who had read Binet and corresponded with Spearman,[17] were probably few and far between. But as many of the examples cited in chapter 8 showed, a substantial number seized on intelligence tests or intelligence-test-type questions as a way of extending or

---

[16] *Education* 6 Feb. 1920, pp. 102-3. The competition for free places at Manchester Grammar School remained a separate competition from that for free and special places at other grant-aided secondary schools in the Manchester area — see Ed 77/62.

[17] Above, p. 237.

livening up the standard format for interviews and orals. For the candidates' sakes, one must hope that not too many interviewers proceeded in the manner of 'Secondary Headmaster', who wrote to *The Times Educational Supplement* in 1921 as follows:

To each of thirty-five candidates, the most highly recommended out of ninety, from the elementary schools of my neighbourhood I gave as an oral test in a free place examination last week this question which they read in print from a paper:—

'Captain Cook made three voyages to the South Seas. On one of these voyages he was killed. On which one?'

Only six of the thirty-five candidates could answer this question correctly. The candidates were aged between ten and twelve years. Which is wrong — the test or the intelligence of the children?[18]

The officials serving local education authorities were a less homogeneous group, in terms of background and career experience, than either elementary or secondary teachers; and paradoxically, it seems somewhat easier to discern the dim outlines of two camps on the subject of mental measurement and testing. The Association of Directors and Secretaries of Education contained two distinct groups: on the one hand, the older breed of lower-middle-class, upwardly socially mobile ex-elementary-school teachers, ex-NUT officials, ex-school-board clerks, if graduates, mature students and often London external students; on the other, slightly younger middle-class graduates of the more conventional kind, with perhaps some token years of teaching experience, who, fifty years earlier, might have become public schoolmasters, briefless barristers, or even, immediately after 1870, HM Inspectors of Schools.[19]

Among the former group could be counted Thomas Walling at Newcastle-upon-Tyne, Spurley Hey at Manchester, Thomas Boyce at Bradford, Percival Sharp at Sheffield and A.R. Pickles at Burnley.[20] Among the latter group were Salter

[18] *The Times Educational Supplement* 28 May 1921, p. 240.

[19] Until 1919 there were actually two rival professional associations — *Education* 30 July 1926, p. 116. See also the tension reflected in the job description eventually agreed with the AEC by the end of 1938: ibid., 20 Mar. 1936, pp. 348-50; 12 Feb. 1937, pp. 190, 194-5; 9 July 1937, pp. 35-6; 10 Sept. 1937, p. 252; 3 Dec. 1937, p. 584; 4 Nov. 1938, p. 479. For the HMIs recruited immediately after 1870, see Sutherland, *Policy-Making 1870-95*, ch. 3.

[20] *Education* 21 Nov. 1925, pp. 369-70 (Hey); 13 Feb. 1925, pp. 158-9 (Sharp); 30 July 1926, p. 116 (Pickles); 30 Jan. 1931, pp. 132-3 (Boyce); 8 Jan. 1932, pp. 32-3 (Walling).

Davies in Kent, Keith Innes in Wiltshire, W.R. Brockington in Leicestershire, G.H. Gater in Lancashire and then at the LCC, and, by election, Henry Morris in Cambridgeshire.[21] Those in the latter group were, in the main, officers of authorities who took intelligence tests seriously. Leicestershire was notably early in the field with its own tests, moving later to use Moray House Tests – as did Cambridgeshire, when the decision to test was eventually taken in 1938. Kent and Wiltshire both sought advice from recognized experts in the early 1930s.[22]

But the fit was far from perfect. The LCC's approach to attainments testing was exceedingly sophisticated; but Gater it was who effectively killed the proposal to add an intelligence test to the junior county scholarship examination in 1933.[23] On the other hand, the ex-elementary-school teachers Walling and Boyce, at Newcastle-upon-Tyne and Bradford respectively, presided over examination systems in which intelligence tests were used.[24] A.R. Pickles's authority, Burnley, seems to have begun to test, in 1922.[25] And he showed himself to be very well informed about mental measurement and the whole field of examination technique when he addressed the North of England Conference on Education in 1931. He discussed at length theories about the relationship between general and specific abilities, concluding, 'it is therefore likely that selection for further education at the age of eleven will remain based on range of central capacity rather than type of special ability'. Then he went on:

There is great scope for experiment and research into the methods of transfer from junior schools. No course of senior grade can be properly planned without knowledge of the basis of attainment and capacity reached in the fundamental subjects of the curriculum, and the question of what the normal pupil can or cannot be expected to do assumes a new significance. It will be necessary to know what a pupil can actually do as well as what he is capable of doing. As internal examinations are 'tightened up' the school record will become increasingly valuable; but some form and measure of standardization

[21] Ibid., 17 July 1925, pp. 74-5 (Gater); Seaborne, 'William Brockington'; Weaver, 'Education; Retrospect and Prospect', pp. 3-4, 6-7 (Innes and Davies); and Harry Rée, *Educator Extraordinary: The Life and Achievements of Henry Morris 1889-1961* (London, 1973), esp. pp. 7-11.
[22] Above, pp. 209-10, 239-41.   [23] Above, pp. 263-4.
[24] Above, pp. 133, 212.   [25] Above, pp. 229-30.

will still be desirable. Intelligence tests are still on their trial. Whilst attainment may possibly be tested apart from capacity, it is certain that capacity cannot be ascertained apart from attainment. It is yet doubtful whether intelligence tests measure real capacity; they rather tend to show up sharpness and quickness of reaction, to be by way of puzzles rather than problems. '*If your grand-father's only child was your uncle, draw a square, if not, draw a circle.*' Whilst there may be a permanent place for intelligence tests in the educational scheme, it is probable that a good examination can test intelligence and capacity quite as well as these artificial aids. But the sponsors of intelligence tests are undoubtedly showing how examinations can be reformed.[26]

There is little in this with which either Godfrey Thomson or HM Inspectorate would have chosen to disagree.

Officials' attitudes to mental measurement were almost certainly muffled, too, by their involvement in the coalition that was the Association of Education Committees. The Association of Directors and Secretaries of Education had a separate existence principally to bargain over pay and conditions of service. On other matters and against the rest of the educational world the officer and elected members usually stood together, as Eustace Percy acknowledged by referring to them collectively as 'the local Nestors of Education', later singling out in particular, 'that model Kentish partnership of squire, magnate and scholar, Mark Collet, Lord Sackville and their Director, Salter Davies, who made their difficult mixed county a pattern for the nation'.[27]

From 1925 the full-time Secretary of the AEC was Percival Sharp, formerly Director of Education for Sheffield. The almost embarrassingly laudatory article on Sharp in 1925, in *Education*'s series on 'Educational Administrators' remarked,

Had not Directors of Education passed a self-denying ordinance that they would decline nomination in the election of President or Vice-President, there is little doubt but that Mr Sharp would, by this time, have received the highest honour in the gift of the Association.

As it was, he had been a member of the Executive since 1910.[28]

To point to the involvement of Sharp and others like him (also hymned in the series 'Educational Administrators') and

[26] *Education* 16 Jan. 1931 pp. 62, 64, his emphasis. Cf. the West Suffolk paper quoted above, pp. 252-3. [27] Percy, *Some Memories*, pp. 121-2.
[28] Education 13 Feb. 1925, pp. 158-9.

to the organizational backbone provided for the AEC by the officials is not to suggest that councillors and aldermen were simply their officers' front men or puppets. But the contribution made by the experienced elected members of the larger authorities was as much a reflection of their general standing in the local — and national — community as of particular expertise. However committed and informed councillors and aldermen might be, or become, about their chosen specialism, their local government work remained ultimately voluntary and more or less part-time. The absence of even a common occupational description makes them more difficult to characterize and 'weight' separately than either officials or teachers.

It is, however, possible to say a little about their standing in their communities. County and county borough councillors and aldermen were firmly part of the local élite. The reform of English local government at the end of the nineteenth century had brought about no social revolution. The county councils, at least up to 1974, remained remarkably aristocratic bodies. In industrial and the more heavily urbanized areas business and professional men gradually elbowed out the old squirearchy, but without necessarily bringing much change of style.[29] Among the most prominent and active aldermen and councillors in the AEC in the inter-War years were men like the substantial textile manufacturer, Alderman Sir Percy Jackson, Chairman of the West Riding Education Committee from 1917 to 1937; the local solicitor, Alderman Lieutenant-Colonel W.E. Raley, Chairman of the Barnsley Education Committee from 1904 to the end of the 1920s; and Councillor W. Byng Kenrick, nephew of Joseph Chamberlain and director of the family hardware firm, who succeeded another uncle as Chairman of the Birmingham Education Committee in 1921.[30] Among this company, even

[29] Bryan Keith-Lucas, *English Local Government in the Nineteenth and Twentieth Centuries* (London, The Historical Association, 1977), p. 23. For detailed studies of two authorities, see J.M. Lee, *Social Leaders and Public Persons. A study of county government in Cheshire since 1888* (Oxford, 1963) and G.W. Jones, *Borough Politics: A Study of the Wolverhampton Town Council 1884-1964* (London, 1969).

[30] P.H.J.H. Gosden and P.R. Sharp, *The Development of an Education Service: The West Riding 1889-1974* (Oxford, 1979), pp. 23-4 (Jackson); *Education* 24 Apr. 1925, pp. 388-9 (Raley); ibid., 23 Jan. 1925, pp. 92-3 (Kenrick).

the self-made men are rare and I have so far only identified two, Alderman E.G. Rowlinson, the railway trade-union official, Chairman of the Sheffield Education Committee from 1926; and George Tomlinson, the Lancashire weaver and union official, a member of the Lancashire Education Committee from 1930 and the successor to Ellen Wilkinson as Minister of Education in the Labour Government in 1947.[31]

Rowlinson, like Tomlinson, was a solid Labour man. But there has emerged no simple or necessary correlation between progressive politics — or, indeed, any other sort — and a predilection for the new technology in education. Rowlinson's fellow alderman from Sheffield, H.W. Jackson, embarrassed him badly when he launched a thoroughgoing attack on psychologists in general and child guidance clinics in particular at the AEC meetings in 1938 and 1939.[32] And Sheffield, as we have seen, did not use an intelligence test in its eleven-plus examination.[33]

The incomplete and cryptic nature of so many Education Committees' Minutes may conceal real enthusiasms and substantial patterns of interests. There was the mysterious committee at Bradford.[34] But so far, Dr Andrew Messer, the member of the Northumberland Education Committee who first drew Godfrey Thomson's attention to the whole question of selective examinations, seems *sui generis*.[35]

The AEC was thus an extremely diverse coalition, very much more so even than the NUT — which it faced regularly across the table in the salary negotiations of the Burnham Committee. It is small wonder, then, that like the NUT, the AEC did not even attempt to achieve a collective view on mental measurement.

*

A brief consideration of the decentralized nature of government in education and of the people involved in decision-

---

[31] Ibid., 17 June 1932, p. 697 (Rowlinson). For the working coalition between Jackson, Rowlinson, Lady Simon of Wythenshawe, Brockington, and R.H. Tawney on the Consultative Committee in the 1930s, see Joan Simon, 'The Shaping of the Spens Report on Secondary Education 1933-38: An Inside View', *British Journal of Education Studies* xxv (1977), pp. 63-80, 170-85.

[32] *Education* 24 June 1938, p. 825, 23 June 1939, pp. 807, 809, 811.

[33] Above, p. 266.   [34] Above, p. 212.   [35] Above, p. 194.

making in the localities serves, at first sight, only to twirl the patterns of the kaleidoscope faster. And awareness of these structures and relationships is essential to an understanding of the variety and fluctuations of responses to mental measurement. But the parts played in educational selection by secondary-school heads, local councillors and the newer breed of official also point us back to one of the major themes explored in the chapter on the rise of the eleven-plus examination: secondary education as the education of an élite group. If it is possible to move beyond a *description* of the reception of mental measurement in England in the inter-War period to an *explanation* of the nature of the reception, then that explanation is surely to be found in the distinctively élitist nature of English secondary education. The chapter that follows, the final one, attempts to sketch such an explanation.

Chapter 10

The Peculiarities of the English

The English did not embrace mental measurement in the same whole-hearted and complete way after the First World War as the Americans did. But neither did they reject it or ignore it — as the Welsh seem to have done. It remains finally to see whether the characterization of response attempted in chapters 7 and 8, and the sketch of local decision-makers in chapter 9, can help towards some explanatory hypothesis. How might one begin to explain the peculiarities of the English in this particular respect?

The patchy and uneven understanding and reception of mental measurement in England has surely much to do with the extent to which English secondary education remained highly and distinctively élitist. To put it very crudely, the uses of mental measurement were not that obvious to those in control of the English educational system between about 1900 and 1940; many of them reckoned they could manage quite well without it. This is not quite the crude functionalist tautology it seems; and it will perhaps begin to make more sense if we stand back and consider the ways in which the educational system examined in this book was élitist. Here the comparison with the United States is extremely instructive.

In the first decades of the twentieth century, American teachers and school administrators were struggling to build a system to cope with and contain a rapidly expanding population of staggering heterogeneity. The situation of the Army authorities in 1917, overwhelmed by volunteers and needing to make quick decisions about who should go where, in order to get on and actually fight the war, was exactly paralleled in the educational world. The people clamouring for education had somehow to be classified, categorized, organized into manageable groups so that they could be taught something. It is not difficult to imagine the appeal of so-called objective tests in offering ways of getting some purchase on this situation.[1]

---

[1] This is a huge subject and under scrutiny in a major research project directed

The English population was not expanding in this period; and in racial and cultural terms it was quite remarkably homogeneous, by comparison not only with the United States but with much of Europe also. Demand there was for more education but it was utterly insignificant compared with the demand in the United States, and most successfully contained and directed. The English 'scholarship ladder' was broader in 1940 than it had been in 1900 and fewer of its rungs were missing; but it was recognizably still the same structure. The involvement of government in the provision of secondary education did not radically alter the nature or objectives of that education. The effect of the Education Act of 1902 was almost certainly to strengthen existing structures, both in education and more generally in the society at large. The partial implementation of the Education Act of 1918 consolidated LEAs' powers while economic depression prevented them from using these powers in radically new ways. The period from about 1900 to 1940 saw an increase in the opportunities for upward mobility via the educational system, but it was a gradual expansion, owing as much to the fall in the child population as to any increase in the number of places provided.[2]

Upward mobility was not only gradual but also controlled and structured in very precise ways. The constitution of county and county borough councils as education authorities, together with rate and grant aid for secondary schools greatly extended the powers and patronage at the disposal of local élite groups, not only those substantial landowners, business and professional men who served as councillors and aldermen, but also the secondary-school head teachers. The involvement of the latter in interviews and oral examinations

by Daniel P. Resnick, Professor of History at Carnegie-Mellon University, Pittsburgh; see his 'History of Educational Testing' in Alexandra K. Wigdor and Wendell R. Garner, eds., *Ability Testing; Uses, Consequences and Controversies* (National Research Council, Committee on Ability Testing, Washington, DC., 1982), Part II, pp. 173–94; see also Clarence J. Karier, 'Testing for Order and Control in the Corporate Liberal State', *Educational Theory* xxii (1972), pp. 154–80, reprinted in *The I.Q. Controversy* ed. Ned Block and Gerald Dworkin (London, 1977), pp. 339–69. On the US Army tests, see above, pp. 54–5.

[2] A.H. Halsey, A.F. Heath, and J.M. Ridge, *Origins and Destinations. Family, Class, and Education in Modern Britain* (Oxford, 1980), p. 196; Appendix I below.

and the relish and idiosyncrasy with which many of them conducted their inquisitions, underlines the extent to which selection for secondary education entailed a very direct exercise of patronage.

As the element of patronage in the process of selection suggests, English educationists might propose the equation of ability with merit, of talent with virtue, but their notions of ability and talent had social and cultural as well as more narrowly intellectual dimensions. Sometimes the encrustations can be plainly distinguished. In 1910, in one of its earliest issues, *The Times Educational Supplement* approved the principle of the free-place system but warned:

> To insist all at once upon so large a proportion as 25% of 'free-placers', *ex hypothesi* boys or girls from working class homes, in an average secondary school to which middle class parents send their children, is, under present conditions of English life, to say the least of it, 'a large order'. . . . In an old country like England, where lines of social distinction are sharply drawn, they cannot be ignored or set aside in practice, however anxious we may be to open the best educational advantages to everyone. Most secondary school headmasters would welcome a contingent of capable working class boys to be absorbed into the life of the school and profit by its tone and teaching, but many of them are alarmed lest, if it be known or surmised that the numbers thus coming up from below are large enough to affect the tone and character of the school, the parents of paying pupils will hold aloof and the finances of the school become disorganized. Our administrators and reformers should be careful in the matter not to force the pace.[3]

Fifteen years later, in 1925, it was put more crudely. Dr Terry Thomas, the new headmaster of Leeds Grammar School — who was to remain there until the middle 1950s — moved and carried at the Headmasters' Conference a resolution to the effect that a substantial extension of the free-place system in existing schools would be unwise: 'They must be careful that their schools were not swamped. They had a great body of boys from middle class homes who might not be scholars but who were very valuable in building up a right tone in the school.'[4]

The defence of social privilege in secondary education is

---

[3] *The Times Educational Supplement* 16 Spet. 1910, p. 19, 'The New Secondary Education'.

[4] *Education* 2 Jan. 1925, p. 7.

quite explicit in these two comments. But arguments about the importance of qualities additional to 'scholarship' could be put both more loftily and more neutrally. A defence of 'tone' and 'character' could be transmuted quite easily into a defence of high culture in the strictest Arnoldian sense – as J.L. Paton's account of his interview technique and objectives showed.[5] The more neutral version was proffered by W.P. Alexander to a meeting of the NUT in 1938:

there are three questions to answer in selecting a pupil for any type of post-primary school; first, has he enough knowledge to make a start in the particular school for which he is being selected; second, has he sufficient ability of the appropriate type; and third, has he enough determination, or, if you would prefer it, is his character suitable to back up his ability and enable him to achieve the success which would normally be expected?[6]

In the course of the London experiments Dr A.G. Hughes had argued that attainments tests were a better guide than intelligence tests to a child's ambition, motivation and application. Like Alexander, he saw the conditions for success in the secondary school as three:

1. A good degree of innate intelligence.
2. A certain standard of academic attainment on entry.
3. Some sturdiness of character, preferably combined with physical vigour and satisfactory home conditions.

A child lacking one or more of those advantages listed under '3', he saw as suffering from 'permanent extraneous handicaps', the kind of child who might show up well in an intelligence test but not in an attainments test, and likely to be no more successful in the secondary school than in the elementary school.[7]

It was a point which had been put much more simply and directly by one of the Examiners in the first Leicestershire experiments with intelligence tests in 1925:

[5] Above, p. 276.

[6] *Education* 14 Jan. 1938, p. 32. Alexander was at this stage Director of Education for the Part III authority of Margate, at the beginning of his administrative career.

[7] LCC Papers, EO/PS/3/38 'Intelligence Tests and the Junior County Scholarship Examination – 1930 Experiment', Report by Dr A.G. Hughes 16 Apr. 1931, pp. 12-13; see also above, pp. 262-3.

in most cases where the written examination gave a worse result than the Group Test, the pupil was either retarded by home influences or was deficient in response to teaching – both factors which might continue to operate in further education.

However, in Leicestershire, in contrast to London, the response of the Director of Education – Brockington – was crisp: 'It is the duty and privilege of the Local Education Authority to counteract so far as possible adverse home influences; and a secondary school should be counted upon to improve a pupil's response to teaching.'[8]

Brockington, however, was something of an exception. Altogether, it is easier to characterize the élitism of the English educational system as aristocratic rather than meritocratic; and it becomes the less surprising that arguments for equality of opportunity in the interests either of the individual or of the state were infrequently heard and usually ineffective. It might have been expected that the debates on post-War reconstruction, although in the end bearing so little fruit, would have brought arguments about the gain to the state from investment in education into more general currency than before 1914. Certainly between 1915 and 1920 *The Times Educational Supplement* had declared at regular intervals that in future the nation could not afford to waste its 'child capital'.

But after 1920 statements of this kind largely disappeared. If the interests of the state were invoked at all in discussions of secondary education after 1920, it was as likely as not to be in arguments about the risks of over-education. Such a point was put with great elegance during the debate on the 1922 Education Estimates by Sir Martin Conway, Conservative MP for the Combined English Universities:

It is not, in fact, a ladder that we want from the lowest slum to the highest university honour, what we want is a sieve, so that we may be quite sure that not a grain is kept above the sieve that can get through it, and that not a grain large enough to remain in the top of the sieve gets lost. We want to sift the millions of children born in this country to discover, to isolate, to bring out, to help in every way, all the finest ability in the country, and allow none of it to escape. If you succeed in

---

[8] Leicestershire Education Committee Minutes and Papers, QR 92 Report to the Education Committee 1926-7, Appendix C, p. 48, comments of Examiner no. 9.

getting that, you really get all that is required, because the number of really able and most highly developed and educated people that are wanted will never be very many.[9]

As economic depression deepened and unemployment increased, comments about the 'saturation' of professions and black-coated occupations became more explicit.[10]

The government Inspectorate had first embarked upon its investigation of free-place examinations in 1921 in an effort to ensure that scarce secondary-school places were allocated as fairly as possible. In 1936 it contended that: 'The purpose of the examination is the selection at the age of 11+ of children fit to profit by secondary education. The importance of accurate selection is vital and the main business is to get the right children.'[11] But we have seen just how difficult the Inspectorate found it to persuade some authorities to act on this; and throughout the period a significant number of authorities declined to take the obvious step of examining the entire eligible age group.

Likewise, by no means all local authorities responded to the introduction of 'special' means-tested places by declaring all their secondary-school places 'special' and selecting for them by a uniform method. The AEC recommended that all authorities do so; but the language of the *AEC Memorandum on Special Places* can only be described as wistful:

It is desired — apart altogether from the enunciation of the simplest principles of justice — to emphasize that it is merely an elementary part of economic, social and political prudence to provide that the places in secondary schools maintained or aided by the nation should be allocated to children on an equal basis of merit. This is an ideal in secondary education which should not be forgone even in times of gravest national difficulty.[12]

---

9 Quoted in *Education* 12 May 1922, p. 282.
10 Ibid., 8 Jan. 1926, p. 24, report of address by J.F. Duff to the Eugenics Education Society; ibid., 5 Oct. 1928, p. 290, R.B. Henderson, 'Some reflections on the Scholarship System'; ibid., 14 Sept. 1934, p. 228, report of address by Dr Cyril Norwood to the British Association; cf. also ibid., 3 Dec. 1937, p. 585, 'Local Authority Notes'.
11 Above, pp. 155, 160.
12 *Education* 21 Oct. 1932, pp. 378–80, 'Selection for and Tuition Fees in Secondary Schools'. Cf. also ibid., 13 Jan. 1933, p. 41 (from the comments of Sharp at the North of England Conference); 23 June 1933, p. 708 (from Rowlinson's presidential address to the AEC AGM), and 18 Mar. 1938, p. 332 (the arguments at Brighton).

Against this broad background it becomes easier to see why the English response to intelligence tests and mental measurement, as providing ways of classifying normal children, was so patchy and sometimes so casual. The English educational establishment, with its various levels, was pretty much in control anyway; it had no special need for new tools and technology.

The claims of the new technology to objectivity were not unattractive, however. And 'general intelligence', whatever technical content it had recently acquired, was a term already in widespread use. It was a very handy shorthand for the bundle of qualities scholarship boys — and girls — had been expected to possess, ever since the Taunton Commission had offered the first sketch of an educational ladder for pupils of 'real ability'. It was almost too easy for Directors of Education to talk of tests of intelligence, use the term 'general intelligence', in describing what they were already doing in the selection process, dressing their procedures up, giving them just the right overtones of modernity and signalling an appropriately progressive stance. There is really nothing to choose between this kind of exploitation of the fashionable catch-phrase and that attempted by the Singer Sewing Machine Company with their 1927 advertisement: 'The Needlework Lesson now seems to develop general intelligence, too!'![13]

Slowly a more informed and more critical awareness of the *technology* as distinct from the *idea* of mental measurement spread, the principal missionaries being the HMIs and Moray House. This awareness, in turn, contributed to an increased preoccupation with rigour and objectivity in examining methods in general. But even among local authorities where this preoccupation was well developed and examining methods sophisticated by the standards of the day, a knowledge of the techniques of mental measurement did not automatically lead to the use of a group intelligence test. Here it is important to remember that the children going to secondary schools by means of scholarships and free and special places were a very highly selected group — in England even more so than in Wales.[14] Those children who carried off

[13] Above, p. 149.   [14] Above, p. 267.

the top prizes, who led the lists, would probably have survived most systems of selection. The problems lay, as most authorities recognized, at the borderline — in practice a huge group of candidates, between whom some dividing line had to be drawn. Enthusiasts for mental measurement argued that this line was a less arbitrary one when the results of an intelligence test were used as a cross-check on the results of attainments tests; but it was a nice point and much debated. As Dr Hughes remarked to the LCC subcommittee experimenting with intelligence tests, 'No method which is reasonably simple administratively, can do more than rough justice to the candidates.'[15]

In the inter-War years English education authorities were operating methods of selection which had their roots in patterns and precepts developed in the second half of the nineteenth century. Although these methods and the patterns and precepts from which they grew came under increasingly critical scrutiny, they were at no point before 1940 subjected to fundamental challenge, either of a political or of a demographic kind. Hence it was possible for English educational authorities to be somewhat selective and cavalier in their reception of mental measurement. Some treated it as a useful propaganda device. Others treated it like a new toy. Yet others came to see how it might help them sophisticate and refine existing methods of selection. There, too, however, they picked and chose, some attaching great weight to intelligence tests, others concerning themselves primarily with the standardization of attainments tests. In the years before 1940 mental measurement did not take the English educational world by storm. Rather, when it was noticed at all, it was exploited, bent to the service of existing élite structures and methods of selection.

[15] Above, p. 262.

Appendix I
Tables and Figures

The sources, except where otherwise stated, are the Statistics of Public Education for England and Wales, published until 1916 and again from 1927 to 1939 as Parliamentary Papers, and from 1927 presented as an appendix to the Board of Education's Annual Report. The statistics for 1920–6 were simply an HMSO publication.

1. *Access to grant-aided secondary education*

Commentary

To show the changing opportunity for access to secondary education one needs to look at the number of pupils in that age band in which entry will have almost certainly taken place if it is going to take place at all, i.e. over thirteen and under fourteen. The number of thirteen-year-olds in secondary education can then be compared with the total population in that age group, distinguishing between boys and girls.

If instead we looked at the yearly changes in the total secondary-school population (in some relevant age range) then the known tendency for the length of school life to increase — between 1924 and 1935 the average length of a pupil's school life increased from three years seven months to four years eleven months — would be incorporated, i.e. the opportunity increase would be exaggerated.

Again, if we looked at the new intake each year, any variation in the age at which secondary education *started*, would affect the changes thus shown in the overall opportunity changes from year to year. But the new intake series is useful in its own right, as showing the physical provision that had to be made for the entry cohort; and also for the associated calculation of the rising proportion of free places gained at entry — though this had still not reached one half by 1938.

The published official sources chose initially to calculate:
(1) pupils in grant-aided secondary schools as a percentage of the total population; and (2) ex-public elementary-school (ex-pes) pupils admitted to grant-aided secondary schools as a percentage of the public elementary-school pupils aged over ten and under eleven. But (1) is open to objection when those aged 10–15 are not a constant proportion of the total population. (2) is particularly objectionable since significant proportions of those admitted to grant-aided secondary schools were aged over eleven, but that age cohort is not included in the denominator. Thus, the percentages given in the Statistics of Public Education exaggerate the extent to which ex-pes pupils entered secondary education. For example, the data for 1921–2 (Table 61) show 11,772 ex-pes pupils of *all* ages admitted to secondary schools in England and Wales during 1921–2 and this is put as 9.5 per cent of the 653,115 pupils registered in public elementary schools on 31 March 1921 aged ten and under eleven. But Table 62, 1921–2, records only 28,137 full-time pupils in secondary schools (from *all* schools) aged over eleven and under twelve in 1921–2; and the Census shows 729,133 in that age cohort; i.e. only 3.9 per cent of that age group were in secondary schools.

What is shown here, therefore, as Table 1.1, is the annual intake to secondary schools and free-place holders as a percentage of this; and as Table 1.2, a time series showing the numbers of boys and girls over thirteen but under fourteen in full-time attendance at grant-aided secondary schools, and the percentage of the total cohort of that age, where known, represented by these numbers. The underlying population figures, although official, are necessarily estimates in non-Census years; and the 1931 Census is not in itself wholly reliable. Over the period 1921–38 the total population of school age (5–14 years) declined by about one and a third million — see Fig.1 below. Table 1.2 shows that advantage was taken of this demographic opportunity and that about 50 per cent more of the thirteen-year-olds were in secondary education in 1938 than in 1921; but the percentage was still no higher than 13.2 in that year. It can also be seen from Table 1.2 that the probability that a thirteen-year-old boy would be in secondary education was throughout somewhat higher than the probability that a thirteen-year-old girl would be there.

Table 1.1: *Total annual intake to grant-aided secondary schools and annual intake of pupils holding free places in England and Wales 1914–38*

School year	Total intake	Number of free-place holders	Free-place holders as a percentage total intake
1913–14	60,453	18,310	30.3
1919–20	96,283	28,539	29.6
1920–1	95,561	33,254	34.8
1921–2	90,601	28,829	31.8
1922–3	80,754	26,116	32.8
1923–4	80,340	27,191	33.8
1924–5	84,567	32,161	38.0
1925–6	86,908	33,743	38.8
1926–7	88,946	37,056	41.7
1927–8	89,253	38,097	42.7
1928–9	84,385	37,014	43.8
1929–30	86,119	39,079	45.4
1930–1	89,682	43,823	48.8
1931–2	96,342	46,946	48.7
1932–3	92,652	43,865	47.4
1933–4	92,490	41,106	44.4
1934–5	94,456	42,304	44.8
1935–6	93,850	42,327	45.1
1936–7	97,115	45,957	47.3
1937–8	98,820	46,707	47.3

Table 1.2: *Pupils aged over thirteen and under fourteen in full-time attendance at grant-aided secondary schools in England and Wales and the proportion they bear to the total population in that age group 1920–38*

School year ending March	Pupils aged 13–14			Total population 13–14			Pupils as a percentage of the population		
	Boys	Girls	Total	Boys (1911 Census)	Girls	Total	Boys	Girls	Total
1920	32,338	27,235	59,573	345,144	345,588	690,732)			
1921	34,839	30,117	64,956	373,527	371,241	744,768	9.3	8.1	8.7
1922	35,814	31,613	67,427						
1923	35,514	30,500	16,014						
1924			63,364						
1925	33,974	29,182	63,156						
1926	35,637	30,101	65,738	355,829	355,386	711,215	10.0	8.5	9.2
1927	37,711	32,072	69,783	356,324	357,004	713,328	10.6	8.9	9.8
1928	37,730	32,820	70,550	356,324	357,004	713,328	10.6	9.2	9.9
1929									
1930	39,280	34,038	73,318	306,210	301,150	607,360	12.8	11.3	12.1
1931	34,787	30,728	65,515				12.8	11.5	12.1
1932	36,127	31,748	67,875				13.5	12.1	12.8
1933	44,878	39,456	84,334				11.9	10.8	11.4
1934	48,153	41,782	89,935				12.3	11.0	11.6
1935	44,790	39,343	84,133				12.2	10.9	11.6
1936	43,495	38,303	81,798				12.7	11.4	12.0
1937	44,310	39,592	83,902				13.3	12.2	12.8
1938	44,749	40,229	84,978				13.8	12.7	13.2

Fig. 1. *Child Population of England and Wales (aged 5–14)*

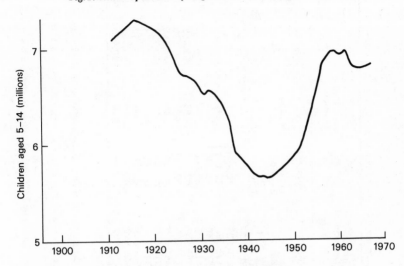

Reproduced, by kind permission, from A.H. Halsey, A.F. Heath, and J.M. Ridge, *Origins and Destinations — Family, Class, and Education in Modern Britain* (Oxford, 1980), p. 196.

2. 'Reorganization' following the Hadow Report

Table 2: *Public elementary schools in England and Wales: reorganization of departments on lines recommended in the Hadow Report, 1927–38*

(1)	Senior Departments.			Junior Departments.			All-age Departments with Senior Divisions.		Percentage of the total of Cols. 3, 7 and 9 to total number of pupils 11 and over.
	Number.	Number of pupils 11 and over.	Percentage of Col. 3 to total number of pupils 11 and over.	Number.	Number of pupils 8 and under 12.	Number of pupils 11 and over.	Number.	Number of pupils 11 and over.	
	(2)	(3)	(4)	(5)	(6)	(7)	(8)	(9)	(10)
									%
March, 1927 ··	649	163,106	8.5	1,776	150,923	10,830	No figures available.		
„ 1928 ··	713	174,574	9.5	1,868	175,773	12,164			
„ 1929 ··	883	209,899	12.6	2,518	277,330	15,230			
„ 1930 ··	1,017	238,681	15.3	3,212	416,405	26,500	1,225	120,440	24.7
„ 1931 ··	1,352	319,620	19.5	4,049	565,730	62,535	1,483	152,052	32.5
„ 1932 ··	1,915	519,151	28.1	4,994	739,739	95,336	1,408	162,510	42.1
„ 1933 ··	2,344	699,077	34.7	5,586	855,549	120,689	1,346	164,450	48.8
„ 1934 ··	2,612	800,651	39.1	5,922	913,039	129,103	1,322	158,759	53.2
„ 1935 ··	2,744	792,474	41.3	6,215	942,871	129,782	1,304	149,593	55.8
„ 1936 ··	2,864	794,972	43.6	6,553	967,769	132,225	1,341	143,765	58.8
„ 1937 ··	2,962	805,335	45.9	6,937	998,979	133,025	1,400	140,562	61.5
„ 1938 ··	3,074	818,827	48.3	7,471	1,039,664	138,473	1,136	120,443	63.5

Source: Board of Education List 49, 1938. (HMSO 1939)

Notes:

1. In addition there were still, in 1938, 11,642 unreorganized departments in England and Wales, containing 856,636 pupils under eleven and 618,654 pupils over eleven.

2. The inclusion of children over eleven in Junior Departments (col.7) and of pupils over eleven in all-age departments with senior divisions (col.9) in the percentages calculated for col.10 is surely stretching the notion of 'reorganization' somewhat. The number of pupils aged eleven and over in 'Junior Departments' actually increases significantly during the period.

3. In Addition to this initial summary table, List 49, 1938 provides a detailed breakdown by LEA area revealing the peculiar problem of Anglican village schools.

3. Special Schools

Table 3: *Accommodation for mentally defective children in special schools (day and residential) in England and Wales, 1915–38*

Year ending 31 March	Number of places
1915	14,626
1916	14,598
1917	15,051
1918	15,329
1919	15,249
1920	15,551
1921	16,328
1922	16,281
1923	16,209
1924	16,372
1925	16,746
1926	17,168
1927	17,337
1928	17,035
1929	17,008
1930	16,536
1931	16,644
1932	16,893
1933	16,839
1934	16,587
1935	16,466
1936	16,542
1937	16,407
1938	16,375

Appendix II
The sources of evidence for the use of mental tests in free and special-place examinations 1919–40

Three sets of sources purporting to be national in their coverage of test use were initially examined: the survey conducted by Sir Philip Hartog and Gladys Roberts for the International Institute Examinations Enquiry and published by them in 1937 as *A Conspectus of Examinations in Great Britain and Northern Ireland*; the records of the testing organization Moray House; and the papers in the Public Record Office files Ed 77/17–137 and Ed 110/1–147, relating to the confidential inquiries made by HM Inspectorate into free and special-place examinations throughout the period. An attempt was made to complement these by means of a questionnaire about inter-War selection procedures (and the employment of psychologists) sent to all LEAs in England and Wales in May 1975 – GSQ 1975; and a further questionnaire about the location of records, sent to all appropriate local archive offices in England and Wales in June 1976 – GSQ 1976. The immediate aftermath of local government reorganization was not an easy time and the response was varied; but a number of officers of a number of authorities went out of their way to search out material and/or find people who could answer the questions asked; and I hope the publication of this study will stand as some recompense for their time and effort.

Only thirty-four LEAs responsible for the provision of secondary education declared themselves to Hartog and Roberts as using something they chose to call an intelligence test. A trawl of the other sources, treating 'test use' in its loosest and most all-embracing sense (see chapters 7 and 8) brought this total up to seventy-five. The problem then remaining was that of devising a strategy for sampling LEA archives. Mapping the information suggested that there had been no use of testing in Wales outside Monmouthshire. Otherwise, there was no discernible geographical pattern. Attempts to classify LEAs according to the provision of secondary-school places per head of the relevant age group in their areas during the period and then to look for possible correlations between these proportions and the use of testing, failed. Systematic information on age structure, broken down by LEA area, cannot be found in the published Board of Education and Census Reports and to extract it from the unpublished material would be an independent research project in itself.

It was eventually decided to approach the problem pragmatically, through a pilot study in East Anglia, of the records of ten authorities. These initial ten record sets, representing six authorities known to use tests and four not known to use tests, suggested that while it was unlikely that authorities who used tests would give details of their reasons for doing so, it was even more unlikely that those who did not would give their grounds for *not* doing so.

Subsequent work entirely confirmed this impression. LEA committee minutes, especially the nearer one approaches to the present day, primarily report decisions taken and seldom give much indication of the background of discussion. Thus where full sets of committee and subcommittee minutes and papers do exist, they are often rather cryptic. In a number of cases the LEA records are incomplete and/or in a state of some disorder. Only in 1972 did the Local Government Act lay a mandatory responsibility on authorities to make proper provision for their own administrative records. Local government re-organization followed only two years later; and the financial cuts of the later 1970s have not been kind to archive services in particular. The net result of all this is that much material has been destroyed or mislaid; some still remains in local authority offices and they may choose to refuse access; and some has found its way to local archive offices, although often in a state of great confusion. Thus, however carefully, or on whatever basis, a sample of non-testing authorities was drawn, it might yield very little information about the non-use of tests and whether a decision *not* to test was ever taken.

We decided therefore to concentrate our attention in the first instance on those authorities we knew to have used tests of some kind, bringing to bear also what we had learned about the survival and/or availability of records from the two questionnaires. To ensure a complete geographical spread in England, Hampshire was added; and in Wales we decided to look also at the records of one northern rural LEA and one southern industrial LEA, in addition to Newport and Monmouthshire. During our visits to these authorities' records we looked also, wherever possible, at the records of other LEAs deposited in the same Record Office, or elsewhere in the same town, which were not known to have used tests. Altogether we looked at the records of eighty-two LEAs, plus those of the London County Council.

The additions described in the previous paragraph brought under scrutiny the records of fourteen authorities not hitherto known to have used tests, and six of these authorities turned out to have used tests, bringing our total of known test users — again defined in its broadest and loosest sense — to eighty-one out of 146.

If the percentage of authorities using tests was similar among the sixty-three authorities whose archives were not visited, to that among these fourteen, then there could be as many as twenty-seven further cases of undetected test usage. There is no way of checking this, short of searching the records of all sixty-three authorities — if they have survived. But it is plausible that if the number twenty-seven is wrong it is too high rather than too low. The fourteen authorities, by definition, included an unduly high proportion whose headquarters were in the same town as the headquarters of authorities which did use testing; hence there would be more opportunity for local communication than in the case, say, of neighbouring counties. In addition, Wales appears to be a special case (see pp. 267–8).

To conclude: we looked at some LEA records in every region of England, looking also thereby at the records of at least 70 per cent of those authorities in England and Wales which used testing of some kind in selection for secondary education. We could see no basis for making a further selection among the records of the remaining authorities; while to visit them all seemed likely to yield very little return for considerable effort.

Note: The number of LEAs with responsibility for secondary education was not constant throughout the inter-War period. The 1888 legislation allowed the creation of new county boroughs; and between 1888 and 1926 the number of county boroughs in England alone increased from fifty-nine to seventy-eight. Thereafter the process was halted. (See *Report of the Royal Commission on Local Government in England 1966-69*, para. 82, P.P. 1968-9 xxxviii Cmnd 4040.) It seemed sensible, therefore, to use for purposes of calculation etc. the maximum, the total number of county and county borough councils in existence between 1927 and 1940, that is, 146 (cf. Hartog and Roberts, *Conspectus of Examinations*, p. 2).

The sketch maps in chapters 7 and 8 are based on maps in *Philips' Handy Administrative Atlas, England and Wales*, 1928 edition, pp. 3-4.

Bibliography

MANUSCRIPT SOURCES CITED

(a) Local authority archives

(i) County Council Papers

Buckinghamshire	County Record Office, Aylesbury.
Cambridgeshire	County Record Office, Shire Hall, Castle Hill, Cambridge.
Devon	County Record Office, Exeter.
Dorset	County Record Office, County Hall, Dorchester.
Isle of Ely	County Record Office, Shire Hall, Castle Hill, Cambridge.
Huntingdonshire	County Record Office, Shire Hall, Castle Hill, Cambridge.
Kent	County Record Office, Maidstone.
Lancashire	County Record Office, Preston.
Leicestershire	County Record Office, 57 New Walk, Leicester.
Lindsey	Lindsey County Council Offices, Newland, Lincoln.
London	Greater London Record Office, 40 Northampton Road, Bowling Green Lane, London EC1.
Monmouthshire	County Record Office, Cwmbran, Gwent.
Norfolk	Education Department, County Hall, Norwich.
Northamptonshire	Education Offices, Northampton.
Northumberland	County Record Office, Melton Park, North Gosforth.
Nottinghamshire	County Record Office, County House, High Pavement, Nottingham.
Oxfordshire	County Record Office, New Road, Oxford.
East Suffolk	Suffolk Record Office, County Hall, Ipswich.
West Suffolk	Suffolk Record Office, Bury St. Edmunds Branch, Schoolhall Street, Bury St Edmunds.
Westmorland	Cumbria Record Office, Kendal.
Isle of Wight	County Record Office, Newport, Isle of Wight.

Wiltshire	County Record Office, Trowbridge.
East Riding of Yorkshire	County Record Office, County Hall, Beverley.
North Riding of Yorkshire	County Record Office, County Hall, Northallerton.

(ii) County Borough Council Papers

Barnsley	Metropolitan Borough Council Education Offices, 50 Huddersfield Road, Barnsley.
Barrow-in-Furness	County Record Office, Barrow-in-Furness.
Birmingham	Public Library, Victoria Square, Birmingham.
Bolton	Central Library, Bolton.
Bournemouth	Education Department, Portman House, Richmond Hill, Bournemouth.
Bradford	Central Library, Prince's Way, Bradford.
Brighton	East Sussex County Record Office, Lewes, Sussex.
Burnley	Central Library, Grimshaw Street, Burnley.
Cardiff	Central Library, The Hayes, Cardiff.
Coventry	City Record Office, 9 Hay Lane, Coventry.
Croydon	Central Library, Katharine Street, Croydon.
Darlington	Local History Department, Crown Street, Darlington.
Dewsbury	Central Library, Wellington Road, Dewsbury.
Doncaster	Education Offices, Princegate, Doncaster.
Halifax	Central Library, Lister Lane, Halifax.
Hull	City Record Office, The Guildhall, Hull.
Ipswich	Suffolk Record Office, County Hall, Ipswich.
Lincoln	Lincoln Archives Office, The Castle, Lincoln.
Liverpool	Brown, Picton, and Hornby Libraries, Liverpool.
Manchester	Manchester Central Library, St Peter's Square, Manchester.
Newport (Mon.)	County Record Office, Cwmbran, Gwent.
Northampton	County Record Office, Delapré Abbey, Northampton.
Nottingham	County Record Office, County House, High Pavement, Nottingham.
Oxford	Central Library, Westgate, Oxford.
Portsmouth	City Record Office, Guildhall, Portsmouth.
Reading	Berkshire County Record Office, Shire Hall, Reading.

Salford	Local Studies Library, Peel Park, Salford.
Smethwick	Central Library, High Street, West Bromwich.
Southampton	Civic Record Office, Civic Centre, Southampton.
Sunderland	Langham Library, Sunderland Polytechnic, Sunderland.
Worcester	Hereford and Worcester Education Department, County Hall, Worcester.

(b) Other archives
Cranbrook Papers:
Papers of the first Earl of Cranbrook, Suffolk County Record Office, County Hall, Ipswich.
Education Department and Board of Education Papers:
Public Record Office, Kew: files in classes Ed 10/-, 11/-, 12/-, 14/-, 22/-, 23/-, 24/-, 31/-, 50/-, 77/- and 110/-.
Moray House Papers:
Papers of the testing service Moray House, now the Godfrey Thomson Unit for Educational Research, on deposit in Edinburgh University Library. (It may be helpful to explain that the material covering the period to 1940 is of two kinds: a collection of exercise books listing Moray House clients, and eight large leather-bound volumes into which batches of correspondence, tables, graphs, draft test papers, etc. have been pasted or pinned. My references to the latter give volume numbers – Roman – and folio numbers – Arabic – for the leaf or leaves to which the item(s) in question have been attached.)
NUT Examinations Board Minute Books:
National Union of Teachers' Library, Hamilton House, Mabledon Place, London W.C.1.
Papers of the Colleges at Ripon and York:
The College of Ripon and York, St John, The College, Lord Mayor's Walk, York.
Salisbury Papers:
Papers of the third Marquess of Salisbury, Hatfield House.

(c) Unpublished dissertations and papers
Doyle, Denis, 'Aspects of the Institutionalization of British Psychology: The National Institute of Industrial Psychology 1921–1939', unpublished Manchester Ph.D. thesis, 1979.
Hope, Keith, 'The Political Conception of Merit', typescript, 1977, to be published by Russell Sage.
Jefferys, Kevin, draft chapters of 'The Educational Policies of the Conservative Party 1918–1944', to be submitted for the degree of Ph.D. to the University of London.
Taylor, A.I., 'The Church Party and Popular Education 1893–1902', unpublished Cambridge Ph.D. thesis, 1981.
Yeo, Eileen, 'Social Science and Social Change: A Social History of Some Aspects of Social Science and Social Investigation in Britain 1830–1890', unpublished Sussex D. Phil. thesis, 1973.

PRINTED SOURCES

(a) Parliamentary Papers and Official Publications

Annual Reports of the Education Department, 1880–99.

Annual Reports of the Board of Education, 1900–38.

Hansard

The Health of the School Child 1921–38.

Report on the Organisation of the Permanent Civil Service (Northcote-Trevelyan), P.P. 1854 xxvii.

Report to the President of the Board of Control on the Examination of Candidates for the Indian Civil Service, November 1854 printed as Annexe A to *Report on the Selection and Training of Candidates for the Indian Civil Service, 1876,* P.P. 1876 lv ff. 300–6.

Bill to make further provision for the Good Government and Extension of Public Schools (no. 32) and *The Public Schools Bill as amended by the Select Committee (no. 202),* House of Lords Papers 1865 v.

Report of the Select Committee on the Public Schools Bill, House of Lords Papers 1865 x.

Report of the Schools Inquiry Commission (Taunton), P.P. 1867–8 xxviii.

Report of Dr Crichton-Browne on Over-pressure, P.P. 1884 lxi.

Report of the Royal Commission on Elementary Education (Cross), P.P. 1886 xxv.

Report and Minutes of Evidence of the Royal Commission on the Blind, Deaf, Dumb etc. (Egerton), P.P. 1889 xix, xx.

Report of the Royal Commission on Secondary Education (Bryce), P.P. 1895 xliii.

Special Reports on Educational Subjects in England and Wales, vol. 1, P.P. 1897 xxv.

Report of the Departmental Committee on Defective and Epileptic Children, P.P. 1898 xxvi.

62 & 63 Vict., c. 32 (1899 Elementary Education (Defective and Epileptic Children) Act).

Minutes of Evidence etc. of the Royal Commission on the Care and Control of the Feeble-Minded, P.P. 1908 xxix Cd 4202, xxxv Cd 4215, xxxvi Cd 4216, xxxvii Cd 4217 and 4218, xxxviii Cd 4219 and 4220, xxxix Cd 4221.

3 & 4 Geo. V, c. 28 (1913 Mental Deficiency Act).

4 & 5 Geo. V, c. 45 (1914 Elementary Education (Defective and Epileptic Children) Act).

8 & 9 Geo. V, c. 39 (1918 Education Act).

Report on the Departmental Committee on Scholarships, Free Places and Maintenance Allowances (Hilton Young), P.P. 1920 xv Cmd 968.

Report of the Select Committee on the Education (Consolidation) Bill, P.P. 1921 vi Cmd 661.

11 & 12 Geo. V, c. 51 (1921 Education Act).

Board of Education Circular 1190, 1921.

Board of Education Circular 1297, 1923.

Board of Education Circular 1341, 1924.

Mental and Scholastic Tests Among Retarded Children, Board of Education pamphlet no. 44, 1923.

Psychological Tests of Educable Capacity and their possible use in the public system of education, Report of the Board of Education Consultative Committee, 1924.

Board of Education Circular 1371, 1925.

The Education of the Adolescent, Report of the Board of Education Consultative Committee (Hadow), 1926.

17 & 18 Geo. V, c. 33 (1927 Mental Deficiency Act).

Report of the Mental Deficiency Committee (Wood), 3 vols., 1929.

Memorandum on Examinations for Scholarships and Free Places in Secondary Schools, Board of Education pamphlet no. 63, 1928.

Supplementary Memorandum . . ., 1936.

The Primary School, Report of the Board of Education Consultative Committee, 1931.

Report of the Departmental Committee on Sterilisation (Brock), P.P. 1933–4 xv Cmd 4485.

The Education of Backward Children, with special reference to children who are backward because dull, Board of Education pamphlet no. 112, 1937.

Secondary Education with special reference to grammar schools and technical high schools, Report of the Board of Education Consultative Committee (Spens), 1938.

The Reorganization of Public Elementary Schools in England and Wales to year ending 31 March 1938, Board of Education List 49, 1938, 1939.

Report of the Royal Commission on Local Government in England 1966–69 (Redcliffe-Maud), P.P. 1968–9 xxxviii Cmnd 4040.

(b) Periodicals
British Journal of Educational Psychology
British Journal of Psychology
Education
The Schoolmaster: from 1915 *The Teacher*
The Times
The Times Educational Supplement

(c) Primary sources (place of publication London, unless otherwise stated)
Alexander, William, *The Educational Needs of Democracy*, 1940.
Ballard, P.B., *Mental Tests*, 1920; *The New Examiner*, 1923; *Things I cannot forget*, 1937.
Burt, Cyril, 'The Measurement of intelligence by the Binet tests', *Eugenics Review* vi (1914), pp. 36–50, 140–52; *The Distribution and Relations of Educational Abilities*, 1917; *Mental and Scholastic Tests*, 1921; *Report of an investigation upon backward children in Birmingham*, Birmingham, 1921.
Carlyle, Thomas, *Chartism*, 1839.

Carr-Saunders, A.M., and Caradog Jones, D., *A Survey of the Social Structure of England and Wales as illustrated by statistics* 2nd edition, Oxford, 1937.

Cattell, J.M., 'Mental Tests and Measurements' *Mind* xv (1890), pp. 373-80 — with 'Remarks' by Francis Galton pp. 380-1.

Cattell, Raymond B., *The Fight for our National Intelligence*, 1937.

Charity Organization Society, *The Education and Care of Idiots, Imbeciles and Harmless Lunatics*, 1877; *The Feeble-Minded Child and Adult*, 1893.

Church Congress, Authorised Report of the Proceedings, 1912.

Fisher, H.A.L., *An Unfinished Autobiography*, 1940.

Galton, Francis, *Hereditary Genius*, 1869, 2nd edition, 1892; *Inquiries into Human Faculty and Its Development*, 1883; *Memories of my Life*, 1908.

Gray, J.L., and Moshinsky, Pearl, 'Studies in genetic psychology: the intellectual resemblance of collateral relatives', *Proceedings of the Royal Society of Edinburgh* liii (1932-3), part ii, pp. 188-207; 'Ability and Opportunity in English Education', *Sociological Review* xxvii (1935), pp. 113-62; 'Ability and Educational Opportunity in Relation to Parental Occupation', *ibid.*, pp. 281-327 (these two latter articles were reprinted in L. Hogben, ed., *Political Arithmetic*, 1938.

Gray, J.L., *The Nation's Intelligence*, 1936.

Hartog, Sir Philip, and Rhodes, E.C., *An Examination of Examinations*, 1935; *The Marks of Examiners*, 1936; Hartog and Roberts Gladys, *A Conspectus of Examinations in Great Britain and Northern Ireland*, 1937.

Hayward, F.H., *A First Book of School Celebrations*, 1920; *A Second Book of School Celebrations*, 1920; *An Educational Failure*, 1938.

Herrman, L., and Hogben, L., 'The intellectual resemblance of twins', *Proceedings of the Royal Society of Edinburgh* liii (1932-3), part ii, pp. 105-29.

John Langdon Haydon Down, 'Observations on an Ethnic Classification of Idiots', *London Hospital Reports* 3 (1866), pp. 259-62, reprinted in Down, *Mental Affections of Childhood and Youth*, 1887.

Lapage, C. Paget, *Feeblemindedness in Children*, 1911.

Lee, Jennie, *This Great Journey*, 1963.

The Works of Lord Macaulay, 12 vols., 1898.

Maguiness, Olive, *Environment and Heredity*, 1940.

Markham, Violet, *Friendship's Harvest*, 1956.

Mearns, Andrew, *The Bitter Cry of Outcast London*, 1883, reprinted with commentary by A.S. Wohl and supplementary material, Leicester, 1970.

Annual Reports of the National Union of Teachers 1895-1936.

Penrose, Lionel, *The Influence of Heredity on Disease*, 1934; *The Biology of Mental Defect*, 1949.

Percy, Lord of Newcastle, *Some Memories*, 1958.

Philips' Handy Administrative Atlas. England and Wales, 1928.

Philpott, Hugh B., *London at School. The Story of the School Board*

1870–1904, 1904.

Pinsent, Ellen F., 'On the Permanent Care of the Feeble-Minded', *The Lancet* 21 Feb. 1903, pp. 513–15.

A History of Psychology in Autobiography, 4 vols., 1–3 ed. C.A. Murchison, 4 ed. E.G. Boring, H.S. Langfeld, H. Werner and R.M. Yerkes, Worcester, Mass., 1930–6, 1952.

Sadler, Sir Michael, *et al.*, *Essays on Examinations*, 1936.

Sandford, E.G., ed., *Memoirs of Archbishop Temple by Seven Friends*, 2 vols., 1906.

Scottish Council for Research in Education Publications, V *The Intelligence of Scottish Children*, 1933; XXX *The Trend of Scottish Intelligence*, 1949; XXXV *Social Implications of the 1947 Scottish Mental Survey*, 1953; XLI *Educational and Other Aspects of the 1947 Scottish Mental Survey*, 1958; XLII *Eleven-Year-Olds Growing Up*, 1958; XLVI *The Level and Trend of National Intelligence*, 1961.

Selby-Bigge, Sir L.A., *The Board of Education*, 1927.

Shuttleworth, G.E., *Mentally Deficient Children*, 1895, 2nd edition 1900.

Spearman, Charles, '"General intelligence" : objectively determined and measured', *American Journal of Psychology* xv (1904), pp. 201–92; 'Heredity of abilities', *Eugenics Review* vi (1914), pp. 219–37; *The Nature of Intelligence and the Principles of Cognition*, 1923.

Spencer, F.H., *An Inspector's Testament*, 1938.

Tawney, R H., ed., for the Educational Advisory Committee of the Labour Party, *Secondary Education for All*, 1922.

Thomson, Godfrey, *Instinct, Intelligence and Character*, 1924; *A Modern Philosophy of Education*, 1929.

Tredgold, A.F., *Mental Deficiency*, 1908.

Trollope, Anthony, *An Autobiography*, 1883.

Warner, Francis, 'A Method of Examining Children in Schools as to their development and Brain Condition' *British Medical Journal* 22 Sept. 1888, pp. 659–60; *Lectures on the Growth and Means of Training the Mental Faculty*, Cambridge, 1890; 'Mental and Physical Conditions among 50,000 children', *Journal of the Royal Statistical Society* lix (1896), pp. 125–68; *The Nervous System of the Child; its growth and health in education*, New York, 1900.

Weaver, Toby, 'Education: retropsect and prospect: an administrator's testimony', *Cambridge Journal of Education* ix (1979), pp. 2-17.

Webb, Beatrice, *My Apprenticeship*, 1936.

Winch, W.H., 'Binet's mental tests', *Child Study* vi (1913), pp. 113–17, vii (1914), pp. 1–5, 19–20, 29–45, 55–62, 87–90, 98–104, 116–22, 138–44, viii (1915), pp. 1–8, 21–7, 50–6, 86–92.

(d) Secondary sources (place of publication London, unless otherwise stated)

Abrams, Philip, *The Origins of British Sociology 1834–1914*, Chicago, 1968.

Allen, Bernard M., *Sir Robert Morant. A Great Public Servant*, 1934.

Ausubel, Herman, *In Hard Times. Reformers Among the Late Victorians*, 1960.

Banks, Olive, *Parity and Prestige in English Secondary Education*, 1955.

Barker, Rodney, *Education and Politics 1900-1951. A Study of the Labour Party*, Oxford, 1972.

Best, Geoffrey, *Mid-Victorian Britain 1851-75*, 1971.

Blaug, 'The Myth of the Old Poor Law and the Making of the New', *Journal of Economic History* xxiii (1963), pp. 151-84; 'The Poor Law Report Re-examined', ibid. xxiv (1964), pp. 229-45.

Blewett, Neal, *The Peers, the Parties and the People: The General Elections of 1910*, 1972.

Brain, Lord, 'Chairman's Opening Remarks: Historical Introduction' in *Mongolism: In Commemoration of Dr John Langdon Haydon Down*, ed. G.E.W. Wolstenholme and Ruth Porter (1967), pp. 1-5.

Bridgeland, M., *Pioneer Work with Maladjusted Children*, 1971.

Briggs, Asa, *Social Thought and Social Action. A Study of the Work of Seebohm Rowntree 1871-1954*, 1961.

'A Balance Sheet on Burt', Supplement to the *Bulletin of the British Psychological Society* xxxiii (1980).

Chester, D.N., *Central and Local Government. Financial and Administrative Relations*, 1951.

Symposium on the Child Guidance Service, *British Journal of Educational Psychology* xxii (1952) and xxiii (1953).

Clarke, A.D.B. and Clarke, A.M., eds., *Readings from Mental Deficiency: The Changing Outlook*, 1978.

Coleman, D.C., 'Gentleman and Players', *Economic History Review* 2nd ser. xxvi (1973), pp. 92-116.

Colleges of Education: A Checklist of Archives, History of Education Society, Leicester, n.d. [1981].

Collini, Stefan, *Liberalism and Sociology. L.T. Hobhouse and Political Argument in England 1880-1914*, Cambridge, 1979; 'Political Theory and the Science of Society in Victorian Britain', *Historical Journal* xxiii (1980), pp. 203-32.

Cruickshank, M., 'Mary Dendy 1855-1923', *Journal of Educational Administration and History* viii (1976), pp. 26-9.

Cullen, M.J., *The Statistical Movement in Early Victorian Britain: the Foundations of Empirical Social Research*, Hassocks, Sussex, 1975.

Dubois, P.H., *A History of Psychological Testing*, 1970.

Dyhouse, Carol, *Girls Growing Up in Late Victorian and Edwardian England*, 1981.

Eaglesham, Eric, *From School Board to Local Authority*, 1956.

Evans, Brian, and Waites, Bernard, *IQ and Mental Testing. An Unnatural Science and its Social History*, 1981.

Fletcher, Sheila, *Feminists and Bureaucrats. A study in the development of girls' education in the nineteenth century*, Cambridge, 1980.

Finer, S.E., *The Life and Times of Sir Edwin Chadwick*, 1952.

Flugel, J.C. and West, Donald J., *A Hundred Years of Psychology*, 1964.

Forrest, D.W., *Francis Galton: The Life and Work of a Victorian Genius*, 1974.

Foster, C.D., Jackman, R., and Perlman, M., *Local Government Finance in a Unitary State*, 1980.

Freeden, Michael, *The New Liberalism. An Ideology of Social Reform*, Oxford, 1978.

Gilbert, B.B. *The Evolution of National Insurance in Great Britain. The Origins of the Welfare State*, 1966; *British Social Policy 1914-1939*, New York, 1970.

Gillie, Oliver, 'Sir Cyril Burt and the great IQ fraud', *New Statesman*, 24 Nov. 1978, pp. 688-94.

Gosden, P.H.J.H., *The Development of Educational Administration in England and Wales*, Oxford, 1966; *Education in the Second World War. A Study in Policy and Administration*, 1976; Gosden and Sharp, P.R., *The Development of an Education Service: The West Riding 1889-1974*, Oxford, 1979.

Gould, Stephen Jay, *The Mismeasure of Man*, 1981.

Halsey, A.H., Heath, A.F., and Ridge, J.M., *Origins and Destinations. Family, Class, and Education in Modern Britain*, Oxford, 1980.

Harris, José, *Unemployment and Politics. A Study in English Social Policy 1886-1914*, Oxford, 1972; *William Beveridge: A Biography*, Oxford, 1977.

Hartog, Mabel, *P.J. Hartog: A Memoir*, 1949.

Harwood, Jonathan, 'American Academic Opinion and Social Change: recent developments in the nature-nurture controversy', *Oxford Review of Education* viii (1982), pp. 41-67.

Hearnshaw, L.S., *A Short History of British Psychology 1840-1940*, 1964; *Cyril Burt, Psychologist*, 1979.

Hennock, E.P., 'Poverty and Social Theory in England: the experience of the eighteen-eighties', *Social History* i (1976), pp. 67-91.

Hodgkinson, Ruth G., *The Origins of the National Health Service. The Medical Services of the New Poor Law 1834-1871*, 1967.

Hicks, U.K., *The Finance of British Government 1920-1936*, Oxford, 1938, reprinted 1970.

Jefferys, Kevin, 'Sources for Conservative Party Education Policy 1902-1944', *History of Education Society Bulletin* xxx (Autumn 1982).

Jones, G.W., *Borough Politics. A Study of the Wolverhampton Town Council 1888-1964*, 1969.

Jones, Greta, *Social Darwinism and English Thought: the interaction between Biological and Social Theory*, Hassocks, Sussex, 1980.

Jones, Kathleen, *A History of the Mental Health Services*, 1972.

Kamin, L., *The Science and Politics of IQ*, Potomac, Maryland, 1974.

Kanner, L., *A History of the Care and Study of the Mentally Retarded*, Springfield, Illinois, 1964.

Karier, Clarence J., 'Testing for Order and Control in the Corporate Liberal State', *Educational Theory* xxii (1972), pp. 154-80, reprinted in *The IQ Controversy*, ed. Ned Block and Gerald Dworkin, 1977, pp. 339-69.

Keith-Lucas, Bryan, *English Local Government in the Nineteenth and Twentieth Centuries*, Historical Association, 1977.

Kevles, Daniel J., 'Testing the Army's Intelligence: Psychologists and the Military in World War I', *Journal of American History* lv (1968), pp. 565-81.

Lambert, R.J., *Sir John Simon and English Social Administration 1816-1904*, 1963.

Leavis, F.R., 'Introduction' to *Mill on Bentham and Coleridge*, 1950.

Lee, J.M., *Social Leaders and Public Persons. A Study of County Government in Cheshire since 1888*, Oxford, 1963.

Lewis, Jane, *The Politics of Motherhood*, 1980.

Lowe, R.A., 'Eugenicists, Doctors and the Quest for National Efficiency: an Educational Crusade 1900-39', *History of Education* viii (1979), pp. 293-306; 'Eugenics and Education: a note on the origins of the intelligence testing movement', *Educational Studies* vi (1980), pp. 1-8.

Lynd, H.M., *England in the Eighteen Eighties*, New York, 1945.

MacDonagh, O.O.G.M., 'The Nineteenth Century Revolution in Government: A Reappraisal', *Historical Journal* i (1958), pp. 52-67.

McGregor, O.R., 'Social Research and Social Policy in the Nineteenth Century', *British Journal of Sociology* viii (1957), pp. 146-57.

Mackenzie, Donald A., *Statistics in Britain 1865-1930. The Social Construction of Scientific Knowledge*, Edinburgh, 1981.

Macnicol, John, *The Movement for Family Allowances 1918-45: A Study in Social Policy Development*, 1980.

Matthew, H.C.G., *The Liberal Imperialists. The Ideas and Politics of a Post-Gladstonian Elite*, 1973.

Moorman, Mary, *George Macaulay Trevelyan: a memoir by his daughter*, 1980.

Morgan, Kenneth O., *Consensus and Disunity: The Lloyd George Coalition Government 1918-22*, Oxford, 1979; and Jane Morgan, *Portrait of a Progressive. The Political Career of Christopher, Viscount Addison*, Oxford, 1980.

Mowat, C.L., *The Charity Organisation Society 1869-1913: Its Ideas and Work*, 1961.

Murray, Bruce K., *The People's Budget 1909-10*, Oxford, 1980.

Norton, Bernard, 'Charles Spearman and the General Factor in Intelligence: Genesis and Interpretation in the Light of Socio-Personal Considerations', *Journal of the History of the Behavioral Sciences* xv (1979), pp. 142-54.

Parry-Jones, William Ll., *The Trade in Lunacy. A Study of Private Madhouses in England in the Eighteenth and Nineteenth Centuries*, 1972.

Pearson, Karl, *The Life, Letters and Labours of Francis Galton*, 4 vols., Cambridge, 1914-30.

Pritchard, D.G., *Education and the Handicapped 1760-1960*, 1963.

Prochaska, F.K., *Women and Philanthropy in Nineteenth-Century England*, Oxford, 1980.

'Psychological Services for Children in London from Burt to Underwood', Appendix B to *Report of the County Medical Officer of Health and Principal School Medical Officer to the London County Council, 1959.*

Rée, Harry, *Educator Extraordinary: The Life and Achievement of Henry Morris 1889-1961,* 1973.

Resnick, Daniel P., 'History of Educational Testing' in Alexandra K. Wigdor and Wendell R. Garner, eds., *Ability Testing; Uses, Consequences and Controversies* (National Research Council Committee on Ability Testing, Washington D.C. 1982) Part II, pp. 173-94.

Ryan, Joanna and Thomas, Frank, 'Mental handicap: the historical background' in *The Practice of Special Education,* ed. Will Swann, Oxford, 1981, pp. 80-92.

Roach, John, *Public Examinations in England 1850-1900,* Cambridge, 1971; 'Examinations and the Secondary Schools 1900-1945', *History of Education* viii (1979), pp. 45-58.

Sadleir, Michael, *Trollope. A Commentary,* 1927.

Sampson, O., *Child Guidance: Its History, Provenance and Future,* British Psychological Society Occasional Papers, vol. 3, no. 3, 1980.

Scull, Andrew, *Museums of Madness. The Social Organization of Insanity in Nineteenth Century England,* 1979.

Seaborne, Malcom, 'William Brockington, Director of Education for Leicestershire 1903-47' In Brian Simon, ed., *Education in Leicestershire 1540-1940,* Leicester, 1969, pp. 195-224.

Searle, G.R., *The Quest for National Efficiency,* Oxford, 1971; *Eugenics and Politics in Britain 1900-1914,* Leyden, 1976; 'Eugenics and Politics in Britain in the 1930s', *Annals of Science* xxxvi (1979), pp. 159-69.

Semmel, Bernard, *Imperialism and Social Reform,* 1960.

Sherington, Geoffrey, *English Education, Social Change and War 1911-20,* Manchester, 1981.

Simey, T.S. and Simey, M.B., *Charles Booth, Social Scientist,* 1960.

Simon, Brian, *The Politics of Educational Reform 1920-1940,* 1974.

Simon, Joan, 'The Shaping of the Spens Report on Secondary Education 1933-38: An Inside View', *British Journal of Education Studies* xxv (1977), pp. 63-80, 170-85.

Smith, James V. and Hamilton, David, eds., *The Meritocratic Intellect. Studies in the History of Educational Research,* Aberdeen, 1980.

Soffer, Reba N., *Ethics and Society in England. The Revolution in the Social Sciences 1870-1914,* 1978.

Stedman Jones, Gareth, *Outcast London. A Study in the Relationship between Classes in Victorian Society,* Oxford, 1971.

Sutherland, Gillian, ed., *Studies in the Growth of Nineteenth Century Government,* 1972; *Policy-Making in Elementary Education 1870-1895,* Oxford, 1973; 'Secondary Education: The Education of the Middle Classes' in Sutherland, ed., *Government and Society in Nineteenth Century Britain: Commentaries on British Parliamentary Papers: Education,* Dublin, 1977, pp. 137-66; 'The Magic of

Measurement: Mental Testing and English Education 1900–1940', *Transactions of the Royal Historical Society*, 5th ser. xxvii (1977), pp. 135–53; and Stephen Sharp, ' "The fust official psychologist in the wurrld": aspects of the professionalization of psychology in early twentieth century Britain', *History of Science* xviii (1980), pp. 181–208.

Tillotson, Kathleen, *Novels of the Eighteen-Forties*, Oxford, 1954.

Trevelyan, Sir George Otto, *The Life and Letters of Lord Macaulay*, 1908.

Tropp, A., *The School Teachers*, 1957.

Webster, Charles, ed., *Biology, Medicine and Society 1840–1940*, Cambridge, 1981.

Werskey, Gary, *The Visible College*, 1978.

Wheldon, Sir Wynn, and Thomas, Sir Ben Bowen, 'The Welsh Department, Ministry of Education 1907–1957', *Transactions of the Honourable Society of Cymmrodorion*, session 1957, pp. 18–36.

Wilson, F.P. and Wilson, John Dover, 'Sir Edmund Kerchever Chambers', *Proceedings of the British Academy* xlii (1956), pp. 267–85.

Wolf, Theta H., *Alfred Binet*, Chicago, 1972.

Woodhouse, Jayne, 'Eugenics and the feeble-minded: the Parliamentary debates of 1912–14', *History of Education* xi (1982), pp. 127–37.

Wynne Evans, Leslie, 'The Evolution of Welsh Educational Administration 1881–1921' in *Studies in the Government and Control of Education since 1860*, History of Education Society, 1970.

Young, R.M., *Mind, Brain and Adaptation in the Nineteenth Century*, Oxford, 1970.

Index